THE LEGACY OF H.L.A. HART
LEGAL, POLITICAL, AND MORAL PHILOSOPHY

The Legacy of H.L.A. Hart

Legal, Political, and Moral Philosophy

Edited by
MATTHEW H KRAMER
CLAIRE GRANT
BEN COLBURN
and
ANTONY HATZISTAVROU

OXFORD
UNIVERSITY PRESS

OXFORD
UNIVERSITY PRESS

Great Clarendon Street, Oxford OX2 6DP

Oxford University Press is a department of the University of Oxford.
It furthers the University's objective of excellence in research, scholarship,
and education by publishing worldwide in

Oxford New York

Auckland Cape Town Dar es Salaam Hong Kong Karachi
Kuala Lumpur Madrid Melbourne Mexico City Nairobi
New Delhi Shanghai Taipei Toronto

With offices in

Argentina Austria Brazil Chile Czech Republic France Greece
Guatemala Hungary Italy Japan Poland Portugal Singapore
South Korea Switzerland Thailand Turkey Ukraine Vietnam

Oxford is a registered trade mark of Oxford University Press
in the UK and in certain other countries

Published in the United States
by Oxford University Press Inc., New York

British Library Cataloguing in Publication Data

Data available

Library of Congress Cataloging in Publication Data
The legacy of H.L.A. Hart : legal, political, and moral philosophy/edited
by Matthew H. Kramer ... [et al.].
    p. cm.
Includes bibliographical references and index.
ISBN 978–0–19–954289–5 (acid-free paper) 1. Law—
Philosophy. 2. Justice. 3. Causation (Criminal law) 4. Criminal
liability. 5. Hart, H. L. A. (Herbert Lionel Adolphus),
1907– I. Kramer, Matthew H., 1959–
K235.L434 2008
340'.1—dc22   2008023430

Typeset by Newgen Imaging Systems (P) Ltd., Chennai, India
Printed in Great Britain
on acid-free paper by
CPI Anthony Rowe, Chippenham, Wiltshire

ISBN 978–0–19–954289–5

1 3 5 7 9 10 8 6 4 2

Preface

This book arises from a British Academy Symposium on 'The Legacy of H.L.A. Hart' held at Churchill College, Cambridge, in July 2007, under the auspices of the Cambridge Forum for Legal & Political Philosophy. Early versions of the essays in this volume were written as papers for presentation at that Symposium.

We are very grateful to the British Academy for their support and generous sponsorship; we owe special thanks to Onora O'Neill, Angela Pusey, and Joanne Blore. We are likewise greatly indebted to the contributors to this volume for their fine essays and for their admirable cooperativeness at the Symposium and in the preparation of this book. Also deserving of warm thanks are Trevor Allan, Tony Honoré, Serena Olsaretti, Onora O'Neill (again), and Quentin Skinner, who chaired panels at the Symposium. We are delighted that Hart's son Charlie and grandchildren Justin and Tanya were able to attend part of the proceedings. We are much obliged also to Hart's daughter Joanna for her kind and enthusiastic support of the venture. We are likewise extremely grateful to the numerous people who attended the Symposium as delegates, and we extend our apologies to the many people who could not be taken off the waiting list. The presence of delegates at the Symposium from every continent except Antarctica is indicative of the global reach of Hart's influence.

We extend glad thanks as well to four Cantabrigians who handled a number of logistical matters: Christopher Arias, Kiersten Burge-Hendrix, Rupert Gill, and Mark McBride.

Many people at Churchill College helped to make the Symposium a great success. We are especially grateful to the bedmakers, catering staff, handymen, and porters, and we owe particular thanks to the following individuals: Paul Barringer, Alison Barton, Shirley Blackley, Jillian Blaine, Tim Cooper, Ian Douglas, Dean Flack, Martin Haydon, Paul Howitt, Rosetta Kyriakou, Ivan Martin, Richard Mee, Sandra Parsons, Angela Railton, Steve Ridyard, Carol Robinson, Michelle Tuson, and Paul Willimott. We are also much obliged to several people at the Cambridge University Law Faculty for their extremely valuable assistance: Elizabeth Aitken, Daniel Bates, Matthew Martin, David Newton, and Norma Weir. Hearty thanks are due as well to several people at the Cambridge Centre for Research in the Arts, Social Sciences, and Humanities: Catherine Hurley, Mary Jacobus, and Michelle Maciejewska.

At the Oxford University Press, John Louth and Alex Flach and Lucy Stevenson have been gratifyingly enthusiastic and adroit in their handling of this book. We are very pleased that the OUP, as the publishers of every one of Hart's books, have been so helpfully supportive of this project.

Matthew H Kramer
Claire Grant
Ben Colburn
Antony Hatzistavrou

September 2007

Table of Contents

IV JUSTICE

V. RIGHTS

VI. TOLERATION AND LIBERTY

List of Contributors

R A Duff is a Professor of Philosophy at the University of Stirling, where he has taught since 1970. His research interests lie in philosophy of criminal law, especially in issues concerning the grounds and structures of criminal liability and the aims of criminal punishment. With three colleagues (Lindsay Farmer, Sandra Marshall, Victor Tadros), he recently completed an AHRC-funded project on criminal trials; with the same colleagues he is starting a new AHRC-funded project on criminalization.

Cécile Fabre holds the Chair of Political Theory at the University of Edinburgh. She has published extensively on rights and distributive justice and is currently writing a book on the ethics of war. She is the author of *Social Rights under the Constitution* (Oxford University Press, 2000), *Whose Body is it Anyway* (Oxford University Press, 2006), and *Justice in a Changing World* (Polity, 2007).

John Finnis is Professor of Law and Legal Philosophy at the University of Oxford, a Fellow and Tutor in Law of University College Oxford, Biolchini Professor of Law at the University of Notre Dame du Lac (Indiana), and a Fellow of the British Academy.

John Gardner is Professor of Jurisprudence at the University of Oxford. He has also held positions at King's College London, Yale Law School, Columbia Law School, Princeton University, the University of Texas, and the Australian National University. He is the author of *Offences and Defences* (Oxford University Press, 2007), and recently prepared a new edition of H.L.A. Hart's *Punishment and Responsibility* (Oxford University Press, 2008).

Claire Grant is Reader in Social and Political Philosophy at the University of Warwick. Her many publications deal with issues in legal philosophy and the philosophy of criminal law. She was a founding Editor-in-Chief of the journal *Criminal Law and Philosophy*.

Leslie Green is Professor of the Philosophy of Law at the University of Oxford, where he is a Fellow of Balliol College. He has held visiting professorships at NYU, Berkeley, and the University of Texas at Austin, and remains a part-time faculty member at the Osgoode Hall Law School of York University, Toronto. He publishes widely in jurisprudence and political theory.

Brad Hooker is a Professor of Philosophy at the University of Reading and the author of *Ideal Code, Real World: A Rule-Consequentialist Theory of Morality* (Clarendon Press, 2000).

Matthew H Kramer is Professor of Legal & Political Philosophy at the University of Cambridge; Fellow of Churchill College, Cambridge; and Director of the Cambridge Forum for Legal & Political Philosophy. Among his many books, the most recently published is *Objectivity and the Rule of Law* (Cambridge University Press, 2007).

David Lyons taught philosophy at Cornell University from 1964 to 1995, and in 1979 joined the law faculty. He has since been a member of the law and philosophy faculties of

Boston University. His publications include *Forms and Limits of Utilitarianism* (Oxford, 1965), *In the Interest of the Governed* (Oxford, 1973), *Ethics and the Rule of Law* (Cambridge, 1984), *Moral Aspects of Legal Theory* (Cambridge, 1993) and *Rights, Welfare, and Mill's Moral Theory* (Oxford, 1994).

Susan Mendus is Professor of Political Philosophy and a member of the Morrell Centre for Toleration at the University of York. Her main area of research interest is modern political philosophy and especially theories of toleration. She has recently completed a book entitled *Politics and Morality,* and is currently preparing her 2007 Freilich Lectures on Tolerance for publication under the title *Religious Toleration in an Age of Terrorism.*

Philip Pettit is L S Rockefeller University Professor of Politics and Human Values at Princeton University. His recent books include *Republicanism* (Oxford University Press, 1997), *The Economy of Esteem* (Oxford University Press, 2004) with Geoffrey Brennan, and *Made with Words: Hobbes on Mind, Society and Politics* (Princeton University Press, 2007). He is currently working on a book on group agency with Christian List. *Common Minds: Themes from the Philosophy of Philip Pettit* appeared in 2007, edited by Michael Smith, Geoffrey Brennan, Robert Goodin, and Frank Jackson (Oxford University Press).

Gerald J Postema, Cary C Boshamer Professor of Philosophy and Professor of Law at the University of North Carolina at Chapel Hill, is the author of *Bentham and the Common Law Tradition*, editor of *Philosophy and the Law of Torts*, and associate editor of *Treatise of General Jurisprudence and Philosophy of Law* (eight of twelve volumes published). He is currently writing a history of Anglo-American jurisprudence and editing a collection of Sir Matthew Hale's jurisprudential writings.

Alan Ryan has been Warden of New College, Oxford since 1996, and before that was Professor of Politics at Princeton University. He has written on the ethics and politics of a liberal society in many places, including particularly *The New York Review of Books*, and is the author of several books on J S Mill, Bertrand Russell, and John Dewey.

Hillel Steiner is Professor of Political Philosophy at the University of Manchester and a Fellow of the British Academy. He is the author of *An Essay on Rights* (Blackwell, 1994) and co-author, with Matthew Kramer and Nigel Simmonds, of *A Debate Over Rights: Philosophical Enquiries* (Oxford University Press, 1998). His current research projects include ones on the concept of 'the just price' and the application of libertarian principles to global, and to genetic, inequalities.

Judith Jarvis Thomson is Professor of Philosophy at MIT. Her many books and articles address a wide variety of topics in metaphysics, the philosophy of action, ethics, and political philosophy. Her most recently published book is *Normativity* (Open Court Publishing), which is an expanded version of her 2003 Carus Lectures.

Jeremy Waldron is a University Professor at New York University. He has previously taught at Columbia, Princeton, California-Berkeley, Edinburgh, Oxford, and Otago. Among his many books, the most recently published is *God, Locke, and Equality: Christian Foundations of Locke's Political Thought* (Cambridge University Press, 2002).

W J Waluchow has BA and MA degrees from the University of Western Ontario and a DPhil in Philosophy of Law from Oxford, where he studied under H.L.A. Hart.

He is Professor of Philosophy at McMaster University. His research interests include Legal Philosophy, Ethics, and Political Philosophy. Among his publications are: *Inclusive Legal Positivism*; *Free Expression: Essays in Law and Philosophy*; *The Dimensions of Ethics;* and *A Common Law Theory of Judicial Review: The Living Tree.*

Leif Wenar is Professor of Philosophy at the University of Sheffield. He is the author of 'The Nature of Rights', *Philosophy & Public Affairs* (2005), 'The Value of Rights', *Law and Social Justice* (MIT, 2005), 'Epistemic Rights and Legal Rights', *Analysis* (2003), and the entry on rights in the *Stanford Encyclopedia of Philosophy.*

Richard W. Wright is a Professor of Law at the Illinois Institute of Technology's Chicago-Kent College of Law. He has been a visiting professor or fellow at the Universities of Canterbury, Melbourne, Oxford, Texas, and Torcuato di Tella. He is a member of the American Law Institute and the advisory boards of the *Journal of Tort Law* and the Center for Justice and Democracy.

Introduction

Matthew H Kramer and Claire Grant

Herbert Lionel Adolphus Hart was the world's foremost legal philosopher in the twentieth century, and was also a major figure in political and moral philosophy. Born in the first decade of that century and living until its final decade, he was centrally responsible for reviving the philosophy of law from the doldrums in which it had lain for many years. Both through his own brilliant work and through his mentoring of some of the twentieth century's other great jurisprudential thinkers, he exerted a far-reaching influence on legal philosophy that was comparable to the influence of his friend John Rawls on political philosophy. His work has often been tellingly criticized—indeed, one of the marks of his intellectual excellence lay in his encouragement of students who took strong exception to many of his ideas—but the magnitude of his achievements is beyond any reasonable doubt.[1]

An especially impressive feature of Hart's writings is the breadth of the topics which they encompass. Unprecedentedly, the essays in this volume together cover all the main areas of his philosophical work: general legal philosophy and legal positivism; criminal responsibility and punishment; theories of rights; causation in the law; toleration and liberty; and theories of justice. Though Hart is most famous for his work in the first of these areas—as the greatest proponent of jurisprudential positivism since the days of Jeremy Bentham and John Austin—his publications in the other areas are themselves sufficient to earn him a place in the pantheon of the twentieth century's leading thinkers. Consequently, while the present volume devotes more attention to legal positivism and general legal philosophy than to any of Hart's other concerns, it also examines those other concerns in some depth.

As the title of this book suggests, the contributors focus more on Hart's legacy than on the man himself.[2] Although most of them discuss his writings quite sustainedly, every essay in the volume is predominantly philosophical rather than predominantly exegetical. While paying tribute to Hart at numerous junctures—and while taking issue with him at other junctures—the

---

[1] Our own admiration for Hart, huge though it is, has been far from uncritical. See, for example, Kramer 1998, 69–70, 81–82; Kramer 1999, 21–36; Kramer 2003, 312–13; Kramer 2004, 249–94; Kramer 2005; Grant 2006; Grant 2008.

[2] Hart's life has been the subject of a major recent biography; see Lacey 2004. See also MacCormick 1981.

contributors look principally toward the future rather than principally toward the past. They tackle philosophical problems that preoccupy contemporary thinkers. Hart, who memorably warned against the notion that 'a book on legal theory is primarily a book from which one learns what other books contain' (Hart 1994, vii), would doubtless have approved of this way of exploring his legacy.

*****

At the July 2007 British Academy Symposium from which this book has emerged, several legal practitioners as well as numerous philosophers were in attendance. One of the practitioners, Stephen Hockman, asked a particularly perceptive question about the applicability of Hart's abstract categories to the more concretely focused endeavours of people who participate in the operations of legal and governmental institutions. Such a question well captures an important aim that Hart pursued. On the one hand, Hart during his academic career was a philosopher who remained at high levels of abstraction in his analyses of legal and social institutions. Some of his concerns as a philosopher were quite remote from the everyday activities of lawyers and governmental officials. On the other hand, he spent several years as a practicing barrister and was thus in a position to develop a vividly informed sense of the characteristic objectives and interests of people who deal with the pressures of practical affairs. A salient element of his thought in every area of philosophy explored by this book is his emphasis on the outlooks of the participants in the practices which he discussed.

Perhaps most famous is his insistence on the centrality of the internal perspective of participants as an object of investigation by jurisprudential theorists. Without ever losing sight of the importance of other perspectives, he criticized Oliver Wendell Holmes and others for neglecting the ways in which legal concepts are understood and used by the people who run the sundry components of legal-governmental systems. Any satisfactory philosophical account of such systems has to take into consideration not only the external vantage point of an observer but also the internal viewpoint of a committed participant. By rendering salient the latter viewpoint, Hart enriched legal philosophy and helped to underscore the differences between such philosophy and certain varieties of legal sociology. Of course, in so doing, he never maintained that legal philosophers themselves have to adopt the internal perspective of a committed participant in a legal system. Such a methodological claim has been pressed by Ronald Dworkin and his followers, but Hart himself wisely eschewed it. He recognized that legal philosophers' analyses typically stem from a moderately external point of view. Still, that moderately external position is marked not least by an attunedness to the outlooks of the people whose practices are being subjected to philosophical scrutiny.

Hart's work on the other topics covered by this volume is similarly alert to the characteristic concerns and judgments of the participants in various activities. In his massive first book, *Causation in the Law*, co-written with Tony Honoré, Hart sought to systematize the factors that lead juristic decision-makers to attribute responsibility for untoward events to individuals or groups (Hart and Honoré 1959). With a host of fascinating examples to illustrate the distillation of general principles, *Causation in the Law* expounds the ways in which the participants in legal institutions construe the ascription of responsibility. Though Hart and Honoré swept too broadly in classifying many straightforwardly moral questions as questions about causation (Kramer 2003, 312–13), their exposition of the often implicit criteria for the imputation of legal responsibility was a landmark in the philosophy of law and was influential among non-jurisprudential philosophers (Mackie 1974, 117–33).

A cognate focus on the typical point of view of participants informed much of Hart's writing on legal rights. His adherence to the Will Theory of rights—a theory that analyses any rights as essentially involving powers to waive or enforce other people's duties—stemmed partly from his effort to understand why rights would matter from the perspective of somebody who holds them. His emphasis on the choices or opportunities open to individuals who are legally empowered to waive or enforce others' legal obligations is reflective of his concern to make sense of rights through the eyes of the people for whom they exist. Of course, to recognize this facet of Hart's approach is not perforce to endorse his embrace of the Will Theory; we in fact reject such a theory (Kramer 1998; Kramer 2001). Nonetheless, whether or not Hart was correct in thinking that the Will Theory is uniquely suitable for capturing the internal perspective of a right-holder, his striking image of the individual right-holder as a sovereign was indicative of his concentration on that perspective.

A similar concentration is evident in Hart's reflections on basic liberties. As is highlighted in the essay by Philip Pettit in this volume, one of the principal hallmarks of any basic liberty—as understood by Hart or by Rawls—is the significance of the liberty for the typical person who possesses it. Under the approach favoured by Hart and Rawls, then, a political philosopher cannot satisfactorily classify any basic liberty as such without placing herself in the position of a typical person for whom such a liberty is to be safeguarded. Just as a satisfactory analysis of the workings of legal systems must take account of the viewpoint of a participant in the running of such a system, a satisfactory theory of justice must take account of the viewpoint of a person to whom the principles of justice assign basic desiderata.

In Hart's work on criminal responsibility and punishment as well, we find an insistence on fathoming the concerns and motivations of the people directly involved in the practices under consideration. Indeed, any credible theory of criminal responsibility has to enter into the outlooks of the people whose responsibility is at issue. Such an approach is prominent in Hart's agency-focused theory of criminal responsibility, which requires that 'as a normal condition of liability to punishment, ... the person to be punished should, at the time of his offence, have had a certain knowledge or intention, or possessed certain powers of understanding and control' (Hart 1968, 210). This understanding of criminal responsibility was linked to Hart's conception of the basic function of law in guiding human conduct. The very focus of Hart on issues of responsibility in his writings on the philosophy of criminal law is a sign of his attentiveness to the thoughts and objectives of the people on whom legal institutions impinge. Among the conditions that must be satisfied for the proper imposition of criminal penalties is the status of someone as a responsible agent; to ascertain whether that condition is fulfilled in any given context, legal decision-makers (and the theorists who analyse their activities) have to place themselves—not necessarily sympathetically, but always empathetically—in the position of any person whose agency is under scrutiny. To a considerable extent, they must seek to grasp what it was like to be that person in the specified context.

In a largely similar vein, Hart in his political-philosophical work on toleration and liberty called for a more capacious understanding of the outlooks and concerns of the people who fall prey to intolerance. Here, however, he was appealing for a sympathetic understanding as well as for empathy; his endeavours as a political philosopher were predominantly prescriptive. He drew attention to the misery caused by intolerance (especially in connection with the legal proscription of homosexual intercourse and other unorthodox sexual behaviour), and, like Bentham before him, he urged that such misery is unwarranted when the production of it is not necessary for averting or remedying the commission of any wrongs. Whereas Hart's opponents had concentrated on the benefits to a society that stem from the strict enforcement of its code of proper behaviour, Hart highlighted the perspective of the people at whose expense those ostensible benefits are gained. He recognized that deviant conduct may elicit feelings of distaste or offence in others, but he maintained that—without more—those feelings are not enough to justify the suppression of activities that are so important from the viewpoint of the individuals who engage in them. The viewpoint of those individuals should not be obliterated from a liberal-democratic system of criminal law.

In short, in every area of legal and political and moral philosophy covered by this book, Hart sought to emphasize the need for theorists to grasp the ways in which the workings of institutions are characteristically perceived by the people who are involved in those workings. As Hart wrote, for anyone who aspires to come up with an illuminating philosophical exposition of the sundry dimensions of legal-governmental institutions, 'what is needed is a "hermeneutic" method which involves portraying rule-governed behaviour as it appears to its participants' (Hart 1983, 13). Of course, to say as much is scarcely to maintain that the viewpoints of the participants in social practices are the only things worthy of attention in such practices. On the contrary, Hart was keenly alert to the regularized patterns of interaction that constitute such practices. Those regularities, and the participants' outlooks that shape them and are shaped by them, can always be approached through external critiques that reject the participants' self-understandings. For some purposes, such external critiques are plainly apposite. Nonetheless, no such critique will be minimally satisfactory if it ignores the participants' perspectives. Though the proponent of an external critique might deride those perspectives as deluded or otherwise inadequate, the derision will be superficial and ineffective if the perspectives have not been carefully fathomed.

More broadly, whether a theory of the institutions of law and government is condemnatory or supportive, its cogency will depend on its taking account of the ways in which the people who operate those institutions—and the other people who are affected by them—are reflective beings with characteristic aims and concerns. Hart's insistence on this point was one of his major contributions to legal and political philosophy. Admittedly, his point may sound obvious when it is stated in the abstract. In various contexts, however, it had been neglected by many of the people who write on these matters. One of Hart's great achievements lay in revealing so forcefully the distortions and intellectual impoverishment that ensue from such neglect.

*****

Because the principal essays in this volume are grouped under the areas of scholarship mentioned at the outset, we shall not prolong this Introduction by seeking to summarize each of them separately. Readers should be able to locate quite readily the chapters that are of most interest to them. Suffice it for us to say that the contributors to this book are among the most eminent writers on their topics, and that they have adopted a variety of approaches in their discussions of those topics. We are delighted to present their essays as a collective tribute to Hart.[3] That tribute is paid even by the chapters which are

---

[3] Of course, to state as much is hardly to suggest that we agree with everything in each of the essays. We disagree strongly with some of the analyses in some of the essays. We shall here mention only one small point. Leif Wenar, in footnote 11 of his chapter, insinuates that Matthew Kramer has displayed inconsistency by 'appeal[ing] to the purpose[s] of legal norms to make sense of [certain] cases . . . , where a few pages earlier he had said that purposes had no "determinative bearing" and were "quite immaterial" in his theory'. In fact, there is no inconsistency whatsoever between the two passages (in Kramer and Steiner 2007, 289–90 293–4) to which Wenar refers. In the passage from which Wenar takes his snippet quotations, Kramer is denying that a *necessary* condition for the conferral of a legal right upon some person X by a legal norm is that the underlying purpose of the norm is to benefit X or people like X; the existence of such an underlying purpose is not a *necessary* condition for the conferral of a right upon X. By contrast, in the passage that appeals to the purpose of a law L, Kramer is maintaining that that purpose can combine with the terms and the predictable effects of L to constitute a *sufficient* condition for the holding of a right by X thereunder. In circumstances where the terms and the predictable effects of L are not themselves enough to form such a condition, they can be supplemented to that end by L's purpose. In short, contrary to the impression conveyed by Wenar with his snippet quotations, the passages to which he adverts are perfectly compatible.

sustainedly critical of him or which say little directly about him, for the former chapters fully recognize his towering stature as a thinker, while the latter chapters address problems on which he produced trailblazing work. This collection as a whole reveals how richly multifarious and stimulating the legacy of H.L.A. Hart is.

PART I

LEGAL POSITIVISM AND GENERAL JURISPRUDENCE

1

On Hart's Ways: Law as Reason
and as Fact

John Finnis

1

I remember Hart saying to two or three of his colleagues, over tea and biscuits in the Senior Common Room, that every ten years or so, going back a long way, he read the whole of Proust's *À la recherche du temps perdu*. I don't think he said why—why should he have?—but central to what led him, repeatedly, through all seven of these novels, on the long way from *Du côté de chez Swann* to *Le Temps retrouvé*, will surely have been their reflexive, self-referential deployment and exploration of interiority, of the first person singular. As Neil MacCormick justly says in the first edition of his *H.L.A. Hart*, the 'fulcrum' and 'central methodological insight' of Hart's 'analytical jurisprudence' is that, as a 'descriptive legal or social theorist,' one can and must '[hold] apart one's own commitments, critical morality, group membership or non-membership', and 'portray the rules for what they are in the eyes of those whose rules they are' (MacCormick 1981, 37–8). One's account of law, as Hart himself puts it in *The Concept of Law*, must 'refer to the internal aspect of rules seen from their [the members of the group's] internal point of view' and 'reproduce the way in which the rules function in the lives' of those members, that is, in their 'claims, demands, admissions, criticism... all the familiar transactions of life according to rules', life as led by those for whom the rules count as reasons for action, and violations of those rules count as a reason for hostility (Hart 1994, 90).

Somewhat less well known than Hart's prioritizing of the internal attitude or attitudes to law are his works on self-reference (especially self-referring laws [1]), and on intention (especially in relation to criminal liability, and to human causation). But these aspects of interiority are as central to his thought. In response to a remark of mine about, I think, how significant self-referential consistency is to the testing of philosophical positions,[2] he told me that what started his interest in philosophy, as a boy, was the breakfast cereal packet.

---

[1] On self-referring laws, see Hart 1983, 15–16, 170–8.
[2] See, latterly, Finnis 2004.

From the 1890s,[3] packets of Quaker oats have depicted a substantial Quaker man holding a Quaker oats packet depicting a substantial Quaker man holding a packet of Quaker oats... (and so on 'to infinity', claims someone talking about these packets in Aldous Huxley's 1928 novel *Point Counter Point*)[4]. In relation to crime and punishment, causation, and self-referring laws, Hart's attentiveness to our inner lives of thought, judgment, and decision was a motive for, and supplied arguments to advance, his resistance to more or less behaviourist currents of (as he often put it)[5] 'scepticism' about central aspects and institutions of law, a resistance which has been generally decisive for subsequent legal theory: a great legacy. When summing up his vindication of responsibility against the sceptic Barbara Wootton in a lecture delivered in 1961, he articulates what he calls 'an important general principle':

Human society is a society of persons, and persons do not view themselves or each other merely as so many bodies moving in ways which are sometimes harmful and have to be prevented or altered. Instead persons interpret each other's movements as manifestations of intention and choices, and these subjective factors are often more important to their social relations than the movements by which they are manifested or their effects. (Hart 1968, 182)

This talk of intention and choice complements and corresponds to what *The Concept of Law*, published in the same year, says about the

whole dimension of the social life of those [who]...look upon [the red traffic light] [not merely as a sign that others will stop, but] as a *signal for* them to stop, and so a reason for stopping in conformity to rules which make stopping when the light is red a standard of behaviour and an obligation. (Hart 1994, 89)

Here Hart italicizes *signal for*, and later on the same page he italicizes its equivalent: '*reason* for'. 'Reason' is italicized more than any other noun in the book (Hart 1994, 11, 55, 90, 105, 194); it signifies practical reasons, the propositional element in thoughts of the form appropriate to guiding deliberation and eventual (possible) action. The first and fourth of the book's five italicizings of 'reason' are to make the argument that Hart was so eager, indeed impatient, to put forward even while he was setting up the three 'recurrent issues' about law—the argument that is his answer to the 'realist' scepticisms which reduce law to prediction. Sceptical 'realism' is poor as legal theory because it shuts one's eyes to the fact that 'the judge, in punishing, takes the rule as his *guide* and the breach of the rule as his *reason* and *justification* for punishing the offender'; a 'judge's statement that a rule is valid is an internal statement..., and constitutes not a prophecy of but

---

[3]   I knew what he meant, because an Australian cereal packet in the 1950s had the same feature, but with a frog not a Quaker.

[4]   Huxley 1928, 294.

[5]   See my review of his *Punishment & Responsibility* (Finnis 1968); the word 'scepticism' appears in virtually every one of these essays.

part of the *reason* for his decision' (Hart 1994, 11, 105). By the time of *Essays on Bentham*, twenty years later, Hart had recast his theory of authority and law so as to emphasize yet further the centrality to it of reasons for action (peremptory and content-independent reasons).

...an authoritative legal reason...is a consideration (which in simple systems of law may include the giving of a command) which is recognized at least in the practice of the Courts, in what I term their rule or rules of recognition, as constituting a reason for action and decision [, a reason] of a special kind. Reasons of this kind...constitute legal guides to action and legal standards of evaluation.[6]

Now reasons of this kind, *as* articulated in commands or *as* manifested verbally or non-verbally in the practice of the courts, are historical facts. Like other historical facts about thoughts, decisions and actions, they can, and often must, be understood, thoroughly, without being endorsed or approved, condemned, or disapproved—just understood and faithfully described. Adulterating one's understanding of other people's valuations (or of one's own past evaluations) with one's own present valuations is sheer folly for the general, the advocate, the detective, the assessor (judge of fact), the historian. There should be no question here of 'interpretative charity' or 'making it the best of its genre', let alone morally best.[7] As Hart puts it in the posthumous *Postscript*, 'Description may still be description, even when what is described is evaluation' (Hart 1994, 244). True, to bother investigating and describing *this* evaluation by *this* person or group, from among all the welter of other facts available for investigation and description, presupposes an evaluation by the investigator, not to mention the audience.[8] But that presupposed evaluation remains external to the evaluative thought—the concept, action, or practice—described. So description can and, for many purposes, should be value-free even when it describes the values and consequent actions of persons—of others or of oneself giving an account of one's own beliefs and conduct.

But Hart went further, both in the *Postscript* and earlier. As he puts it in the *Postscript*:

...the descriptive legal theorist must *understand* what it is to adopt the internal point of view and in that limited sense he must be able to put himself in the place of an insider; but this is not to accept the law or share or endorse the insider's internal point of view or in any other way to surrender his descriptive stance. (Hart 1994, 242)

[6] Hart 1982, 18. Here Hart uses 'evaluation' much more broadly than 'statements of value' in his contrast of the latter with 'statements of validity' at Hart 1994, 108 (see text and n 25 below).
[7] All this has been clear to me since I read R G Collingwood's 1939 *Autobiography* in the early or mid 1950s. See Twining 1998, 603.
[8] 'It is the historian's judgments of value that select from the infinite welter of things that have happened the things that are worth thinking about' (Collingwood 1999, 217). Weber's version of this thought is better known.

Here there has been a shift which Hart never seems to have attended to, and perhaps would simply deny is a shift, from the description that is the stock in trade of the detective, the assessor, the translator, or the historian to what Hart calls 'descriptive general theory' (Hart 1994, 239–40). This shift is both real and important. I am not going to dwell upon it in this paper; it is the burden of chapter I of *Natural Law & Natural Rights* and of a number of recent writings of mine (Finnis 2003, 115–25; Finnis 2007, § 5). One's aspiration as a *theorist* about law and legal systems is to identify and affirm *general* and warranted propositions about a human practice or institution thoroughly shaped by thought. Developing a general theory requires one to select among all the particular and very various vocabularies and concepts that have been employed in social life both to shape and to describe the various practices or institutions which, as a theorist, one judges it accurate, illuminating and theoretically fruitful to call and treat as instances of (say) law or legal system. This theoretic judgement is not settled by the concepts or criteria articulated and/or used by those whose thought and practice is being named and treated in this way—taking those one by one, or taking the whole disorderly series of them. It is a judgement that requires one as a theorist to select and adopt one's own concept and criteria, and to do so for reasons, as Hart does in working up his theory of law in *The Concept of Law*.[9] What he offers us in that book is a *new and improved concept* of law, corresponding closely to the concept of law already employed in societies he thought reasonably organized and reasonably and critically self-aware. But even in relation to the concepts widely employed in such societies, Hart's concept of law did 'add value', that is, provided an improved understanding of the cluster of features he identifies as the central idea and reality of law, and of why those features can well cluster together—an understanding of the social functions which that kind of clustering serves and promotes, in remedying defects and affording facilities for advancing human purposes.

---

[9] In remarks published in 1983, Hart accepts, as part of his correction of what he had come to consider errors involved in his 'early invocation in jurisprudence of linguistic philosophy' (Hart 1983, 5), that 'the methods of linguistic philosophy, which are neutral between moral and political principles and silent about different points of view which might endow one feature rather than another of legal phenomena with significance' were, precisely by reason of that neutrality and indifference to non-neutrality, not suitable for resolving or clarifying those controversies which arise, as many of the central problems of legal philosophy do, from the divergence between partly overlapping concepts reflecting a divergence of basic points of view or values or background theory.... For such cases what is needed is first, the identification of the latent conflicting points of view which led to the choice or formation of divergent concepts, and secondly, reasoned argument directed to understanding the merits of conflicting theories, [or] divergent concepts or of rules. (Hart 1983, 6)

Though it is not entirely clear how far this passage refers to concepts of law itself (the nature of law), the passage fairly clearly accepts the reality of and need for selection of concepts for use in a general theory of a subject-matter instantiated in varying forms because of the varying concepts (ideas) of those persons and groups in whose life that (range of) subject-matter(s) is instantiated.

The extent to which Hart's descriptive explanation of law depends for its explanatory power on presuppositions about good and bad in human affairs was hidden from Hart in some measure by, it seems to me, some assumption he made or thesis he held about *concepts*. In the notebook which seems to record the genesis of key parts of *The Concept of Law* the word 'Concept' appears a number of times in large capitalized form.[10] It was as if, in these preparatory thoughts, the investigation or identification of a Concept somehow lifted one's understanding, one's account, one's theory, above an investigation of what particular people or groups (or any merely statistical-frequency-based selection of them) have meant, or have intended, above their conceptions of what it is important to promote as desirable (good) and avoid as undesirable (bad), and above the theorist's own 'pre-theoretical' judgments about importance and desirability (good and bad), into a realm of timeless—truly *general*—essences or forms somehow available for adoption on inspection, a neutral, value-free and 'theoretical' perception. This, I believe, is nowhere affirmed in *The Concept of Law*; if it is implied, as I think it is (and not only by the notebook and the book's title), it can and should be regarded as a philosophical myth, an illusion. In this respect, I think Hart's ideas about method in legal theory regressed from the position he had affirmed in 1953: that 'the fundamental issues of legal philosophy' are those 'discussed and reflected upon' by intelligent students of (and surely because they are issues raised and discussed in) Plato's *Republic* and Aristotle's *Nicomachean Ethics* (Hart 1953, 357). Hart knew what he meant: he lectured in 1951 on Plato's ethical and political theory, where, as in Aristotle too, whatever is said or implied about the concepts, nature, or essence of government, constitutionality, law and so forth is controlled by the respective philosophical author's *normative* moral and political theory. As Plato and Aristotle make clear, a theorist's judgments that certain conceptions of political community, government, constitutionality, and law should have primacy in the theoretical description, and the strongly evaluative (morally evaluative) grounds that Plato and Aristotle adduce for those judgments, in no way block the theorist's descriptions of other conceptions of polity, government, and law. In particular, those philosophers of human affairs can, and did, provide careful and illuminating accounts of the defective and inferior kinds and conceptions of polity, government, and law that are so frequently articulated or manifested, despite their normative inferiority (sometimes gross immorality), in the life and history of the human groups available for empirical study in their day.

---

[10] For one instance ('the *Concept* of law') see the transcription of an important passage from the 1950s notebook in Lacey 2004, 222. With that passage's account of how to identify 'a *standard* legal system...without *prejudiced* description' compare the late-1985 ms note at ibid, 351, and the similar passage published in 1983 and quoted above in note 9.

2

Instead of pursuing further that well-trodden path, I want to turn in this paper to another question arising out of Hart's interest in the internal point of view and consequently in law's character as one kind or family of reason(s) for action. The question is this: even when his account in *The Concept of Law* is enhanced by his adoption of something tantamount to Raz's concept of the detached professional perspective, neither external nor internal, in the central senses of those terms, *how well do Hart's accounts enable us to understand that kind of point of view* and that kind of reason for action? The issues I want to explore are not precisely those taken up by Neil MacCormick in the appendix to his *Legal Reasoning and Legal Theory*, where he disambiguates what he calls cognitive and volitional elements run together in Hart's relatively undifferentiated 'internal attitude' (MacCormick 1978). But, while nervous lest there be a Humean implicature to his distinction between cognition and volition, I take for granted, and accept, the many clarifications with which MacCormick there and in chapter 3 of his *H.L.A. Hart* equips us for understanding what Hart was trying to articulate in his over-simple distinction between 'the internal' and 'the external' points of view.[11]

In January 1958, Stuart Hampshire and Hart published in *Mind* 'Decision, Intention and Certainty'. Though Hampshire's name comes first, perhaps as alphabetically prior, it is certain that Hart fully owned the paper's argument: while in Harvard the previous academic year, he had not only worked on the article but spoken at a philosophy seminar on 'Knowing what you are doing', which is the article's theme and thesis (Lacey 2004, 187, 190). That thesis is: one has a knowledge of, and certainty about, what one is doing, one's own voluntary actions, which is not an observer's knowledge, and is not based like the observer/spectator's on empirical evidence or on the observation of one's own (the acting person's) movements: it is *practical* knowledge.[12] First-person statements about an action have the same meaning as third-person statements, but as with 'many concepts involving reference to states of consciousness' there is an 'asymmetry between first-person and third-person statements' about actions, corresponding to the radical difference between the 'means of verification' of the respective statements, the kind of knowledge they articulate (Hampshire and Hart 1958, 10). For the same reason, the article contends, there is a 'necessary connexion' between intending to do something and certainty about what one will do—certainty based not on reflection upon and induction from the evidence of one's

---

[11] For my own, overlapping clarifications, drawing like MacCormick's on work by Raz, see Finnis 1980, 233–7.

[12] Hampshire and Hart 1958, 1, 5, 6, 8–9. The thesis can also be found prominently in Anscombe 1957, but, unlike Hampshire and Hart, Anscombe proceeds to a robust examination of practical reasoning and its upshot, intention.

experience (as might be the case with one's more or less *in*voluntary behaviour), but instead on one's having reasons for doing what one has decided to do: 'practical certainty about what to do' (Hampshire and Hart 1958, 1, 4, 5, 12).

Although neither 'internal' nor any cognate term appears in it, the article is plainly a portrayal and exploration of what *The Concept of Law* will call the internal attitude or point of view as it bears, not on rules or rule-guided action, but on any sort of voluntary action. The article explores other truths important to *The Concept of Law*: the importance of distinguishing that first-person perspective from the perspective or viewpoint or 'attitude' of any observer or spectator (Hampshire and Hart 1958, 5), and the parallel difference between stating an intention—thereby evidencing one's acceptance of reasons for action—and making a prediction that one will act. The article is illuminating and sound, furthermore, in much that it stresses about the empirical reality of practical knowledge and 'free-will', and about the connection between freedom of decision and having reasons for decision (Hampshire and Hart 1958, 4–5). But it has deep and pervasive mistakes, which shed much light on some principal features of contemporary legal philosophy, features manifested in and partly shaped by *The Concept of Law*.

At the very point where Hart and Hampshire bring us face to face with the reality and distinctness of one's practical knowledge of what one intends to do, or is doing, they mix up that practical knowledge with certainty; worse, the certainty they speak of is predictive. Moreover: since *will*, which culminates in choice (what they call decision), is really part and parcel of *reason* (for willing is one's responsiveness to what one believes to be reasons), it is unsurprising that, having conflated practical knowledge and predictive certainty, they make the acting person's choosing consist in (be 'constituted' by) 'becoming certain' about 'what he will do' (Hampshire and Hart 1958, 3, 2). Just when they are announcing that reason can be practical as well as descriptive/predictive, they dissolve its practicality into the descriptive/predictive. One's decision, like one's consequent intention (and thus of course one's disposition to act and one's action), is unhinged from the reasons that precede, and in an unexplored sense result in,[13] the deciding/choosing.

Though it is true that, as the authors underline (Hampshire and Hart 1958, 2), someone who has not yet decided between two or more courses of action must be uncertain about what he will do, it is fallacious to conclude, as they do, that deciding is constituted by becoming certain about what one will do. Indeed, it is not even true that my deciding to do *phi* entails, as they assert, that I am 'certain that I will do this, unless I am in some way prevented'. For I know that I may change my mind, reverse my decision, make a contrary choice. Hart and

---

[13] Hampshire and Hart 1958, 3: 'The [agent's] certainty [about what he will do] comes at the moment of decision, and indeed constitutes the decision, when the certainty is arrived at...as a result of considering reasons, and not as a result of considering evidence.... When he has made his decision, *that is,* when, after considering reasons, all uncertainty about what he is going to do has been removed from his mind, he will be said to intend to do whatever he has decided to do...'

Hampshire, without signalling their shift, later acknowledge this, saying that once I have made my decision, which occurs when 'all uncertainty about what [I am going to do] has been removed from [my] mind, I will be said to intend to do whatever [I have] decided to do, unless either [I fall] into uncertainty again, as a result of further reasons suggesting themselves, *or until [I] definitely [change my] mind*' (Hampshire and Hart 1958, 3). But neither the conditionality of conditional intentions (Finnis 1994) nor the standing significant possibility of change of mind (reversal of decision) is elucidated or even discussed by Hart and Hampshire.[14] The authors are left both asserting and denying that to decide and intend is to make a prediction (become certain) about what one will do.

The truth is that choosing, forming a definite intention, is settling not the indicative-future question 'What will I do?', but the gerundive-optative, *practical* question 'What am I to do?', 'What, in these or more or less specific future cir-cumstances, *should* I do?', 'What is-to-be done [*faciendum, agendum*]?' It is com-patible with uncertainty about the merits of the option chosen, and in that sense, compatible with uncertainty about *what to do*. For choice between alternative options, in the focal sense of 'choice' (*electio*, selection and resolve) is really only necessary when (so far as the chooser can see) the reasons in favour of one option are not all satisfied, or as well satisfied in all dimensions of intelligible good, by the other option(s) (Finnis 1992, 146–7; Finnis 1997, 219–20). Choosing is also compatible with uncertainty about what one will do; for, especially when the car-rying out of one's intention is conditional on contingent future circumstances, one can reasonably be alive to the possibility that one will sometime before then find reason to reverse one's choice (perhaps even reasons that one had consid-ered when making one's original decision). Hart and Hampshire were right to point out the certainty one can and normally does have about what one is doing, but wrong to extrapolate to certainty about the future fulfilling of one's inten-tions; their error leads them to substantial self-contradiction about the allegedly predictive character of statements of intention, and to belated and unintegrated acknowledgement of changes of heart/mind.

Nor do they adequately explicate one's certainty about what one is doing. One knows what one is doing, I would say, because one's doing (in the case of fully vol-untary actions) is the *carrying out of* the proposal/plan that one adopted in one's decision/choice. A plan is a rational structure, in thought, of ends and means. As Aristotle and Aquinas have brilliantly illuminated, each end except the one most ultimate (relative to some particular behaviour) is also a means to some more ultimate end, and each means, except the exertion involved in the very behav-iour itself, also stands as an end relative to the means next more proximate to

---

[14] They pertinently put to themselves the objection that, because 'deciding' and 'changing my mind' represent an act, something that I *do*, 'deciding cannot be adequately characterized as simply becoming certain about one's future voluntary action after considering reasons, and not consider-ing evidence'. But their response restricts itself to asserting that it is unclear what is meant here by 'do', and never confronts the core objection.

that exertion.[15] Moreover, in the deliberation that shapes alternative proposals for choice, ends and means figure propositionally, as reasons for the respective courses of action envisaged in the rival proposals. Each reason articulates a supposed benefit, a supposed intelligible good, promised (not guaranteed!) by the proposed course of action supported by that reason. Within each proposal that one shapes for oneself in deliberation, every means (and thus virtually every end) is transparent for the end which gives point to that means. So too, when one has chosen one proposal in preference to the other(s), the reasons favouring that proposal and course of action remain in play, giving one reason to exert oneself to carry out the chosen action, whether now or when appropriate circumstances arise. The propositional expression of this is not Hart-Hampshire's 'I am certain that *this* is what I will do,' but Aquinas's *imperium*, '*This* is the thing for me to be doing—what I should be doing' (not necessarily a moral 'should')—the directive (*imperium*, command), from oneself as rational self-determining chooser to oneself as rational agent,[16] to do what it takes to achieve the intelligible benefits with an eye to which one chose (adopted the proposal one did), benefits one believed and believes attainable by or in such conduct (attainable if one's means prove to have the efficacy one envisaged for them in one's plan/proposal).

Under pressure of Hobbesian, Humean, and Kantian misunderstandings of practical reasoning, choice, and (consequently) action, all this was much neglected in the period when Hart was turning his philosophical attention to the relation between reason and action, and correspondingly to the way in which behaviour becomes intelligible when understood as it is understood by the acting person, that is, 'from the internal point of view'. But as the role of reasons, though constantly pointed out, remains essentially unanalysed and incompletely integrated in the Hart-Hampshire treatment of intention and practical knowledge, so their role, though again constantly signalled, remains incompletely analysed and integrated in *The Concept of Law* and even, I think, in the later work explicitly focused on peremptory content-independent reasons for action.

3

Consider Hart's canonical account or definition of the internal attitude. As it bears on rules, it is the attitude of those who 'accept and voluntarily co-operate in maintaining the rules, and so see their own and other persons' behaviour in terms

[15] On their understanding of means as nested ends, see eg Finnis 1991; Finnis 1998, 58–71, esp 64 n 20.

[16] On the important and neglected reality of *imperium* in personal choice and action, see Finnis 1980, 338–40. Hart, in conversation with me (again in the tea room), once lightly mocked my account as replacing 'push' theories of motivation (and obligation) with a 'pull' theory. But in understanding practical reason, and willing (which is *in* it, *in ratione*), we must in the last analysis treat as misleading all metaphors borrowed from sub-rational motivation, let alone those from sub-human forms of motion. Reason's directiveness, in practical as in theoretical reason, is *sui generis*, and so, accordingly, is willing, one's responsiveness to reasons (intelligible goods).

of the rules'.[17] And, says Hart, 'the acceptance of the rules as common standards for the group may be split off from the *relatively passive* matter of the ordinary individual acquiescing in the rules by obeying them for his part alone' (Hart 1994, 117, emphasis added).

What should strike us, however, is the relatively passive character of even the officials' internal attitude as characterized by Hart. True, they accept the rules not simply as commonly accepted standards but as common standards *for* themselves *and others*;[18] they use the rules to appraise their own and others' conduct. But in Hart's account they at most cooperate in *maintaining* rules that Hart's account treats as out there, available for acceptance and maintenance. What is striking is the contrast between this and the classical theory of law which treats as central and primary the *positing* of legal rules, and—rightly, I believe—takes their epistemologically and ontologically primary mode of existence to be their existing as a proposal adopted by the choice/decision of their maker; adopted, that is to say, as a kind of plan of conduct for the community and its members and officials. Once made, promulgated, the rules will of course have to be maintained. But this very maintaining is to be understood as a kind of (re)novation of the making. That understanding is in line with Aristotle's definition of the citizen as one who is entitled to share and does share in governing the political community. Hart's notion of accepting rules *as common* standards for oneself *and others* is the nearest his core legal theory gets to the classical notion of law's existence: as a kind of extending of the law-making activities of the rulers, an extending by a kind of interior personal re-enactment, person by person, of the ruler's or rulers' legally decisive adoption of their own legislative or other law-positing proposals.[19]

---

[17] Hart 1994, 91; see also 90, 98, 102, 109–10, 115, 116, 201.

[18] MacCormick 1978, 34–5, begins his explanation of the 'stronger case' of acceptance of a rule, 'willing acceptance': 'Not merely has one a preference for observance of the "pattern", but one prefers it as constituting a rule *which one supposes to be sustained by a shared or common preference* among those to whom it is deemed applicable' (emphasis added). Later, at p 41, MacCormick adjusts this to make the more important point: 'the element of "preference" involved in the "internal point of view" tends to be conditional: one's preference *that a given pattern of action be adhered to by all* may be conditional upon the pattern's being and continuing to be supported by common or convergent preferences among all or nearly all the parties to the activity contemplated' (emphasis added). This justified adjustment is carried forward on p 43: 'Where there is common acceptance of certain standards envisaged as being shared or conventional standards, those who accept them belong to a "group" but so "from the internal point of view" *of these accepters* do all those to whose conduct they deem the standards applicable, and commonly that in turn depends on the possession by human beings of some characteristic which is not necessarily a voluntarily acquired characteristic. Hence Hart's crucial conception of a "group" appears not to be prior to or definable independently of his conception of a rule.' This is illuminating, though the final 'hence' is not altogether clear to me, since members of a group of the kind in which the central case of law is instantiated are characteristically able to identify their group (nation) even when a good many rules, including at least some of the group's former rules of recognition, have broken down.

[19] Finnis, 1998, 254–6: 'Aquinas proposes and argues for a definition of law: an ordinance of reason for the common good of a [complete] community, promulgated by the person or body responsible for looking after that community. But in supplementing and explicating that definition, Aquinas immediately stresses that law—a law—is "simply a sort of prescription {dictamen} of practical reason *in the ruler* governing a complete community", and that "prescriptions" are

A law may, of course, as the classics constantly remind us, be a barely articulate belch of malevolence against a minority (or indeed a perhaps sheeplike majority), a decree mouthed by the terrorist ruler or rulers to a group of henchmen, officials, and 'people's' judges, and communicated by these officials only fragmentarily and in deliberately confusing form to the subjects, perhaps to induce some self-herding towards the slaughterhouse. But it would advance no theoretical purpose to take *such* decrees and such forms of governance as representative laws and legal governance when asking why it makes sense to transit from Hart's 'pre-legal' form of governance to what he calls the central case of law and legal system, or when reflecting on what would be lost in transiting from law to Marxian post-legal society, or when considering the point and worth of the principles 'which lawyers term principles of legality' (Hart 1994, 207), or joining the millennial debate about the respective advantages of the rule of law and the rule of legally unfettered rulers.

But leave that aside. After all, everyone knows that there have been and are—it's a matter of fact—rules laid down as laws, and described by makers and subjects alike as law, which were and are deeply unreasonable, unjust, immoral; it can happen that some of them do not even profess to be reasonable, just, or morally decent. That fact has nothing like the theoretical significance Hart thought it did. As a matter of *fact*, there is no necessary connection between arguments and logic or validity as argumentation; arguments worthless as argument—as *reasons* for a conclusion—can be found all over the place. As a matter of *reason*, an invalid argument is no argument. Again: as a matter of *fact*, there is no necessary connection between medicines and healing; countless medicines do not heal and many of them in fact do nothing but damage health. As a matter of reason, such deleterious medicines are not medicines and are not referred to in discussions of whether there is good reason to devise medicaments and make them available. So too: as a matter of *fact*, there is no necessary connection between

---

simply universal propositions of practical reason which prescribe and direct to action. His explications also add that government (governing, governance) by law means, equally concretely, that these practical propositions conceived in the minds of those responsible for ruling must be assented to by the ruled, and adopted into their own minds as reasons for action. The assent may have been induced only by fear of sanctions, though such unwilling (reluctant) assent cannot be the central case of cooperation in government by law.... the present point is simply that law needs to be present in the minds not only of those who make it but also of those to whom it is addressed—present if not actually, at least habitually—as the traffic laws are in the minds of careful drivers who conform to them without actually thinking about them. The subjects of the law share (willingly or unwillingly) in at least the conclusions of the rulers' practical thinking and in the plan which the rulers propose (reasonably and truthfully or unreasonably and falsely) as a plan for promoting and/or protecting common good. For just as an individual's choice is followed and put into effect by the directive {imperium} of that individual's reason, so a legislature's or other ruler's choice of a plan for common good is put into effect by way of citizens taking the law's directive {imperium; ordinatio} *as if* it were putting into effect their own choice. The central case of government is the rule of a free people, and the central case of law is coordination of willing subjects by law which, by its fully public character (promulgation), its clarity, generality, stability, and practicability, treats them as partners in public reason' (notes, citations, and cross-references omitted).

law and reasonableness, justice or morality; irrational and unjust laws abound, as natural law theory insists from earliest time until today. As a matter of practical reason, unreasonable (and therefore unjust and immoral) laws and legal systems are not what we are seeking to understand when we inquire into the reasons there are to make and maintain law and legal systems, and what features are essential if law and legal systems are to be acceptable—worthy of acceptance—and entitled to the obedience or conformity of reasonable people. (Of course, the study of arguments as reasons will include a study of fallacious arguments, the study of pharmacology will include the study of bad medicines, and a study of law, legality, and the rule of law will include a subordinate study of the ways in which bad laws and official abuse of legality and legal institutions corrupt law, legality, and the rule of law and need to be guarded against by laws and legal institutions designed for the purpose.)

In that light, we can see that laws and law-makers systematically offer their subjects *at least* four different kinds of reason for compliance.[20] (It goes without saying that, as Hart constantly said, laws like every other social fact provide the occasion for many other kinds of motivation for doing the same thing as the law requires to be done: conformism and conventionalism, careerism and cowardice, to name some of the motives, which Hart gave other names.[21]) Where the posited law attaches definitions and either penalties or other negative consequences to *mala in se* (say, rape), it invites its subjects to treat abstaining from these forbidden kinds of act as something required by the very same practical reason that the law-maker judged inherently sound and sought to refine and reinforce, *as well as* by the next three kinds of reason. Secondly, when we are in the zone of, broadly speaking, *mala prohibita*, the posited law offers to promote common good (including, as common good always does, what justice demands as proper respect for rights) by forbidding or requiring some kind of act which is not already, as such, or always and everywhere, excluded or required by well-judging practical reason. In this zone the law offers its subjects the opportunity to accept and comply with it both (a) for the same sufficient though often *not* rationally conclusive, dominant, or compelling reason(s) as the law-maker(s) *decided* to give effect to in preference to the competing reasons for some competing alternative legislative scheme, and (b) for the next two kinds of reason.

Thirdly, then, in the same zone of *mala prohibita* or 'purely positive' laws, the rules in the second of these four categories are also held out to subjects who consider the reasons in favour of the rule insufficient to warrant the law-maker's

---

[20] I discuss here only obligation-imposing norms/rules, and leave aside both (a) power-conferring norms/rules and (b) the question of the collateral moral obligation (not to be seen to defy the positive law) that may subsist *in some of the instances* of laws so unjust that their legal validity is deprived of the moral entailment that, presumptively and defeasibly, it would otherwise have (Finnis 1980, 361).

[21] See Hart 1994, 231, 203, 114.

adoption of it; for such subjects there remains, nonetheless, a kind of reason, often sufficient, to accept the rule as a common standard for themselves and others in the same country, the reason afforded by the fact that the rule is a valid part of the country's legal system.[22]

Fourthly, in respect of *mala in se* and *mala prohibita* alike, the law usually though not invariably offers its subjects, public or private, the kind of reason afforded by the prospect (and undesirability) of undergoing punishment or other penalties or authorized kinds of negative consequence. That kind of reason differs markedly from the reasons which the law-maker has for threatening and (usually different reasons) for imposing such penalties, and the reasons that people amenable to the first three kinds of reason have for complying with the rule to which the penalty is attached. For as Hart points out in the clearest of his rather slender explorations of law's place in the flow or network of practical reason(s),

'Sanctions' are...required not as the normal motive for obedience, but as a *guarantee* that those who would voluntarily obey shall not be sacrificed to those who would not. To obey, without this, would be to risk going to the wall. Given this standing danger, what reason demands is *voluntary* co-operation in a *coercive* system. (Hart 1994, 198)

This passage, illuminating though it is, is not very clear, for it shifts to and fro, without signalling, from viewpoint to viewpoint. Its first and third sentences address the perspective of the law-maker, and of the subject (citizen or friendly alien resident) who shares the law-makers' perspective; the first sentence also *alludes to* the perspective of those (who may even be the 'normal' majority) for whom the normal motive for obedience *is* fear of sanction. The passage's second sentence addresses the perspective of the subject as subject, contemplating obedience or disobedience. The passage's conclusion, about what 'reason demands', presupposes, strikingly but ineluctably, that the designer of the legal system, and anyone willing to adopt the designer's viewpoint and purposes, envisages (has as an end or objective) a system with a content (including forms and procedures) worthy of the *voluntary* cooperation of a *reasonable* subject. Hart here takes for granted that law, the central case legal system that is the real subject-matter of *The Concept of Law*, is an arrangement rationally prescribed, by those responsible for the community, for the common good of its members: *ordinatio rationis ad bonum commune, ab eo qui curam communitatis habet promulgata.*[23]

Notice that Hart does not specify what is bad in the 'danger' that those who voluntarily cooperate would 'go to the wall'; the passage gets much of its force from the plausible implication that it is, in some large part, the evil of unfairness to them (for the disobedience of the scofflaws would, by hypothesis, be going unpenalized). It is like the passage earlier in the book (Hart 1994, 93–4), stating the 'defect' for which the 'remedy' is courts and 'secondary' rules of adjudication.

---

[22] This is explored in some depth in Finnis 1984 (whose analysis is defended, against Raz's critique, in Finnis 1989).

[23] Aquinas, *Summa Theologiae*, 1–2, q. 90 a. 4c; see Finnis 1998, 255–6.

For though Hart labels it inefficiency, what makes the absence of *judicial* means of resolving disputes about rule-violation a defect is surely, in some large measure if not predominantly, the unfairness to the party whose wronging causes the dispute and/or who, being the weaker, would probably be wronged if the dispute were ended by some non-judicial means. In each of these cases, the fairness being appealed to just beneath the surface of Hart's text is essentially the justice that he elucidates in his account of the justice of compensation for injury: the injury upsets the 'artificial equality' or 'equilibrium' established by moral (and, Hart should have added, legal) rules which put the weak and simple on a (normative) level with the strong and cunning; the upset is itself unfair/unjust, and it would be unfair/unjust to leave it unrectified by compensation.[24]

To understand Hart's legacy, however, one needs to notice that he never invites his readers to reflect on the relation—within the one book *The Concept of Law*, let alone within his writings as a whole—between what he says there about justice, what he says about reason, and what he says about the central case of law and the 'defects' it 'remedies' and the 'amenities' it provides. This neglect of pertinent questions parallels other refusals to raise questions. When judges around the English-speaking world needed the help of legal theory to respond to the juridical challenge of *coups d'état* and revolutions, they could find nothing illuminating in Hart's theory of the rule(s) of recognition.[25] For though that 'ultimate' rule is explained by Hart as the answer to a question, namely the question—which follows fittingly the lawyer's sequence of inquiries seeking the reason for the validity of by-laws and ministerial legislation—why a parliamentary enactment is valid, the answer, namely that the courts and officials (if not also private persons) *have the practice* of *using* the rule that what Parliament enacts is to be recognized as law, is treated by Hart as 'a stop in inquiries' (Hart 1994, 107). What he has in mind is *not only*, as he reasonably says, a stop in inquiries seeking further, more ultimate posited rules, *but also*, as he disappointingly takes for granted, inquiries seeking other *juridically relevant* reasons for continuing, discontinuing, or modifying the practice in which the rule of recognition consists. When we entertain, for reasonable affirmation or denial, the proposition that the rule (and the system based on it) is 'worthy of support', we have simply moved, according to Hart, 'from a statement of validity to a statement of value'.[26]

---

[24] Hart 1994, 164–5. Hart should have recalled all this when considering the justice of retribution as a general justifying aim of punishment, but seems never to have done so: see Finnis 1980, 262–4; Finnis 1998, 210–15.

[25] So they turned, albeit inappropriately and fruitlessly, to Kelsen, whose general theory at least attempted to give a juridical account of the source of the validity of an existing constitution, ie of the relation between a 'momentary' legal system and the diachronic legal system in which each momentary system takes its place. See Finnis 1973; Eekelaar 1973.

[26] Hart 1994, 108. [After delivering this paper, I read Simmonds 2007, which at 126–36 develops a valuable complementary critique of Hart's truncation of 'the domain of the juridical' (126). There is much illuminating argument and reflection in the book; it is mistaken, however, in saying (56 n 28) that, in the theory of law developed in the central chapters of my *Natural Law and Natural Rights*, the treating of the common good as central to the understanding of law is 'a

In the idiom of the book, that is a way of saying we have moved outside legal theory, outside the law, outside the juridical, and have nothing to offer the judge who is asking, as judge, whether and when and how a successful *coup d'état* alters the law of the land. Nor anything, indeed, to say to judges who, in altogether ordinary times, ask themselves why they should continue their practice of using the rule(s) of recognition and the criteria of legal validity and juridical argumentation embodied therein or pointed to thereby. For the book's legal theory, its account of law and the juridical, includes no systematic engagement with 'value'—only episodic forays into disintegrated topics such as justice, and later a minimum natural law for 'survival', which have no articulated connection with each other or with the explication of what makes law law.

In short: *The Concept of Law*, the *Essays on Bentham*, and Parts I–III and V of *Essays in Jurisprudence and Philosophy* display a legal theory or general jurisprudence that, having identified its own descriptive dependence on the internal point of view and attitude (in which rules are reasons for action), leaves those reasons largely unexplored, and rests largely content with reporting the fact that people have an attitude which is the internal aspect of their practice. Having so fruitfully gone beyond the observer's or spectator's perspective on bodily movements and behaviour, it rests officially content with a *report* that the participants have reasons for their behaviour and their practice. It does not seek to understand those reasons as reasons all demand to be understood—in the dimension of soundness or unsoundness, adequacy or inadequacy, truth or error. To have been consistent in its abstinence from engagement with that dimension—from 'statements of value'—Hart's method should have restricted him to the observation that people often think they have reasons, that many people think or have thought that a pre-legal set of social rules is defective, think that secondary rules are the remedy, and so forth. But his book's engagement with its readers would then have been very different. And, since by no means everyone everywhere has the same beliefs about reasons, the question why select for report *these* supposed reasons rather than others would have become deafening; it would have broken up the party.

4

Before turning, finally, to the question why Hart so truncated his enquiry into legal reasons, I should say a word about what Hart's successors, in their reflections on the nature of law, have made of his legacy. (Perhaps the word 'legacy'

consequence of' the methodological claims I advanced in chapter I about descriptive general theory. Though chapter I of my book treats general legal theory which is descriptive in purpose as a legitimate enterprise (provided it acknowledges its dependence on evaluations internal to its method of concept-selection), the later chapters on law do not have a descriptive purpose, but (for reasons underlined in Finnis 2003) are normative/evaluative in purpose as well as method, and are not at all dependent on the argument of chapter I.]

in this volume's title was intended, not in the lawyer's sense of what the testator chose to give, maybe with latent defects of which he was unaware—the sense on which I've been relying—but in the loose sense of what his successors made of it all.) Some have maintained (LP1) that 'in any legal system, whether a given norm is legally valid, and hence whether it forms part of the law of that system, depends on its sources, not its merits (where its merits, in the relevant sense, include the merits of its sources)'.[27] Others have maintained (LP2) that 'determining what the law [in a given time and place] is does not necessarily, or conceptually, depend on moral or other evaluative considerations about what the law ought to be in the relevant circumstances' (Marmor 2001, 71). The first thesis (LP1) seems the more strenuous: 'never by reference to merits' is a stronger claim than 'not necessarily by reference to merits,' and that helps explain why John Gardner, sponsor of (LP1), ascribes to the thesis, and to its approach to law, 'comprehensive normative inertness'.[28] It corresponds to Hart's sharp distinction between 'statements of validity' and 'statements of value'. But in Hart that distinction seemed to have the purpose, and more clearly had the effect, of restricting the theory of law to accounting for social-fact-source-based validity without proposing any statement of value.[29] In Gardner, however, as in Leslie Green's similar account of legal theory, and Joseph Raz's, in his own way,[30] too, the affirmation of this sources thesis, (LP1), is said to be in no way 'a whole theory of law's nature'. (LP1) is compatible, they affirm, 'with any number of further theses about law's nature, including the thesis that all valid law is *by its nature* subject to special moral objectives and imperatives *of its own*' (Gardner 2001, 210, emphases added), and compatible with the thesis that 'in some contexts "legality"...names a moral value, such that laws may be more or less valid depending on...their merits', and with the thesis that 'one must capture this moral value of legality...in order to tell the whole story of law's nature'.[31] It thus becomes clear that (LP1) can and should

---

[27] Gardner 2001, 201. This seems to be practically equivalent to Raz's 'sources thesis', often called by others 'exclusive positivism'.

[28] Gardner 2001, 203; cf my comparison of his and Brian Leiter's uses of this phrase in Finnis 2003, 115–28.

[29] The *Postscript's* embrace (Hart 1994, 250–4) of soft or inclusive positivism does not significantly qualify this restriction, since it is a social-fact source that, in such a view, licenses the jurist to look beyond such sources to moral standards, and the legal *theory* of the kind that Hart undertook is restricted, by the descriptive purpose so emphasized in the *Postscript*, to reporting the social fact that the societies under study bring to bear, at this point in their legal reasoning, the relevant moral beliefs they have and are licensed to refer to.

[30] Consider his distinction between applying the law (restricted to social-fact sources) and judicial argument *according to law* (which properly embraces moral reasons and reasoning about maintaining, developing, or amending the law): see, for example, Raz 1993.

[31] Gardner 2001, 226. The final paragraph of Green 2003 similarly affirms: 'Evaluative argument is, of course, central to the philosophy of law more generally. No legal philosopher can be *only* a legal positivist. A complete theory of law requires also an account of what kinds of things could possibly count as merits of law (must law be efficient or elegant as well as just?); of what role law should play in adjudication (should valid law always be applied?); of what claim law has on our obedience (is there a duty to obey?); and also of the pivotal questions of what laws we should have and whether we should have law at all. Legal positivism does not aspire to answer these questions,

be formulated more precisely, converting its universal quantifier to an existential one: (LP′) There is a 'technically confined' and 'intra-systemic' sense of 'legal validity' such that validity in this sense can be predicated of a supposed rule by reference only to social-fact sources, without reference to what ought to be the law (or the sources of law) according to some standard not 'based on' social-fact sources.

(LP′) is entitled, it seems to me, to the assent of everyone everywhere.[32] Certainly it is what was taken for granted by those who said *lex injusta non est lex*, which, understood as its authors understood it,[33] asserts that if a rule which is legally valid in the (LP′) sense is sufficiently unmeritorious it lacks the entitlement to be counted as personally decisive for them by judges, officials, and citizens, an entitlement to directive decisiveness that is central to the reasons we have for establishing and maintaining legal systems.

5

I return to the rule of recognition, which exists—and is the answer, ultimate for Hart's legal theory, to the question 'What is the reason for the validity of the highest rule of change, if not of all the rules, of this legal system?'—by being used as such in the practice of courts and other officials.

Like any other fact about what happens or is or has been done, *practice*, whether idiosyncratic, widespread, or universal, provides by itself no reason for its own continuation. From such an *Is* no *Ought* (or other gerundive-optative) can be inferred without the aid of another *Ought* or gerundive-optative *Is-to-be-pursued-or-done*. The fact that it is raining is in itself no reason to carry an umbrella, no reason at all, even in conjunction with the fact that without an umbrella I'll get wet. But facts like these can play their part in the reason, the warranted conclusion (that I should [had better] carry an umbrella) which gets its directive or normative element from some practical, evaluative premise such as: it's bad for one's health

---

though its claim that the existence and content of law depends only on social facts does give them shape.'

[32] See Finnis 1980, 290; Finnis 2002, 8–15; Finnis 2003, 128–9; and more precisely Finnis 2007, § 3.1.

[33] Nothing could be stranger than Hart's decision to treat the saying as an invitation to treat all positive law as morally binding: Hart 1994, 210–11. For my critique, see Finnis 1980, 364–6; for Hart's reply, see Hart 1983, 11–12. Yet MacCormick is right to give prominence to the thought that motivates Hart in his attempted critique of the tradition, the thought that we must '[hold] all laws as always open to moral criticism since there is no *conceptual* ground for supposing that the law which *is* and the law which *ought* to coincide', with the result that 'the ultimate basis for adhering to the positivist thesis of the conceptual differentiation of law and morals is itself a moral reason...to make sure that it is always open to the theorist and the ordinary person to retain a critical moral stance in face of the law which is' (MacCormick 1981, 24–5). See likewise the opening paragraph of MacCormick 2007a. Since that moral concern was fully shared by the tradition assaulted by so many theorists calling themselves legal positivists, much of the history of jurisprudence over the past two hundred years or more is a tale of wasted zeal.

to get wet, or: it's bad for one's ability to think and function to get uncomfortably wet and cold. *By virtue only of that* or some similar truth (as one supposes) about good and bad, the plain fact that an umbrella can prevent these evils by keeping me dry can contribute to the normative conclusion that I have reason to, or ought to, carry an umbrella. Though David Hume himself thoroughly misunderstood and frequently ignored or violated it,[34] the inaptly named 'Hume's Law' remains valid and indispensable for an understanding of reason and normativity, ethical or otherwise.

In his last writings, Hart identified accurately enough the way in which his legal theory is enmeshed in something much more truly Humean: Humean psychology, Humean conceptions of practical reason, and Humean scepticism. His essay 'Commands and Authoritative Legal Reasons,' the last (number 10) of the *Essays on Bentham*, concludes that 'judicial statements of the subject's legal duties need have nothing directly to do with the subject's reasons for action', a conclusion he rightly anticipates will seem paradoxical, confused, and open to the objection that it 'whittle[s] down the notion of [say, the judge's] *acceptance* of the legislator's enactments as reasons for action' to something very different from the essay's own explanation of what it is to accept some directive as a content-independent peremptory reason for doing what the directive directs—an objection which Hart virtually concedes, professing a lack of 'sufficient grasp of the complexities which I suspect surround this issue' (Hart 1982, 267, emphasis added). The objection can be reformulated: as against the thesis of *The Concept of Law*, that at least officials (including presumably judges) must accept the rules as common standards for their own *and others'* conduct, this final essay holds that judges (and presumably other officials) need not do more than speak (and think!) in 'a technically confined way', that is 'as judges, from within an institution which they are *committed* as judges to maintain', stating not what the subject has reason to do but only 'what . . . may legally be demanded or exacted from him' (Hart 1982, 266, emphasis added). But commitment, and appointment and practice as a judge, are all just facts, which of themselves afford no reason to act, no reason to stay committed or practice as a judge. So the account strips away not only (as Hart admits) the subject's reasons for compliance with law but also (as Hart does not signal) the judge's reasons.

Admittedly, this paradox or confusion *partly* arises from something distinct from the issues of reason and fact that concern me here, something only methodologically significant: namely, Hart's disorderly neglect of central-case analysis, his resort, pervasive in these late essays, to the question whether judges, officials, or anyone else *need* do or think or say such and such. To this question the answer will usually and all too easily be 'No, that way of acting, thinking or speaking is not necessary'. After all, countless kinds of less than fully reasonable ways of

---

[34] See the detailed but evidently much ignored section II.5 in Finnis 1980, 36–42, along with 33–6 and 47–8.

acting, thinking, and speaking can and sometimes or even often do occur. But insistence that nothing save the logically or ontologically necessary can be given any descriptive-explanatory priority would devastate descriptive social theory, leaving it babbling about what is possible and silent about the important, central, and fully rational, and the main ways of diverging from that.

However, undiscussed retreat from central-case analysis is only one of the causes of Hart's final position about the internal attitude on which he had built his legal theory. That position can be reformulated as the claim that the central case of law, as also of adjudication, involves no proposing, not even a pretended proposing, of reasons for the subject's deliberation and action. But that more focused formulation still leaves it indeed a paradoxical position, and one that *misdescribes* what it is for judges to *accept* a rule in their practice of adjudication. Of course, Hart formulated it as a thesis not about judicial acceptance or attitudes, but about judicial speech. However, before judges can speak, in a technically confined way or otherwise, to litigants, witnesses, counsel, and spectators, they must resolve, in deliberation, in the presence, so to speak, of their own consciences, whether and how to speak. 'They are committed as judges', as Hart observes right here, to maintain the legal institution within which they work, and in the last analysis their work is not mere speech but interpersonal action which harms some and helps others in very palpable ways. What are they to *say to themselves*, one may ask, about their commitment?[35] The plain fact that they made that commitment, publicly and no doubt privately, by itself settles nothing, nothing at all, about what they have sufficient *reason* to do, that is, about what is to be done, had better be done, and in any relevant sense ought to be done by them. No *Ought* from a mere *Is*.

At this point, just before his admission of the appearance of paradox (which he cannot resolve), Hart suggests that his position would be quite different if legal reasons for acting (often action contrary to one's interests and inclinations) were 'objective, in the sense that they exist independently of [one's] subjective

---

[35] It might seem as if Hart himself, on the previous page, had raised or identified this very question, when he says that 'it would be extraordinary if judges could give no answer to the question why in their operations as judges they *are disposed to* accept enactments by the legislature as determining the standards of correct judicial behaviour and so as reasons for applying and enforcing particular enactments' (Hart 1982, 265, emphasis added). But their question, if it is pertinent, should and will rather be of the form—or at least should rather have the meaning—'*Should* I be disposed to accept, apply and/or enforce particular enactments…?' Are there sufficient reasons for my doing so, and if so what are they?' [Simmonds 2007, 129–35, takes the decisive question to be, not what reason judges have for applying the law, but what justification they can offer others, notably the litigants before them, for applying it. I agree that the latter question is of high importance, and very pertinent to the assessment of Hart's position. But the judge's own first-person singular question is *at least* equally important in itself and at least equally relevant to the theoretical debate. Simmonds 2007, 134–5 is as relaxed as Hart about the fact that judges' reasons for adhering to the law 'may be non-moral reasons grounded in self-interest'. Of course they 'may' and doubtless often are. But self-interest can never require more of judges than that they *appear* to be applying the law, and the opportunities for plausibly and 'deniably' corrupting the law's application are so great that here the first-person question—the question that is conscience—is also of high public importance and decisive for understanding the 'archetype' or central case of law and legal system.]

motivations'.[36] The implication of this and the whole paragraph, that Hart did not believe in objective practical reasons, legal or moral, was to be thoroughly confirmed by the last-written piece of work he published, his hard-working review of Bernard Williams, *Ethics and the Limits of Philosophy* for the *New York Review of Books* in July 1986. The review firmly endorses Williams's ethical subjectivism, while emphasizing its controversial character. I quote just one passage in relation to which the points I have been making about practices, commitments, and the first-person perspective may again seem pertinent:

> ...the question, 'What should I do in these circumstances' is essentially 'first-personal' and not a mere derivative of and replaceable by 'What should anyone do in these circumstances?' For the 'I' of practical deliberation that stands back from my desires and reflects upon them is still the 'I' that has those desires, and, *unless I am already committed to the motivations of an impartial morality, reflective deliberation will not lead me to it.* To hold otherwise is to confuse reflection with detachment; and that confusion has encouraged the mistaken idea that if our moral beliefs are to be more than mere prejudices they must be regulated by some general ethical theory *au dessus de la mêlée* of our ethical practices. (Hart 1986, 50, emphasis added)

The French phrase perhaps recalls the title of a once famous pacifist tract by Romain Rolland, published in 1915 and alluded to directly in the last volume of Proust's great book. Be that as it may, the passage shows again how inadequately Hart's work represents the first-person perspective, in particular the form that reasons take in that perspective (when I am concentrating on reasons in the search for a right answer), and the way in which reasons can lead me to change my mind and, if they are practical reasons, acquire new motivations. The claim that 'unless I am already committed to the motivations of an impartial morality, reflective deliberation will not lead me to it' is simply wrong. Could it be plausible to anyone who does not accept the Humean dogma that reasons cannot motivate?

As a general thesis about reason and will, that dogma is made to seem tolerable, if not credible, by the assumption that the impossibility of rational and rationally motivating *ends* leaves intact motivation by 'instrumental reasons', reasons which identify suitable and efficient means to sub-rationally desired (and therefore 'subjectively motivating') ends. But that assumption is illusory. If I have no reason for my ends, I have no *reason* for adopting or being interested in instrumental means

---

[36] Hart 1982, 266–7: 'Of course, if it were the case, as a cognitive account of duty would hold it to be, that the statement that the subject has a legal duty to act in a way contrary to his interests and inclinations entails the statement that there exist reasons which are "external" or objective, in the sense that they exist independently of his subjective motivation, it would be difficult to deny that legal duty is a form of moral duty. At least this would be so if it is assumed that ordinary non-legal moral judgments of duty are also statements of such objective reasons for action. For in that case, to hold that legal and moral duties were conceptually independent would involve the extravagant hypothesis that there were two independent "worlds" or sets of objective reasons, one legal and the other moral.'

to them, clever though the techniques embodied in some of those means may be. As I put it recently, adopting an argument of Christine Korsgaard:

'…unless something attaches normativity to our ends, there can be no requirement to take the means to them.'[37] Such ends, moreover, have to be '*good*, in some sense that goes beyond the locally desirable'.[38] For 'I must have something to *say to myself* about why I am [willing an end, and am committed and remain committed to it, even in the face of desires that would distract and weaknesses that would dissuade me]—something better [to say to myself], moreover, than the fact that this is what I wanted yesterday'[39] (or indeed a moment ago or even, in the struggle of feelings, right now).[40]

What am I to say to myself? That question comes to mind when reading the final section of Hart's review of Williams. Having endorsed the author's main arguments for denying that ethical/moral beliefs have rational foundations, Hart asks 'What bearing on practice will and should these arguments have?' His answer begins by noting one of the fears that

have been excited by such skeptical thought.… [the fear] that if it becomes widespread we shall have nothing—or not enough—to say to the immoralist, whether he is the coldly selfish egoist of private life, or the brutal advocate of oppression in public life. But there is surely something laughable in the idea that anything we could draw from philosophy could weigh with such characters bent on having their way at others' expense. Why should it matter to them that there is a philosopher's proof that, in acting as they do, they are irrational, inconsistent, or flying in the face of some moral truths? As Williams says, 'What will the professor's justification do when they break down the door, smash his spectacles, take him away?' (Hart 1986, 52)

But the interesting question is not: what have I to say to the barbarians to persuade them that they should desist? It is: what have I to say to myself when I ask myself whether I shouldn't perhaps be on the winning side and team up with them?[41]

---

[37] Korsgaard 1997, 251.

[38] Korsgaard 1997, 250–1. Korsgaard, at 251, 252, is tempted to resile from this to allow for a 'heroic existentialist act' of 'just tak[ing] one's will at a certain moment to be normative, and commit[ting] oneself forever to the end selected at that moment', 'for no other reason than that [one] wills it so'. But she should concede that unless such a person considers that there is something worthwhile in doing so, some good in or reason for doing so, such an 'act of commitment' and of subsequent 'taking [it] as normative' is not rational but irrational.

[39] Korsgaard 1997, 250.

[40] Finnis 2005a, 113–14. For my criticism of Korsgaard's attempts to develop a non-Humean conception of practical reason, see Finnis 2005a, 114–18.

[41] Hart's next paragraph speculates about the reactions not of the immoralist or the egoist but of 'more ordinary people who with various degrees of conviction, difficulty, and backsliding manage to live up to the moral standards they have acquired and developed in their social life and to transmit them to their children', and gradually he locates 'us', the first-person plural, among them: when they/we discover the truth of ethical scepticism, 'the sense of necessity (the moral "I must") in which the recognition of moral obligation often terminates, will have to be seen as coming not from outside, but from what is most deeply inside us even though it is normally also supported by others who share our practices and beliefs. The fear is that this will not be enough and that when

Williams and, more hesitantly, Hart attribute to certain ethical beliefs some
measure of immunity from their scepticism: what they call 'substantive' or 'thick'
ethical concepts, as used unreflectively and uncritically in 'a simple traditional
society': concepts such as 'cruelty, lying, brutality, treachery, and gratitude', as distinct from 'abstract all-purpose evaluative concepts of "ought" and "right" and
"good"'. But in this marshalling by Hart and Williams of practical predicates for
classification between thick and thin we find omitted yet again, as in Hume and
Kant and chapter IX.1–2 of *The Concept of Law*, the intelligible goods of knowledge, life and health, friendship, reasonableness in one's inner life and one's outer
actions, and the other fundamental reasons we all have for choosing and doing
anything worthwhile we do or should do. These ends, taken in their fundamental
intelligibility as good not only for me but for anyone, and all the more when taken
in their reflective implications as the elements of human flourishing and so the
key to adequately understanding our nature as persons (Finnis 1998, 29–34, 53,
90–2), are so substantive, 'thick', and so far from being merely 'abstract', that they
are the 'deep inside' of all that we can and should 'say to ourselves' to warrant our
decisions as law-makers, law-appliers (executive or judicial), and citizens. The pursuit of these basic goods needs and can be given rational integration by the Golden
Rule and other principles of that reasonableness we call ethical/moral, and by the
call of reason to be attentive to architectonic facts such as the possibility of free
choice, and the subsisting of personal, familial, and (in different ways) national
identity (partly given and partly constituted as the intransitive implications of free
choices) (Finnis 2005b). Such integration reinforces and makes more pointed the
rational directiveness of the initial normativity entailed by the intelligible desirability of the basic human goods, that is, from their priority as reasons both for action
and for abstention from what by entailment from them are basic forms of harm by
conduct or neglect. These basic reasons for action are the rational ground for the
Hartian primary rules restricting violence, theft, and fraud, and in their implications are the ground also for the Hartian remedies called secondary rules.[42]

Was the moral scepticism to which Hart gives restrained but clear voice in his
last work a change of direction for him, something extrinsic to the architecture of

we come to think of our moral standards as resting on no further foundation, we shall disregard
them whenever they stand in the way of our getting or doing what we want'. Hart's response to
this fear begins: 'How likely this is, is a question of moral psychology about which we know little
enough ...', and never gets round to considering what one *should* think about the directive force
of one's 'moral standards' once one discovers, through philosophical argumentation, that they
merely 'come from what is most deeply inside us' and reflect motivations and 'concerns' which one
just happens to have but which plenty of other people do not have, and which collide with other
motivations and lively interests one has deep inside one.

[42] Hart's position in the Postscript, Hart 1994, 249, that it is 'quite vain to seek any more specific purpose which law as such serves beyond providing guides to human conduct and standards
of criticism of such conduct', is simply incompatible with the theory of law set out in *The Concept of
Law*: see Finnis 1980, 6–7. It is part and parcel of the disorderly retreat from central-case analysis
that we see in Hart 1982 (which I have discussed above).

his main work in the philosophy of law? I feel sure it was not.[43] In the notebook from which *The Concept of Law* emerges, immediately before the key paragraph beginning 'I have the dim . . . outline of this book in my mind', are two sentences, on separate lines:

One side saying: you are blind

The other: you are seeing ghosts.

Midway between those years and the final years, his way of articulating the issue, on the one occasion when our conversation touched explicitly on ethical object-ivity, was the same: it's a matter of 'You're blind' versus 'You're seeing things'. The ghosts he had in mind as *The Concept of Law* began to take shape surely included[44] the 'complex' and 'debatable' conceptions of 'the human end or good', conceptions entertained by philosophers before 'other thinkers, Hobbes and Hume among them, . . . [were] willing to lower their sights' (Hart 1994, 191). And as we know, what Hobbes, not to mention his disciple Bentham, found when the sights were right down and he looked inside was the brute fact of desires, will as no more than the desire that last precedes action, and, to make possible some unified theory, some desire by postulation dominant, such as (in early Hobbes) the desire to surpass others for the sake of surpassing them, or (in later Hobbes) to avoid death.

Trying to understand the internal point of view makes, I would say, no sense as a method in social theory unless it is conceived as trying to understand the intelligible goods, the reasons for action, that were, are, and will be available to any acting person, anyone capable of deliberation or of spontaneously intelli-gent response to opportunities. Once these reasons are understood, along with the accompanying, potentially reinforcing, potentially disruptive, subrational inclin-ations (passions, emotions), theorists are equipped to understand the myr-iad ways in which the practices of individuals and groups can, do, and doubtless will respond, reasonably and more or less unreasonably, in the ever-variable but far from random circumstances of human existence. Social theory may be fun-damentally contemplative ('descriptive') in purpose, or it may be fundamentally practical, intending to guide action—the theorist's as much as anyone else's—by

---

[43] His official position remained, to the end, that 'legal theory should avoid commitment to con-troversial philosophical theories of the general status of moral judgments and should leave open, as I do in this book ([Hart 1994, 168]), the general question of whether they have what Dworkin calls "objective standing"' (Hart 1994, 253–4). But this was always an implicitly partisan neutrality. For, as the review of Williams I think concedes, to withhold the affirmation of such standing is to depart from the internal point of view of those who accept moral standards as binding—depart in a way they would consider fundamental. Joseph Raz, who knew Hart far better, I believe, than I did, speaks less cautiously about Hart's subjectivist and (not unlike Williams) naturalist (I would say scientistic) view on these fundamental matters and about their implications for his jurisprudence, in Raz 2001, 4–6.

[44] To be sure, the sentences in the notebook (which I quote from Lacey 2004, 222) doubtless also refer to the Realists' view (mistaken, as Hart says) that obligation and associated reasons even for official (eg judicial) action are illusory projections of feelings, psychological compulsions, etc.

identifying at least some outlines and principles of right and wrong, better and worse. But descriptive social theory will be unable to get beyond an endless video of local histories—or a merely statistical ordering of them—unless it makes the judgments about reasonableness that are fundamental to practical social theory. (Hart's theory makes and relies on some.) And practical, morally oriented social theory will be a half-blind guide unless it profits from the practical insights, and the transmissible experience of inner and outer causes and effects, that are made available by history and social theory, perhaps distilled and by imagination and intelligence enhanced in great works of literary art.

The asymmetry between the first-person and the third-person viewpoint goes deeper than Hart and Hampshire identified. In the last analysis, it is this: the third-person view terminates in facts, including facts about the beliefs and attitudes, intentions and commitments of other persons; but in the first-person view 'I believe that *p*' is transparent for '*p*'.[45] The 'I believe' drops out, leaving '*p*', usually not just one proposition but a network of propositions some of which are reasons for believing others. One is looking not at oneself, one's attitudes and beliefs, as facts about oneself, but at the proposition(s) under consideration, the reasons there are for affirming it and the reason(s) it gives for making it one's belief, one's attitude, and one's action, whether the theoretical-practical action of judging it true or the practical-practical action of following and putting into effect the intelligent and reasonable guidance it gives, the good (benefits and goals) towards which it directs one. And because the first-person (practical) viewpoint is concerned not, in the end, with facts about oneself but with reasons (for action) that are both available to and bear on the good of anyone like me (generically, all human beings), it is the domain of *common* good and so the engine-room, the most proximate efficient cause,[46] of law.

In that perspective there is no reason to be found for stopping at the supposedly 'minimum' set of reasons which Hart appeals to, not simply in his reflections on the 'minimum content of natural law', but much more importantly in his account of primary rules, private and public secondary rules, and the union of them that constitutes law in its central instantiation and concept(ion). I argued earlier in this long paper that that account gets its persuasiveness partly from its suppressed appeal to reasons which, though largely unarticulated or, where articulated, unintegrated in the legal theory proposed in *The Concept of Law*, are reasons (good and not so good) pervasive in Hart's other writings and indeed in his own life. His work is a standing invitation to develop legal theory's critical account and promotion of those considerations of justice, of concern for

---

[45] On this transparency, see Finnis 1983, 70–4.

[46] In respect of the law's positivity, it is also the formal (shaping) cause. Even wicked law will almost invariably purport to be for common good, and should be juridically and morally assessed by reference to the standing requirements of the common good that yield the principles of legality or the Rule of Law, and the general principles of law common to civilized peoples.

common good, which include the general principles of legality and law com-mon [47] to *civilized* [48] peoples and make law salient [49] as a means of governance and a reasonable exercise and acceptance [50] of authority.

[47] In Finnis 1980, 286–9, I articulated some of those principles, and did so by reference to pub-lic international law. But their primary domain is, and will in justice remain, the legal system of what Hart called *countries*, that is, the nation state, the political community of persons who regard themselves as one people and organize their law and legal system to be theirs as distinct from other peoples'.

[48] Failure today to take seriously this qualifier makes freshly resonant the memoir contrib-uted by Lord Wilberforce to the privately printed record of the memorial meeting for Hart in the University Examination Schools, Oxford, in 1993, recalling their friendship in the 1930s: 'We shared . . . a sense of coming disaster which we knew would destroy our way of life. . . . In 1938 we were together, with some lawyers and clerks, when the news came that Mr. Chamberlain was returning with "Peace for our time". There was applause, there was talk of going to the airport to cheer him home. We just looked at each other with tears in our eyes—it was unnecessary to speak.' See Lacey 2004, 57. The reference by Williams and Hart to smashing the professor's spectacles and taking him away doubtless alluded, most immediately, to the destruction which befell the nation under the Khmer Rouge, in Cambodia—far away, unlike that of which it is (in one sense) 'unnecessary to speak' today.

[49] On this salience, see Finnis 1984 and Finnis 1989.

[50] On the not merely 'conceptual' reasons why authority entails obligation, and an earlier reflec-tion on Hart's stopping short in the identification of reasons, see Finnis 1987.

2

The Legal Entrenchment of Illegality[1]

David Lyons

When a legal theory accounts for existing law, it also determines what counts as unlawful conduct. That there is so direct an implication may help to explain why illegality does not receive much attention from legal theorists. This paper concerns a special subset of unlawful conduct, namely, *official* practices that are *clearly* unlawful, largely *open* (not hidden), and deeply *entrenched* (tolerated for a long period of time). I call this phenomenon the legal entrenchment of illegality.

Much official misconduct falls outside those bounds. Some unlawful conduct by officials is kept out of the public eye (though it may be widely known by officials and a limited number of lay persons). In the US this includes, for example, bribe-taking and solicitation as well as covert programs against political dissidents that range from unlawful surveillance to assassination. Such practices may be maintained for a very long time; but when they are publicly exposed they may become a political embarrassment and even a legal liability. Typically, the government then denounces the practice and informs the public that it has been ended, although experience often argues to the contrary. The examples I shall discuss are different. The system of racial stratification called *Jim Crow* was part of the American way of life from the 1890s to the 1960s[2]—much the better part of a century. Some of its entrenched practices involved clear and open violations of law, by officials and others, including the systematic failure by officials to enforce some unproblematic laws, such as those against rape and murder, when the victims were African Americans, and the non-enforcement decisions could not plausibly be seen as a reasonable exercise of official discretion.

---

[1] A draft of this paper was presented at the July 2007 British Academy Symposium on 'The Legacy of H.L.A. Hart: Legal, Political, and Moral Philosophy'. I am grateful to Charles Hunter and Lauren Ingoldsby for research assistance and to participants in philosophy and law workshops at Boston University and at the Hart Symposium for comments on previous drafts.

[2] *Brown v Board of Education* (1954) condemned racial segregation only in public schools, not more generally. The first major civil rights act confronting Jim Crow became law ten years later (Civil Rights Act of 1964). Although its enforcement was strongly and often violently resisted, its enactment represents the beginning of the end of official acceptance of the racial stratification that began with the creation of race-based chattel slavery three and a half centuries earlier.

The existence of plainly unlawful practices that are openly tolerated within what is usually regarded as a normally functioning legal system suggests the need for theoretical reflection.[3] One of the central points of Hart's legal theory is that we cannot understand law without recognizing the crucial role of officials' attitudes towards the norms, especially the basic elements, of their respective legal systems. Officials 'accept' the foundational rules of their system and employ them 'as guides to conduct', including their own. A derivative species of 'acceptance' is conferred upon the system's non-foundational rules, such as those laid down in legislative enactments. Officials regard all of the system's 'valid' rules as standards to be followed by the society as a whole. When clearly unlawful practices are openly tolerated or engaged in by officials, however, the result is a significant clash of attitudes involving the foundations of the legal system. The legal entrenchment of illegality thus threatens to falsify Hart's widely endorsed legal theory.

This paper has four parts. Part 1 reviews crucial components of Jim Crow. Part 2 notes neglected aspects of some historically important Supreme Court opinions. Part 3 explores some theoretical ramifications of the legal entrenchment of illegality. Part 4 offers some further reflections.

A preliminary point is needed. I wish to focus on official practices that are clearly unlawful, but my reference to Jim Crow might suggest otherwise. The Jim Crow system is often referred to as 'racial segregation', but racial segregation *per se* could not be regarded as *clearly* unlawful during the Jim Crow period. Although officially mandated racial segregation was ultimately ruled unconstitutional, and thus unlawful, it would be unreasonable to ignore the legal role of earlier judicial decisions that upheld the practice. Most importantly, in 1896 the US Supreme Court held, in *Plessy v Ferguson*, that state-mandated racial segregation was lawful. Although at the time one could reasonably have regarded the Court's reasoning as problematic and its holding as unsound,[4] the Court's authoritative ruling means that one could not thereafter reasonably regard the maintenance of racial segregation as *clearly* unlawful conduct. That presumably changed when the Supreme Court declared, in 1954, that racial segregation in public schools was unconstitutional.[5]

None of this affects the Jim Crow example, because I am not concerned here with racial segregation *per se*. In promulgating its 'separate but equal' doctrine, the *Plessy* court made clear that racially segregated public services and facilities must be substantially equal. Systematic and open violation of *that* legal requirement, which was characteristic of Jim Crow, was a *clearly* unlawful official practice. To take another example that I've mentioned, public officials' toleration of, and sometimes direct involvement in, lynching likewise exemplified the legal entrenchment of illegality.

---

[3] I doubt that Jim Crow is an isolated case, but I shall not pursue that issue here.

[4] I discuss an aspect of this decision in Part 2 below.

[5] The Supreme Court's condemnation of racial segregation was soon extended. In a 1956 case (*Gayle v Browder*), occasioned by the Montgomery, Alabama, bus boycott, for example, the Court ruled against racial segregation in a municipal bus system.

1 Jim Crow[6]

Americans lived under the system of racial subjugation known as chattel slavery
for two centuries. Following the Civil War, however, US federal law, including a
substantially amended Constitution, called for a 'reconstruction' of society, with
radical implications for the former slave states. The law conferred upon African
Americans, including four million former slaves, equal rights in many areas—from
contractual conditions and judicial procedures to participation in governance of
the community.

There was widespread resistance within the former slave states to the mandated
reforms, including organized violence. Despite this, change occurred. Some
former slaves acquired farms, and those who managed to retain them beyond the
reconstruction period achieved a measure of economic independence. African
Americans voted, served on juries, and held public office. Political parties com-
peted for their votes. Black-white coalitions developed. Racial relations were in
flux (just as they had been two centuries earlier, before racial stratification was
officially imposed[7]).

Federal agencies, such as the Freedman's Bureau, as well as federal troops were
crucial to the progress of social reconstruction. In the early 1870s, for example,
federal forces routed organized bands of violent white supremacists. But support
for reconstruction weakened in the wider community and the political price of
federal action became unacceptable to the ruling Republican Party. This led to
the *de facto* abandonment of reconstruction. The disputed presidential election
of 1876 was settled the following year when the Democrats agreed to accept
the Republican candidate on the understanding that the federal government
would stop trying to enforce African Americans' legal rights. Federal troops were
accordingly withdrawn from the South.

Within a few years the former slave states began openly to construct a
system of racial subordination that could survive legal challenge under the post-
Civil War constitutional amendments (as federal courts were applying them) by
avoiding explicit references to race. Efforts to exclude blacks from government
and from effective use of the courts were largely successful. Between 1896 and
1904, for example, the roll of black registered voters in Louisiana declined by
99 per cent. Blacks' political leverage declined drastically.

As Congress had rejected any form of reparations for the former slaves, including distribution of land the slaves had cleared and worked, most became sharecrop-
pers or tenant farmers, which ended their economic and political independence.
In non-agricultural pursuits, African Americans were paid substantially less than

---

[6] This Part draws upon Foner 1988, Myrdal 1944, Kennedy 1997, President's Committee on
Civil Rights 1947, and Woodward 1955.
[7] Which occurred half a century after Africans first arrived in Jamestown (Lyons 2007, 33–5).

whites for comparable work and were also excluded from many industries and job categories. In some areas, sheriffs would rent black prisoners to local employers and would arrest blacks without cause in order to secure labour for the purpose.

Resistance to the development of the Jim Crow system, by whites as well as blacks, was overcome by a campaign of terror. A crucial weapon was lynching, which occurred with increasing frequency. At its peak, in the 1890s, lynching claimed two persons per week. Fewer lynchings occurred after the first decade of the new century, but the change was not a result of increased law enforcement. Once Jim Crow was consolidated, there was less need for actual lynchings. The ever-present threat was sufficient.

Lynching is, of course, murder. At no point under Jim Crow was lynching lawful. No court threw out a lynching-based homicide charge on the ground that no law would have been broken by action of the sort that was alleged to have occurred. Most importantly, many lynchings were public affairs; some were even advertised in advance. In many cases participants were easily identifiable; in some, involvement was pictorially recorded. Participants were openly photographed, *facing* the camera, and prints were widely distributed through the US mail as picture postcards, with incriminating messages (Allen 2000). Lacking fear of prosecution, participants posed with impunity. Prosecutions were in fact rare and, thanks to jury nullification, convictions were rarer still. The few officials who attempted to enforce the law in such cases were subjected to social, political, or economic sanctions.

Public officials sometimes participated in lynchings. Some publicly expressed support for the practice as needed to maintain the prevailing way of life—white supremacy. Anti-lynching legislation was frequently proposed in Congress but never reached a Senate vote. Senators from the Jim Crow South defended the system, including its extra-legal modes of enforcement (Holden-Smith 1996). As late as the 1950s, a prominent Southern senator reacted to a voting rights campaign by openly calling for the sort of 'night riding' that was associated with Ku Klux Klan terror (Dittmer 1994, 2).

No fair description of Jim Crow would fail to mention *pogroms*, events that in the US are usually called 'race riots'. A pogrom has been defined as an 'organized, often officially encouraged massacre or persecution of a minority group, especially one conducted against Jews' (American Heritage Dictionary 1992, 1397). The term applies to attacks on African American communities, a substantial number of which occurred between 1898 and 1946.[8] These frequently were

---

[8] Wikipedia (2007) lists 'race riots' between 1890 and 1954 in Wilmington, NC, Lake City, NC, and Greenwood County, SC in 1898; New Orleans, LA, and New York City, NY in 1900; Atlanta, GA and Brownsville, TX in 1906; Springfield, IL in 1908; East St. Louis, IL, Chester, PA, Philadelphia, PA, and Houston, TX in 1917; Washington, D.C., Chicago, IL, Omaha, NB, Charleston, SC, Longview, TX, Knoxville, TN, and Elaine, AR in 1919; Tulsa, OK in 1920 and 1921; Rosewood, FL in 1923; Harlem, NY in 1935; Detroit, MI, Los Angeles, CA and Harlem, NY in 1943; Columbia, TN in 1946, in addition to riots around the US following Jack Johnson's defeat of Jim Jeffries for the heavyweight boxing championship in 1910.

followed by the prosecution of blacks who defended themselves and little if any prosecution of white attackers.[9]

The less overtly violent aspect of Jim Crow included the open, established practice by state and local governments of providing substantially inferior public facilities for blacks, when they provided any at all. In the Jim Crow South, budgetary allocations per black student were a fraction of those for white students. School buildings, equipment, and transportation for black students were substantially inferior to those for whites. Black teachers received substantially lower salaries and were assigned a substantially greater number of students than white teachers. Near the middle of the century, the President's Committee on Civil Rights (1947, 63) reported that segregated school districts failed to provide black students with a proper public education.

Similar inequalities characterized other public services and facilities at the state and local levels. Only a fraction of public libraries served blacks—a fraction much smaller than their portion of the population. Public parks and playgrounds for blacks were substantially inferior or not provided. Streets in black neighborhoods were poorly maintained compared with streets in white neighborhoods. State and local government services for blacks were either inferior or denied. The 'separate but equal' doctrine of *Plessy v Ferguson* clearly implied that these Jim Crow practices were unlawful.

The operation of the criminal law was openly inequitable. Officials enforced the law more vigorously when crime victims were white than when they were black. Blacks were more likely than whites to be subjected to unwarranted arrests, abusive search and seizure practices, and unnecessarily extended detentions prior to arraignment. Police brutality was widespread against blacks. Criminal trials of blacks were much more likely than those of whites to be perfunctory. Courts frequently admitted unacceptable evidence against blacks, including coerced confessions. The sentencing of blacks was much more likely to be disproportionate to the crime as well as greater than punishments for whites convicted of similar crimes. These practices were deeply entrenched in the Jim Crow system.

Racial discrimination in and by the federal government was widespread (especially after the Wilson administration), but it was *not clearly* unlawful until the Supreme Court's 1954 decision in *Bolling v Sharpe* subjected the federal government to equal protection requirements.

2 The Supreme Court

To suggest dominant official attitudes in the last third of the nineteenth century, I will discuss briefly three Supreme Court decisions that contributed substantially to the development of Jim Crow. My point is not the familiar one that these

[9] For the Tulsa 'race riot' of 1921, for example, see Brophy 2002.

decisions reduced significantly the federal government's acknowledged authority to secure civil rights for African Americans (although that is true). It is, rather, that the Court's majority opinions included statements that would have been seen *at the time* to be so implausible as to raise serious doubts about the Court's sincerity and its willingness to enforce African Americans' constitutional and statutory rights.

It will be useful to first review Chief Justice Taney's opinion (just prior to the Civil War) in *Dred Scott v Sandford* (1857, 393–454). John Emerson had taken his slave Dred Scott with him for several years in US territories that prohibited slavery. After Emerson later died, back in Missouri, his widow refused Scott's offer to purchase his own freedom. Scott then sued for his freedom in the Missouri courts, on the ground that slaves were emancipated when they were taken into territories that prohibited slavery. That doctrine had routinely been respected by several slave states, including Missouri, so Scott had good reason to be optimistic about the result. In Scott's case, however, the Missouri Supreme Court, with a new Chief Justice, reversed its own precedents and ruled against him. Scott then took his case to federal court. This seemed possible because Scott's new owner, John Sanford,[10] was a citizen of New York State and Scott had been treated by both state and federal courts in Missouri as a citizen of that state. Under the federal Constitution's 'diversity clause',[11] federal courts have jurisdiction when a citizen of one state sues a citizen of another state.[12]

Taney argued, however, that federal courts lacked jurisdiction because *no* person with African ancestry, like Scott, *could* be a citizen under the US Constitution. So far as the federal government was concerned, African Americans 'had no rights which a white man was bound to respect' (*Dred Scott v Sandford* 1857, 407). That infamous statement was followed by a less frequently noted claim:

This opinion was at that time fixed and universal in the civilized portion of the white race. It was regarded as an axiom in morals as well as politics, which no one thought of disputing, or supposed to be open to dispute; and men in every grade and position in society daily and habitually acted upon it in their private pursuits, as well as in matters of public concern, without doubting for a moment the correctness of this opinion (*Dred Scott v Sandford* 1857, 407).

Taney argued that, as these ideas were shared by the framers of the Constitution, they had the effect of excluding African Americans, free as well as enslaved, from membership in the political community.

Taney's historical claim was not just wrong but *plainly* false. Although he cited many racially discriminatory provisions in state and federal law as evidence of white supremacist ideology, he did not establish that the ideology had been 'fixed

---

[10] Sanford's name was misspelled in the official report.
[11] Article III, Section 2 says that 'The judicial power shall extend to all Cases…between Citizens of different States.'
[12] For the history of *Dred Scott*, see Fehrenbacher 1978.

and universal in the civilized portion of the white race'; nor could he have done so. And Taney, a learned man, would have known better.

Taney would have known that, during the Constitutional Convention of 1787, delegates from the Lower South, especially Georgia and South Carolina, had demanded constitutional protections for slavery because they reasonably feared the abolitionist movement, which was making practical progress at the time.[13] He might well have known that anti-slavery sentiment was significant even in slave states of the Upper South, such as Virginia, where abolitionist-inspired manumissions had become commonplace, and that two delegates to the Convention, including one from Virginia, had voiced support of abolition. In any case, he presumably knew that, just days prior to the Constitutional Convention, the Continental Congress, in the same city, had enacted the Northwest Ordinance, which prohibited slavery in that territory. He would have known that by 1787 the Northern states had begun to abolish slavery and that several of the new Western states would soon do the same. So Taney knew that his historical claim was false. Anyone paying attention—and much attention was paid at the time to the *Dred Scott* case[14]—would have seen Taney's historical claim as expressing his own unwillingness to acknowledge the rights of African Americans, not a unanimous view of 'civilized' late eighteenth century white society.

It seems to me that Taney provided a model for *post*-Civil War Supreme Court opinions that interpreted the constitutional and legislative changes which laid the legal groundwork for Reconstruction. Consider the three principal cases in that category:

Slaughterhouse Cases (1873) was about monopolies, but the Supreme Court addressed the constitutional amendments that guaranteed, in more general terms, legal equality for African Americans (because the amendments were invoked by the aggrieved parties). In holding that the fourteenth amendment's privileges and immunities clause concerns only a very narrow class of federal rights (*Slaughterhouse Cases* 1873, 73–4),[15] Justice Miller, writing for the Court, maintained that the amendments did not substantially increase federal authority vis-à-vis the states (78), which, he said, would continue to have primary responsibility for 'the regulation of civil rights' (82). That was an astonishing claim. As Justice Field noted in dissent, 'The amendment was adopted...to place the common rights of American citizens under the protection of the National government' (93). Miller's opinion denied what was plainly true. That crucial aspect of the Court's position could not reasonably have been taken as an honest construal

[13] Madison's notes on the Convention proceedings had been published in 1840; see Kammen 1986, 88. My thanks to Carol Lee for this reference.

[14] There was enough public interest in the case to warrant the publication in book form of all nine opinions, edited by the Court's Reporter (Howard 1857).

[15] The Court lists 'the prohibition against ex post facto laws, bills of attainder, and laws impairing the obligation of contracts' plus 'a few other [unnamed] restrictions' (*Slaughterhouse Cases* 1873, 77).

of the Constitution, but rather indicated the majority's unprincipled resistance to Reconstruction.

Next, for present purposes, comes Justice Bradley's opinion for the Court in *The Civil Rights Cases* (1883). This concerned Congress' authority to prohibit racial discrimination in privately owned public accommodations, such as inns, theatres, and railroads, which Congress did in the Civil Rights Act of 1875. The Court had earlier decided that the relevant parts of the fourteenth amendment concern 'state action' only.[16] It now applied that ruling to hold that the Civil Rights Act exceeded Congress' authority, because racial discrimination by privately owned inns, theatres, and railroads does not constitute state action.[17] Bradley further remarked:

There were thousands of free coloured people in this country before the abolition of slavery, enjoying all the essential rights of life, liberty, and property the same as white citizens; yet no one, at that time, thought that it was any invasion of their personal status as freemen because they were not admitted to all the privileges enjoyed by white citizens, or because they were subjected to discriminations in the enjoyment of accommodations in inns, public conveyances, and places of amusement (*Civil Rights Cases* 1883, 25).

That there had been severe, extensive, systematic discrimination against free blacks during the ante-bellum period, in the North as well as in the South, had been noted in detail by Chief Justice Taney in his frequently cited *Dred Scott* opinion. Taney's review refutes Bradley's claim that free blacks enjoyed the same basic rights as whites. It is difficult to take seriously Bradley's claim, that no person of colour regarded such discrimination 'an invasion of their personal status as freemen'.

Another part of the same passage in Bradley's opinion likewise boggles the mind. He wrote:

When a man has emerged from slavery, and by the aid of beneficent legislation has shaken off the inseparable concomitants of that state, there must be some stage in the progress of his elevation when he takes the rank of a mere citizen, and ceases to be the special favorite of the laws, and when his rights as a citizen, or a man, are to be protected in the ordinary modes by which other men's rights are protected (*Civil Rights Cases* 1883, 25).

This passage cynically trivializes the widespread, organized terror and discrimination that was then being experienced by blacks, and which had been checked only by the deliberate application of federal military power. The Court's opinion helped

---

[16] Beginning with *United States v Reese* (1875).

[17] In a dissenting opinion (*Civil Rights Cases* 1883, 25–62), Justice Harlan reminded the Court of the well-established doctrine that, as railroads, inns, etc, perform a public function, they act as agents of the state and are routinely subject to governmental regulation, including conditional licensing. These familiar points were being applied by courts in the US during the nineteenth century in cases occasioned by the development of railroads. That no member of the majority even acknowledged Harlan's argument suggests that they lacked a plausible rejoinder.

to justify the federal government's withdrawal from efforts to secure African Americans' civil rights.

My third example is provided by Justice Brown, writing for the Court in *Plessy v Ferguson* (1896). The most striking passage of his opinion reads as follows:

> We consider the underlying fallacy of the plaintiff's argument to consist in the assumption that the enforced separation of the two races stamps the colored race with a badge of inferiority (*Plessy v Ferguson* 1896, 551).

This sentence was written during a period marked by an intense campaign of white supremacist propaganda and a lynching almost every other day. It is difficult to suppose that the Court majority believed the statement it was publicly endorsing.

It is easy to criticize on purely legal grounds many of the Court's important decisions. My point in this section is different. Some assertions made on behalf of the Court in these leading cases are so implausible as to indicate that the majority simply did not believe the positions they endorsed and were determined to undermine the legal measures taken after the Civil War to establish civil rights for African Americans.

After the ill-fated Civil Rights Act of 1875, Congress gradually withdrew from seeking to ensure that African Americans could enjoy the rights that were supposedly guaranteed by the amended Constitution. In 1877 the executive branch withdrew from enforcement of those rights. Given its 1873 decision in *Slaughterhouse Cases*, the judicial branch appears even earlier to have rejected the officially adopted project of reconstruction. The Supreme Court's record during the second half of the nineteenth century indicated at the time that a majority of justices were willing to dissemble in order to permit the re-establishment of racial subjugation. In thus providing ideological support for the creation of Jim Crow, the Court did not, however, legally legitimate that system's clearly unlawful practices.

3 Legal Theory

I want now to relate officials' attitudes towards legal norms under Jim Crow to Hart's central claim that officials of a legal system 'accept' its norms.[18]

Hart (1994) refers to three special categories of legal norms that most directly concern officials: rules of change, which confer (eg, on legislatures) the authority to make law; rules of adjudication, which confer (eg, on courts) the authority to apply law; and rules of recognition, which collect the criteria that are recognized and employed by officials to determine whether a given putative norm is a legally 'valid' rule of the system. Hart believes, reasonably, that it is unrealistic to assume

---

[18] I am grateful to Matthew Kramer for comments that led me to revise this Part substantively.

that ordinary subjects are familiar with the details of these norms. Officials, especially judges, are assumed to possess the requisite legal sophistication.

Hart's distinction between officials and other subjects of the law fits with his further claim, that the contents of a legal system's rules of change, adjudication, and recognition are determined by the argumentative and decisional practice of officials. The ultimate rule of recognition of a legal system, for example, represents the complex fact that officials consciously use certain tests for determining what else counts as law within the system and regard such use as appropriate. Articulate official practice *determines* the criteria of legal validity.

These distinctions are assumed in Hart's concise summary of his general theory, when he says that there are

two minimum conditions necessary and sufficient for the existence of a legal system. On the one hand, those rules of behaviour which are valid according to the system's ultimate criteria of validity must be generally obeyed, and, on the other hand, its rules of recognition specifying the criteria of legal validity and its rules of change and adjudication must be effectively accepted as common public standards of official behaviour by its officials (Hart 1994, 116–17).

We are concerned here primarily with the second condition.

Hart holds that officials have related attitudes towards rules that they believe belong to their system by virtue of satisfying the system's criteria of legal validity. An official who believes that such a rule is part of her legal system regards it as likewise establishing a 'common public standard of behaviour' (Hart 1994, 56–7, 89–90, 102, 108, 201).

We need to look more closely at what this means. In the original text of *The Concept of Law*, Hart referred to the relevant attitude that officials take towards the rules of their system as 'acceptance'. He says that one's acceptance of legal norms, or one's taking the 'internal point of view' towards them, involves 'a critical, reflective attitude' which 'should display itself in criticism (*including self-criticism*), demands for conformity, and in acknowledgements that such criticism and demands are justified'. One acknowledges *'the legitimacy of such criticism and demands when received from others.* For the expression of such criticism, demands, and acknowledgement a wide range of "normative" language is used', eg, ' "*I (You) must do that*", "*That is right*", "*That is wrong*"' (Hart 1994, 57, italics added).

Hart's use of the terms I have italicized seems to imply that one who 'accepts' norms regards them, not as *merely* legal standards, but as standards that are properly, unqualifiedly employed in the evaluation of behaviour.

Hart acknowledges, of course, that 'the certification of something as legally valid is not conclusive of the question of obedience' (Hart 1994, 210). In other words, acceptance does not commit one to supposing that legal rules override all other considerations that might apply in particular circumstances. That would be implausible. But acceptance, as Hart has explained it, is compatible with the notion suggested by his last-quoted remark, that there is something like a moral presumption favouring obedience to the laws that one recognizes as legally valid and thus 'accepts'.

That notion does not sit well with Hart's understanding of 'the separation of law and morals'. His recognition of outrageously unjust and inhuman laws is not plausibly combined with a moral presumption favouring obedience to laws regardless of their character, content, or acknowledged consequences. This suggests that Hart has not clearly expressed (or has not clarified for himself) the notions of 'acceptance' and of the 'internal point of view'.

I will now show that understanding Hart's notion of 'acceptance', as we have so far understood it, generates problems for his legal theory. Under that interpretation, the theory denies that officials might systematically disapprove of or violate the law as, I will suggest, some subsets of officials can reasonably be supposed to have done during the Jim Crow period.

(As I will go on to show, however, these counter-examples are neutralized once we take account of Hart's Postscript, which suggests how better to understand official 'acceptance' of law.[19] Under the revised interpretation, Hart's theory accommodates the range of officials' attitudes towards law under Jim Crow.)

For present purposes it will suffice to consider the attitudes of those who fully approved of Jim Crow and of those who strongly disapproved of that system. I will refer to these two groups as *white supremacists* and *racial egalitarians,* respectively.

After the *Brown* decision and related legal developments, some officials strongly resisted racial desegregation and publicly endorsed white supremacy. But European Americans have never been ideologically homogeneous. Some in the Southern colonies had opposed the development of race-based chattel slavery, and disapproval by whites of racial subordination was manifested under slavery and Jim Crow. But racial egalitarians risked severe physical as well as economic sanctions. As a consequence, some fled the South while others kept silent. Continued support for racial equity was shown, however, by the readiness of many white Southerners to accept desegregation, despite militant (and frequently violent) opposition by white supremacists.

It seems reasonable to suppose that some white supremacist officials approved of the legal system's basic norms, including the federal Constitution, at least in part because they understood them to sanction white racial domination. It is also quite possible, however, that other white supremacists disapproved of the legal system's basic norms insofar as they believed those norms could be used to undermine Jim Crow. This means that some officials did not 'accept' all of the system's basic norms. They continued to occupy public offices, perhaps because they wished to use their legal authority to prevent egalitarian reform.

---

[19] I will hereafter place quotation marks around 'accept' when the term is to be understood in the way we have so far supposed Hart meant it to be understood.

Now consider the attitudes of white supremacist officials towards non-basic norms that were systematically violated under Jim Crow, such as the *Plessy* doctrine that racially segregated public facilities must be substantially equal and colour-blind criminal prohibitions of rape and murder. Some public officials who approved of racial subordination not only recognized the legal validity of such norms but tried to enforce them, eg, by prosecuting those responsible for lynchings or by attempting to prevent lynch mobs from seizing prisoners. Those officials can be understood to have 'accepted' those norms. Their efforts were rarely successful, however, and they were generally unable to remain in office. It seems reasonable to suppose that some other white supremacist officials recognized the validity of those norms (which, after all, were not legally challenged under Jim Crow) but nevertheless approved of their systematic violation. Those officials could not be regarded as 'accepting' the relevant norms.

How important is such non-'acceptance'? I do not assume that Hart's theory should be understood to require absolutely universal, unqualified 'acceptance' by officials of all the norms that they regard as law. That would be an unrealistic, unnecessary, and therefore ungenerous reading of Hart's theory. What seems significant about conjectures like those sketched above is that the *lack* of 'acceptance' would not have been aberrational or idiosyncratic; it would have been systematic, relating to deeply entrenched official practices that were both open and plainly unlawful.

Now let us consider the attitudes of racial egalitarians who occupied official offices under Jim Crow. It seems reasonable to suppose that some approved of the legal system's basic norms, at least in part because they believed them capable of being used to undermine Jim Crow. It is also quite possible, however, that other racial egalitarians disapproved of the system's basic norms insofar as they believed that those norms permitted racial subordination. This means that they did not 'accept' all of the system's basic norms. Despite that, they might have preferred to occupy public offices, at least in part because they wished to use their legal authority, when possible, to mitigate the burdens that Jim Crow imposed on its victims.

Now consider the attitudes of racial egalitarians towards non-basic legal norms. It seems reasonable to suppose that some favoured adherence to the *Plessy* doctrine, insofar as it required a more equitable distribution of public facilities and services, and that they favoured colour-blind applications of the criminal law. However, it would have been impossible for them to use those norms as 'common public standards of behaviour'; for others would effectively resist egalitarian reform. Therefore, one could not accurately say that they 'accepted' the relevant norms.

It therefore seems likely that a number of officials during Jim Crow systematically *failed* to 'accept' important norms of their system. They did not approve of some norms, they did not regard them as common public standards of behaviour, or both. For those reasons, Jim Crow would seem to falsify Hart's legal theory.

That problem arises because we have understood 'acceptance' to involve embracing and following legal norms much the way one internalizes and follows the moral norms one endorses. I want now to suggest that we read Hart differently, as a result of which such counter-examples would dissolve.

In his posthumously published Postscript to *The Concept of Law*, Hart acknowledged that the original text had failed to distinguish between the attitude an official must have towards the basic norms of her legal system and her attitude towards the moral principles she endorses (Hart 1994, 254–6). Hart came to the view that the basic norms of a legal system are conventional in the sense that 'the general conformity of the group to them is part of the reasons which its individual members have for acceptance' of them (Hart 1994, 255). I understand this to mean that one might function as an official if one is prepared to apply the same tests for law that other officials regularly apply, and does so apply them, *even if* one would prefer (perhaps on moral grounds), that somewhat different tests were used.

The change improves Hart's theory. In general, it is unrealistic to suppose that the attitudes of officials towards the law must be morally loaded. Individuals who become officials have been acculturated within an existing legal system. They would not be able to function as officials unless they normally employed its rules in conventional ways. Moral approval of them is not necessary and would sometimes be utterly inappropriate.

If we say, along with Hart, that officials regard the norms of their system as 'common public standards of official behaviour', we must recognize that they might qualify that characterization by adding the prefix *legal* to those standards. They would thereby recognize, along with Hart, that the law under which they live and function as officials does not necessarily possess any moral merit and that its authority, along with theirs, is merely legal. They would recognize that 'criminal justice' refers to criminal *law*, warts and all. Depending on the circumstances, they might so function conscientiously.[20]

Thus an official need not approve of all of her system's norms. This would seem to accommodate the attitudes of federal judges who held the Fugitive Slave Act to be valid US law, and who applied it accordingly, while professing to be abolitionists. They accepted the conventional view, that the Supreme Court's ruling in *Prigg v Pennsylvania* (1842) settled the constitutionality of fugitive slave law.[21] Conversely, some officials who approved of chattel slavery may well have

---

[20] This assumes that an official's oath to uphold the law need not generate a moral obligation or, if it does, that the obligation can be overridden.

[21] Not only the 1793 enactment that Prigg concerned, but also the 1850 Act. However, it is not easy to understand judicial acceptance of the 1850 provisions, as some (eg, barring testimony for the alleged fugitive and providing twice the remuneration for commissioners when they find for the slave owner than when they find against him) plainly violate the due process clause of the Fifth Amendment.

disapproved of the system's basic norms, insofar as they believed they might permit the abolition of slavery.

It may help to note the limited legal authority and political leverage of various officials. In the US system, individual occupants of federal office are limited in their capacity to initiate or effect legal change. In addition, the US system limits the ability of federal officials to affect state and local law and officials at the state and local levels to affect federal law. It is therefore possible that many officials during Jim Crow disapproved of at least some of the clearly unlawful practices by officials but were unable to do anything about them through the exercise of their legal authority. Jim Crow, including its unlawful supporting practices, was well entrenched.

The question is what attitude officials must necessarily take towards well-entrenched but clearly unlawful aspects of their legal system. Hart's revised theory suggests an answer: officials must regard such practices as *conventionally* accepted in the system. Like it or not, *that's the way things are done here.* What this means is that officials simultaneously recognize the *illegality* of those practices. This combination of attitudes seems incoherent and inherently unstable. Those consequences are not an artefact of Hart's theory. They reflect moral and intellectual tensions that should plague any individual who functions officially within such a system.

4 Further Reflections

This paper has focused on a special subset of illegal official behaviour—clearly unlawful practices that are open and entrenched. I employed that narrow focus because I wished, first, to explain some merits of an important revision that Hart made in his notions of 'acceptance' and the 'internal point of view'.

There is a second reason for the special focus of this paper. I wanted to establish, by means of a clear class of cases, that governments may openly and systematically violate their own laws for long periods of time. Once we confront that fact, we can consider such cases along with other commonplace, troubling examples of official nonfeasance and malfeasance.

The involvement of officials in clearly unlawful practices presents a problem for political theory and practice, most clearly in relation to the idea of a moral obligation to comply with law. Theorists generally agree that the existence of such a 'political obligation' is compatible with some measure of injustice in a system. That accords with the point of positing political obligation, which is invoked to demand compliance with the law, even when it is unjust.

A plausible case for political obligation would seem to assume that the injustices which are supported by the law are not grievous, systematic, or well-entrenched and that the government, through its officials, generally respects its own law, which it applies evenhandedly. The Jim Crow example and the wider range of cases to which it points appear incompatible with those conditions. They challenge the assumption (commonly made by Americans), that the US provides a model of respect for the rule of law and exemplifies a system that supports political obligation.

We can go further. As I've noted, Jim Crow maintained a system of white supremacy that was accepted or embraced by most of the nation's political leaders from the independent nation's eighteenth century beginnings. The retention of that racial hierarchy after the abolition of chattel slavery required systematic violations of the rule of law as well as grievous injustice. Despite this, it has been commonplace for political leaders to invoke the idea of a moral obligation to obey the law. This requires, and promotes, moral myopia.[22]

I doubt that US history, in this regard, offers a case for American exceptionalism. Comparable practices have probably existed in all societies that have been divided by race, caste, class, or gender.

The Jim Crow example may also be misleading. It may suggest that entrenched unlawful practices are always morally pernicious and that officials who systematically subvert the law do so for morally bad reasons. That need not be assumed. Plausible examples to the contrary involve the deliberate non-enforcement of legal prohibitions that are reasonably and widely regarded as outdated, unwise, or morally objectionable, such as laws against private gambling and departures from harsh sentencing requirements. It may be noted, however, that such practices differ from lynching under Jim Crow insofar as they do not serve as part of a pervasive system.

---

[22] I have addressed this issue more generally in Lyons 1998.

3

Conformity, Custom, and Congruence: Rethinking the Efficacy of Law

Gerald J Postema

At its foundations, law rests on social practice; we might even say that law at its foundations is a matter of convention, if we are willing to allow a very broad notion of convention. This *conventionalist thesis* is thought to capture something essential about the nature of law. It is no mere tautology, yet it represents something of a plateau of agreement in contemporary English-speaking jurisprudence. Firmly positioned on this plateau, as we might expect, are positivists wearing Hartian colours, but positivists of other stripes and many anti-positivists locate themselves on this plateau as well. Jurisprudential debate has focused not on the truth of the conventionalist thesis, but on how best to understand it.

Since Hobbes, modern positivist jurisprudence has tended to favour a formalist, or centralist, interpretation of the conventionalist thesis. For the classical positivists, the social practice or convention on which law is grounded was thought to be that of the regular obedience of the sovereign law-giver by its subjects. This is a formalist or centralist interpretation in the sense that it takes the focus of the social practice to be the exercise of authority or power by what is assumed to be the most important (ie, the law-defining) legal institution. For Hobbes, this obedience was rooted in an agreement among subjects to take the sovereign's commands as law, while Bentham thought of this practice as a kind of convention in the narrow sense of relatively stable equilibrium in a complex network of mutual expectations (Postema 1986, 232–7). It is important to note that, for classical positivists, this sovereignty-constituting social practice not only provided the legal system's criteria of validity, but also secured its *efficacy*, its ability to operate in and through the decisions and actions of law-subjects. For classical positivists, the ground of law's efficacy was *wide*, anchored in the society-wide practice of obedience, which was taken to be essential to its existence.

Hart, and many positivists after him, retained the centralism of the classical view but moved claims about law's efficacy to the margins of the conventionalist thesis. Hart narrowed the conventional foundations of law to the practice of law-applying officials in the limited enterprise of recognizing legal norms as valid in the system, although he added, in what might strike some as an afterthought, that general conformity of the behaviour of the populace to the officially-recognized law is also necessary for its existence (Hart 1994, 116–17). Over the past two decades or so, although the *nature* of law's conventional foundations has been the focus of much dispute, the question of its scope has attracted very little attention.

This consensus stands in sharp contrast to ancient and (some) modern thought about law. Aristotle, for example, assumed it was a commonplace that '*nomos* [enacted law] has no power without the force of *ethos* [custom]' (Aristotle, *Politics* II.8, 1269a20), in which point he followed the Athenian in Plato's *Laws* (793b–c), who maintained that well-established, unwritten laws and customs bind together and underwrite a polity's formal laws and make possible the introduction of newly enacted laws into the existing structure of law. Informal social norms, they argued, are the infrastructure of law and of the polity it orders. The view is echoed in the Twelfth Century *Decretum* (D 4, pc 3): 'Laws are instituted with promulgation', Gratian wrote, but they are 'firmly established when they are approved by the practice of those who observe them' (Porter 2007, 92–3). The 'approval' in question (like Aristotle's 'common agreement'—*homologia*) is not a matter of the acquiescence, let alone the assent, of individuals to formal, enacted laws governing them, but rather a matter of law's integration into their ordinary, daily practice. It is possible to find much the same view at the core of common-law jurisprudence both in its classical form, represented by Sir Matthew Hale, for example (Postema 2002, 172–6), and in Fuller's modern version (Postema 1994). Common-law jurisprudence, like its ancient and medieval antecedents, insisted on a wider and more substantial conventional foundation for law than that recognized by classical positivism and its latter-day versions.

Yet, this wider conventionalism is likely to strike most of us as quaintly antique; plausible, perhaps, for an era and for forms of social and political organization long gone, but clearly out of touch with more complex and sophisticated modern legal systems, and therefore false as a claim about the nature of law. There is some truth in this criticism, and we surely do not want to make the mistake, ruthlessly exposed by Bentham, of confusing *custom in pays* with *custom in foro* (Bentham 1977, 182–3, 216–18, 330–5; Postema 1986, 273–5). That said, however, I believe the current orthodoxy regarding law's efficacy is no less problematic. We would do well to rethink the notion of the efficacy of law. I will not defend in full the conventionalism of common law jurisprudence, but I will argue for a richer and wider notion of law's efficacy and defend a more central role for it in the conventional foundations of law.

1 The Problem of Efficacy

To begin I will sketch the outlines of the problem of law's efficacy using Hart's familiar account as a convenient starting point. First, however, because confusion over terminology bedevils discussion in this area, I propose to regiment our language in the following way. We must distinguish between the efficacy of law, on the one hand, and its effectiveness, on the other. Efficacy is the power or capacity of something to produce an effect that adequately answers to its purpose. When it does so with some degree of success, it is efficacious or effective; the more successful, the more effective it is. Effectiveness is manifested in the effects or outcomes of a process or productive activity, and a measure of effectiveness is a measure of the success of the process in producing the effects. Efficacy concerns the properties or structures of a thing that give it the power in question; it must not be confused with efficiency. If we judge something efficient, we judge it as especially good at producing the intended effects and, more specifically, as producing them at an optimal ratio of cost to benefit.

1.1 The Efficacy of Modern Law: Hart's View

With this in mind, consider two contrasting modes of efficacy of legal norms. Consider, first, customary international law. Norms of customary international law are *practically concrete* (Postema 2007, 290–1). That is, necessarily, they are not only anchored to concrete deeds in the social world that they govern, but their existence, content, and practical force are determined by these deeds—deeds that are widely performed in the relevant community, or performed by parties distinguished in no special way from others in the community and thus regarded as acting for the public. Any articulation of such norms, even if it is official and formal is answerable to these deeds. Moreover, it is impossible to mark with precision a line between the formation of customary norms and their application.

Practice is what creates [customary law], and practice is how it is applied: so it may be hard to distinguish which aspect one is dealing with. Similarly, established customary rules are rarely simply abolished: they are normally replaced by other rules. The customary process is in fact a continuous one, which does not stop when the rule has emerged, even if one could identify that moment.... Even after the rule has 'emerged', every act of compliance will strengthen it, and every violation, if acquiesced in, will help to undermine it (Mendelson 1998, 175).

Deeds create and sustain norms of customary international law, but they also modify, refine, and replace them. Often it is through what are reasonably regarded as violations that the norms are changed and replaced with new ones: *ex iniuria ius oritur*. From this it follows that the efficacy of customary international law consists in their manifest effectiveness—their being *practiced* in the relevant community; this is essential to their existence and constitutive of their being norms of this kind.

This account of the mode of efficacy and existence of customary norms is familiar to readers of Hart's *Concept of Law*, although he argues that in these respects social rules are fundamentally different from legal norms (Hart 1994, ch 5.3). He argued that a society governed by such rules alone lacks the defining institutional structure of law, its law-making, law-applying, law-enforcing, and, crucially, law-recognizing institutions (all defined by distinctive kinds of secondary rules, governing and maintained by officials). Because legal norms are products of law-constituting activities of these officials, it is possible to distinguish relatively sharply between the formation of legal norms and their application and thus to distinguish clearly between violations of legal norms and actions taken to change them. According to Hart, unlike customary norms, the existence of individual legal norms does not depend on their being practiced by those who are governed by them. Their legal status or validity is strictly a matter of satisfying criteria laid out in a rule of recognition, which is not a rule of the legal system, but rather a *social* rule underwriting it, constituted by the practice of law-applying officials. The existence and legal status of each norm of the system, and the persistence through time of the legal system as a whole, depend on officials who accept and practice the foundational rule of recognition. Since ordinary citizens do not participate in the practice constituting the rule of recognition, they contribute to the existence of the legal system, at a minimum, through their general conformity to its norms, although 'in a healthy society' law-subjects may accept them as common public standards.

Thus, Hart recognizes two minimum necessary conditions of the existence of a legal system: (1) the foundational rule of recognition must be accepted and practiced by law-applying officials, and (2) the behaviour of most of the population governed by these norms must be in broad conformity with the system of legal norms traceable to the rule of recognition (Hart 1994, 116–17). Hart is largely silent about the status of the second condition and the relationship between the two conditions. But it is clear that he took the general conformity condition to be a conceptually necessary condition of the existence of a legal system.

Brian Tamanaha, however, argued that he should abandon this claim because it flies in the face of facts about legal systems like that of post-war Micronesia (Tamanaha 2001, xi–xii, 145–6). Micronesia's law was imported in its entirety from the United States by Americans and most of its active participants were American (especially, American lawyers), while the Micronesian people were almost entirely ignorant of the law, feared and avoided the part they knew, and generally regarded it as an alien, mostly irrelevant presence. It was of marginal significance in maintaining social order in the countryside and confined its attention largely to the operations of government in the capital. Day-to-day affairs of the people of Micronesia were ordered by social norms that had almost no connection with the formal law. The legal system of Micronesia, Tamanaha insists, functioned but was ineffective and generally ignored by the population.

We must resist Tamanaha's proposal, I believe. The argument for this conceptual necessity of law's efficacy for its existence is fairly straightforward. Law is a normative system—a structured set of norms—that defines an ordering of social life. It is not merely a set of norms *for*, ie, concerned with, and in that sense governing, a particular society; rather, it is a set of norms *in force* in that community. 'A legal system exists', Raz correctly pointed out, 'if and only if it is in force' in some community (Raz 1979, 104). It is capable of doing its normative work just in virtue of the fact that it is in force in the community. The idea of an abstract normative proposition that is never used or followed, one that is valid or true but not yet adequately entertained or seriously considered by any rational agent, is surely an intelligible idea, but the idea of a legal system that is never used or practiced, or no longer practiced, is hardly intelligible. It is, rather, 'like a piece of music never played, an offer that has languished for want of acceptance' (Jones 1969, 4). To abstract a set of legal norms from the social context of their normal operation is, at best, to consider a possible, hypothetical, or virtual legal system, but not a real one. Thus, if a system of norms fails to order the social life of a community to a substantial extent, we must conclude that that set of norms is not the legal system in that community, even if a self-appointed elite treats it as such.

1.2 When is Law in Force in a Community?

This argument forces a new question to the foreground: what is it for a legal system to be in force in a community? David Lewis once asked what relation must hold between a possible language and a given population such that that language is the actual language of that population (Lewis 1969, 176–7). The obvious answer, that the people must *use* it, he argued, is hardly adequate, for they might use it privately to bring on sleep, or use it together to sing operas (without understanding the words). Not just any way they might use the language would make it theirs—*as a language*, we might say. They must use it *in the right way*, Lewis insisted. They must use it in a way appropriate to its nature as a language. Lewis argued that language is used in the right way when people use it together in conformity to a truthfulness convention, which is 'something everyone in P does because he expects his conversational partners in P to do it too, and because a common interest in communicating leads him to want to do his part if they do theirs' (Lewis 1969, 177). Using the language is not something done by individuals taken separately, but by members of a community of speakers. The network of expectations is produced and sustained through participation in the practice and through inducting and apprenticing new members in the practice. The norms of the language function as norms for individuals just because they are recognized as norms for the community of speakers of which they are a part.

Lewis's question, transposed to the jurisprudential key, offers a useful starting point for our quest. To be in force in a community, law must be *used* in that community *in the right way*, where doing so involves some *convention*, that is, some complex network of expectations of regular users of the law. But immediately two questions demand attention: what is the focus of the convention and who are its (necessary) participants? Hart proposes that law is 'used in the right way' just when officials practice a convention of law-recognition and the conduct of most citizens conforms to the system's norms mostly. But this proposal is mistaken.

The main problem is that Hart's conformity condition is too weak to measure the effectiveness of law. The condition is meant to be satisfied by strictly behavioural descriptions, determinations of whether the behaviour is consistent with the governing norms without considering the motivations or reasons of agents engaging in it.[1] There may be nothing that can be said *in general* about the internal points of view of law-subjects (Hart 1994, 117). However, a measure of effectiveness is a measure of the success *of law* in some respect. So, merely coincidental correlations of behaviour with standing legal norms fail to manifest law's effectiveness. To do so, it must be possible to attribute the behaviour to law's efforts and operations, traced to properties or powers of law. Moreover, since effectiveness is said to be essential for the existence of law, these properties or powers must be part of the nature of law. If conformity is a necessary mark of the existence of law, the behaviour it comprises must bear some significant relation to necessary features of law.[2]

Moreover, the relation between law and conforming behaviour must be of a certain sort. Imagine a society governed by a set of general norms, where the behaviour of its members largely conforms to those norms but only through the efforts of a vast army of enforcers standing beside each member issuing particular commands (accompanied by incentives to follow them) every time some norm bears on their actions. If we can truly imagine such a society—there is reason to doubt the possibility—we would have to conclude, nevertheless, that the members' behaviour, although not inconsistent with legal norms, does not exhibit their effectiveness; thus, it is not a mark of their efficacy. For, under the conditions described, the norms are not in any way guiding the behaviour of the members of the society, but only (if at all) the actions of the enforcers. The problem in this case is not that coercion is deployed to motivate conformity, but rather that the legal norms do not function as norms for—ie they are not used by—those to whom they appear to be addressed. If the legal norms play any role in the direction of conduct of ordinary members of the group it is as standards by which the enforcers determine how they should act with respect to those members, just as circus rules direct trainers' treatment of tigers and elephants.

We can explain this problem in the following familiar terms. The core *modus operandi* of law is to guide the actions of intelligent, self-directing agents by addressing to them general norms to which their actions are expected to conform. It is not always necessary for such agents to *comply* with these norms in

---

[1] Hart speaks of 'obedience' rather than 'conformity', but his discussion of Austin makes clear that he treats the two terms as equivalent and regards conformity as something that can be observed from the 'extreme external' point of view.

[2] Indeed, without some significant internal relation between the behaviour and the law to guide us, it is not clear that we can intelligibly judge it to be in conformity with legal norms. Viewed 'externally', any stretch of behaviour can be described in an indefinite number of ways, so without more said, there is no reason to select one such description portraying it as conforming to the law. The most that we can say of it is that it is not in violation of law, but that bare privative gives us no information about the law at all, let alone confirms its efficacy.

the sense that they seek to make their behaviour conform to the norms *by acting specifically on* the reasons those norms provide them. Nevertheless, the right relationship between the general norms and their addressees' conforming behaviour must obtain. The mediating efforts of the army of enforcers issuing at each concrete instance specific incentive-backed commands is not the right kind of relationship, because the capacities of the addressees for intelligent self-direction are not in any way engaged. Thus, the general norms are not in force for them and the enforcers may use the law, but not *as law*. Thus, we are still left with the question: what is it for law to be in force, to be used in the right way, in a community?

1.3 Distance, Alienation, and Modern Law

We must sharpen this question further. Following the line of thought just introduced, we may be tempted to say that a body of law is in force in a population just when those governed by it mostly comply with it in the sense that they seek to bring their behaviour into conformity with it, or that the legal norms figure non-accidentally as premises in their practical deliberations. But this is not correct either, for reasons Hart fully appreciated and took pains to highlight.

Hart's reasons for insisting on his thin condition of effectiveness are instructive and indicate factors we need to keep in mind as we seek a more adequate account. From the heuristic story he told in chapter V of *The Concept of Law* highlighting the defining characteristics of law, Hart drew a sobering moral. According to Hart, each of the primary rules in a pre-legal society exists on its own bottom, as it were, in the general acceptance of those who practice them. But, as a result of the institutionalization, centralization, and formalization characteristic of law a two-fold gap is opened up between legal norms and the people they govern. Legal norms are valid, not insofar as practiced, but just insofar as they meet the conditions laid out in the rule of recognition, a rule practiced by law-applying officials. Thus, it is likely that first-order social rules are not merely *supplemented* by a structure of second-order, institution-creating and -maintaining rules, a template laid over an already established network of customs and practices, but rather *supplanted* by primary rules of the officials' own making. Legal norms, even primary ones, are likely to be 'disembedded' (Berman 1983, 86)—or perhaps we should say unembedded, since they may never have been embedded in ordinary, informal social practices. 'Conventional norms cannot diverge much from what people actually do', MacCormick writes, 'because their existence is determined by what people actually do. Institutionalized norms can so diverge, even if the basis of their institutionalization does depend on a common habit of respect for the constitution and even if the latter habit is quite widespread' (MacCormick 2007, 70).

If this is true of modern law, we can expect that ordinary law-subjects would not know, or even have a rough idea, of the rule of recognition in the legal system that governs them, let alone accept it; after all, it is not their practice, but rather the practice of a legal elite. Moreover, we might expect many law-subjects to have only rudimentary knowledge of the substantive legal norms. The 'sobering truth' of law, Hart concludes, is that the advantages of formalization and institutionalization of social order offered by law come at a high price, for with law comes a serious risk that the legally constituted and centralized power may well be used for the oppression of large numbers of people whose support it can dispense with (Hart 1994, 117, 201–2). The inevitable *distance* between law and those it governs opens the further possibility of their more or less radical *alienation* from that law.

Although radical alienation is seen by Hart to be the extreme case, the difference between it and less extreme cases lies largely in the degree of oppression and injustice of the legal system in question. The 'internal attitude' of ordinary citizens will not be greatly different in the two cases, because in almost all cases it is unlikely that ordinary citizens will be in a position to take the internal point of view with respect to the law, since they will have only the most rudimentary knowledge of it. 'The very fact of institutionalization of legislative power means that the results of exercise of that power may be statutory texts that are very imperfectly, if at all, observed as working norms from any norm-user's point of view', observes MacCormick; 'it is very much an open question how much of the official law is any part of the working consciousness of lay persons' (MacCormick 2007b, 70, 71). Scott Shapiro argues further that this is not surprising, since law as a whole, not just the rule of recognition, is fundamentally the exclusive practice of legal officials. Even ordinary citizens who willingly conform to the law are not participants in the legal system, he argues, because the 'business of law is the creation and exercise of authority, and its participants are the officials who operate the levers of legal power. Compliant citizens are best regarded as cooperative participants in the social life of the community', but not participants in the legal system (Shapiro 2002, 418).

Shapiro offers, to my eye, a seriously distorted view of law, albeit one that is arguably within the spirit of Hart's account. However, the deficiencies of this view do not diminish the fact that Hart has called attention to familiar features of the ordinary lives of citizens lived in the shadow of law. Rarely do citizens have more than a rudimentary grasp of much of the law, and certainly little or no grasp of its more technical features. They rarely have access to legal materials and would not know how to handle them if they did. Thus, they are unlikely to understand the normative propositions to which these texts and other materials point, when properly related and understood. It would seem, then, that it is difficult to maintain that ordinary citizens can be said to accept these normative propositions, treating them as common standards for their conduct and that of their fellow citizens.

The arguments of the previous few pages yield an antinomy, or at least force on us a stark dilemma: 'use [of the law] in the right way' cannot be understood to involve widespread acceptance and practice of the law, as Hart understands these notions, because of the inevitable distance between formal law and ordinary social practices and the likely alienation of ordinary citizens from that law; but on the other hand, it is also a mistake to limit 'use' to acceptance by officials supported only by mere conformity of the population at large (coincidental correlation of their behaviour and formal legal norms), as Hart insisted.

I propose to prepare a pathway between the two horns of this dilemma. In what follows, I will sketch the outlines of a view of law's efficacy that will enable us to do that. My sketch proceeds in three stages. In the first, I identify some important features of law's distinctive mode of normative guidance. In the second, I argue that, in view of this mode of normative guidance, it is a necessary condition of the existence of law that there exist a substantial degree of congruence between formal legal norms and the informal customs and practices of ordinary life in the society governed by them. The extent of such congruence, I shall argue, is a measure of the efficacy of law. In the third stage, I shall argue that efficacious law not only presupposes such congruence, but that law does its normative work *through* the mediation of informal social practices. This will give us a general idea of what it is for a community to use its law in the right way.

2 Normative Guidance

I begin from what I shall assume is jurisprudential common ground, namely, the view that it is a conceptually necessary fact about law that it seeks to do whatever tasks are assigned to it by providing normative guidance to rational and intelligent self-directing agents. This feature of law is not *a function* of law, not even its most important function—it does not make sense to attribute to law the (more or less self-sufficient) *aim* of securing compliance—rather, it defines the law's distinctive instrumentality, the distinctive manner in which law undertakes to perform whatever functions are assigned to it. The key to resolving the above antinomy and explaining what it is for law to be in force in a community—for that community to 'use it in the right way'—is an understanding of how law purports to guide ordinary citizens. However, our intuitive idea, which takes for its model that of a direct command, is too simple to capture law's distinctive mode of normative guidance. It is not possible to explore this matter in detail here, but for present purposes the following remarks may be sufficient.

On the command, or authoritative directive, model, legal norms are *addressed to* individual law-subjects, as if someone in authority issued a command to another person subject to that authority. The command is *effective* if it is obeyed, where obeying involves at a minimum that the prescription figures appropriately in the subject's practical thinking. It may only inform the subject of requirements on his or her action ('epistemic guidance') or, more typically, it provides reasons for the subject to act in accord with those requirements ('motivational guidance') (Shapiro 1998, 490). In either case, the prescription plays an important role in the subject's 'on-line' practical reasoning, that is, practical reasoning leading to action. This may be due to the fact that the subject accepts the prescription itself, or recognizes some reason to follow it, or because the subject acknowledges the authority of the party to issue the directive. In either case, the relationship between the prescription and the agent is direct in two respects: the subject 'accepts' the directive (perhaps via accepting the authority of the issuer) and the subject obeys the directive by following it (her behaviour conforms to it because it figures in an important way in his or her on-line practical reasoning).

To understand law's distinctive mode of normative guidance we must recognize features not explicitly captured by the simply authoritative directive model. I will mention just three features here, although a more thorough investigation may uncover others. First, the command model tends to recognize that law's directives are *general*, prescribing types or classes of actions (perhaps also for classes of subjects), but it does not explicitly recognize that they are addressed to some more or less well-defined *public* of law-subjects. That is, legal norms are not simply addressed to each law-subject individually but typically address individuals whose law-relevant conduct is linked to that of other individuals in complex and interdependent ways. Law plies its trade only in certain kinds of circumstances: it is addressed to rational, self-directing agents when and insofar as they are engaged in thick networks of interdependent social interaction. These circumstances—the nature of the parties addressed and the social context of their practical activity—are not merely contingent features of the milieu in which law typically works; rather, they are essential to even the most basic operations of law. If human beings were fundamentally different either in their psychological, cognitive, or practical capacities, or in respect to the ways they live their lives, that is, if they were able to carry on their lives without social interaction, or if that interaction was not characterized fundamentally by the kind of interdependence with which we are familiar, then social life would not be ordered by the distinctive instrumentality of law. There would be no point in deploying this instrumentality. Law addresses individual rational, self-directing agents not one-by-one, as it were, but rather as participants in this public.

Second, it is tempting for us, especially if we are partial to the positivist jurisprudential point of view, to think of *law* as a set or collection of *laws*, that is, of more or less discrete legal norms (or authoritative directives). Bentham wanted to think of law in this way, and so insisted that to understand what it is for law to exist we must first consider what it is for *a* (single, discrete) law to exist (Bentham 1776; 1970b, 1). He soon discovered, however, that tracing some publicly manifested directive to the law-making efforts of the sovereign, no matter how carefully he worked out the conditions of sovereignty and the manner, forms, and conditions of law-making, he could not capture what a single law is. For that, he was forced to concede, we need to think about how the products of such law-making efforts are systematically related, not by connections of authorization, but by connections of *content*. What Bentham came to grasp, if only dimly, was that law is not a set of norms, but a *normative system*. To understand the meaning of any given legal proposition requires that it be located in its proper place in that system tied in contentful ways to other elements of the system (Bentham 1996, 299; 1970b, 233–4). The overall systemic coherence of a body of law is, of course, always imperfectly realized, but even in an imperfectly realized system norms relate to those they address very differently from the way discrete and independent norms or rules do. The law addresses law-subjects as a system, and the normative guidance it offers takes the form of providing a framework of practical reasoning rather than that of a discrete general command.

Third, the command model explicitly recognizes only one form of normative guidance, the *directive* mode: the law lays out prescribed classes of actions and either (if merely 'epistemic guidance') piggy-backs on, or (if 'motivational guidance') provides, substantial reasons to act in particular ways as specified by the norms. Typically, legal norms are practical-reasons-constituting norms. But there are at least two other modes of guidance, closely related to the directive but distinct from it, that are at least as important for understanding law's distinctive normative instrumentality. One of these we might call the *evaluative* mode. This is a relatively complex, but not unfamiliar, idea. The basic idea is that law provides standards by which law-subjects evaluate their behaviour and that of others (including officials). These evaluations are important because sometimes they enable law-subjects (or officials) to justify their actions to themselves, which typically (in the social circumstances presupposed by law) requires at the same time (at least making a pretence of) justifying themselves to others in the community. At the same time, they provide the standards for condemning the actions of others and holding them publicly accountable. This evaluative mode adds a dimension to law's normative guidance not fully captured by the directive mode with its own value and importance.

Finally, and most important for our purposes, law's normative guidance has a *constitutive* mode. Normative systems, law among them, often guide not just by explicitly directing, but also by giving normative significance to certain actions, activities, and especially roles and relationships. They define normative statuses or competences, and accord to actions meaning as claims against or responses to the actions of others, as falling within or outside the pale of the relationship, calling for, authorizing, or blocking certain responses, and the like. In this way, normative systems do not so much *direct* actions as provide the infrastructure or context for meaningful interaction. Law, for example, constitutes relations between employer and employee, marriage partners, family members, municipal citizens, and the like, and networks of such relationships, some of which are further integrated into discrete institutions and systems of institutions. To represent such constitutive guidance on the model of a command distorts its role in practical reasoning. For often it functions not as an explicit premise of deliberation, but as the context within which deliberation takes place and from which the elements prominently figuring in it have their practical significance.

Much more needs to be said about these three modes of guidance, especially the last mentioned, but I wish to add here only one more word about the law's characteristic constituting activity. It is useful to distinguish two domains in which law's constituting activity is involved. The most familiar, perhaps, is the political, 'constitutional' domain: law organizes and regulates how political power is established, conferred, removed, exercised, and constrained. It constitutes political relations of and within government, between government and citizens, and among citizens. Just for ease of reference we might call this the 'vertical' dimension of law's constitutive activity. There is also a 'horizontal' dimension. We might refer to this as the civil or *commutative* dimension, putting us in mind of the exchange or interchange of activities of citizens in the public sphere. Law in this domain constitutes relationships defined by contract, property, and tort, but also family, marriage, master-servant, employer-employee, and a host of other non-political relationships and networks of relationships.

With this richer understanding of law's normative guidance we can return to our attempt to explain what it is for a legal system to be 'used in the right way' in a population. The pivotal notion in my explanation is *mediation*. A legal system is 'used in the right way' if it offers effective normative guidance to those governed by it, but it offers this normative guidance *indirectly* through the mediation of the network of informal social customs, conventions, and practices that structure the daily lives of those governed by law. Law guides, in the three modes I mentioned above, in substantial part but not exclusively, by giving shape to, and taking its shape from, the network of informal social practices; and individual law-subjects are guided, in substantial part but not exclusively, through participation in those social practices. When law is sufficiently congruent with and reciprocally interacts with background social practices of a society and when those governed by that law participate mindfully in those practices and thereby, if indirectly and partially, follow and navigate their social world with the help of the law, then law is 'used in the right way' in that community. The remainder of this essay is devoted to explaining the nature of this mediation.

3 The Congruence Thesis

The first step in this explanation is to defend the congruence thesis. If the congruence thesis is true, we can explain the efficacy and effectiveness of law in its terms. The *efficacy* of law can be understood as a function of this congruence, that is, the ability of law to function at least to a minimum level of adequacy, and so to produce its characteristic effects, depends on this congruence. The effectiveness of law, exhibited in the general compliance with that law of people governed by it, can then be understood as a reliable mark of its efficacy.

The *congruence thesis* holds that a substantial degree of congruence between the norms and modes of reasoning of a legal system and the informal social customs, practices, and modes of reasoning that predominate in the society governed by it is a necessary condition of the existence of that legal system. The notion of congruence is, admittedly, rather vague, but we can say a few things to lift most of the fog. Congruence is a matter of the at least partial overlap of and interaction between the legal system and important networks of informal social customs and practices. Of course, congruence is a matter of degree: more or less of the law can be congruent with informal social practices that are of wider or narrower scope in the community; moreover, law and social practices can also be more or less tightly interwoven.

Congruence as here understood is not a matter of legal norms *mirroring* informal social norms. Congruent norms are not identical in content, even *modulo* their very different normative modalities of law and informal social practices; neither must they serve in their own ways fundamentally the same values. It is reasonable to think that a society's legal system may take on quite different tasks than those served by informal social practices, and the values it serves may vary significantly from those of social customs and practices. Moreover, congruence is not likely to be a matter of one-to-one correspondence. Neither law nor most important social practices are sets of discrete rules. We have already noticed that the content of legal norms tends to be shaped by the role they play in the system of norms of which they are members. Something similar is true for many informal social norms and practices. Thus, the congruence we have in mind is congruence of these systems or portions of them, rather than a simple one-to-one mapping of legal to social norms.

I will say more in the next section about the nature of this congruence, but with this general idea in mind, let us proceed to consider the argument for the congruence thesis. The argument begins with the claims about law's normative guidance discussed in the previous section. In sum: necessarily, law provides intelligent self-directing agents, engaged in thick patterns of social interaction, with norms forming a systematic framework of practical reasoning, directing their actions, constituting their relationships and the context of their actions, and enabling them to evaluate their own actions and those of others.

From this thesis regarding law's distinctive instrumentality we can derive four important implications. (1) Law's efficacy—its ability to provide at least minimally the reasons, standards, and normative relations that can guide its addressees—depends on the up-take by its addressees. So, (2) the norms by which law seeks to guide social behaviour must be *practically intelligible* to addressees. That is, what is called for by the norms must to a minimal degree at least make sense to them, such that they know how to carry out its directions, deploy its standards, or navigate its relations in concrete cases. Moreover, (3) the norms must be *publicly accessible*, both synchronically and diachronically.[3] Law cannot do its job of

---

[3] Just how wide the relevant 'public' must be, however, is determined by the likely scope of potential interactions among the intended addressees. It need not include the entire political community, if only some of its members are likely to engage in the activities governed by the norms or are likely to interact with only some of those who do regularly engage in them.

public normative guidance by addressing private signals to individual members of society. The reason for this is that the kind of social interactions with which law is concerned depend essentially on *public understandings*, matters that are common knowledge for those who engage in them. Thus, each agent must have a sufficient degree of confidence that each of the others with whom she interacts grasps the practical import of the legal norm in a way that meshes with her own and that they have confidence in the meshing of their grasp with hers. Finally, (4) if law is institutionalized, with officials charged with making, applying, enforcing, and maintaining it, then the relationship between officials and the law's addressees is itself characterized by a distinctive form of interaction such that what it makes sense for parties on one side to do depends on what they expect parties on the other side to do, while, at the same time, what it makes sense for the latter to do depends on what they expect their counterparts to do.

With this background in place, we can show why a substantial degree of congruence between legal norms and informal social customs, practices, and modes of reasoning is essential for the existence of law. The argument in outline is that legal norms are practically intelligible and publicly accessible to those governed by them only if, taken together (as a system), they are *normatively coherent* and *practically congruent*. Normative coherence is a matter of the norms fitting together substantively in a coherent way. I will not defend this condition here or discuss it any further because that would take us far from our appointed course. The practical congruence necessary for law's efficacy takes two forms. The one is familiar from Fuller's familiar canonical list of the eight essential features of the rule of law (Fuller 1969, 38–41, 81ff). It is congruence between the formally announced rules, the rules on the books, as it were, and the actions of officials applying and enforcing them. This is crucial not only for proper control and accountability of the exercise of official power—a primary concern of the rule of law—but also for law's efficacy. For, if there is a significant degree of incongruence of this kind, and if officials intervene in the social interactions of people governed by law to a significant degree, then the incongruence will necessarily shift the attention away from the general norms of law to the specific, anomalous actions of officials. At that point, the game of law is over and an analogue of 'scorer's discretion' takes its place (Hart 1994, 141–7).

The second form of practical congruence is that between legal norms and the informal social practices and customs of ordinary social life. Recall that law provides normative guidance by promulgating *public norms*, public guides for self-direction, justification, and navigation of social relations. But public norms presuppose *public understanding*, and public understanding and practical reasoning utilizing public norms are possible only through recourse to what we might call an 'informational commons' (Postema 2008). That is, normative propositions can play an active role in practical reasoning only against the background of intelligible and familiar patterns and examples. Norms are grasped to the extent that they can be located in a familiar network of normative inferences made concrete in a normative practice. For the understanding to be public, the normative practice must be public.

Hobbes's failure to understand this dynamic is instructive. Hobbes thought the state of nature was not only anarchic, lacking a common governing power, but also, in consequence, radically anomic, lacking all public standards and measures—in Nigel Simmonds' words, 'a chaos of subjectivity'. Hobbes mistakenly thought that law could, by itself, *create* the necessary but missing public language. Absent any common normative practice, 'people would be completely opaque to each other'. In that case, general commands of a sovereign could not supply the needed public language (Simmonds 1991, 313–14). Hobbes understood that to establish the sovereign, it was not enough that each party in the state of nature transfer his or her rights of judgment to the same person, for each must be confident that (enough of) the other have done the same; that is, he recognized that the authorization of the sovereign had to be public and common. What he failed to see was that this transfer was not sufficient to escape the 'chaos of subjectivity', for the sovereign must then create the general public norms that are notably absent in the state of nature, but this is not possible. The sovereign's commands have public practical significance only if its subjects can be confident that the significance given them by their fellows generally meshes with their own, and that in turn requires common knowledge of the resources from which that significance is drawn.[4] This essential pool of common knowledge rarely comes from sharing general principles and values, but rather from participating in common practices that give shape and order to daily life and interactions.

The sovereign might attempt to direct social interactions by addressing specific commands to each subject in each instance of social interaction calling for sovereign intervention. But this strategy is fatally flawed, for it would amount to abandoning Hobbes's project of remedying the anomic chaos of the state of nature through institution of a sovereign who rules *through law*. Moreover, the strategy is utterly unworkable for two reasons. First, it puts all the sovereign's money on *directive* guidance. But explicit directive guidance can work only against the background of understandings implicit in the competences and relationships that give intelligible practical shape to the circumstances and available actions to which the directives are addressed. Directive normative guidance presupposes constitutive guidance. Second, that guidance must be largely (albeit not exclusively) in the deliberative background of those governed by law. Constitutive guidance guides by defining horizons for deliberation, parameters within which reasons

---

[4] Bentham entertained the fantasy that the problem of securing public understanding could be solved by regimenting the language of legal instruments (and theoretical reflection on law). He insisted that questions of law were at bottom questions of the import of words. But even he recognized that not just any ostensibly clear and determinate language would do the trick. The language he insisted upon for this purpose was 'the language of utility', which he naïvely assumed was 'natural' and hence fully public language of all those governed by law (Bentham 1996, 32–3; 1998, 256; 1838–43, i, 163, vi, 238).

are considered and weighed and directives are interpreted and applied. They cannot be brought into explicit focus and submitted to expert advice at every practical juncture without eviscerating the guidance.

Of course, even when general legal norms are promulgated, intervention will be necessary to resolve disputes and to provide interpretations of the norms, but the institutions charged with such interventions can perform their task even minimally well only if they work on the margins. The institutional mechanisms would be overwhelmed, would seize up and collapse, if they were required to address all matters of interpretation and all disputes that might arise. Law depends for its efficacy on a vast reservoir of public understanding among intelligent, self-directing law-subjects. This reservoir is necessary, as Waldron pointed out, if individual citizens are to determine when to seek the assistance of legal experts and, if necessary, the formal institutions of law. 'The citizen has got to be in a position to know for himself what sorts of situations call for expert legal advice and what sorts of situations he can reliably handle on the basis of his own knowledge' (Waldron 1989, 91). However, this understanding is possible only if the law's demands are broadly familiar, reasonably constant over time, and consonant generally with familiar informal social customs and practices. Law cannot create on its own this reservoir of public understanding; it presupposes it (although, as we shall see, it does much to shape it). Congruence, therefore, is necessary for the efficacy of law's normative work.

This, then, is the main argument for the congruence thesis; however, a few words in clarification of this argument are in order. The congruence for which I have argued does not require that people generally affirm or agree with legal norms. It does not require convergence of the law's values with popular social values such that law-subjects are encouraged to endorse, at least in broad strokes, the law's efforts. Congruence is said to be necessary for law's practical, public intelligibility, and hence of its efficacy. It is an argument, ultimately, to establish a certain condition of the existence of law. The thesis makes no claim regarding conditions of law's legitimacy either *de facto* or *de jure*. The public, practical intelligibility of law is necessary not only for the 'good citizen' but also for the 'bad man', not only for obeying the law, but also for gaming it. From a demonstration of a substantial degree of congruence it does not follow that people generally affirm or accept it; neither does it follow that congruence is, or is widely taken to be, a *reason* for compliance.

4 The Mediation Thesis

Congruence, we have seen, is a matter of degree and the degree of congruence necessary for law's efficacy is something short, perhaps well short, of that typical of medieval law, which was thickly interwoven with the customary practices of medieval social life. Modern law, linked more closely with centralized, formally institutionalized political authorities, has become more detached from informal social customs. Bentham, and many after him, argued that the professionalization of law put enormous power into the hands of the legal class ('Judge & Co'), inclining them to make the law complex, unintelligible, and detached from the customs and practices of ordinary social life in order to drive up the demand for their services (Bentham 1977, 509; Tamanaha 2001, 73). Radical alienation of the population from law maintained by, and solely for, the legal elite is, according to Hart, more than merely conceivable. Even when the law seeks explicitly or implicitly to incorporate customary structures into the law, the result often is not convergence of law and pre-existing custom, but transformation of custom and forcing it to serve alien values.

These considerations challenge the congruence thesis and we must take the challenge seriously, but some of its sting can be drawn if we keep in mind that congruence does not entail identity of content: law and informal social practices may be sufficiently congruent without mirroring each other. Likewise, although the congruence thesis holds that law depends for its efficacy on background social practices, it does not deny that law can also have a profound effect on those practices. It is not committed to the Romantic claim that law can function just insofar as it plays along with ancient and unchanging customs. The congruence thesis recognizes that the relationship between law and informal social practices is not merely a matter of overlap or intersection, but rather a matter of interaction of powerful reciprocal forces. Anthropologist Paul Bohannan keenly observed that it is a 'fertile dilemma of law that it must always be out of step with society, but that people must always...attempt to reduce the lack of phase' (Bohannan 1965, 37). Rather than undermine the congruence thesis, this 'dilemma' tends to confirm it. For the fact that the law's attempt to establish standards and control conduct, ignoring or even directly challenging existing social practices, is in powerful tension with the forces that those practices exert on the law is a measure of law's need for congruence. Because congruence is necessary for law's efficacy, law must seek to guide conduct through assimilating and transforming social practices and in doing so make itself vulnerable to being tailored to fit the dimensions of informal social practice.[5]

These reflections on congruence give us some insight into what it is for law to be 'in force', to be 'used in the right way', in a community and how to deal with the possibility of serious alienation of individuals from the law. The argument for the congruence thesis strongly suggests that a substantial part of law's

---

[5] Hart, like Bentham, thought that informal social practices and customs (the 'regime of primary rules') are static, but this is often clearly not the case. Precisely because they are informal and close to the ground of daily interactions, social customs (that is, individuals engaged in dynamic interactions structured by them) are often better able to respond adroitly to changes of circumstances and to change again if the initial change proves inadequate. Thus, informal social practices and customs, rather than resisting and retarding change, can often be powerful agents of social change.

normative guidance must be indirect, *mediated* by the informal social customs and practices in which law-subjects participate.[6] We can approach this mediation from two directions. First, one measure of law's being 'used' is its influence on and involvement in the social practices and norms that more directly shape the lives of law-subjects. This can take a wide variety of forms. We need only mention a few.

(1) In some cases, it gives formal expression to the norms, articulating them and incorporating them into the body of law. In this way, formal law makes explicit what may be only implicit in the practices of law-subjects. This not only facilitates the enforcement of these norms, but, as Cardozo pointed out, it enables citizens publicly to reaffirm their commitment to obligations they expect themselves and others to honour and to reflect together on those obligations and the consequences of living up to them (Goldberg 1990, 1327).

(2) In some cases it directly influences the emergence or entrenchment of particular social norms. Through articulating new norms, or attaching incentives of various kinds to emerging but not yet established social norms, it can create new equilibria of expectations which over time can encourage a shift in social attitudes regarding what is proper social behaviour. (Shifts in American attitudes towards smoking in public places, for example, may be due in part to legal influences.)

(3) By raising (or lowering) what are broadly perceived to be the minimal conditions of socially appropriate behaviour, or through publicly announced incentives giving assurance of certain regularities of social behaviour, the law can affect the viability of social norms, encouraging their development, enhancing their staying power, or accelerating their decline.

(4) Legal institutions often put the law and social practices into direct contact by integrating representative participants in informal social practices into their operations. The result of such contact can be that the law is refined to fit more comfortably with the informal practices or the practices are adjusted to the new outlines of the law. The classic example of such contact is the jury throughout the history of Anglo-American law; and a similar phenomenon can be found in Continental commercial law, where courts of first instance are composed of lay judges drawn from the business community. Litigant-driven adjudication, typical in private or civil law, has the same effect. Such adjudication is brought to bear only on those issues raised and pressed by litigants and the interpretations and arguments considered by the courts are greatly (if not exclusively) shaped by what litigants take to be salient for their ordinary practice.

---

[6] This is especially true if law's primary, if least visible, mode of guidance is constitutive, since, arguably, it is with respect to the constitution of non-political relationships and networks of relationships that the forces for consilience are strongest. Some evidence for the truth of this claim lies in the fact that legal systems often retain their ability to structure non-political life despite radical *political* revolutions (ie, despite extra-legal changes in the political constitution including rules of recognition), in virtue of the consilience of civil and private law with background social practices.

While we might enumerate other ways in which law shapes (and is shaped by) informal social practices, I propose that we shift focus to consider law's social-practice-mediated normative guidance from the second direction, namely from the perspective of law-subjects. Recall the problem we identified in the first section of this essay: for a legal system to be in force in a community it was not sufficient that the conduct of law-subjects generally conforms with its norms, but it was too much to require that they accept them (in the sense familiar to readers of Hart). It is even too much to require that ordinary law-subjects have extensive general knowledge of the law, if by that we mean that they grasp it, as it were, *in sensu composito,*[7] for that would require acquaintance with legal texts and with techniques for extracting true legal propositions from them that are available to only a relatively small (legally trained) sub-set of them. Law is, after all, a complex system of norms the content of which is determined by their location in the system. With respect to informal, largely customary, systems it might be reasonable to expect widespread knowledge of its norms *in sensu composito*, but modern law's increased complexity and formal institutionalization puts this form of knowledge beyond most law-subjects. What is possible is that law-subjects grasp *in sensu diviso* much of the law that pertains to them, enough at least to enable them to judge when they should consult legal experts and when they can rely on their own assessment of what they ought to do (and the legal consequences of their actions and the actions of others), without having to do so at every practical turn. In doing so, they must also be reasonably assured that their grasp meshes with the grasp of other law-subjects with whom they are likely to interact. It is necessary, then, that they grasp legal norms *in sensu diviso* as public standards for their conduct and the conduct of others in the community.[8]

For this to be the case for the generality of law-subjects, they must come to learn the law (insofar as it pertains to them) through their ordinary daily interactions. And this is possible only if law is customized for law-subjects in two respects. (1) Legal norms must be tailored to schemata that individual law-subjects can readily understand and apply to standard instances of the norms that they will encounter or to exemplars from which they can intuitively and implicitly reason by analogy, and (2) these schemata or exemplars will typically be found in or related to informal customs or practices that law-subjects learn through participating

---

[7] I rely here on the distinction David Lewis (1969, 64–8), following Abelard, drew between general propositions that are grasped *in sensu composito* and those grasped *in sensu diviso*. If I believe *in sensu composito* that every F is G, then the content of my belief is the general proposition that every F is G. If, however, I believe *in sensu diviso* that every F is G, I may not actually grasp any general proposition, but it may nevertheless be true that for every F I encounter I believe of it that it is G. By extension, I want to claim, while a person may not grasp very much of the law's norms *in sensu composito*, she may still grasp it *in sensu diviso*, ie, grasp it to the extent that in most instances in which law puts her under obligation, she understands herself to be obligated to act as it requires, and to some extent also understands that law, perhaps *inter alia*, requires it.

[8] It is not necessary, however, that they be committed to or otherwise accept these standards on their merits.

in them, or through observation of others participating in them. Law-subjects initially learn of the law's demands indirectly through learning informal norms or expectations that are more or less congruent with those legal norms. This understanding is refined through encounters with specific legal demands that may confirm, or extend, or in some cases contradict this initial understanding and call for a revision of it. In this way, law-subjects will come to have a roughly adequate, concrete (ie, *in sensu diviso*) grasp of the law's requirements and of the law as requiring them (albeit not necessarily in sharp distinction from other sources of normative expectations) as the law touches their ordinary daily lives. With this understanding they can have a reasonably good working understanding of when they can rely on their own lay understanding of the law and when they need to consult legal experts.

Law's normative guidance, then, is indirect, mediated by the informal social norms and the practices in which they are embedded, social norms that more directly give shape and direction to the lives of law-subjects. From these informal normative practices, law-subjects learn how to grasp and respond to normative demands generally, and the law's normative demands in particular, and they acquire a background working knowledge of law's normative demands and resources for refining and building on this working knowledge as time goes on and their experience broadens. The law's normative relationship with its law-subjects is mediated by the informal normative social practices in which they participate in two respects: (1) it is through participation in those informal practices that law-subjects begin to develop a working knowledge *in sensu diviso* of law's demands and (2) relying on resources drawn from those practices they extend, refine, and correct their understanding of demands, sometimes, where necessary (and they can afford it) working into their understanding advice from legal experts and, more rarely, direct or indirect knowledge of the decisions and actions of formal legal institutions.

If this sketch of how informal social practices mediate the relationship between the system of formal legal norms and the practical deliberations and decision-making of the intelligent self-directing agents governed by those norms is correct in broad outline, then we have some idea what it is for behaviour which is not inconsistent with legal norms to *comply* with them and thus to manifest their effectiveness as law. In a population governed by those norms and complying with them in this way we can reasonably say that it is used or practiced in that community 'in the right way', that is, in a way that funds and confirms our saying that law exists and is effective in that community. For this to be true the formal law and informal social practices must be to a substantial degree congruent and it is in this congruence that the efficacy of law consists.

If this is correct, then, we have not only asserted that effectiveness of law, understood as general compliance with its norms, is a necessary condition of its existence in a community, but we have also explained why effectiveness of that sort is necessary for its existence. We have done so by tracing it to an account of the efficacy of law that is logically tied to a conceptually necessary feature of law, namely, its ability to provide normative guidance to those it claims to govern. The effectiveness of law is a complex matter of empirical social fact to be confirmed through empirical inquiry, but its jurisprudential relevance is determined by its relation to necessary features of law's distinctive mode of operation.

4

Hart and the Principles of Legality

Jeremy Waldron[1]

1

H.L.A. Hart's contributions to the philosophy of law are so considerable and his reinvigoration of this whole field has been so extensive and important that it may seem churlish to draw attention to—let alone complain about—any gaps or inadequacies in his jurisprudence. For why should anybody be expected to cover everything? And why should someone who has given us the practice theory of norms, the internal aspect of rules, a robust insistence on the difference between being obliged and being obligated, law as the union of primary and secondary rules, the minimum content of natural law, the core and penumbra, a new conception of the separation between law and morality, and a lot more besides—why should anyone who has given us all that be criticized for failing to give us even more? The old phrase from the song in the Passover service comes to mind: *Dayeinu.* Had God given us the Torah and not led us into the land of Israel, *Dayeinu!* If God had just done *this* for us, it would have been enough.[2] If Hart had just given us the union of primary and secondary rules, and not the minimum content of natural law, *Dayeinu!*

Yet gaps there are in Hart's jurisprudence: two or three quite big ones in my view, and they are of concern not because they attest to the limits on his god-like contribution, but for the effect they have had on the tradition of analytic legal philosophy in Hart's wake. (The subject of this volume is, after all, Hart's *legacy.*) Those who base their own credentials on Hart's glory too often take *his* failure to

---

[1] A slightly shorter version of this chapter was presented at the Symposium on 'The Legacy of H.L.A. Hart' at Cambridge University in July 2007. A much longer version was presented at a conference on the 'Fiftieth Anniversary of the Hart/Fuller Debate' at New York University in February 2008. That longer version is forthcoming in the NYU Law Review (October 2008) and is available at <http://www.law.nyu.edu/conferences/hart-Fuller/docs/Positivism_and_Legality_Waldron.pdf>.
[2] 'Had God brought us out of Egypt and not divided the sea for us, *Dayeinu*
Had God divided the sea and not permitted us to cross on dry land, *Dayeinu*
Had God permitted us to cross on dry land and not sustained us for forty years in the desert, *Dayeinu*
Had God sustained us for forty years in the desert and not fed us with manna, *Dayeinu...*' [and so on].

address a topic as a reason for thinking that it is not worth addressing rather than as a challenge to build upon the legacy of his work in an area which, as it happened, was not among the ones where he made his most significant contribution.

One gap is huge and, mercifully, it is not my subject today. I mean Hart's failure to say anything at length on the issue of precedent and *stare decisis*. There are a few observations, scattered throughout *The Concept of Law*;[3] but nothing indicating any sustained interest in the issue of why a system of social governance might commit itself so strongly to a principle of consistency with past decisions, and why this should be regarded as so distinctive of the legal method, at least in our tradition. In this regard it is to the work of Hart's successor at Oxford, Ronald Dworkin, that we have to turn if we want fresh insight into the connection between the concept of law and the idea of keeping faith with past decisions. And yet it is deplorable that those who count themselves followers of Hart are usually much more interested in defending his work against some criticisms that Dworkin made than in following Dworkin's example of forward and affirmative movement in this important and still neglected area of jurisprudence.

A second shortcoming is Hart's treatment of international law. Now here we have a different situation. There is a whole chapter devoted to international law at the very end of *The Concept of Law*,[4] but that chapter is, for the most part—there is one exception that I will mention at the end of my remarks today—quite unhelpful. Legal philosophers mostly do not bother with it; indeed legal philosophers in Hart's tradition mostly neglect the subject of international law altogether. Those international lawyers who do bother to read Hart's chapter on international law usually come away with the impression that Hart, like Austin, did not believe there was any such thing as international law.[5] That is not quite correct, but Hart did say that international law is like a primitive legal system—all primary norms and no secondary norms. And that characterization was wrong in 1960 and it is certainly wrong now.

---

[3] See esp. Hart 1994, 134–5, where Hart acknowledges that he is not offering any fresh insights into this topic.

[4] Hart 1994, 213–37. See also Hart 1983, 311–34 (on Hans Kelsen's monism).

[5] See, eg, Barker 2007, 12: 'Hart's own conclusion was that international law could not be considered as a legal system because it lacked the necessary secondary rules and the required rule of recognition.' But cf Zipursky 2006, 1250: 'Although it is currently unfashionable in Hart scholarship to say so, Hart also thought it a distortion of legal reality to deny the existence of international law. It is easy to read from Hart's guarded language in chapter X, combined with his warm embrace of the idea earlier in the book heralding the idea that legal systems should be analyzed as the union of primary and secondary rules, that Hart did not truly believe international law qualified as law. But I think this quite clearly is a mistake. *The Concept of Law* is very naturally read, in fact, as articulating a rich enough theory of legal obligation to permit one to retain the idea that international law is really a form of law. Primary rules exist that purport to impose obligations, and are recognized from the internal point of view as imposing obligations. One of the principal advantages of decoupling the notion of obligation from the existence of a centralized system of sanctions, is that it permits one to retain the view—widely shared by language and lawyers—that there is such a thing as international law.'

This is another example of an area where Hart's own carelessness or indifference has been imitated rather than compensated for, by his followers. Those who regard themselves as working to protect and develop Hart's legacy have shown little interest in subjecting Hart's claims about international law to any sort of careful scrutiny or revision. The neglect of international law in modern analytic jurisprudence is nothing short of scandalous.[6] Theoretically it is the issue of the hour; there is an intense debate going on in the legal academy about the nature and character of customary international law, for example.[7] Analytic legal philosophers seem mostly to have missed this, even when it is evident that they might have a substantial contribution to make. Indeed the contribution could be based on some of the specifics of Hart's jurisprudence. Many of the critiques of customary international law argue that custom is too flabby and inchoate to lie at the heart of a real working legal system; yet it is Hart who gave us a more sophisticated understanding of customary law than previous positivists could provide and it is Hart who showed that something like custom lies at the foundation of every system of law, in the fundamental secondary rules which generate its structure. So analytic jurisprudence is potentially very relevant to these disputes about the character and legitimacy of international law. Yet all the important philosophical work on it is being done by people other than those in the core of modern positivist legal philosophy.[8] Most of those who bask in Hart's glory prefer to fiddle with issues about exclusive and inclusive legal positivism, a discussion that has been following the law of diminishing returns since Jules Coleman initiated it in 1988, rather than address these more urgent and compelling issues.[9]

The third gap, which I *do* want to talk about in this paper, is the issue of legality or the Rule of Law and its relation to the work that Hart did—the god-like work that I have referred to—on the concept of law and on what it means to describe something as a legal system.

Here too we are dealing with an area of jurisprudence that Hart touched on here and there, but passed by rather lightly and carelessly. Or rather, he dealt with

[6] At a time when they are being criticized for the inbred sterility of their work (see Dworkin 2002, 1678–9), it is quite amazing how little attention specialist legal philosophers have given to this real problem. *The Blackwell Guide to the Philosophy of Law and Legal Theory* (Golding & Edmundson 2005) has no chapter on international law and no reference to it in the index. The *Oxford Handbook of Jurisprudence and Philosophy of Law* (Coleman & Shapiro 2002) has an essay on international law (Buchanan & Golove 2002), but it is entirely about normative issues of global justice and intervention etc. The authors explicitly disdain any discussion of analytic or philosophical issues. Analytic philosophy of law since 1999 has had its own house journal, *Legal Theory*, edited by Jules Coleman, Brian Leiter, and Larry Alexander. A quick survey of titles reveals just three articles on international law in its 13 years (that's three out of about 250 articles), and all of them are on normative rather than conceptual or analytic issues. (Two are discussions of Rawls 1999.)

[7] See, eg, Goldsmith and Posner 2006, McGinnis and Somin 2007, and Rabkin 2006.

[8] I am not neglecting the contribution in Finnis 1980, 238–45 (a discussion of customary international law). It is an honourable exception and it illustrates the point that natural lawyers are probably better at thinking usefully about positive law than positivists are.

[9] See, eg, Coleman 1982, Coleman 2001, and Dworkin 2002.

it carefully, but in my view with the wrong sort of care. For him the issue was a defensive one, to block a real or imagined assault upon the Maginot Line of positivist jurisprudence—the separation of law and morality. The aim was to block an assault on the separation of law and morality, launched on the basis of the importance for any adequate understanding of law of what Hart called the principles of legality. Hart's work on this issue was almost wholly defensive. It was directed against a challenge to his work by Lon L Fuller, and the impression I get from reading what Hart wrote about the principles of legality is that, once Fuller's challenge was rebutted, the principles of legality were of little interest, and Hart was quite happy to sponsor their neglect, a neglect which has been continued by many (though not by all) of his followers in modern analytic philosophy.[10]

Some of what he said indicated that Hart did not think that, strictly speaking, legality was really a topic in the philosophy of law at all. At best, it was a topic in moral or political philosophy: it alerted us to principles that might be important in the evaluation of law; but, for that very reason, the principles of legality should be kept firmly apart from our understanding—our positivist understanding—of *what law is.* That, as we will see, is more or less the extent of Hart's affirmative contribution on this topic. Negatively, he was inclined to see a preoccupation with legality and the Rule of Law as a source of confusion in jurisprudence; and he often gave the impression that if anyone offered to talk about principles of legality or the Rule of Law in a philosophy of law class, the responsible thing to do was to shut down that discussion as quickly and firmly as possible. Principles of legality, he implied, may be principles for the evaluation of law; but their study is not part of the philosophical discipline that tries to tell us what law essentially is.

I do not mean that Hart was in any sense hostile to the Rule of Law as a political ideal. Neil MacCormick (1981, 157–8) once got very indignant about a suggestion by Fuller that Hart embraced a managerialist approach to law. Professor MacCormick said this in his book on Hart:

Nobody who gave five minutes' cursory thought to Hart's various but largely self-consistent reflections about the moral relevance of positive law . . . could suppose that he is any less an enthusiast than L.L. Fuller for promoting the vision of a society in which freely communicating individuals willingly collaborate in their common social enterprises and freely grant each other friendly tolerance in their more particularistic or individual activities, and in which the resort by officials to means of mere coercion is minimized. Nobody could deny either the reality of his concern for justice or the firmness of his contentions that a precondition of justice as defined within his critical morality is the existence of a well working legal system and that a consequence of a just legal system's existence is the establishment of a network of mutual moral obligations of respect for law among the citizens within that jurisdiction. (MacCormick 1981, 157–8)

But it is not Hart's personal enthusiasm for the Rule of Law that one misses in his jurisprudence; it is his elucidation of it and his setting in train a sense among his

---

[10] Two exceptions are Raz 1979, 210–29; and Kramer 2007, 101–86. See also MacCormick 2005.

followers that it is a topic worthy of jurisprudential analysis. That's what we look for and what we cannot really find.

2

Let us begin with what there is. The most extensive discussion of the Rule of Law or legality in Hart's writings may be found in a little-known essay called 'Problems of the Philosophy of Law' (Hart 1967c) which Hart wrote originally for Paul Edwards's *Encyclopedia of Philosophy*.

The encyclopedia piece was divided into two parts: the first part dealt with 'Problems of Definition and Analysis' and the second part with 'Problems of the Criticism of Law'. The second part discussed substantive criteria of evaluation for a while and then Hart went on to say the following:

> Laws, however impeccable their content, may be of little service to human beings and may cause both injustice and misery unless they generally conform to certain require-ments which may be broadly termed procedural... These procedural requirements relate to such matters as the generality of rules of law, the clarity with which they are phrased, the publicity given to them, the time of their enactment, and the manner in which they are judicially applied to particular cases. The requirements that the law, except in special circumstances, should be general (should refer to classes of persons, things, and circum-stances, not to individuals or to particular actions); should be free from contradictions, ambiguities, and obscurities; should be publicly promulgated and easily accessible; and should not be retrospective in operation are usually referred to as the principles of legal-ity. The principles which require courts, in applying general rules to particular cases, to be without personal interest in the outcome or other bias and to hear arguments on mat-ters of law and proofs of matters of fact from both sides of a dispute are often referred to as rules of natural justice. These two sets of principles together define the concept of the rule of law.... (Hart 1967c, 273–4)

Hart's taxonomy is a little confusing. I would call the principles that deal with generality, proximity etc, *formal* rather than procedural; the procedural ones are the principles Hart refers to as principles of natural justice or as we Americans redundantly say procedural due process.[11] But the general picture is pretty clear. There are principles about the form that legal norms should take and there are principles about the broad character of the procedures that should be used in their application to particular cases: and together those principles of legality and due process add up to what people call the Rule of Law.

The first set of principles—the formal ones—are roughly what Lon Fuller referred to as the 'inner morality of law'. I have always found it odd that Fuller said so little about the procedural side of the Rule of Law in chapter 2

---

[11] Hart 1994, 160 also has brief reference to principles of natural justice such as *audi alteram partem*.

of *The Morality of Law* (Fuller 1969, 33–94), especially in view of his own very intense and focused interest in the forms and limits of adjudication (Fuller 1978). And by the way, Fuller (1969, 96) also made the mistake of calling the formal principles procedural, as though everything which is not substantive is procedural. Be that as it may, the formal principles that Hart mentions are roughly what Fuller (1958, 659) referred to as the 'inner morality of law', and these comments in the *Encyclopedia* essay (Hart 1967c) are about as close as Hart ever came to acknowledging the importance of Fuller's contribution.

Hart dealt with the principles of legality in the *Encyclopedia* essay rather less briskly than he had done, some years earlier, in a very offhand passage in *The Concept of Law* (Hart 1994). There, in the course of his discussion of various ways in which law might be related to morality, Hart invited us to consider

what is in fact involved in any method of social control...which consists primarily of general standards of conduct communicated to classes of persons, who are then expected to understand and conform to the rules without further official direction. If social control of this sort is to function, the rules must satisfy certain conditions: they must be intelligible and within the capacity of most to obey, and in general they must not be retrospective, though exceptionally they may be. (Hart 1994, 206–7)

Of these requirements, Hart said: 'Plainly these features of control by rule are closely related to the requirements of justice which lawyers term principles of legality.' But in *The Concept of Law* Hart had no interest in explicating what 'principles of legality' might mean. His main interest was to squelch any inference from the principles of legality to a position like Fuller's about law's overall moral potential. He alluded briefly to Fuller's own view of these principles—'one critic of positivism has seen in these aspects of control by rules, something amounting to a necessary connection between law and morality' (Hart 1994, 207 and 303n)—but he made no comment of his own except to say, acidly, that these formal requirements are 'unfortunately compatible with very great iniquity' (Hart 1994, 207). That, he indicated, was more or less all that needed to be said on the matter. Fuller was wrong in thinking that the imposition of these requirements necessarily placed any limits on the evil that could be done under the auspices of the rule of law. And Hart's followers have imitated him in that: that particular anti-Fuller point is all they are interested in too. The crucial thing is to protect the separability thesis. Once that is done, the principles of legality have little interest for jurisprudence.

Hart said something similar—'compatible with very great iniquity'—about the principles of legality in the *Encyclopedia* article too; but there he said it much less dismissively. In that context Hart said that, even if these principles are very important, we must not infer that 'it will always be reasonable or morally obligatory for a man to obey the law when the legal system provides him with [the] benefits [of principles of legality and natural justice], for in other ways the system may be iniquitous' (Hart 1967c, 274). That, as I say, is much less dismissive. For one thing, it acknowledges that there *are* important moral values underpinning the principles of legality (even though they may be outweighed by this ubiquitous 'iniquity' that he harps so heavily upon). I will come back to this in a moment.

3

One interesting thing about both the cursory discussion in *The Concept of Law* and the somewhat less cursory discussion in the *Encyclopedia* essay is that Hart seems fastidiously careful not to use the term 'principles of legality' himself; he mentions it but almost always attributes its use in this context to others. He speaks of 'the requirements of justice which lawyers *term* principles of legality' (Hart 1994, 207) and principles which are '*usually referred to* as the principles of legality' (Hart 1967c, 274). I am not sure why he did this. It is as though he could not bring himself to use the term in his own voice, for fear that 'legality' would connote a more intimate connection between these principles and the very idea of law than he was comfortable with. (In Hart's review of Fuller—Hart 1965a, 1284—we are told that 'principles of legality' is Fuller's term, but Hart does go on to say that he himself certainly prefers it to the phrase 'the inner morality of law'. We will go into his reasons for that preference shortly.)

Hart also mentioned the principles of legality in his writing on the philosophy of criminal law,[12] and there—where the jurisprudential stakes were a little less fraught—he seemed happier to use the term 'principles of legality' in his own voice. So, for example, in his debate with Lord Devlin about the use of criminal law to enforce morality (Hart 1963), Hart considered the decision of the House of Lords in *Shaw v DPP* (the 'Ladies' Directory' case, where the Law Lords dredged up a non-statutory common law crime of conspiracy to corrupt public morals). Hart said this about the decision in *Shaw*:

[The House of Lords] seemed willing to pay a high price in terms of the sacrifice of other values for the establishment...of the Courts as *custos morum* [guardian of morals]. The particular value which they sacrificed is the principle of legality which requires criminal offences to be as precisely defined as possible, so that it can be known beforehand what acts are criminal and what are not. (Hart 1963, 12)

Or consider what Hart said about what would happen if Barbara Wootton's proposal that strict liability should comprehensively replace ordinary criminal liability were to prevail:[13]

Among other things, we should lose the ability which the present system in some degree guarantees to us, to predict and plan the future course of our lives within the coercive

---

[12] See Stewart 1999 for a most helpful discussion.
[13] For her views, see Wootton 1981.

framework of the law. For the system which makes liability to the law's sanctions dependent upon a voluntary act not only maximizes the power of the individual to determine
by his choice his future fate; it also maximizes his power to identify in advance the space
which will be left open to him free from the law's interference. (Hart 1968,181–2)[14]

This is the same principle as the one that is referred to in his discussion of *Shaw*,
only it is characterized in a slightly different way: it is now a principle that informs
us about the extent of our freedom, as opposed to a principle that informs us
about the specification of crime. But these are more or less the same thing. And
the point is that in these two contexts Hart does seem to take that principle or
pair of principles seriously.

4

Yet, when it comes to general jurisprudence—and specifically the debate with
Lon Fuller—Hart seems determined to minimize and even mischaracterize these
principles.

In his review of Fuller's book, for example, Hart said that he was puzzled by
Fuller's association of the word 'morality' with the principles of legality. He said
'the author's insistence on classifying these principles of legality as a "morality" is
a source of confusion both for him and his readers' (Hart 1965a, 1285). In a vivid
analogy, Hart said if we were to come up with a set of craft principles for poison-
ers, that wouldn't be a 'morality' of poisoning:

Poisoning is no doubt a purposive activity, and reflections on its purpose may show that
it has its internal principles. ('Avoid poisons however lethal if they cause the victim to
vomit,' or 'Avoid poisons however lethal if their shape, color, or size is likely to attract
notice.' But to call these principles of the poisoner's art 'the morality of poisoning' would
simply blur the distinction between the notion of efficiency for a purpose and those final
judgments about activities and purposes with which morality in its various forms is concerned. (Hart 1965a, 1286)

The analogy depends, of course, on seeing Fuller's principles simply as principles
for the efficient pursuit of a given purpose. (And some of what Fuller says about

---

[14] The same point was presented in a somewhat more sustained way in Hart 1965b, 1330: 'In
a system in which proof of *mens rea* was no longer a necessary condition for conviction the occasions for official interferences in our lives would be vastly increased.... [E]very blow, even if it was
apparent that it was accidental or merely careless... would in principle be a matter for investigation
under the new scheme. This is so because the possibilities of a curable condition would have to be
investigated and if possible treated. No doubt under the new regime prosecuting authorities would
use their common-sense; but a very great discretion would have to be entrusted to them to sift from
the mass the cases worth investigation for either penal or therapeutic treatment. This expansion of
police powers would bring with it great uncertainty for the individual citizen and, though official
interference with his life would be more frequent, he will be less able to predict their incidence if
any accidental breach of the criminal law may be an occasion for them.'

the craftsmanship and carpentry analogy encourages that reading: see Fuller 1969, 96.) And if they *were* just principles of efficiency—How to Do Things with Rules—then it *would* be inappropriate to call them a morality, at least (as Hart said) without showing that 'the purpose of subjecting human conduct to the governance of rules, no matter what their content' was 'of ultimate value in the conduct of life' (Hart 1965a, 1287).

But then a little later, when Hart wants to respond more defensively to Fuller's characterization of legal positivism as insufficiently concerned with legality— that is, when he wants to respond to Fuller's accusation that positivists ' "cannot even explain what would be wrong with a system of laws that were wholly retro- active," and that we cannot give any adequate explanation of why normally legal rules are general' (Hart 1965a, 1290, quoting Fuller 1969, 147)—he says that it is perfectly possible to develop an account of what would be wrong with such a system. And, though he does not say so explicitly, the account that he intimates is firmly located within the realm of the moral. Hart says this:

Why, to take the simplest instances, could not writers like Bentham and Austin, who defined law as commands, have objected to a system of laws that were wholly retroactive on the ground that it could make no contribution to human happiness and so far as it resulted in punishments would inflict useless misery? Why should not Kelsen or I, myself, who think law may be profitably viewed as a system of rules, not also explain that the normal generality of law is desirable not only for reasons of economy but because it will enable individuals to predict the future and that this is a powerful contribution to human liberty and happiness? (Hart 1965a, 1291)

Hart imagines that Fuller might complain that Hart's own or Bentham's use of these principles is not really moral, because it is just oriented to human happi- ness—in other words, that the principles of legality 'are valued so far only as they contribute to human happiness or other substantive moral aims of the law' (Hart 1965a, 1291) but they are not really moral in themselves. Hart, I think, regards that quite rightly as a distinction without a difference.

Sometimes indeed Hart is very explicit about the moral status of these principles. In a solution he proposes (1958, 618–21) to the Grudge Informer case, which he and Fuller discussed in their 1958 exchange, Hart toys with the idea of a retro- spective statute for the post-war era making the wife's conduct, which was legal in 1944, unlawful. (The case raised the question of whether to punish a woman in 1949 for having denounced her husband to the authorities in 1944 under prepos- terously oppressive Nazi statutes enacted in 1934 and 1938 respectively.)[15] Hart took the position that instead of declaring the Nazi statutes to have been nullities, it might have been better to enact a statute after 1945 and apply that statute retro- actively to the informer's case to punish her. He acknowledges that this would violate the principle of legality which prohibits retroactive legislation and he says

[15] Fuller 1958, 652–7 gives a good account of this case; the relevant statutes are set out at Fuller 1958, 653 and 654.

that would involve 'sacrificing a very precious principle of morality endorsed by most legal systems' (Hart 1958, 619). 'A very precious principle of morality'—that is how he characterizes legality.

But if that is Hart's position, then he should not have maintained the view that he set out a few pages earlier in the review that Fuller was wrong to give a moral characterization of these principles. For his own account now shows that he and Bentham and many other positivists do regard them as moral, in the most straightforward sense of the term. They are oriented to human happiness and liberty, and as such they are part of the principles of critical or censorial jurisprudence.

They are certainly not just principles of efficiency, or if they are, they are principles constraining the ruler for the sake of efficiency for the subjects—the efficient pursuit of their own aims within clear parameters of freedom—and that in itself is a moral matter (so far as the ruler is concerned). The poisoning analogy assumes that the principles are oriented to efficiency only for the purposes of the ruler or the poisoner; but the principles of legality, as Hart stressed in his discussion of *Shaw v DPP* (Hart 1963, 12) and in his discussions of strict liability (Hart 1965b, 1330; and Hart 1967c, 181–2), have the purpose not of advancing the ruler's own aims but of making room in the ruler's calculations—respectful room—for the purposes of the individuals who live under his power. And all this is quite incompatible with his taking Fuller's characterization of these principles as 'moral' as a ground for criticizing Fuller. What I am saying, then, is that Hart's criticism of Fuller for emphasizing the moral character of legality depends on its being separated by two or three pages of distracting argument from the places where Hart himself says that we *can* give a moral account of why these principles are important.

In the *Encyclopedia* article I mentioned (Hart 1967c), the characterization of the principles of legality is much more honest. Hart says two things about them, but he no longer equivocates. He says, on the one hand, that 'general rules clearly framed and publicly promulgated are the most efficient form of social control' (Hart 1967c, 274). That is efficiency from the point of view of the ruler. But then he goes on immediately to say that 'from the point of view of the individual citizen, they are more than that'.

[T]hey are required if [the citizen] is to have the advantage of knowing in advance the ways in which his liberty will be restricted in the various situations in which he may find himself, and he needs this knowledge if he is to plan his life. (Hart 1967c, 274)

Also Hart says that generality helps the individual citizen because it gives him information about what others will be held to, which 'increases the confidence with which he can plan his future' (Hart 1967c, 274). Well, if that is not a moral characterization of these principles or of the rationale of these principles, then I do not know what is. They may not be fundamental moral principles; they are not the principle of utility or the categorical imperative; they may operate in the service of human happiness or dignity or autonomy; but they are none the less moral for that.

5

So the principles of legality *are* moral principles or can be seen in that light. Perhaps what Hart really objects to in Fuller's characterization is that they are a special morality *of law*. Maybe they are just a general part of political morality; but if we call them a morality of law, then again we are creeping towards the Maginot Line of a separation between law and morality which Hart thinks needs to be defended at all costs.

But I do not understand why Hart should be committed to denying this. Consider the principle of generality,[16] which he thinks is one of the principles of legality. At the end of the review of Fuller's book, when Hart was being honest about the moral character of Fuller's principles, he said that a positivist might acknowledge that 'the normal generality of law is desirable not only for reasons of economy [I think he means administrative economy], but because it will enable individuals to predict the future and that this is a powerful contribution to human liberty and happiness' (Hart 1965a, 1291). But in Hart 1994, he also observed that this requirement of generality is deeply and intimately bound up with law. He observed that law had something formal in common with justice, inasmuch as both proceed according to rules and both embody the formal idea of 'treating like cases alike' (Hart 1994, 157–67). 'We have', he said, 'in the bare notion of applying a general rule of law, the germ at least of justice' (Hart 1994, 206). Now it is not the link with justice that I want to talk about here; for the moral character of the generality principle, *qua* principle of legality, is not that it will yield just results but rather that—just or unjust—at least people will have a better appreciation of their position. The principle contributes to human liberty and happiness via predictability not via the germ of justice hypothesis, which is much more Fullerian than Hart is usually willing to be.[17] It is not the link with justice that I want to talk about. It is rather this sense that generality as a requirement

---

[16] In Hart 1994, 8, 21–3, there is discussion of the common insistence that nothing be called a law unless it is general in character, and Hart suggests (like Austin) that this is based on the impracticality of the alternative: '[N]o society could support the number of officials necessary to secure that every member of the society was officially and separately informed of every act which he was required to do' (Hart 1994, 21). Hart inferred that particularized orders (without a general basis) were exceptional and ancillary relative to the concept of law as he was expounding it.

[17] Cf Hart 1958, 624: 'So there is, in the very notion of law consisting of general rules, something which prevents us from treating it as [if] morally it is utterly neutral, without any necessary contact with moral principles.' But he backtracked a bit in Hart 1994, 161, where he said: 'This close connection between justice in the administration of the law and the very notion of a rule has tempted some famous thinkers to identify justice with conformity with law. Yet plainly this is an error...' For critical views of the 'germ of justice' hypothesis, see Lyons 1973; Kramer 1999, ch 2; Green 2005.

put forward in the name of political morality is not just incidentally applicable to law but applicable on account of what law is and inherently aspires to be: law itself in its declared character looks forward to being evaluated on this basis. To that extent, generality does seem to be a principle of the morality *of law*, and not just political morality in the abstract.

The same may be true of the other principles of legality, like the requirements of publicity or prospectivity. They certainly seem to be oriented towards law; law seems to be their special target. It is not as though they are principles of perfectly general application that just happen to apply to law among other things. They are a part of political morality that lies specially in wait for law. There is no reason at all why political morality should not have a special subset of evaluative criteria dedicated in this way; they may be part of what Bentham (1970a, 294) meant by the principles of censorial jurisprudence. In a very fine essay, John Gardner (2001) pointed out not only that positivists are not debarred from thinking that 'unclarity, uncertainty, retroactivity, ungenerality, obscurity and so forth are demerits of a legal norm', but also that legal positivists are 'not debarred from agreeing with Fuller that these values constitute law's special inner morality, endowing law with its own distinctive objectives and imperatives' (Gardner 2001, 210). Raz said something similar in his discussion of the Rule of Law (Raz 1979, 210–29). He claimed that the Rule of Law is intended to correct dangers of abuse that arise from law as such:

The law inevitably creates a great danger of arbitrary power—the rule of law is designed to minimize the danger created by the law itself. Similarly, the law may be unstable, obscure, retrospective, etc., and thus infringe people's freedom and dignity. The rule of law is designed to prevent this danger as well. Thus the rule of law is a negative virtue:...the evil which is avoided is evil which could only have been caused by the law itself. (Raz 1979, 223–4)

Personally I think Raz is wrong about this (Waldron 2006b). The Rule-of-Law ideal (or the principles of legality) are intended to correct dangers of abuse that arise in general when political power is exercised, not dangers of abuse that arise from law in particular. Indeed the principles of legality aim to correct abuses of power by insisting on a particular mode of the exercise of political power—namely, governance through law—which is thought more apt to protect us against abuse than (say) managerial governance or rule by decree. On this account, *law itself* seems to be prescribed as the remedy, rather than identified as the problem (or potential problem) which a separate ideal—the Rule of Law—seeks to remedy.

You might think that even if I am right here about the formal principles of legality—that they aim to make governmental measures look more like law, rather than merely aiming to make things *that purport to be law* like law—I must be wrong about the procedural principles: the principles of natural justice. They seem inherently to apply only to legal proceedings. But actually I think I am right about that too. The principles of natural justice don't simply say that *if* you have a legal tribunal, it must follow principles like non-bias, or *audi alteram partem* (as though it would be perfectly alright to have a tribunal that was biased and was deaf to one side of the issue as long as it was not categorized as a legal tribunal). No: the principles of natural justice are principles for making all entities that make determinations which adversely impact on individual citizens behave more like legal tribunals. The aim of the Rule of Law in general is not to make laws and legal institutions more law-like; it is to make government and government institutions more law-like.

The sense in which I would argue, then, that the principles of legality constitute a special morality *of law*, is not that law is their natural target, but that law is *the result of their successful application*—these are principles which are designed to make governmental measures law-like (for the sake of the liberty and dignity and happiness of the subject).

6

This points me now towards a final confrontation with Hart. I am inclined to say that a system which commonly violates the principles of legality may undermine its right to be called a legal system. It may indubitably be an effective system of rule, but I do not think it can usefully be regarded as a system of rule by law.

If one has a system of governance that ordinarily proceeds to make important decisions *ad hoc* without reference to general norms, or if it keeps general norms and policies secret, or only concocts them under pressure after the fact; if it deals with individual situations and impacts upon citizens and firms in a way that is peremptory and in procedural terms disrespectful and bears no resemblance to any sort of process of fair adjudication; if there are no officials set up in what we would recognize as the position of an independent judiciary; and if the overall ethos is just to manage the mass of subjects by shouting orders at them and getting the orders obeyed by whatever means work, including terror and manipulation—if that is the system by which a people is ruled, would there be any sense in calling it a legal system (only a bad one)? Would it not be more illuminating to say this was a system of rule, in the sense of ruling or domination, but not a system of rules and certainly not a system of rule by law? And wouldn't the consistent flouting of principles of legality and principles of natural justice be the main basis of our inclination to say that?

Hart of course would balk at this point, and so too would many positivists, because it does sound now that we are making moral principles—which we have established is what the principles of legality are—into criteria of legal validity. But actually I do not think that that is what my proposal does. It does not say that the measures that I am imagining by this unscrupulous regime are *not valid law*; my proposal says instead that the measures and the system that generates them do not really get into the ballpark of being law at all. That is, they do not get into the ballpark where validity or invalidity would be an issue.

Think, for a moment of the pre-legal society, the 'primitive' society, described in chapter V of *The Concept of Law* (Hart 1992, 91–4). Such a society may be ruled by certain primary rules, but not ruled by them in the character of law, and the issue of the validity of any one or more of these customs or primary rules simply wouldn't arise. *Ex hypothesi*, the society does not have the sort of apparatus in play which would make sense of judgements of validity. And the effect of the absence of that apparatus is not to condemn all these measures as invalid, but to remove one of the presuppositions for validity. It seems to me we could say something exactly similar about the unscrupulous managerial or terroristic regime it envisaged. There is nothing really here to apply the terms 'valid' and 'invalid' *to*. So strictly speaking we are not committing what is of course the mortal sin in the eyes of Hart and his followers, viz, making a moral principle a condition of legal validity. What we are doing is making moral principles part of our general criteria for categorizing systems of government, and that I think has been traditionally one of the main functions of the discourse of legality, certainly one of the main functions of the Rule of Law.

Now of course the situation I have been describing is very extreme. Usually we are dealing with something less than that: we are dealing with an ordinary functioning legal system, occasionally violating norms of legality to a certain degree. What do we say about that? Well, we say two things: first, we say that its normal operation and its normal observance of legality in most instances does give us a field where the concepts of validity and invalidity can operate, and that there is no reason to suppose that the principles of legality enter into the application of those principles. But secondly, we say that the principles of legality may enter into a sort of *warning* we could imagine issuing to such a system (if anyone was interested) to the effect that its violations of legality, while not fatal, are beginning to undermine or erode its claim to be regarded as a legal system.

Hart might say, 'Big deal!' or some gentlemanly equivalent of that. The status of a system of governance as a legal system was always exaggerated anyway. Remember he said that Gustav Radbruch's post-war denunciation of positivism depended on an enormous over-valuation of our ability to describe a system as a system of law, as though that settled the matter of obedience, or as though that settled the question of whether it was just or legitimate (Hart 1958, 618). He is right about that narrow point. Legality may not settle the matter of obedience or even the issue of justice. But I think Hart's own honest characterization of the principles of legality, together with his appreciation that these principles are specially oriented towards the legal enterprise, does mean that there is something here which operates rather as Lon Fuller imagined the inner morality of law operating. And it operates in that way whether we call it by the terms that Fuller used or not. Once again, I am not concerned with Fuller's *other* claim, namely, that legality (or whatever we call it) comes close to guaranteeing justice or legitimacy

(Fuller 1958, 636–8); legality may have an important moral role to play even if it does not achieve that result. (It may be a necessary but not sufficient condition of justice or legitimacy; or it may tend always to make things better from the point of view of justice or legitimacy even if they remain pretty dire.) Even so it amounts to an important and distinctive dimension by which social systems are to be evaluated. And I think it is a pity that Hart became convinced that it was necessary to deny this, even when so much of what he said explained why it was true.

7

It would be wrong to end on such a negative note. Though Hart did not discuss it as such, one of the most important contributions that he made to the Rule-of-Law tradition was in his critique of the idea of sovereignty, in the early chapters of *The Concept of Law*.

You may recall that in medieval through early modern discussions of the Rule of Law, a key question was always whether the prince or sovereign of a state was to be subject to the laws, or whether he was in the technical sense absolute— *princeps ab legibus solutus*. The high-water mark of the absolutist tradition was in the work of Thomas Hobbes (1988), who held it to be an 'opinion, repugnant to the nature of a Common-wealth..., That he that hath the Sovereign Power, is subject to the Civill Lawes' (Hobbes 1988, 224). It was far from a new doctrine; a version of it can be found in Aquinas.[18] And we find continuing debate about it throughout medieval jurisprudence: how could the maker of the laws be subject to the laws that he has made? We know that for Hobbes, the difficulty here was partly political: the thought that any doctrine that the sovereign was subject to the laws would undermine the unity of sovereign authority, generating lines of legal responsibility whose own relation to the law might be problematic. Such a doctrine, he said, 'because it setteth the Lawes above the Soveraign, setteth also a Judge above him, and a Power to punish him; which is to make a new Soveraign; and again for the same reason a third, to punish the second; and so continually without end, to the Confusion, and Dissolution of the Common-wealth' (Hobbes 1988, 224). And it was partly a logical claim: '[T]o be subject to Lawes, is to be subject to the Common-wealth, that is to the Soveraign Representative, that is to himselfe; which is not subjection, but freedome from the Lawes' (Hobbes 1988,

---

[18] See Aquinas 1959, 70: 'The sovereign is said to be "exempt from the law," as to its coercive power; since, properly speaking, no man is coerced by himself, and law has no coercive power save from the authority of the sovereign. Thus then is the sovereign said to be exempt from the law, because none is competent to pass sentence on him, if he acts against the law. Wherefore on Ps 50:6: "To Thee only have I sinned," a gloss says that "there is no man who can judge the deeds of a king."...Again the sovereign is above the law, in so far as, when it is expedient, he can change the law, and dispense in it according to time and place.'

224). Above all it was a difficulty imagining that the source of all positive law could also be constrained by positive law; it was a difficulty imagining that and it was a difficulty imagining that there would be any shape to a legal system that did not require some sort of sovereignty in that strong sense.

Well, for reasons that I imagine had little to do with the vindication of the Rule-of-Law position, Hart simply knocked the stuffing out of the logical presuppositions of absolute Hobbesian sovereignty. In *The Concept of Law*, he made room for the Rule of Law position. He showed that sovereignty—where it exists—depends on rules, is constituted by rules, and so cannot intelligibly be regarded as the source of all the rules that make up the legal system (Hart 1994, 51–61). The rules did not just *affect* the sovereign or *pertain to* the sovereign; some of them actually *constituted* the sovereign. They were in that sense constitutive rules of the legal system.[19] That was the lesson of Hart's critique of Austin, among others, in chapter IV of *The Concept of Law*.

Now, once we acknowledge that sovereigns are constituted by rules, we might entertain the possibility that the foundations of some legal systems can be constituted by rules in a way that exhibits a fundamentally different shape—ie, in a way that does not yield anything looking remotely like a sovereign. We can then see through to the possibility that a legal system need not have *a constituted sovereign* at its base (though some do); it may just have a constitution. (This, I believe, is how we have to think about the legal system of the United States, for example.[20] Hannah Arendt (1973, 153) is right: the American constitution works on the basis of the systematic abolition of sovereignty, at least so far as the internal features of the legal system are concerned.)

Of course, the fact that the sovereign—where there *is* a sovereign—is constituted by rules does not guarantee that the ruler will be subject to law in the way that the Rule of Law theorist demands. The sovereign Parliament in the United Kingdom in Albert Venn Dicey's time was law-constituted; but Dicey (1982, 268–73) was probably over-optimistic in seeing this, in and of itself, as sufficient to reconcile sovereignty and the Rule of Law. But Hart's move opens up space for the sovereign to be legally constrained. It knocks the stuffing out of the logical and jurisprudential thesis, associated with Hobbes, that the Rule of Law in this sense is an incoherent impossibility.

It is ironic, by the way, that the Rule of Law position that Hart made room for is usually regarded as a much more ambitious version of the Rule of Law than the version associated with Fuller. The version associated with Fuller and with the principles of legality is something like this: if people are going to rule us, it would be better if they were to rule us through law, as defined in part by the principles of legality. But the position that Hart's assault on sovereignty makes room for is the old ambition to imagine a society where *people* do not rule us at all, but law

---

[19] See also the discussion in Waldron 2006a.
[20] For Hart's awareness of the importance of this implication, see Hart 1994, 66–78.

rules—King Nomos. It enables us to credibly imagine *the rule of law, not men*. That is the very ambitious position that Hart's demolition of sovereignty makes room for. And I wanted to pay tribute to that, even in the midst of my quite severe critique concerning the equivocations in Hart's discussion of other aspects of the Rule of Law and legality.

If space permitted, I would also say that Hart's discussion of external sovereignty in what is otherwise the justly maligned tenth chapter of *The Concept of Law* does us the service of understanding that phenomenon too in rule-governed terms: '[W]e can only know which states are sovereign, and what the extent of their sovereignty is, when we know what the rules are' (Hart 1994, 223). We must not begin from a pre-legal assumption of absolute sovereignty in the international realm and organize our understanding of international law in a way that is constrained by that. Hart does not quite get to an equivalent of the position he argues for in municipal law, namely, that sovereignty is constituted by legal rules. In the international realm, he holds the slightly cruder position that the sovereignty of a state is just what is left over when its international obligations are taken into account (Hart 1994, 224). I think it would be better to argue that external sovereignty itself is a legal construct of international law, not just the idea of a residue left over once the claims of law have been acknowledged. In this sense, sovereignty might conceivably constrain the extent and content of international law; but the nature and basis of such constraint would itself be a legal, rather than a pre-legal doctrine. But to begin arguing in detail about international issues would take us too far afield.

The message of this paper that I hope readers will find helpful is that there is more to legality, the principles of legality, and the Rule of Law than Hart was sometimes prepared to acknowledge. As I have argued, Hart's position on all this was shifty and equivocal. That opens up an opportunity, I think. In the midst of Hart's inconsistencies, we will do better to take seriously his positive remarks about the moral and legal importance of the principles of legality than to set too much store by his sporadic and unjustified attempts to dismiss them as having little real interest for jurisprudence.

5

Legality, Morality, and the Guiding Function of Law

W J Waluchow

1 Conceptual and Normative Questions

In his classic work, *The Province of Jurisprudence Determined*, John Austin famously proclaimed the separation thesis: that the existence of law is one thing; its merit or demerit is another thing entirely. A simplistic reading of Austin's thesis might lead one to view him—and his positivist descendents—as saying that morality and law have absolutely nothing to do with one another. But of course this is nowhere near the truth of the matter. Not only do positivists agree that law and morality are intimately connected with one another in a variety of different ways; in addition many contemporary positivists go on to assert that the same is true of the relationship between morality and legal theory. For a good many years now, positivists have defended theories about the role of moral norms in the development and evaluation of legal theories. Liam Murphy, for example, has argued that disputes between the two main positivist rivals, Inclusive and Exclusive Positivism, have reached a stalemate, with no valid conceptual arguments available for choosing between them. Given this impasse, Murphy argues, positivists ought to seize the opportunity to develop or engineer the concept of law in such a way that its use, in both legal theory and practice, will have the best moral consequences. In his view, the best moral consequences will be realised if we opt in favour of Exclusive Positivism.[1] This kind of argument is reminiscent of what I once called 'Bentham's causal-moral argument' (Waluchow 1994, 86–98). This is the argument for preferring positivism to natural law theory Bentham employed in *Anarchical Fallacies* to discredit the *French Declaration of the Rights of Man*. According to Bentham, adopting positivism allows us avoid the 'terrorist language' he took the *Declaration*, and the natural law theory it embodied,

---

[1] Murphy 2001, 371. Cf MacCormick 1985, 1. Brain Leiter has argued that we should move on from trying to assess theories of law on the purely 'conceptual' grounds presupposed by many positivists. We should instead embrace a kind of 'naturalized jurisprudence', which in Leiter's view, also favours Exclusive Legal Positivism. See Leiter 2007.

to represent. In his earlier writings, Hart followed Bentham's lead in arguing that the adoption of positivism not only increases our chances of avoiding terrorist language—what Hart less colourfully called 'anarchist thinking'—but also renders it less likely that we will succumb to the opposite extreme of permitting our sense of the morally right to collapse into our sense of the legally valid. This other extreme he referred to as 'reactionary thinking' (Hart 1982, 7 and 1983, 53). Most positivists—including the later Hart, he once told me—are uneasy with causal-moral arguments. They prefer instead to remain more firmly within the confines of conceptual argument and descriptive explanation. But even these positivists are happy to suggest a different, and quite robust, role for moral norms in the development of legal theories. Jules Coleman and Julie Dickson, for example, argue that there is nothing amiss in positing moral norms as providing the basis for an explanation or interpretation of legal practices, say American tort law (Coleman 2001b, 175–9 and Dickson 2001, *passim*). One can posit certain moral norms as ones which a legal practice embodies or seeks to realize without in any way suggesting that the practice is for that reason morally justified, or that we will achieve better moral consequences if we interpret it in that way. One can still, in other words, maintain some version of the separation thesis at the level of legal theory and analysis. Stephen Perry and Ronald Dworkin both argue that the conceptual distance between legal and moral concepts presupposed by this kind of approach is a pure myth, that one cannot posit the pursuit of particular moral norms as the point of a legal practice without in some way endorsing them. That is, positivists such as Coleman are wrong when they accept Hart's contention that 'Description may still be description, even when what is described is an evaluation' (Hart 1994, 244). According to Perry and Dworkin, one cannot, in effect, explain an evaluative practice such as tort law as embodying a particular moral norm without thereby evaluating it morally. To explain law is to interpret it, and to interpret it is to show it in its best moral light. To quote Dworkin, 'Telling it how it is means, up to a point, telling it how it should be' (Dworkin 1996, 38; for Perry's views, see Perry 2001, 311).

So Positivists—including early versus later Hart—are split on the role of moral norms in the development and evaluation of legal theories. Another area in which Positivists have divided is over how far and in what ways moral norms can figure, not in the development and evaluation of legal theories, but in the actual legal practices which positivist theories attempt to analyse or explain. In a famous passage from *The Concept of Law*, Hart reminds us of the following:

The law of every modern state shows at a thousand points the influence of both the accepted social morality and wider social ideals. These influences enter into law either abruptly and avowedly through legislation, or silently and piecemeal through the judicial process. In some systems, as in the United States, the ultimate criteria of legal validity explicitly incorporate principles of justice or substantive moral values; in other systems, as in England, where there are [or at least there were, in Hart's time] no formal restrictions on the competence of the supreme legislature, its legislation may yet no less scrupulously conform to justice or morality. The further ways in which law mirrors morality are myriad, and still insufficiently studied…No 'positivist' could deny that these are facts, or that the stability of legal systems depends in part upon such types of correspondence with morals. If this is what is meant by the necessary connection of law and morals, its existence should be conceded. (Hart, 1994, 20–34)

Modern positivists all agree with Hart that morality and legal practice are connected in a number of different ways. But that's perhaps as far as the agreement goes. How one understands the various connections is one of the main questions dividing Legal Positivists today. Of particular note is the division over how to interpret Hart's provocative suggestion that in some systems of law, as in the United States, the ultimate criteria of legal validity explicitly incorporate principles of justice or substantive moral values. How one interprets this idea is the main ground on which the conceptual debates between defenders of Inclusive and Exclusive Positivism have been waged since John Mackie first brought the possibility of different readings to our attention (Mackie 1977, 3). Defenders of Exclusive Positivism, such as Raz (1979), Green (2003), Shapiro (1998, 469 and 2000, 127), and Giudice (2002, 69), suggest that the concept of law demands that moral norms can never figure in the task of identifying valid laws. These Exclusive Positivists proclaim the 'sources thesis', that the existence of legal norms must depend exclusively on whether they have the appropriate source in, eg, precedent or parliamentary legislation.[2] Moral tests are excluded because these will almost inevitably make reference to a norm's merit, not its source. There are, however, important roles for moral norms in legal decision-making according to defenders of Exclusive Positivism. As I will explain more fully in a moment, moral norms can figure in arguments for or against changing or developing the law, and judges can even be required by law to consult moral norms directly in deciding legal disputes. But the moral norms which figure in these ways are not part of the law on the Exclusive theory. Their satisfaction never counts, on that view, towards establishing the present state of the law, what it presently *is*.

This account of the role of moral norms in legal decision-making has been seized upon by Exclusive Positivists to explain the constitutional challenges to validity alluded to by Hart in the long passage I quoted above. These are challenges to the validity of what purports to be valid law on the ground that the norm in question—eg, a statute duly passed by Parliament and having received Royal Assent—fails to satisfy moral conditions for validity to which reference is made in a constitutional charter or bill of rights. There is, of course, no reason in

---

[2] In what follows I will speak of the existence and validity of a legal norm interchangeably. In so doing, I will follow the usual practice among positivists of assuming that the existence conditions for a legal norm are identical with its validity conditions, that is, that a legal norm does not exist unless it is valid. For the sake of ease of expression, and unless the context plainly suggests otherwise, I will also use the terms 'rules' and 'norms' interchangeably. Strictly speaking, rules are but one kind of legal norm, the latter category including, eg, principles and variable standards, as well as rules.

principle why the relevant moral norm must be enshrined in a written, constitutional document. A practice might well develop among judges and other legal officials of denying validity to directives and decisions which flout specific, well established moral norms which have never been formally expressed. It is arguable that in the UK, conformity with certain fundamental moral norms was for many years informally recognized as a binding condition of validity, despite the fact that these were not then included within any written document with constitutional standing. They were instead part of what is sometimes referred to as the UK's 'unwritten constitution'.

In any event, it seems undeniable that charters and bills of rights do make reference to norms of political morality. Examples include the one Hart mentions, namely, the due process clause of the American Bill of Rights. One might now add Section 7 of the comparatively new *Canadian Charter of Rights and Freedoms*, which specifies rights to life, liberty, and security of the person and the companion right not to be deprived thereof except in accordance with the principles of fundamental justice. Section 7, like the American due process clause, clearly invokes norms of political morality. Now it might seem as though this undeniable fact is fatal to Exclusive Positivism—since we seem to have validity depending on much more than source-based considerations. But appearances are said to be deceiving. Exclusive Positivists are actually quite happy to acknowledge a robust role for moral norms in constitutional challenges to validity. They simply dispute the Inclusive Positivist's account of this common feature of legal practice and the implications, for legal theory, which that account is said to entail.[3] According to Inclusive Positivists, constitutional challenges based on norms of political morality illustrate that legal validity both can and sometimes does depend on conformity with such norms, thereby undermining the Exclusive Positivist's claim that sources alone can determine the content of law. Defenders of Exclusive Positivism reply by denying this inference. Constitutional charters and bills of rights do not, it is said, require conformity with the relevant moral norms as a condition (sufficient or necessary) for legal validity. Rather, they establish moral conditions under which judges are empowered, by what Joseph Raz calls a 'directed power' (Raz 1996b, 242), to *change* the law, most notably by invalidating what was, till the act of a judge's striking it down, perfectly valid law—perfectly valid because it satisfied all the relevant source-based criteria. In other words, constitutional charters do not help establish the content of existing law, they specify conditions which trigger the exercise, by judges, of their Hohfeldian power to rid the law of a morally unworthy legal norm (or a part thereof). The existence of a law still depends exclusively on its sources—including judicial acts of 'striking down'—even though moral norms can and do figure prominently in legal decisions to eliminate or otherwise change it.

---

[3] For an explicit Exclusive Positivist account of the *Canadian Charter*, see Giudice 2002.

So defenders of Exclusive Positivism have what looks like a promising way of accommodating constitutional challenges which invoke specified norms of political morality. But I am not sure that this avenue is one they are well advised to pursue. I wonder whether Exclusive Positivists have, in pursuing this particular line of response, undermined some of their central arguments against their Inclusive cousins. To illustrate, I'll focus on Scott Shapiro's argument concerning the law's essential 'guidance function' (Shapiro 2000) though I think much the same point could be made, for example, in relation to Raz's quite similar authority argument—the argument according to which Inclusive Positivism is inconsistent with the authoritative nature of law (Raz 1996c, 210). The problem with Inclusive Positivism, Shapiro claims, is that it allows the existence of a valid legal norm to depend on controversial moral questions that law's introduction was supposed to have eliminated. The legal norm, not the controversial moral norms it replaces, is supposed to be our practical guide, at both the motivational and epistemic levels. But if the existence and content of a legal norm can be ascertained only by asking (some of) the very questions it was supposed to rule out, then the intended guidance cannot possibly be realized.

Defenders of Inclusive Positivism have, of course, replied to Shapiro's argument in a variety of different ways, and there is no need to rehearse those arguments here.[4] Instead, I'd like to address the following two questions. First, I'd like to consider whether Shapiro's argument over-states the role that practical guidance both plays, and *should* play, in legal practice. Second, I'd like to consider whether the argument can in fact be turned against those versions of Exclusive Positivism which rely on the directed powers account of constitutional challenges. My argument will be that any potential for guidance which is supposedly sacrificed by the Inclusive Positivist's moral tests for validity would be equally lost by the Exclusive Positivist's directed powers, thus leaving us with no valid reason for preferring the latter.

2 The Emergence of Law: A Double-Edged Sword[5]

Much as Hobbes did when he asked us to ponder our emergence from the state of nature, Hart asks us to consider life without law, and how the introduction of a rudimentary legal system can help overcome a number of so-called 'defects' inherent in a hypothetical, pre-legal society.[6] Among these are uncertainty about the identity and content of the rules governing social behaviour, their immunity from deliberate change, and the inefficiency of diffuse social pressure as a means

---

[4] See, eg, Coleman 2001a, 99, Kramer, 17–24 and 45–74, and Waluchow 2000, 45.

[5] The following two sections draw heavily on Waluchow 2007.

[6] I say 'hypothetical' because Hart's argument in no way rests on the historical claim that pre-legal societies ever did (or do now) exist. Pre-legal society serves as an analytical device, not an historical reality.

of enforcing them. The defect of uncertainty can be overcome, Hart suggests, by introducing a rule of recognition. Overcoming this defect is by no means guaranteed, of course, but the potential is there—a potential which cannot exist absent a rule of recognition. Similar points can be made about rules of change and adjudication. Success is not guaranteed here either—indeed, it may be highly unlikely if, eg, the rules governing the introduction or elimination of legislative rules are cumbersome, vague, or ambiguous, or require an unattainable level of consensus among legislative bodies. But again, the potential is there if both the rules and the social conditions are right. In having us consider, in this way, the emergence of law from a pre-legal society, Hart hoped not only to illuminate the distinctive features of modern, domestic legal systems, but to illustrate their great social significance and potential value. The union of primary rules with fundamental secondary rules of recognition, change, and adjudication not only transforms society, it does so in a way which creates the potential radically to improve the social condition.

Yet Hart was all too aware that the promise of law is purchased at a potentially heavy cost. The very features of law by which it achieves its promise also create the worrisome possibility that a community's law will war with its sense of morality or with the demands of reason, critical morality, or common sense.[7] Hart's reflections on the 'pathology of a legal system' are a salutary reminder of the ever present dangers inherent in the structures introduced by law. Once accepted social rules—which cannot exist absent widespread acceptance among those to whom they apply—are replaced with rules satisfying a rule of recognition, the distinct possibility emerges of a complete divorce between validity and acceptance, between the rules which are valid and hence to be applied in judging behaviour, and the beliefs (and interests) of those to whom they are applied. This is because the rule of recognition can require, for legal validity, nothing more than formal enactment by the appropriate person or bodies of persons. If so, then there is nothing to guarantee that the rules adopted will be ones which citizens will find acceptable. Nor is there anything to guarantee that the rules will in any way serve the real or perceived interests of justice, fairness, or utility. In extreme cases, the community's governing rules might be ones which no one, save the officials who adopt and enforce them, actually accepts or believes to be justified. In such a situation, Hart notes, we may end up no better than sheep led to the slaughterhouse. So the emergence from a pre-legal society to one with law is, at best, a very mixed blessing.

Yet another danger of law famously highlighted by Hart arises from the means by which law characteristically communicates its expectations. Ignorance of fact and indeterminacy of aim combine, he said, to create the ever present possibility that general legal rules will lead, upon application to specific cases, to absurd or

---

[7] One of the most thoughtful discussions of this element of Hart's thinking is found in Waldron 1999, 169.

highly undesirable results. These are often results which those who introduced the rules would have wished to avoid had they foreseen them in advance. Think here of Hart's toy motor car in the park. The example is usually taken to show the empty promise of legal formalism and the necessity of relying on judicial discretion, but its real power, I suggest, lies in the way it highlights the *moral* shortcomings of the formalist ideal. Rules so tightly crafted that they leave, at point of application, no room for an informed discretion, represent a thoroughly unworthy ideal. In some scenarios we can foresee that situations are likely to arise in which pre-commitment to a particular legal result would have been foolish or morally problematic. We can know this *general* fact, even though we cannot anticipate the particular unwanted results that are bound to arise. In such circumstances, Hart counsels, anyone whose role is to introduce binding general rules will be well-advised to frame rules which incorporate open-textured terms like 'reasonable' and 'fair'. Such rules provide some measure of antecedent guidance while allowing both citizens and judges, later called upon to apply the norm, to avoid the patently undesirable results to which a more closely-textured rule might have led. Whether or not some such device is employed, however, one fact remains: we cannot always anticipate the results to which our general rules will lead, a point it would be foolish to ignore in thinking about how best to bring about legal regulation.

3 Lessons to be Learned

Among the many valuable lessons to be drawn from Hart's thoughts on these matters is this: despite its undeniable potential for good, law is an inherently dangerous social tool. By its very nature, it has the potential insisted upon by Austin—the potential to separate the legal validity of a norm both from its moral and rational merit, and (we might add) from its general acceptability among the society over whom it governs. The union of primary and secondary rules creates this very real possibility. Law also has the potential to drift towards the ideal of formalism and its associated longing for certain guidance, while ignoring the benefits of allowing a degree of flexibility in the application of general rules. Fair enough. But now an important question comes to the fore: are these not risks which we simply must bear if we are to reap the benefits of legal guidance? Is it not true that law just is, by its very nature, a social practice which achieves its intended benefits only by separating the validity and application of legal norms from contestable questions of reason, morality, and common sense? If so, then do we not just have to live with the attendant risks if we wished to be governed by rules? Must we not, in other words, follow the Exclusive Positivists in flatly rejecting the idea that law is the kind of phenomenon which is compatible with moral conditions of legal validity and application?

I don't see why. Recall Hart's thoughts on the competing considerations at play whenever we attempt to determine the appropriate level of practical guidance to be expected from our legal norms:

[A]ll systems, in different ways, compromise between two social needs: the need for certain rules which can, over great areas of conduct, safely be applied by private individuals to themselves without fresh official guidance or weighing up of social interests, and the need to leave open, for later settlement by an informed official choice, issues which can only be properly appreciated and settled when they arise in a concrete case . . . [W]e need to remind ourselves that human inability to anticipate the future, which is at the root of this indeterminacy, varies in degree in different fields of conduct, and that legal systems cater for this inability by a corresponding variety of techniques. (Hart 1994, 130–1)

That law must in some way serve what Scott Shapiro calls its essential 'guidance function' is undeniably true (Shapiro 2000). It wouldn't be law unless some measure of guidance of the sort Shapiro describes were provided. But as Hart correctly notes, legal systems typically realize that there are always competing considerations at play, and that ignoring these may leave one vulnerable to the pitfalls of formalism. There is no doubt that a society might sometimes have ample reason to pursue the formalist ideal as far as possible. One needn't contemplate the Hobbesian war of all against all to recognize the wisdom, in some sets of circumstances, of employing hard and fast rules whose validity depends exclusively on clear, source-based tests and whose concrete requirements leave no room for judgement—especially moral judgement—at point of application. The wisdom of such a regime is evident in less brutish situations in which, for example, there is widespread, fundamental disagreement on the relevant matters of reason, morality, and common sense, and where the need for antecedent certainty about the identity and requirements of the relevant legal rules is at a premium, as it arguably is when the law in question concerns itself with things like estates, taxes, or criminal procedure. In such areas of the law, an adequate level of the kind of guidance whose value is recognized by Hart and upon which Shapiro seizes may be well nigh impossible should moral norms enter into questions of legal validity or application.

But what if things are different? Suppose, for example, that the prospects for agreement are not quite so bleak: that there is, or would be were people to think long and hard enough about the relevant matters, some measure of agreement on the relevant questions of reason, morality, and common sense. Or suppose that certain moral tests of validity are adopted which require, for a finding of invalidity, that a *compelling* case be made that a rule fails the relevant moral tests. We might even contemplate a system in which a rule which satisfies the appropriate source-based tests is, as Fred Schauer puts it, 'presumptively valid', a condition that is overridden whenever a compelling moral case is made.[8]

---

[8] What I have in mind here is a version of what Schauer calls 'presumptive positivism'. See, Schauer 1991, 196–206.

Hobbesian fears notwithstanding, it is not at all clear why we should think that the law cannot do its work if it sometimes retains a degree of flexibility. Nor is it clear why we should allow the undeniable need for antecedent guidance always to trump all other considerations. After all, rule-makers seldom set out intentionally to violate what most everyone agrees are important norms of morality and rationality, but this is sometimes the unanticipated result of the legal norms they introduce. Their ignorance of fact and indeterminacy of aim make this unavoidable. Now if it is wise to draft a rule banning vehicles from the park in such a way that we do not end up sending children in motorized toy cars to the slammer, then surely there is something to be said for seriously considering some of the options I just described. In particular—and this brings us back to Hart's thoughts on the American constitution and its rule of recognition—there is something to be said in favour of arrangements whereby a condition of the validity and/or application of at least some of our legal norms, is their conformity with important norms of political morality. As Hart clearly saw, to forgo this kind of option in at least some circumstances would be

to secure a measure of certainty or predictability at the cost of blindly prejudging what is to be done in a range of future cases, about whose composition we are ignorant. We shall thus indeed succeed in settling in advance, but also in the dark, issues which can only reasonably be settled when they arise and are identified. We shall be forced by this technique to include in the scope of a rule cases which we would wish to exclude in order to give effect to reasonable social aims . . . (Hart 1994, 129–30)

On the other hand, in pursuing the kinds of options I described a moment ago, we can narrow the feared gap between validity, on the one hand, and moral and rational acceptability on the other. And we can do so without at the same time eliminating entirely the law's capacity to guide our actions.

So antecedent guidance is not the be all and end all of rule by law. Even if, as Shapiro and others suggest, the kinds of moral tests for validity sanctioned by Inclusive Legal Positivism sometimes reduce the level of antecedent guidance we can expect from our laws, this may not be such a bad thing after all. We can still have our laws, and we can still have an appropriate degree of practical guidance. Which now brings me to my second question: can Shapiro's argument be turned against those versions of Exclusive Positivism which rely on the directed powers account of constitutional challenges? I think that it can, because any potential for guidance which is sacrificed under the Inclusive Positivist's moral tests for validity will be equally lost under the Exclusive Positivist's directed powers. So if the one theory—Inclusive Positivism—is to be rejected because it fails to explain law's capacity to guide our actions, then the other—Exclusive Positivism—must be rejected on these very same grounds.

4 Exclusive Positivism, Directed Powers, and Practical Guidance

Recall that, on the Exclusive account, presiding judges are sometimes duty bound, in cases of norm application, to determine whether conditions requiring a declaration of invalidity apply, and then to decide the case accordingly. Instead of being required to determine whether the relevant moral conditions *of validity* are fully satisfied, judges are required, on the Exclusive account, to determine whether the relevant conditions *of invalidation* apply. If those conditions obtain, then the judge will be required to exercise her directed power to change or eliminate the law and decide in accordance with the newly created state of the law. To be sure, the judge's decision in such a case will be conceived of differently than on the Inclusive account. According to the latter, the judge will be said to have *discovered* a pre-existing absence of legal validity, whereas on the Exclusive account, she will be seen to have *created* this state of the law when and if the decision to invalidate is acted upon. But—and this is the point I want to stress—on the issue of antecedent guidance, there would appear to be no practical difference. My reasons for saying this are as follows.

If I am a citizen who looks to the law for practical guidance—ie who wants to know what I should do, and which actions I will be expected to have performed should I ever find myself before a court of law—then the bottom line for me is the identity of the legal norms under which I will be judged in that context. To this extent, it seems to me, the early American realists had things right when they stressed our concern with predictions about what courts are likely to decide should we find ourselves before them. To see this point more clearly, consider the following scenario. Suppose that a reasonable case can be made that a statute which applies to my case in fact conflicts with a contentious moral norm found in a constitutional charter or bill of rights. On the Exclusive account the judge is required to consider invalidating the statute when she applies it to my case. If, in her judgment, the statute violates the moral norm, she must exercise her power to strike the statute down, to declare it no longer valid. On the Inclusive account, on the other hand, the judge is required to consider, not whether she should invalidate the statute, but whether the statute *already is* invalid owing to a conflict with the superior moral norm. Now ask the following question: does the statute provide any more guidance under the Exclusive understanding than it does under the rival Inclusive account? I fail to see why. I can no more be guided by a statute which a judge may end up invalidating on contentious moral grounds when she considers applying it to my case (the Exclusive account) than by a statute which a judge may instead declare to be already invalid on the basis of these very same grounds (the Inclusive option). What interests me, so far as the issue of practical guidance is concerned, will always be the following question: which norms will I be held legally accountable for having observed or broken when and if my case finds its way into court? And the answer to that question seems no more obvious or settled under the Exclusive account than under the account provided by Inclusive Positivism.

It is perhaps worth pausing to note the extent to which this argument can be generalized to cover other situations in which moral norms figure in legal cases. Take, for example, the many cases where new or significantly altered judge-made law emerges from the process of adjudicating disputes. Common-law judges typically possess the power to distinguish or overrule relevant precedent(s), and they sometimes do so on moral grounds like fairness, absurdity, or 'repugnance'. If so, then a similar question emerges: what is my situation with respect to the law's practical guidance in cases governed by judge-made law? If my aim is to be guided by norms by which I may ultimately be held accountable, I will be far less interested in knowing which norms *presently* satisfy the relevant source-based tests of validity than in knowing the identity of the norms which are likely to survive the adjudicative process where more than source-based considerations can easily come into play. Will the norms which emerge be the same as those which currently satisfy source-based tests? Will they be the same norms but in a slightly different form, say with a new condition of application added to account for a now-evident moral absurdity, or subject to a wholly novel interpretation of some key phrase or provision? Perhaps the norms under which my case is decided will be completely different, as when a high court overrules a previous line of decisions and substitutes a whole new way of looking at the relevant legal landscape. I should think that if my concern is practical guidance, then I would be foolish to be guided by norms which *currently* satisfy source-based validity criteria, but which might be changed, eliminated, or re-interpreted by judges employing their directed powers. My focus should be on whatever norm(s) are likely to emerge from the adjudicative process and be applied to my case. And to identify *those* norms, I will have to address the moral questions which may trigger the judge's directed powers—ie the very same moral questions which, on the Inclusive account of legal validity, I must ask to determine legal validity. In short, the law offers me no less guidance as to the *relevant* legal duties, rights, privileges and so on under the Inclusive account of judge-altered law than it does under the rival Exclusive account. Whether we view such cases as ones where valid laws are eliminated or changed by courts exercising directed powers, or cases where laws thought to be valid are judged to be already invalid, or in need of re-interpretation because of a now evident pre-existing conflict between laws as they are currently being interpreted, on the one hand, and legally recognized moral norms, on the other, the point remains: laws whose validity or understanding are determined as the Inclusive account proposes provide no less guidance than laws subject to the directed powers invoked by the Exclusive Positivists. There may be sound reasons for preferring the latter theory to its Inclusive cousin, but the guidance argument is not one of them.

In closing, I'd like briefly to consider a response to my argument by which an Exclusive Positivist might be tempted. A defender of that view may want to reply as follows. Whatever a judge ultimately decides to do with the relevant pre-existing law in deciding a case, the fact remains that the law, on the Exclusive account, provides guidance of a sort that is simply not possible on the rival Inclusive account. True, the law may be changed, re-interpreted, or invalidated at point of application. But I can nevertheless be guided by pre-existing law as it is determined by the relevant source-based tests, *till such time as a judge changes, invalidates, or re-interprets that law in adjudicating a case.* Not only is it possible for me to do so, this is the only rational thing for me to do. Judges seldom change the law; and when they do, it is more often than not pretty clear that a change is called for or is long past due. In light of these facts, it is perfectly rational for me always to be guided by norms which currently satisfy the relevant source-based tests of validity, unless it is clear how the judge will exercise her directed power to change the law, in which case I should be guided, not by the law, but by what I know will be the new law emerging from the judge's decision. But none of this is true if the Inclusive account is correct. Since the content of pre-existing law is partly determined by moral considerations, there is nothing for me to rely on.

Tempting as this line of argument might be, it is far from clear that it can save the guidance argument. And the reason is this: there is nothing to prevent a defender of Inclusive Positivism from providing exactly the same practical advice, though she will, to be sure, couch her advice in slightly different terms. An Inclusive Positivist can easily urge, as a matter of sheer practical rationality, that we presume to be valid and act upon—at least for purposes of our day to day activities—any and all norms which have passed the relevant source-based tests of validity, eg those which have been duly passed by Parliament, received Royal assent, rest on long-established precedents, and so on. We should pursue this strategy till such time, if such a time ever comes, when a particular rule's conflict with a recognized moral norm becomes obvious or is formally recognized by a court. In light of the often contentious nature of the cases under which morally based challenges arise, it would almost always be sheer folly to rely on my possibly misguided, and no doubt controversial, belief that the relevant rule, perhaps understood in the way in which it has hitherto been interpreted, really does fail the relevant moral tests of validity—and that I (or someone else) will be able to convince a court of that fact. On the contrary, it almost always makes sense to be guided by the possibly invalid norm till such time as an official ruling of invalidity is made or is very likely to be made. Indeed, there is nothing to prevent the law from actually requiring such behaviour of me—to require that I act on a presumption that norms which satisfy all the relevant source-based criteria are valid, even though the law fully recognizes the possibility that this presumption is false and open to rebuttal in court. It might sound odd to suggest that the law might require me to observe what it freely acknowledges could later be determined to be invalid law. But the law often operates on the basis of presumptions, and I see no reason why this strategy should be ruled out in this kind of case. I fail to see why it should be ruled out any more than it should be ruled out if the Exclusive account of such cases is correct. On that description, the law may require that I act on what *currently* satisfies all relevant source-based conditions—even when I am exceedingly confident that the judge is going to exercise her directed power to change the law upon which I will be expected to have acted. There is no reason that I can think of to rule these strategies out as ones required by law or recommended by the norms of practical rationality.

If the above reflections are correct, then defenders of Exclusive Positivism cannot consistently maintain both their account of constitutional challenges *and* their claim that the argument from guidance provides compelling reason to reject Inclusive Positivism. As a result, Exclusive Positivists seem to be caught in a bit of a dilemma. They must either accept that moral norms do in fact play a vital role in arguments surrounding the issues of legal validity and application—in which case they acknowledge what seems an evident fact, but seriously weaken their case against Inclusive Positivism; or they bite the bullet and deny that moral norms can function in arguments surrounding these issues of legal validity and application—in which case they might rescue the validity of their argument against Inclusive Positivism, but only at the cost of denying an evident fact stressed by Dworkin and acknowledged by all reasonable legal theories, including, as we saw, the theory developed by the man we honour by this book, H.L.A. Hart. Moral norms often *do*—and for a variety of reasons often *should*—play a role in arguments concerning the validity and application of legal norms in many cases. These include those cases where moral norms figure prominently in constitutional challenges.

PART II

CRIMINAL RESPONSIBILITY AND PUNISHMENT

6

Responsibility and Liability in Criminal Law

R A Duff[1]

Hart's *Punishment and Responsibility* was published in 1968 (Hart 1968), and its continuing significance is evidenced by the fact that a new edition, introduced by the current occupant of the Chair of Jurisprudence that Hart held, has been published forty years later (Hart 2008). Looking back at *Punishment and Responsibility*, two features of the collection are striking.

The first striking feature is the extent to which those eight essays, plus a Postscript, set the terms of theoretical debates about criminal responsibility and punishment during the ensuing decades. Quite apart from the substantive merits of the positions for which he argued, Hart suggested ways of thinking about, for instance, the structure of justificatory theories of criminal punishment, about different types of responsibility and their significance, about the concept of action as it figured in criminal law, about *mens rea* and its various forms, which his successors were able to develop fruitfully—whether they were following his substantive leads or reacting against them. The agenda-setting impact of *Punishment and Responsibility* says something, of course, about the state of philosophy of criminal law in the 1960s; but it also attests to the originality and significance of Hart's philosophical approach to issues in criminal law theory.

The second striking feature, visible with the benefit of more churlish hindsight, concerns what is missing from *Punishment and Responsibility*. One thing that is missing is the kind of critical reflection on the structure of criminal law that has been a feature of Anglo-American philosophy of criminal law since Fletcher's *Rethinking Criminal Law* (Fletcher 1978), ten years after *Punishment and Responsibility*. How should we understand, and should we retain, the traditional distinction between '*actus reus*' and '*mens*

[1] This paper is based on work done during my tenure of a Leverhulme Research Fellowship; a much fuller discussion of the issues over which it skates can be found in Duff 2007. Grateful thanks are due to the Leverhulme Trust for its support, and to participants in the Hart Symposium for useful comments.

rea' as the two components or two dimensions of criminal offences (see eg Smith 1978, Lynch 1982, Robinson 1993)? Should we also recognize a substantive distinction between 'offences' and 'defences'; or should we treat that distinction as merely a presentational device (see eg Williams 1982, Campbell 1987, Gardner 2004, Tadros 2005, ch 4)? How clear, how useful, how exhaustive, is the distinction between justificatory and excusatory defences (see eg Greenawalt 1984, Gardner 1998, Berman 2003, Baron 2005, Tadros 2005, chs 9–13)? Should we distinguish 'rules for citizens' from 'rules for courts'—and, if so, which kinds of rule should figure in which category (see eg Dan-Cohen 1984, Alldridge 1990, Robinson 1997)?

The second striking absence (though this one is also a feature of much of the subsequent philosophical discussion) is the criminal process. There is in *Punishment and Responsibility*, as there is in subsequent philosophical writing on criminal law, much about the substantive criminal law and the principles of criminal liability; there is much about criminal punishment: but there is surprisingly little about the criminal process that connects crime to punishment, and in particular about the criminal trial as the forum in which criminal liability is formally determined and criminal punishment is assigned.[2] This is not the place in which to speculate about possible reasons for this relative neglect, at least by philosophers of criminal law, of the criminal trial, but one reason might be that many of them share the view (or assumption) that the 'criminal law . . . comes down to a single, basic question: who is liable for what?' (Dubber 2002, 5)—or, if they are more explicitly normative, 'who should be liable for what?'. If this is the 'single, basic question' in or about criminal law, it is easy to regard the process by which liability is determined as having a purely instrumental significance—and thus as having little theoretical interest in its own right: the trial aims (subject no doubt to various side-constraints set by other values) to determine who is properly to be held liable, and punished, for what.

I will suggest that these two absences from *Punishment and Responsibility* are connected; but also that by building on Hart's own discussion of responsibility, we can see both how they are connected and why they matter. By attending to the logic of the criminal trial, we can gain a clearer view of some important aspects of criminal responsibility, and of the significance of some of the structural dimensions of the criminal law noted above.

Before I try to substantiate that claim, however, I should say something brief about the relational conception of responsibility on which it depends.

---

[2] One notable exception is Burns 1999; three colleagues and I have also tried to start filling this gap in Duff et al 2007, on which I draw heavily in what follows; grateful thanks are due to my co-authors—Lindsay Farmer, Sandra Marshall, and Victor Tadros (and to the Arts and Humanities Research Council, which funded the project).

1 Responsibility and Liability

We should, I will argue, pay more attention than theorists often pay to the distinction between responsibility and liability,[3] and to the relational dimensions of responsibility.

My concern here is with responsibility for actions or states of affairs that are untoward, rather than for deeds that are good or right; and it is with criminal liability to conviction and punishment, and its moral analogue of liability to blame and criticism, rather than with 'civil' liability (either moral or legal) to pay compensation or to be required to do what one promised or contracted to do. It is with responsibility and liability as they are determined by criminal courts, and by moral agents who appraise and criticize their own and others' conduct.

Liability presupposes responsibility: I am liable only for that for which I am responsible. Criminal liability might be imposed without *moral* responsibility, as when it is vicarious—imposed for the actions of others over which the defendant lacked control. But it still presupposes criminal responsibility: I am vicariously liable only if the criminal law holds me vicariously responsible (and I cannot be morally liable if I am not morally responsible).

However, responsibility does not entail liability: I can admit responsibility (criminal and moral) for an action, but avert liability by offering a defence. I might offer a justification: I deliberately broke down your door, but that was the only way to bring help to your mother, who had collapsed inside the locked house. Or I might offer an excuse: I committed perjury, but only as a result of a kind of duress that, whilst it did not suffice to justify my action, was sufficiently frightening to render me non-culpable for giving in to it. In both cases, I admit responsibility for my action, which is to say that I recognize it as something for which I must answer; but I offer an exculpatory answer that, if it is acceptable, blocks the transition from responsibility to liability, and thus averts both moral liability to blame and criminal liability to conviction and punishment.[4]

To be responsible is to be answerable. I may be called, and must be prepared, to answer for that for which I am responsible; I am then liable to moral criticism or criminal conviction if I cannot offer a suitably exculpatory answer.[5] Responsibility often creates a presumption of liability, but that presumption is defeasible: I am liable unless I can offer an exculpatory answer, but can avert liability by offering such an answer.

---

[3] I should perhaps say 'a distinction' rather than 'the distinction', since I do not claim that this is the only way in which 'responsibility' and 'liability' are properly used; all that I need to claim is that the distinction that I draw here is a substantive and significant one, however it is labelled.

[4] The distinction drawn here is related to Hart's distinction (1968, 212–22) between 'role-responsibility' and 'liability-responsibility'.

[5] On responsibility as answerability, see Lucas 1993, Watson 2001; contrast Tadros 2005, 24–31.

Once we attend to the distinction between responsibility and liability, we can distinguish more clearly two quite different types of question about the scope and content of the criminal law. The first concerns that for which we are, or should be, criminally responsible: for what kinds of conduct (or condition, or state of affairs) can or should we be held answerable, on pain of conviction and punishment, by the criminal law? The second concerns the transition from responsibility to liability: what kinds of plea can, or should, avert liability for that for which we admit responsibility? We can also, however, attend to the various relational aspects of responsibility as answerability.

There are of course non-relational notions of responsibility. We can talk of responsible agency, or of what it is to be a responsible agent; we can also talk, in commendatory terms, of responsible parents or responsible teachers or responsible citizens. Both these notions can be explained in terms of a relational conception of responsibility. Responsible agency is a matter of having the characteristics and capacities that are necessary if one is to be held responsible (ie answerable) for one's actions. Hence the attractiveness of accounts of responsibility as a matter of reasons-responsiveness:[6] a responsible agent is one who is capable of responding to the relevant reasons that bear on her actions, and of answering for those actions by reference to those reasons and to her reasons for acting as she did. A responsible parent or teacher is one who takes her responsibilities seriously and discharges them conscientiously: she pays due attention to, and takes due care for, those matters for which she is responsible, and is thus well placed to answer for her actions in relation to those matters.[7]

The relational conception of responsibility on which I want to focus here is not merely dyadic, but triadic: I am responsible *for X, to S*—to some person or body who has the right, the standing, to call me to answer for X. Furthermore, as we will see, I am responsible for X to S as Φ—in virtue of falling under some normatively laden description, my satisfaction of which makes me both prospectively and retrospectively responsible for X to S.

The 'for X' dimension of this triadic relationship is familiar and obvious enough: I can be held responsible for a wide range of 'objects of responsibility', including actions, omissions, thoughts, feelings, conditions, and states of affairs. One important question that I will not try to pursue here concerns the general conditions of responsibility: if I am to be properly held responsible for X, whatever X might be, must it for instance be true that X is or was in some sense within my control; must it be true that I knew or could have known that and how I could

---

[6] For different versions of which see eg Scanlon 1988, Wallace 1994, Fischer and Ravizza 1998, Morse 1998.

[7] The responsibilities that she takes seriously are her prospective responsibilities—those matters or affairs that it is up to her to attend to and take care of, and for her conduct in relation to which she is then retrospectively responsible (answerable). Compare Hart 1968, 212–14; also Casey 1971.

affect X?[8] My concern here is not with such general conditions, but rather with the ways in which the objects, the directions, and the grounds of responsibility differ between different contexts: with the ways in which I can be responsible as Φ for X, but not for Y (although the control condition and the epistemic condition are satisfied in relation to both X and Y); or responsible to S for X, but not for Y; or responsible for X to S, but not to T.

To illustrate. We can try to specify the responsibilities I have as a university teacher. That specification will consist in part in an account of my prospective responsibilities: as a teacher, it is my responsibility to, for instance, keep up to date with my subject, plan courses that will contribute appropriately to the curriculum, prepare and conduct my classes in pedagogically effective ways, mark my students' work, play my part in my department's collective affairs, and so on. We can disagree about just what does or should fall within my responsibilities as a teacher, but any account will set some limits to them: as a teacher in a secular institution, for instance, it is no part of my responsibility to attend church services; as a philosophy teacher it is no part of my responsibility to play football on Saturday for a local amateur team—though these may be among my responsibilities as a member of a church or as a member of that local football team. To say that these are my prospective responsibilities as a teacher is to say that I may be called, and must be ready, to answer as a teacher for my conduct in relation to these matters—for my discharge of (or my failure to discharge) these responsibilities.

Such a specification of my responsibilities must also, if it is to be complete, include a specification of the people or the bodies to whom I am responsible as a teacher—which will also by implication specify those to whom I am not responsible as a teacher. I am responsible as a teacher to my students, to my colleagues, to my employer: they have the right, the standing, to call me to account for the ways in which I discharge, or fail to discharge, my pedagogical responsibilities; they can, for instance, properly call me to answer for failing to turn up to a class, or for giving an ill-prepared lecture. However, first, I am not responsible as a teacher to a passing stranger, or to my aunt, or to other members of the football team, or to the Pope: which is to say that they have no right to call me to account for missing the class or for giving a bad lecture—if they challenged me about that, or demanded that I answer to them for it, I could properly reply that it was none of their business.[9] Second, I am not responsible to my students, my colleagues (qua academic colleagues), or my employer for my conduct as a member of a church

---

[8] On control see eg Fischer and Ravizza 1998, and (in relation to criminal responsibility) Husak 1987, ch 4; on the epistemic condition see eg Feinberg 1986, 269–315 and Zimmerman 1988, 74–91. On why the control condition is indeed a general condition of responsibility, whereas the epistemic condition can figure as a condition not of responsibility but of liability, see Duff 2007, ch 3.3.

[9] Contrast Gardner 2003, 165, on 'basic responsibility' as not requiring or being limited to any *particular* interlocutor, since I can 'assert my basic responsibility by offering the same account of myself to everyone I come across'; in response see Duff 2007, 25–6.

or a football team. There will be some person or some body to whom I am responsible as a member of a church, for my religious beliefs and practices: depending on the character of my religion, that might be my priest, fellow members of my congregation, or only God. There will also be people to whom I am responsible as a member of the football team—my fellow members, our supporters if we have any: depending on the kind of team it is, I might be responsible to them not just for how I play (and whether I turn up to play), but also for keeping fit, and for taking part in practice and training. But I am not responsible to my fellow footballers for my performance as a teacher; nor am I responsible to my academic colleagues or employer for my performance as a footballer.

The responsibility-laden descriptions (teacher, parent, friend, colleague, member of this church or of that sporting group . . .) that help to structure our lives determine the content and the direction of our responsibilities: they determine what we are responsible for, to whom (or what). Such determinations extend our responsibilities: as a member of this football team I have responsibilities that I would not otherwise have, and am responsible to people to whom I would not otherwise be answerable. But they also limit our responsibilities: there are matters that fall within my control and knowledge, even matters that bear on my students' welfare, for which I might deny that I am responsible as a teacher (I might insist, for instance, that it is not my responsibility to offer them advice about their sexual relationships, or to ensure that they attend classes); and there is only a limited range of people or bodies to whom I am responsible as a teacher.[10]

(The strong thesis about the relational character of responsibility, which I am tempted to assert, is that responsibility is *always* to some person or body—though it will sometimes only be to oneself, or to God; if there is no S to whom A is responsible for X, A is not responsible for X. The weaker thesis, which is all that this paper requires, is that we can always properly ask 'to whom or what is A responsible for X?', and can normally expect an answer specifying an appropriate S; but it allows that there might be exceptional cases in which A is responsible for X, but is not responsible to any S. All I need claim for present purposes is that the criminal law is not such an exceptional case.)

Once we recognize the way in which liability depends on responsibility, and the relational dimensions of responsibility, we will see that in the context of criminal law we must therefore ask not just what we should be criminally *liable* for, but for what we should be criminally *responsible, as what,* and *to whom.* To ask that question is in part to ask who has the standing or right to call us to answer for our criminal wrongdoings, and what the relevant normative description is under which we are thus called to answer.

---

[10] We may of course disagree about what I am responsible for, and to whom, as a teacher, or under any other normatively laden description: nothing in my argument depends on claiming that the content or direction of our responsibilities can be uncontroversially specified.

The start of an answer to this question is that in what aspires to be a liberal democracy we should be criminally responsible as citizens, to our fellow citizens, under a criminal law that is our 'common' law;[11] we should be criminally responsible for the commission of wrongs that count as 'public' wrongs in the sense that they are properly the business of our fellow citizens simply in virtue of our shared citizenship—in the context of the civic enterprise in which we are collectively engaged as citizens.[12] This is, of course, only the start of an answer: partly because the relevant ideas of a common law, of citizenship, and of public wrongs need to be explained (and their use in this way justified); and partly because the answer also needs to be qualified and extended to deal with the ways in which temporary visitors to a polity's territory are both bound and protected by the criminal law without being citizens, and with the claims of international criminal law and claims to universal jurisdiction sometimes made by domestic criminal courts.[13] But those further explanations, justifications, and qualifications cannot be provided here; I want instead to discuss the ways in which criminal responsibility, as thus understood, is determined and assigned.

2 The Criminal Trial: Calling to Answer—and Refusing to Answer

A criminal trial summons a defendant to answer a formal charge of public wrongdoing.[14] The defendant is expected (although no longer forced) to enter a plea of 'Guilty' or 'Not Guilty': this is the first manifestation of a crucial feature of the criminal trial—that it is not merely an inquiry into whether this person is (provably) guilty of the alleged offence, but a process in which he is called to take part as someone who is to answer a charge, and to answer for his commission of the alleged offence if it is proved against him.

By entering a plea, the defendant recognizes the authority of the court to try his case and to pass judgment on him in relation to the charge; he formally recognizes this as a forum in which he is properly called to answer. That is why a defendant sometimes insists on refusing to plead: to make clear that she does not accept the court's authority, and will play no part in this—as she sees it-illegitimate procedure. That is also why it matters that the defendant is 'fit to

---

[11] On the idea of a 'common' law see Postema 1986, chs 1–2; also Cotterrell 1995, ch 11.

[12] On this conception of 'public' wrongs, see Marshall and Duff 1998.

[13] On international law see Altman and Wellman 2004, Luban 2004, May 2005, Besson and Tasioulas 2008.

[14] My comments here are based on the formal structure of 'adversarial' criminal trials, and would need to be adapted to apply to more 'inquisitorial' systems. It should also be clear that they are normative, rather than descriptive of criminal trials as they actually take place (or more often do not take place) within our existing systems of criminal justice—though they appeal to norms internal to the structure and rhetoric of the trial.

plead'—that he is competent to understand the trial and to take part in it, either in his own voice or through the counsel whom he instructs. The trial addresses him as a responsible agent: not yet as someone who is responsible *for* committing a crime (he is so far presumed innocent of that), but as someone who can be expected to respond to the charge, and to answer for his commission of the crime if it is proved. If a defendant is, when he is called to trial, so mentally disordered that he cannot respond with understanding to the charge or answer for his own conduct, he cannot legitimately be tried—even if he was sane and competent at the time of the alleged offence, and even if his guilt could be proved beyond reasonable doubt without his present participation.[15]

Unfitness to plead constitutes just one of several possible 'bars to trial'. Bars to trial are not defences that entitle the defendant to an acquittal: for a defence constitutes an exculpatory answer to the criminal charge, and an acquittal presupposes that the defendant was properly called to answer; but a bar to trial constitutes a legitimate reason for refusing to answer to this charge, or before this court, and thus renders the trial illegitimate. The defendant might plead that she has diplomatic immunity, and is therefore not answerable in this court,[16] or that the alleged crime fell outside this court's geographical or temporal jurisdiction;[17] or she might argue that the state's own prior actions, such as a prosecutorial promise of immunity, now bar the trial,[18] or that prior misconduct in relation to the alleged crime or its investigation would render her trial an 'abuse of process'.[19] None of these pleas or claims constitute a denial of her guilt, or a defence to the charge; they deny the legitimacy of the trial itself. They thus concern criminal responsibility, rather than criminal liability: they concern, that is, not the conditions given which a defendant should be convicted at the end of the trial, but the prior conditions on which the trial itself depends, as a process of calling this defendant to answer to this charge.

I have referred so far to various legally recognized bars to trial—bars that are also morally justified if they render the trial morally illegitimate. But we must also ask whether there might be moral bars to trial—conditions that, whether or not they are legally recognized as bars to trial, render the trial morally illegitimate. This offers a fruitful approach to the continuing controversial issue of whether and how penal justice can be done in an unjust society.

---

[15] On fitness to plead, see Sprack 2006, 287–8, Robinson 1984, vol II, 501–8.

[16] See Diplomatic Privileges Act 1964 s 2(1), Consular Relations Act 1968.

[17] See eg Model Penal Code §§ 1.03(1)(f), 1.06.

[18] See eg LaFave et al 2004, chs 8.11, 21.2.

[19] See Ashworth 2002, Dennis 2007, ch 2(E); also *R v Horseferry Road Magistrates' Court, ex p Bennett* (1994) 98 Cr App R 114. See generally Robinson 1984, vol I, 55–7, 102–14, 179–87 and vol II, 460–543. We might explain the significance of entrapment in this way: it should preclude conviction not as a defence (for it does not render the entrapped defendant less culpable, or his action less wrong), but as a bar to trial, on the ground that the state is ill-placed to call someone to account for a crime that its own officials incited. But see Squires 2006, Duff et al 2007, 242–7.

Suppose we recognize that many of those who appear in our criminal courts, who have indeed committed criminal offences without what the law defines as a defence, have also been in various systematic (albeit not intended) ways excluded from full, or adequate, participation in the various dimensions of citizenship: they have been and continue to be subject to various kinds of systemic social injustice; they have not been treated—we have collectively failed to treat them—as full members of the polity. Should this cast doubt on the legitimacy of their conviction and punishment? Some argue that it should, because we should treat the injustice that they have suffered as grounds for at least a partial defence—of 'duress of circumstances', for instance.[20] There is, however, another and perhaps often more plausible explanation for the uneasiness that we should indeed feel: that the legitimacy not merely of their conviction and punishment, but of their very trial, is put in doubt, since our collective standing to call them thus to answer for their offences is put in doubt by the injustices they continue to suffer. The point is not simply that our collective hands are dirtied by our complicity in that injustice ('let those who are without sin...'). It is, rather, that the criminal trial calls the defendant to answer, as a citizen, to his fellow citizens for a wrong that he has allegedly committed against the values by which the polity of which they are all supposedly members defines itself; but if his fellow citizens have radically failed to accord him the respect and concern due to him as a fellow member of the polity, if they have failed to treat him as a fellow citizen, they are now ill placed to assert their standing as his fellow citizens by calling him to account in this way.

That is not to say that we should simply recognize serious social injustice as a bar to trial: for to do so would be to betray the victims of those crimes, to whom we also collectively owe it to call those who wronged them to account. But it is to suggest that we should recognize the way in which such systemic social injustice casts doubt on the legitimacy of summoning its victims to trial even for the criminal wrongs that they have committed without justification or excuse; and that if we are to claim the standing to try them, we must (apart from seeking to remedy those social injustices) find ways in which we can answer to them for the wrongs that they have suffered at our (collective and often passive) hands, just as we call them to answer to us for the wrongs that they have committed. If that cannot be done within the trial process itself,[21] then it must be a dimension of the processes of sentencing and punishment that follow on conviction.[22]

By focusing on criminal responsibility rather than criminal liability, and by understanding responsibility as a matter of being answerable to some person or

---

[20] See eg Hudson 1995; see also Bazelon 1976, Delgado 1985. For a useful general, and critical, set of discussions see Heffernan and Kleinig 2000. One barrier to accepting such arguments too quickly is that the victims of the crimes of the disadvantaged are very often similarly situated themselves: are we really to say to such victims that the wrong they have suffered is excusable in virtue of conditions by which they are just as oppressed as the offender?

[21] See eg Norrie 2001 (esp chs 2–3, 8, 10) and Christodoulidis 2004, on some of the problems in the way of raising such issues in the trial.

[22] See further Duff 2001, 179–201.

body with the standing to call one to answer, we can throw light on the significance of the criminal trial, as the forum in which we are called to answer by and to our fellow citizens for alleged criminal wrongdoing; and on the conditions that can undermine the legitimacy of the criminal trial as such a process of calling to answer. We can also throw light on some the structural features of the substantive criminal law that have been prominent in recent theoretical debates, and that reflect structural aspects of the trial as a process of calling to answer; these will be the focus of the next two sections.

3 Offences, Defences, and Strict Responsibility

Given the Presumption of Innocence,[23] the defendant has nothing *for* which she must formally answer unless and until the prosecution proves beyond reasonable doubt that she committed the offence charged. She is expected to answer *to* the charge, by entering a plea; if the prosecution can adduce evidence that would suffice, if not rebutted, to prove her guilt, she will have to make a more substantive answer to the charge if she is to avoid conviction—and such an answer might have to include explaining, and so answering for, conduct that the prosecution portrays as guilty (it is proved that in the course of a heated argument D pulled the trigger of his loaded shotgun, which was pointing at V, with the result that V was killed; the evidence might well suffice to entitle a jury to conclude that D acted with the intention of harming V, unless D can explain that, for instance, he thought the gun was unloaded).[24] But there is nothing for which she is formally held criminally responsible until the prosecution proves all the elements of the offence.

If the prosecution does discharge that persuasive burden, however, the position alters: the defendant must now answer for her commission of that offence. That is not to say that she is convicted, since she can still avert criminal liability by offering a defence; but she now bears the formal burden of adducing evidence of any defence that she offers—evidence that would suffice, if not rebutted, to create at least a reasonable doubt as to whether the conditions of the defence were satisfied.[25] Proof of the commission of the offence is, we can say, proof of her criminal responsibility—proof that there is something for which she must answer in criminal court, on pain of conviction if she cannot offer an exculpatory answer; but it is not yet proof of criminal liability, since she can still avert liability by offering such an exculpatory answer.

---

[23] On the Presumption of Innocence and its significance, see especially Roberts 1995, 2002, Tadros and Tierney 2004.

[24] Compare *Moloney* [1985] 1 All ER 1025.

[25] See Simester and Sullivan 2003, 53–5. The defence bears a persuasive burden for insanity, but the standard of proof is now 'on the balance of probabilities' rather than 'beyond reasonable doubt'.

The distinction between offences and defences is therefore not just a matter of convenient exposition on which nothing substantial hangs or should hang.[26] Rather, it marks a substantive difference between issues that go to responsibility and issues that concern the transition from responsibility to liability: offence definitions specify that for which a defendant must answer in a criminal court, whilst defences ground answers that serve to exculpate the defendant. A defendant who denies committing the offence denies criminal responsibility; one who offers a defence admits responsibility (at least by implication), but seeks to avert liability by offering an exculpatory answer that blocks the normal or presumptive transition from responsibility to liability.

How then should the distinction between offences and defences be drawn?[27] In particular, can it be drawn in a way that shows placing such an evidential burden on the defendant to be consistent with the Presumption of Innocence, understood as requiring that the prosecution prove the defendant's guilt beyond reasonable doubt? Such a shift of burden can be consistent with the Presumption of Innocence only if proof that the defendant committed the offence is sufficient to displace that Presumption in favour of a presumption of guilt, entitling the court to convict the defendant unless she adduces adequate evidence of a defence. Since conviction must, on the account of criminal law offered here, mark the judgment that the defendant has been proved to have committed a public wrong, proof of the commission of the offence must therefore constitute proof that she committed at least a presumptive wrong. A 'presumptive' criminal wrong will sometimes be an actual wrong, whose commission still leaves logical space for an excuse or even a justification—a wilful killing, for instance; or it might consist in conduct that we can properly presume to be wrong until we are offered evidence that it was justified, and therefore not wrong all things considered:[28] but we can say in either case that it consists in conduct that in the law's eyes we normally have categorical and conclusive reason to avoid—conduct that warrants a defeasible presumption of culpable wrongdoing: the onus can then properly shift to the defendant to offer evidence to defeat that new presumption; but the original Presumption of Innocence still has force, since what is required to defeat the new presumption of guilt is not proof of innocence, but merely evidence that suffices to create a reasonable doubt about guilt.[29]

Offence definitions should therefore define presumptive wrongs. If they do so, proof of the commission of an offence suffices to defeat, at least presumptively,

---

[26] See eg Williams 1982.

[27] For useful discussions see Fletcher 1978, 552–79 and 683–758, Campbell 1987, Tadros 2005, ch 4.

[28] This is to reject both the familiar view that justified conduct cannot constitute a wrong, and Gardner's view that 'basic' wrongdoing is 'strict' (Gardner 2004, 824–5; see further Duff 2007, 217–24).

[29] Compare the discussions of whether laying a persuasive rather than only an evidential burden on defendants is consistent with the Presumption of Innocence as enshrined in Article 6 of the European Court of Human Rights: eg *Lambert* [2001] 3 All ER 577, *Sheldrake* [2003] 2 All ER 497; see Roberts 2002, Simester and Sullivan 2007, 32–7 and 53–61.

the Presumption of Innocence: we can then properly demand that the defendant offer evidence of a defence if she is to avoid conviction; there is something, the presumptive wrong, for which we can properly demand that she formally answer to her fellow citizens, on pain of conviction and punishment if she cannot offer an exculpatory answer.

We can throw further light on the significance of this point by noting a contrast between extra-legal moral responsibility and criminal responsibility as it is usually defined. Whereas moral responsibility for harm that I cause is typically strict, criminal responsibility is usually —though not always—non-strict.

I knock over and break *V*'s valuable vase, and am accused of criminal damage. I am of course expected to offer an answer *to* that charge, by pleading 'Not Guilty' or 'Guilty': but given the Presumption of Innocence, and the burden of proof that it places on the prosecution, if I plead 'Not Guilty' there is nothing *for* which I must answer until the prosecution proves that I committed the offence—not just that I damaged the vase, but that I did so intentionally or recklessly.[30] What I am criminally responsible for, what I must answer for, is therefore not damaging the vase as such, but damaging the vase intentionally or recklessly. Responsibility still falls short of liability, since I might have a defence—perhaps I acted under duress that sufficed to justify or excuse my action. But the key point here is that criminal responsibility in such cases is not strict, since it requires proof of *mens rea* as well as of *actus reus*.[31]

By contrast, whilst I am morally *liable* to blame for damaging your vase only if I did so intentionally or recklessly, I am morally strictly *responsible* simply for damaging it. I must, that is, be ready to answer morally to you just so long as I actually damaged it: it would not be proper for me to refuse to answer for it until it was established that I was at least reckless; you can properly expect me to answer to you for it as soon as it is clear that it was I who damaged it. I might well have an exculpatory answer—perhaps that I damaged it through non-culpable inadvertence or accident;[32] but the point is that you have the right to demand an answer from me—to hold me responsible, to call me to answer, for the damage that I caused.[33]

We might then ask why criminal responsibility should not be generally strict, in the way that moral responsibility is. If the prosecution can prove the *actus reus*

[30] See Criminal Damage Act 1971, s 1.

[31] See *Woolmington v DPP* [1935] AC 462, at 481. Responsibility, like liability, is 'strict' if it does not require proof of some suitable *mens rea* or 'fault element' as to every aspect of the offence in question.

[32] I am of course liable to moral blame if I damaged the vase negligently, whereas criminal liability requires intentional or reckless damage; this disanalogy is not important here.

[33] It is worth noting that this is why such factors as non-culpable inadvertence or accident constitute 'excuses' in moral contexts but not in criminal law. An excuse is a defence which admits responsibility but denies liability, by denying culpability (see, eg, Gardner 1998, Tadros 2005, ch 11): that I non-culpably failed to see your vase is a moral excuse, but a negation of criminal responsibility, since it negates an element of the offence. (An exculpatory answer averts moral liability to blame, but I might still be morally liable to pay for a new vase.)

(ie, in simple cases, prove that the defendant's conduct caused some harm or evil of a kind that concerns the criminal law), why should the defendant not then be liable to conviction unless she can offer a suitably exculpatory account of how she came to cause it—for instance an account that denies *mens rea*?[34] We must answer morally to our friends for harms that we actually cause: why should we not also have to answer to our fellow citizens, under the criminal law, for criminal harms we cause—so long as the law makes adequate provision for exculpatory answers that will avert liability?

Familiar answers to this question (familiar defences of the Presumption of Innocence and of requiring the prosecution to prove both *actus reus* and *mens rea*) usually cite the greater importance of avoiding the conviction of the innocent than of ensuring the conviction of the guilty, and the substantial costs that such a shift of burden would lay on defendants. These are significant factors; but we can cast them in a more illuminating light by asking what I should have to answer for to my fellow citizens, in a practice that is focused on public wrongdoing. To make criminal responsibility strict would be to say that the mere causation of harm, even if it does not itself constitute wrongdoing, creates such a strong presumption of wrongdoing that the actor can reasonably be expected to answer for it, on pain of conviction and punishment if he cannot provide an exculpatory answer; but this would be an unreasonable burden to lay on each other as citizens—especially given the costs involved in making sure that one can offer such answers, and the way in which such answers might reveal facts about oneself that would normally be private. Of course I owe it to my fellow citizens not only to refrain from harming them intentionally, but to take precautions against accidentally harming them: but I should not be taken to owe it to them to answer in criminal court, on pain of conviction and punishment, for harms that I cause by non-culpable accident. We might add a further consideration: the imposition of strict criminal responsibility implies a kind of civic mistrust of each other which is at odds with the idea of citizenship. To expect people to answer in a criminal court for the harms they actually cause is to presume that they caused those harms wrongfully, unless they can show that they did not; it is to presume that our fellow citizens are, if not maliciously intentioned, at least lacking in the basic regard for others that the criminal law requires. The Presumption of Innocence, by contrast, embodies an expectation of mutual civic trust: we are to presume our fellows to be non-wrongdoers unless and until the contrary is proved.[35]

Sometimes, however, criminal responsibility is strict. A shopkeeper who is proved to have sold food which failed to comply with food safety requirements is not strictly liable for selling unfit food: under s 21 of the Food Safety Act 1990

---

[34] This was the principle that was rejected with such ringing fervour in *Woolmington v DPP* [1935] AC 462.

[35] This is to suggest that the Presumption of Innocence has force not just within the structure of the criminal trial, but more generally in our dealings with each other as citizens; we cannot pursue here the question of just how far or how powerfully its authority should extend.

she has a defence if she proves that she 'took all reasonable precautions and exer-cised all due diligence to avoid the commission of the offence'. She is, however, strictly responsible for selling unfit food: given proof only that she sold food that was actually unfit, she must offer a suitably exculpatory explanation if she is to avoid conviction; she must answer for her actual selling of unfit food—whereas were responsibility non-strict, she would only have to answer for what was proved to be a negligent selling of unfit food. The offence of possessing a controlled drug was similarly turned from an offence of strict liability to one of strict responsibil-ity by English law in 1971: one proved to have been in possession of such a drug can now avoid conviction by proving 'that he neither knew nor suspected nor had reason to suspect' that it was such a drug, but will be convicted unless he can offer such an exculpatory account of his possession.[36] The same effect can be achieved by creating legal presumptions. If a civil servant accepts a gift from a govern-ment contractor, the gift 'shall be deemed to have been...given and received corruptly...unless the contrary is proved':[37] the civil servant is held strictly crim-inally responsible for accepting the gift (as the donor is held strictly responsible for giving it); she must answer for it, in that she must offer persuasive evidence of the innocent character of the transaction if she is to avoid conviction.

What, if anything, could justify such impositions of strict criminal respon-sibility? On the face of it, they violate the Presumption of Innocence, since the prosecution no longer carries the burden of proving guilt: once the prosecution has proved something much less than guilt (for the conduct proved could have been entirely faultless), the defendant is required to prove her innocence; and even if the defendant's burden was reduced from persuasive to evidential, it seems at odds with the Presumption. No doubt many instances of strict responsibility are unjustifiable, and mark an illegitimate attempt to make it easier to secure convictions. But we can develop an in-principle justification for some impos-itions of strict criminal responsibility, by thinking further about what citizens can properly be expected to answer for to their fellows, under the aegis (and the threat) of the criminal law. Consider two kinds of case.

One is exemplified by the shopkeeper. She is engaged in an optional activity which, while beneficial to the polity, also creates distinctive risks of serious harm. It is also relatively easy for her both to take suitable precautions against causing such harm (in the ways in which she obtains, checks, and keeps the perishable goods that she sells), and to maintain records which will show what care she has taken. It is reasonable to expect her to maintain such records, as a way both of ensuring, and of assuring herself and her fellow citizens, that she is taking all due care: what she owes to her fellow citizens, we might say, is not just to take

---

[36] See Misuse of Drugs Act 1971, ss 5(1)–(2), 28, as compared to Drugs (Prevention of Misuse) Act 1964, s 1(1). For an egregious example of strict criminal responsibility, see Terrorism Act 2000, s 57. Both Acts lay a persuasive, not merely an evidential, burden on the defendant: see at n 29 above.
[37] Prevention of Corruption Act 1916, s 2.

care not to cause harm, but to assure them that she is taking care.[38] One who has maintained such records is then well placed to adduce evidence (indeed, usually to prove) that she 'took all reasonable precautions and exercised all due diligence'; it is not therefore unreasonable to expect her to answer in a criminal court for the danger that she actually created by selling unfit food.

The other kind of case is exemplified by the civil servant. Here the risk involved is not of physical harm but of criminal wrongfulness. Accepting a gift from a contractor is, as she must know, conduct that will reasonably arouse suspicions of corruption, and creates a real risk of corruption; it is also conduct that it is easy to avoid. Whilst it might be unreasonable to expect the recipient to *prove* non-corruption if she is to avoid conviction, is it unreasonable to require that anyone who accepts such a gift must ensure that they can offer evidence (for instance of their lack of connection with or influence over the government's business with the contractor) that it was not corrupt if they are to avoid conviction? It might be unreasonable, given that the conviction would be for actual corruption: whilst accepting a gift does create both reasonable suspicion and risk, it is surely not sufficient to create a presumption of corruption. But such a burden-shifting presumption might be justifiable if conviction would be for a lesser offence of accepting a gift in circumstances that created a reasonable suspicion of corruption: rather than making it an offence for civil servants to accept gifts from contractors at all, the law requires them to answer for accepting any such gifts, since the public must be assured that government business is being conducted honestly.[39]

By attending to responsibility as a matter of answerability we can therefore throw light both on the significance of the distinction between offences and defences, and on the ways in which the criminal law sometimes, and sometimes perhaps justifiably, makes responsibility strict (strict responsibility is as pervasive a feature of our criminal law as strict liability; but it has not received the systematic theoretical attention that it merits).

4 'Deeds' v 'Reasons'

Finally, by attending to responsibility as answerability, we can show how the controversy between 'deeds' theorists and 'reasons' theorists about the conditions of justification in the criminal law has been misguided: on the issue of justification, 'reasons' theorists are clearly in the right; the real question concerns what should be counted as an element of the offence.

---

[38] Compare Braithwaite and Pettit 1990, 63–8, on the importance not just of freedom, but of assured freedom—the assurance that one is and will remain free. One can see a range of 'regulatory' offences as concerned not just with safety, but with the assurance of safety.

[39] Such a provision might be a legitimate instantiation of the form of offence unjustifiably instantiated in s 57 of the Terrorism Act 2000, which imposes strict responsibility for possessing 'an article in circumstances which give rise to a reasonable suspicion' that the possession is for a purpose connected to terrorism.

Don comes up behind Victoria, throws his arms round her, and squeezes very hard; what he intends, out of sheer malice, is to frighten her. In fact, however, he saves her life: for she was choking on a piece of food and the Heimlich Manoeuvre (which Don's action actually constituted) was necessary and sufficient to dislodge it. Had Don known these facts, and acted as he did in order to save her, he would of course have a defence against a charge of assault and battery; but he did not know them. Some theorists hold that Don should still be acquitted of assault and battery, since he did 'the right thing', albeit for the wrong reason;[40] others argue that he should be convicted, since he did not even know the facts that could have grounded a justification, let alone act because of (for the reason constituted by) those facts.[41]

Now if it is accepted that the necessity of Don's action grounds a defence, then 'reasons' theorists are right. It is up to the defendant (Don) to offer a defence, but to offer a defence is to answer for my actions, and to answer for my actions is to answer for those actions as mine—as done with the intentions with which and for the reasons for which I did them. I explain why I acted as I did; if I am claiming a justification, I explain my action by reference to the reasons that I take to have been good reasons for acting thus—reasons sufficient to defeat those against acting as I did. But for Don to point to the fact, which he discovered only after the event, that his action saved Jill's life is not to explain or answer for his action: that fact, being unknown to him, can play no part in an explanation of why he acted as he did.

That is not yet to say, however, that Don should be convicted of assault and battery. It is to say that he does not have a defence against such a charge, but 'deeds' theorists would do better to argue that he should not need a defence: that the life-saving necessity of his action should instead to be taken as negating an element of the offence—ie that the offence should be defined to require something like an unnecessary, or unreasonable, application or threat of force. For if the mere fact that his action was necessary to save Victoria's life should warrant his acquittal, that must be because he commits no criminal wrong in that actual situation, and therefore has nothing for which he must answer in a criminal court. The 'reasons' theorists are right about justificatory defences; but the real debate between them and 'deeds' theorists is, or should be, about which factors that bear on guilt should be defined as elements of the offence, and which rather belong to defences.[42]

The same is true of the kind of case that more often figures in debates about the problem of 'unknown justification' (a label that, if the argument sketched

---

[40] See eg Moore 1997, 65–6, Robinson 1997, 95–124, Schopp 1998, 29–38. Some who would acquit him of the complete offence would convict him of an attempt; I ignore that issue here.

[41] See eg Fletcher 1978, 555–66, Christopher 1995, Gardner 1996, Baron 2005, Tadros, 2005, 273–80.

[42] Note that what *D* must claim, and adduce evidence of, if he is to offer a justification is not merely that he was aware of the relevant facts, but that he acted for the appropriate reason (see Dressler 1984, 78–81, Gardner 1996, Tadros 2005, 274–80). However, evidence of knowledge will in fact typically suffice at least to create a reasonable doubt about intention.

above is sound, is quite inappropriate, since what is unknown cannot constitute a justification)—the case in which *D* kills *V* when *V* is in fact (unknown
to *D*) attempting to kill someone else (or *D* himself), so that *D* could on any
account have justifiably killed *V* as a matter of self-defence or defence of others
had he known the situation; but we can also see in that kind of case that 'reasons'
theorists provide a more plausible account of what should figure in the offence
definition.

If *D* is to justify his killing of *V*, he cannot, I have argued, appeal to the bare fact
that *V* was himself attempting an unlawful killing; if, as 'deeds' theorists hold, *D*
should be acquitted of murder, that fact must be taken to negate an element of the
offence, rather than to ground a defence. We would therefore need to define murder not just as the wilful killing of a human being, but as the wilful killing of an
innocent human being—defining 'innocent' as, roughly, 'not currently engaged
in attacking another's life'.[43] But to adopt such an offence definition would be, in
effect, to make the non-innocent person an outlaw:[44] by engaging in an attack,
he puts himself outside the law's protection; killing him is not a wrong for which
the killer must be called to answer in a criminal court; it is not even clear that on
this view the killing would need to be necessary for it to be lawful. Now it is true
that our existing law of murder does not protect all human beings: the victim
must be 'under the king's peace', so that a soldier who kills an enemy soldier 'in
the heat of war' does not commit the offence of murder, and needs no defence.[45]
However (and quite apart from the fact that enemy soldiers are still protected, to
some extent, by the rules of war), we should not allow ourselves to be (mis)led by
the rhetoric of the 'war on crime' into seeing offenders, even would-be murderers, as enemies or outlaws who have forfeited the law's protection:[46] to use force
against them is still to commit what is at least a presumptive wrong, for which
one should have to answer—and for which one should be condemned if one cannot show that the force used was both necessary and proportionate. The attacker
still has a claim on us, as a fellow citizen who is protected by the law (including
the laws that he is violating), even if we are justified in using what might be fatal
violence against him: we show our recognition of that claim in recognizing the
need to justify our own use of such violence (to him and to our fellow citizens);
the polity shows its recognition of that claim by requiring one who uses such
force to offer a defence if he is to avoid conviction.

If *D* shoots *V*, intending to kill him, and not realizing that he is already dead,
he is clearly not guilty of murder—not because he has a defence, but because he

[43] On 'innocence' in the context of defensive violence, see McMahan 1994, Norman 1995, ch 5.

[44] Compare Blackstone 1765–9, vol IV, ch 5.iii, 71 on the pirate as outlaw, or '*hostis humani
generis*': 'As he has renounced all the benefits of society and government, and has reduced himself
afresh to the savage state of nature, by declaring war against all mankind, all mankind must declare
war against him'.

[45] See Coke 1628, vol 3, 47 (quoted in Ormerod 2005, 429), Ormerod 2005, 433–4.

[46] Although that is how some philosophers, as well as some politicians and the tabloid press,
portray them: see Morris 1991.

does not have the killing of a human being (an essential element of the offence of murder) to answer for.[47] The only viable way to argue that in cases of 'unknown justification' *D* should be acquitted, at least of the complete offence, would be to argue that in such cases an essential element of the offence (the 'innocence' of the victim, for instance) is also missing: but, I have suggested, we should not define murder in that way. The killing of an attacker is a presumptive wrong for which the killer should have to answer; and an exculpatory answer will need to appeal not merely to the existence of the relevant facts, but to his appropriate reasons for acting as he did.

What matters for my present purposes, however, is not whether I am right about how we should define murder, but the more general point about the nature of justificatory defences, and the significance of the distinction between offences and defences: once we understand the criminal trial as a process of calling to answer, and map the distinction between offences and defences onto that between responsibility and liability, we can see why 'reasons' theorists are right about what is required for a justificatory defence—and why it matters whether we count a particular potentially exculpatory factor as negating an offence element or as grounding a possible defence.

(We can also now see, though I cannot pursue this issue here, why we need to distinguish 'excuses' from 'exemptions'.[48] To offer an excuse is to answer for my actions, by explaining my reasons for acting as I did, as well as my failure to recognize or to respond appropriately to the reasons against acting as I did; it is thus to admit responsibility, whilst seeking to avert liability by arguing that, given the particular context of my action, it would be unreasonable to condemn me for my admitted failure to act in accordance with the reasons sanctioned by the law. But one who was, for instance, so mentally disordered at the time of his alleged offence that he was not at that time a responsible, ie reasons-responsive, agent cannot in that sense answer for his actions, since he was not operating within the realm of reasons: if he is fit to be tried,[49] he can offer an answer to the charge; but his answer must be that he should be exempt from criminal responsibility for his disordered actions, since they are not actions for which he can answer.)

I have suggested that we can illuminate some central aspects both of the substantive criminal law and of the criminal process by distinguishing responsibility from liability, and attending to the relational dimensions of responsibility; we can indeed also then see how closely process and substance are connected to each other. I have illustrated that suggestion by showing how it brings out the importance of bars to trial (whether legal or moral), and of the conditions of responsibility that those bars negate; how it highlights and explains the significance

---

[47] It is a further question whether *D* should be convicted of attempted murder: see *Dlugash* 363 North East 2d 1155 (1977, New York).

[48] See eg Gardner 1998, Horder 2004, 8–10, 103–6, Tadros 2005, 124–9.

[49] See at n 15 above.

of the distinction between offences and defences; how it focuses our attention not merely on strict criminal liability, but on the phenomenon of strict criminal responsibility (and on the role and implications of the Presumption of Innocence, and of various legal presumptions that appear to undermine it); and how it enables us to re-conceive the debate about justificatory defences between 'deeds' and 'reasons' theorists. Although much more needs, of course, to be said to explain that suggestion and its implications (and to show the other ways in which it throws light on the structural logic of the criminal law), I hope that I have said enough here to show that the suggestion is worth pursuing.

7

Hart and Feinberg on Responsibility*

John Gardner

In the 1960s H.L.A. Hart and Joel Feinberg made independent attempts to cata-logue various senses of the word 'responsible' and to explore the relationships among them.[1] Both projects hovered between philosophy and lexicography. Feinberg came up with ten or eleven senses in which a person might be labelled 'responsible'. A judicious application of Occam's Razor would have enabled him to reduce the list, as Hart did, to a more manageable four or five. In saying this, I am not doubting that the word 'responsible' has, in idiomatic English, all the possible differences of nuance assigned to it by Feinberg. But only some are of philosophical interest. Only some of the distinctions, as Hart noticed, advance our understanding of the world and our place in it.[2] In mapping the language of responsibility with scant regard for this criterion of selection, Feinberg's project was more lexicographical and less philosophical than Hart's. In another respect,

---

* This paper is descended from material presented at the Joel Feinberg Memorial Conference in April 2005 at Georgia State University. A more recent version of part of the paper (roughly section 1 of what follows) was presented at the British Academy Symposium on 'The Legacy of H.L.A. Hart' in July 2007 at the University of Cambridge. Thanks to the many people who participated in the discussion at both events, especially to Jules Coleman, my commentator in Atlanta, and to Philip Pettit and James Penner who asked questions in Cambridge that gave me significant pause for thought when I came to redraft.

[1] Hart's characteristically economical treatment appeared as 'Varieties of Responsibility' (Hart 1967a), reprinted as part of the postscript to Hart 1968. Feinberg meanwhile wrote three essays adding up (he says) to a 'complete...account of the language of responsibility'. His essay 'Responsibility for the Present and Past' was never published but, according to Feinberg, its con-tents were largely incorporated into his 'Action and Responsibility' and 'Sua Culpa', both included in Feinberg 1970. The companion essays 'Responsibility *Tout Court*' (Feinberg 1988a) and 'Responsibility for the Future' (Feinberg 1988b) did appear in print, but only long after they were written, in 1988. Feinberg apparently did not rework these two essays for their belated publication, and hence did not make any reference to Hart 1967a (or to anything else published after 1966). Feinberg's remarks on how his essays were supposed to fit together are to be found in Feinberg 1988b, 110.

[2] 'Th[e] welter of distinguishable senses of the word "responsible" and its grammatical cognates can, I think, be reduced by division and classification....I hope that in drawing these dividing lines...I have avoided the arbitrary pedantries of classificatory systematics, and that my divisions clarify the main varieties of responsibility to which reference is constantly made by moralists, law-yers, historians and others.' (Hart 1967a, 346)

however, Feinberg's project was more philosophical and less lexicographical than Hart's. Both authors found connections among the various senses of 'responsible'. Both gave explanatory priority to one sense of the word (or one cluster of senses). However only Feinberg saw this as a logical priority, essential to understanding the other senses. For Hart the connections and priorities were matters of contingent association, explaining how the language had come to be used in so many senses but still consistent with understanding each separately.

In spite of these differences, the two authors took some major steps forward in common. They showed that the existing literature on responsibility, both legal and moral, was mired in confusion. Participants were often at cross-purposes, even with themselves, about which sense of the word they were using, permitting improbable claims to pass unnoticed.[3] It was harder to get these claims past Hart and Feinberg. Yet the two writers also shared some misconceptions. In particular they both fell into a trap that has since been exposed by J R Lucas. 'Traditional accounts of responsibility', Lucas observes,

are too blame-centred. People are required to own up to their misdeeds in order that they can be blamed for them. But this is a distortion. Naturally, we are most energetic in disclaiming responsibility when we are in danger of disapprobation, and therefore lawyers earn their fees in fighting ascriptions of ill-doing, but in ordinary life we are concerned not so much to blame as to understand. I want to know who is responsible, answerable, in order to have him answer my question 'Why did you do it?' (Lucas 2007)

In this paper I return to some of the issues in the theory of responsibility that were investigated by Hart and Feinberg. I do so in a way that echoes and expands on Lucas's criticism. I suggest that Hart's and Feinberg's problems began with their respective mistakes—their contrasting mistakes—about what I call 'basic responsibility' (section 1). These mistakes about basic responsibility led them each to overstate the relative importance of a different idea that I call 'consequential responsibility' (section 2). They both advanced, or at any rate gave succour to, the view that basic responsibility takes its importance from its relationship with consequential responsibility. This is only part of the truth, and the shallower part at that. At a deeper level, consequential responsibility takes its importance from its relationship with basic responsibility. By 'importance' here I mean moral importance. I will not be interested, except incidentally, in the logical and lexical priorities that occupy Feinberg and Hart.

---

[3] Alas, Hart's and Feinberg's blandishments fell mostly on deaf ears, and many invocations of responsibility in philosophical literature continue to help themselves indiscriminately to different senses of the word as the argument demands. A later body of literature much afflicted by this confusion concerns the justification of inequality. See, for example, Rawls 1982, 168–9, Kymlicka 1989, 37–40, Cohen, 1989, 922.

1 Basic Responsibility

In one sense—I call it 'basic responsibility'—responsibility is what it sounds like: it is a kind of ability to respond. More precisely it is the ability to explain oneself, to give an intelligible account of oneself, to answer for oneself as a rational being. As a rational being, one is equipped for explanation. One has many things to explain and (depending on the sophistication of one's rationality) many ways of explaining them. All the same, as a rational agent, one only has two ways of explaining *oneself*. The first is to offer a justification; the second is to offer an excuse.

Justification is direct rational explanation. 'Why did you do that?' is the question. The justificatory answer is: 'Because I had undefeated reasons to do it; because all things considered it was the right thing to do.' Excuse, by contrast, is oblique rational explanation. The question is still 'why did you do that?' but the answer is more qualified. 'True, I didn't act for undefeated reasons, but I had undefeated reasons for being so afraid or enraged or confused or upset that that was how I acted. My action was unjustified, but my being disposed to act that way was justified.' Needless to say, not every justification or excuse is a successful one. We often make misguided attempts at justification or excuse, citing reasons that we fondly imagine to have more force than they really have. We may also offer what we now admit to be inadequate justifications or excuses, citing reasons that, we now acknowledge, did not have the force that we treated them as having when we acted. All of this is consistent with our being basically responsible agents. Our responsibility, in this sense, does not lie in our ability to provide successful justifications and excuses, or even credible justifications and excuses. It lies in our ability to provide justifications and excuses full stop. Basically responsible agents can't always give a rationally *acceptable* account of themselves, but they can always give a rationally *intelligible* one.

You may think that this unduly narrows the range of explanations that we should count as self-explanations. Surely one can also give neurophysiological self-explanations (I blinked because of tardive dyskinesia), physical ones (the wind blew me sideways), psychiatric ones (depression drove me to self-harm), psychoanalytic ones (I had repressed anger towards my father that I took out on my children), and a whole raft of others? One can indeed. But in these cases—the psychoanalytic explanation is perhaps a borderline case—one does not explain oneself as a rational being. One explains oneself *away* as a rational being. One casts oneself in the role of object rather than subject; one explains oneself (including one's reasons) in terms of facts that are not reasons, or are not figuring in one's explanation as reasons. They are not reasons, or are not figuring as reasons, because one was not guided by them *qua* facts.[4] They influenced one other than

---

[4] For elaboration see Gardner and Macklem 2002.

in virtue of one's appreciation of them. Maybe one was moved by them, but one was not motivated by them.

Let me illustrate. Suppose *A* hit *B* so that *B* knocked *C* over. One interpretation: *A* hit *B* so that *B* fell, and as he fell he knocked *C* over. A rival interpretation: *A* hit *B*, provoking *B* to knock *C* over; for some reason, he mistook *C* for *A*. *B* has a rational explanation for his having knocked *C* over in the second version of the story, but not in the first. In the first version *B* figures, but he does not figure *qua* rational agent. He might as well have been a fridge. Does it follow that, in the first version, *B* is not basically responsible? Yes and no. So far as we know from the story he is, in general, a basically responsible agent. But he is not basically responsible for having knocked *C* over. At least, he is not basically responsible for having knocked *C* over unless the story of his falling has an untold complication: unless there was some action φ-ing such that, if only *B* had φ-ed in the course of his falling, he would have averted *C*'s being knocked over by him.[5] If there was such an action—such as pushing *C* out of the way, or shouting 'watch out *C*!', or blocking his own fall—then *B* was still, in (not averting) his knocking *C* over, occupying his role as a rational agent, an agent subject to reasons. We can then ask what reasons he had, or took himself to have, for (not having averted) his having knocked *C* over. We can ask for a justification or an excuse. In asking for such a justification or excuse, we are treating *B* as basically responsible for (not averting) his having knocked *C* over. His (not averting) his having knocked *C* over was a manifestation of his rational agency even if his falling in the first place was not.

Ordinarily, if knocked over by another human being, we treat him or her as basically responsible for knocking us over. We begin by asking: 'Why did you do that?' That is because (barring special circumstances) human beings are basically responsible agents. This is a conceptual claim. Being basically responsible is neither a necessary nor a sufficient condition of being human. But it is a defeasibly necessary condition. It is necessary subject to exceptions. Anyone who thinks of the exceptions as anything other than exceptional, even if they are very frequent exceptions, does not fully grasp what it is to be human.[6] So 'why did you do that?' (asked with the expectation of a justificatory or excusatory answer) is the apt, as well as the usual, reaction to being knocked over by a human being.[7]

---

[5] This proviso is sometimes rendered as 'unless *B* could have done otherwise than knock *C* over'. But this is misleading. For *B* to be basically responsible for having knocked *C* over it is not necessary for φ-ing to be an action which *B* had either the capacity or the opportunity to perform. All that is necessary is that if *B* had φ-ed (even *per impossibile*) *C* would not have been knocked over.

[6] See Hart's own discussion of defeasibility in Hart 1948, an article which he later (in my view over-hastily) disowned.

[7] Compare my discussion of defeasibility in the concept of law in Gardner 2007a. There I argued that the fact that law defeasibly creates moral obligations should not lead one to think that it presumptively creates moral obligations. That is because law is an instrument, the value of which depends on the use to which it is put. Human beings, by contrast, are of ultimate value and respecting this value means treating them, presumptively, as fully human, ie as not belonging to one of the exceptions in which their humanity, or an aspect of it, is defeated.

It remains an apt question even if the human being in question was pushed. But there are two kinds of special circumstances in which, even though the question remains apt, a justificatory or excusatory answer is not apt. There are two kinds of exceptional cases in which the defeasibly necessary condition for being human is defeated. Sometimes, as we saw, the addressee is not basically responsible *for* having knocked one over. Sometimes, on the other hand, she is not basically responsible *tout court*. Some human beings are not responsible agents because— for a period of their lives, or throughout their lives—they lack the ability to provide rational explanations for anything that they do.

It is tempting to think that, inasmuch as they lack basic responsibility, children and mentally ill people belong in the second category. They lack basic responsibility *tout court* for as long as their condition continues. No doubt that is true of babies and small toddlers. But from an early age normal human children begin to ask 'why?', and soon afterwards learn to expect the same question to be asked of them, by way of request or demand for self-explanation. This is the stage at which they acquire a sense of themselves. From this stage on, what is at issue is only how much of what they do they are basically responsible for, not whether they are basically responsible *tout court*. As their grasp of the world grows so does the repertoire of actions that they understand themselves to be performing, and with it the range of actions that they can properly be asked to justify or excuse.[8]

Mental illness normally affects basic responsibility in much the same local-ized way. No doubt some extreme psychotic disorders remove basic responsibility *tout court* for as long as they last. But those who suffer less extreme disorders that involve localized delusions or compulsions lack basic responsibility, if at all, only for those actions of theirs that are owed to their delusions or compulsions.[9] Only when they act in the thrall of their delusions and compulsions do they lose their ability to offer rationally intelligible explanations of what they did. There are no facts they can point to either as reasons for doing as they did or as reasons for their being disposed to do it. There are only imagined facts. *D* had not left the door unlocked and had no reason to suppose that he did. He had checked twenty times already. Yet he kept going back for another look. Nothing would shift his belief that the door was unlocked. Nobody was spying on *E* and she had no rea-son to suppose that they were. The CCTV cameras were not tracking her move-ments. Yet still she insisted that they were, and insisted on wearing a disguise in the street. Nothing would convince her to go out undisguised. These examples should put to rest the impression (which may have been given by the example of *B*'s fall) that questions about one's basic responsibility for what one did arise only if, as in *B*'s case, there is some doubt about whether one really *did* it. The compulsive

---

[8] Of course, it may be better, for independent reasons, not to institutionalize this by subjecting children to court appearances and such like. The aptness of a certain reaction does not yet establish that the law (or any other particular agent) is aptly placed to have that reaction. For detailed discus-sion see Duff 2007.

[9] This point is well explained by Anthony Kenny in Kenny 1978, 82–3.

and delusional actions just mentioned are undoubtedly the actions of D and E respectively. Yet D and E are not, as their stories stand, basically responsible for those actions. The only facts in terms of which they will ever be able to explain what they did are not reasons for having done it ('I was in the grip of delusions'). Meanwhile the only 'reasons' they can invoke—and they are reasons only in a peripheral sense—are not facts but figments of their fevered imaginations ('the cameras were tracking my movements').[10]

I have consciously echoed Feinberg in drawing the distinction between being responsible *tout court* and being responsible *for* some particular action. Feinberg tries to classify many of the numerous senses of the word 'responsible' under these two headings. The main pitfall of this approach should already be apparent from what I have said. Basic responsibility is responsibility in a sense that straddles the divide between responsibility *tout court* and responsibility *for*. It cannot be classified under one heading or the other. In trying to classify it under one heading or the other, Feinberg ends up discussing basic responsibility twice, without realizing that it is the same thing he is discussing. He discusses it once under the heading of 'responsibility *tout court*', where it turns into a kind of *competence*. And then he discusses it again under the heading of 'responsibility for', where it becomes (or is assimilated to) a kind of *liability*. Both discussions are severely distorted by their forced separation. I will say something in the next section about Feinberg's mutation of basic responsibility into a kind of liability. Here I want to show how basic responsibility is distorted—and made to seem less basic than it really is—by the other mutation, its mutation into a kind of competence.

Competences, in Feinberg's lexicon, are abilities of a special kind. They are abilities to perform actions with a normative significance (or 'normative abilities' for short). For example,

the police chief (unlike the justice of the peace) lacks the competence to perform marriages. . . . [I]t is not simply that the police chief lacks the knack, or the ability, or the technique to marry people; rather he lacks the qualifying characteristics, under the law, that would give legal effect to his words. (Feinberg 1988a, 88)

Marrying people involves the exercise of a normative power, so one lacks the ability to marry people if one lacks that normative power. The power in turn is conferred by a norm. That norm creates the competence. All competences are relative to the norms that create them. Not all norms that create a competence are, however, power-conferring norms. As Kelsen points out, and Feinberg agrees, one may also lack competence under a duty-imposing norm (Kelsen 1945,

---

[10] Sometimes (eg in criminal law textbooks) denials of basic responsibility based on infancy or mental illness are mistaken for excuses. It is not hard to see why. Both excuses and denials of responsibility, if successful, are exculpatory, and distinguishing the two kinds of exculpation can be tricky at point of application. Conceptually, however, the two kinds of exculpation could not be more different: making a successful excuse is a way of exculpating oneself by asserting, as opposed to denying, one's basic responsibility. See Gardner 2007b, 131–2 and 177–82.

90–1). One lacks competence because, although one has the ability to do what the norm requires or forbids, one's doing it does not qualify as conformity with or violation of the norm, and hence has none of the normative consequences of norm-conformity or norm-violation. Hence:

Dogs, infants, and lunatics lack the competence to commit murder in the same way that…a citizen may lack the legal 'standing' to become a plaintiff when his personal interests have not been directly hurt. (Feinberg 1988a, 88)

Dogs, infants, and lunatics have the ability to kill, and perhaps to do so deliberately. They may, in other words, have the ability to act in ways that, if they were not dogs, infants, or lunatics, would qualify as murder. But they still lack the ability to murder, which is a normative ability. And this, says Feinberg, is the same kind of ability that one lacks if one lacks responsibility *tout court*:

It is not simply that the non-responsible person [*tout court*] is unfit for responsibility judgments [i.e. judgments of 'responsibility for']; rather he is totally disqualified from them. The rules make it impossible for anyone of his description to 'play the game' at all. (Feinberg 1988a, 87)

Notice that, if Feinberg is right about this, responsibility *tout court* becomes responsibility in a derivative sense. One needs an independent analysis of what counts as being responsible *for* something (for example, as a kind of liability to be reproached or punished) in order to identify which norms one is incompetent under if one is not responsible *tout court*. The competence being conferred is the competence to be responsible for things (whatever that may turn out to mean). This feature of what Feinberg says may lead you to suspect that, in these passages, he is not trying to understand basic responsibility at all. For the responsibility he is discussing is responsibility only in some derivative sense, not responsibility in the basic sense that interests us. But I think Feinberg is trying to understand basic responsibility. His mistake in characterizing it as a competence explains his mistake in concluding that it is not basic.

Whenever someone has a competence, in Feinberg's sense, the exercise of that competence supervenes on the exercise of some other (non-normative) ability or abilities.[11] To murder one must (*inter alia*) kill; to conduct a marriage one must (*inter alia*) hold a ceremony; to make a contract one must (*inter alia*) communicate an intention; and so on. Feinberg's analysis leaves open the question of what the relevant non-normative ability or abilities might be in the case of those who are responsible *tout court*. He does this deliberately. According to Feinberg, as according to Kelsen, the non-normative abilities that must be exercised to exercise a normative ability can conceivably include absolutely any non-normative ability that is specified by the norm that creates the competence. There is nothing

---

[11] It may do so indirectly. Sometimes one exercises a competence by exercising another competence.

in the analysis of responsibility *tout court* (or indeed responsibility in any other sense that Feinberg discusses) that tells us who among us is responsible *tout court* and in virtue of what non-normative abilities. So there is nothing to rule out the possibility of a norm under which, for example, only babies and the seriously psychotic are responsible *tout court*. After all, they have abilities that the rest of us lack, notably the ability to be seriously and persistently oblivious to reason. Why shouldn't responsibility *tout court* be associated with these abilities? Why shouldn't there be a norm conferring on babies and the seriously psychotic—but not on the rest of us—the status of responsible *tout court*?

The natural answer is: because babies and the seriously psychotic, unlike the rest of us, are not responsible *tout court*. Unlike the rest of us, they are not the kinds of beings on whom norms can confer competences, because they are not the kinds of beings whose actions can be regulated by norms. One's actions can be regulated by norms only if one is the kind of being who can be guided by norms. Guidance by norms requires guidance by reasons. It requires that one have the ability to justify or excuse one's actions, meaning at the very least the child-like ability to point to a norm as a reason for doing as one does, even if not the more mature ability to point to further reasons why one uses that norm. Babies and the seriously psychotic lack even that child-like ability to justify or excuse. And there is nothing that any norm can do to confer it upon them.

If this answer is sound then responsibility *tout court* is not, basically, a competence. Rather it is an ability which one needs if one is to have any competences. It is a powerful objection to Feinberg's account of responsibility *tout court* that we cannot even make sense of the natural answer, never mind vindicate it, using his analysis of responsibility *tout court*. For on his analysis it makes no sense to give the fact that babies and the seriously psychotic are not responsible *tout court* as the reason why no norm can make them so. For on his analysis, being responsible *tout court* is simply a competence that is conferred by a norm.

There is, however, a possible way of re-engineering the natural answer that seems to make sense of it in Feinbergian terms. One might point out—as Feinberg himself does—that responsibility *tout court* figures in both moral and legal (or more broadly institutional) thought. Morally, babies and the seriously psychotic are not responsible agents because the moral norms that confer the relevant competence—whatever the competence turns out to be—do not confer that competence on babies and the seriously psychotic. We cannot change these norms because we cannot change morality. We are stuck with it. Legal and other institutional norms, however, can be changed by human beings. Conceivably such institutional norms may confer the relevant competence—whatever it turns out to be—on anyone, on the strength of any abilities at all. Why shouldn't there be a legal norm conferring on babies and the seriously psychotic, but not on the rest of us, the status of responsible agents?

Well of course there are plenty of reasons why not. They include, for example, moral reasons. When people give the natural answer—'because babies and the seriously psychotic, unlike the rest of us, are not responsible *tout court*'—they mean *morally* responsible. They are giving a moral reason why babies and the seriously psychotic shouldn't be held responsible *tout court* in law. They are assuming some further moral norm according to which only the morally responsible should be held legally responsible. They are not making a conceptual claim that implicates the very idea of responsibility *tout court*. The claim is not that babies can't conceivably be responsible *tout court*, but only that it's a very bad idea to make them so. That is because responsibility is a competence and it can be conferred by a norm. The norm may still, of course, be criticized for its immorality.

This is a bad reconstruction of the natural answer because it turns it on its head. We hold people responsible in two senses of 'hold'. Often, indeed, we select the word 'hold' precisely so that we can equivocate between these two senses. Sometimes we hold a person responsible in the ('constative') sense of coming to the conclusion that she is responsible. Sometimes we hold a person responsible in the rival ('performative') sense of making her responsible: we confer responsibility on her by an exercise of our normative powers.[12] As we will see in the next section, responsibility in some senses of the word can certainly be conferred. Basic responsibility, however, cannot be conferred. One cannot assume it, impose it, be relieved of it, be exempted from it, or otherwise subject it to the exercise of a normative power. That is true of basic responsibility *tout court* and also basic responsibility *for* things. This is a conceptual constraint. No norm, and hence no person armed with a normative power, can confer a non-normative ability. The law enjoys no exemption from this constraint. There may be legal norms that instruct others (eg officials) to treat some people who are not basically responsible as if they were basically responsible. But these norms do not make those people basically responsible. Instead, they create a legal fiction of basic responsibility. Why must it be regarded as a fiction? We already know the natural answer: norms—legal, moral, or otherwise—cannot conceivably regulate the actions of those who cannot be guided by norms.[13] *Qua* norms, they must be interpreted as regulating the actions of possible norm-users, and in this case the norm-users in question must be those who have occasion to treat some (other) people as if they were basically responsible, since those who are so treated are *ex hypothesi* not possible norm-users, in that they are not basically responsible.

It is often assumed that, because the law is made by human beings, and is thus capable of grave immorality, it is capable of any ridiculous thing at all. But this is a confusion. Law is no more capable of defying its own nature than is anything else. Legal systems are by their nature systems of norms and something that purports to regulate the actions of someone without basic responsibility is (to that

---

[12] The performative/constative distinction is introduced by JL Austin in Austin 1962, 5. Austin found it hard to maintain the distinction and later abandoned it. This collapse came of a mistake in the way he originally drew the distinction. See n 18 below.

[13] This is one of several small truths that is often inflated to yield the large falsehood that 'ought' implies 'can', ie that no norm can conceivably require one to do what one lacks the ability to do.

extent) not a norm, and so cannot be a legal norm. The law, being made up of norms, is capable of regulating only the actions of the basically responsible among us. So there is no such thing as *legal* basic responsibility. When we speak of basic responsibility as 'moral responsibility' (and we sometimes do) this should not be taken to suggest the existence of some legal counterpart called 'legal responsibility'. If anything, we should understand it to mean just the opposite. 'Moral' here just means 'whatever the law (or anyone else) may try to say'. For the incidence of this responsibility is a matter over which the law, whatever its pretensions, has no possible control.

Is it a legalistic bias in his thinking about responsibility that leads Feinberg to mistake basic responsibility for a competence? Perhaps. There are some signs of that bias in his work. But I think there is also another factor at work. In representing basic responsibility as a competence, Feinberg is straining, and in the process overstraining, to avoid an opposite and no less grave mistake to which Hart, in his explanation of basic responsibility, falls victim. 'In most contexts', says Hart,

the expression 'he is responsible for his actions' is used to assert that a person has certain normal capacities.... The capacities in question are those of understanding, reasoning, and control of conduct: the ability to understand what conduct legal rules or morality require, to deliberate and reach decisions concerning these requirements, and to conform to decisions when made. Because 'responsible for his actions' in this sense refers not to a legal status but to certain complex psychological characteristics of persons, a person's responsibility for his actions may intelligibly be said to be 'diminished' or 'impaired' as well as altogether absent. (Hart 1968, 227–8)

It is surely basic responsibility that Hart has in mind here. He calls it 'capacity-responsibility'. He gets some features of it right. He is right to think of it as an ability. He is right to think that it is an ability to use reasons (including norms), and he is right to think that this entails an ability to be guided by those reasons. But the contrast with which the passage ends—between responsibility as a legal status and responsibility as a set of psychological characteristics—is seriously misleading. True, basic responsibility is not a legal status. But it is, in a sense, a moral status. As Hart himself observes, morality cannot *but* give salience to the ability in question. Why is this? Hart says (lamely) that it is because of how 'morality is at present understood' (Hart 1968, 230). But in fact the explanation goes a lot deeper. Let me explain.

A basically responsible agent not only has the ability to offer justifications and excuses for what she does. She is also aptly disposed to offer justifications and excuses for what she does, and such justifications and excuses are aptly expected of her. What, you may wonder, makes these dispositions and expectations apt? In answer it is tempting to imagine a division of labour between empirical questions and moral ones. First there are some non-normative abilities that human beings normally possess ('certain complex psychological characteristics of persons'). Then there is some moral norm that makes these abilities salient for some purposes (such as the acquisition of a liability to punishment or a duty to atone or apologize). This norm confers a moral status—in the sense of a competence—on normal human beings by virtue of their possession of their normal abilities. At this point the question becomes: should we think of our basic responsibility as our being competent under the moral norm (Feinberg's answer) or should we think of our basic responsibility as our possessing the 'complex psychological characteristics of persons' that the moral norm makes salient (Hart's answer)?

Where basic responsibility is concerned there is no such division of labour and no such question, so both answers are mistaken. No moral norm, nor any other reason, makes it apt for us to explain ourselves rationally. The ability to offer justifications and excuses, to put it another way, is an ability that does not need a case to be made for its own exercise. It makes its own case. Imagine someone who asks: 'Why should we use reasons?' The question can only be interpreted as a demand for reasons. So it answers itself. If one isn't already disposed to use reasons then what is the point of asking for one?[14] As rational beings (beings who are able to use reasons) there is nothing else for us to do but use reasons. We are stuck with them. As soon as we appreciate their existence—as soon as we begin to ask our parents 'why?'—they exert their inescapable hold over us. The hold is not just empirically but conceptually inescapable. One can't conceivably have the ability to use reasons, while leaving open whether one should do so. That points to the sense in which being basically responsible is a moral status. It is not something that is relevant to what we should do because of some norm that makes it so. It is relevant whether it is mentioned in any norms or not. So even if we abolished all the practices (trial, punishment, reparation, recrimination, atonement, etc) to which our basic responsibility is supposed to be relevant, and so rendered moot all the moral norms regulating those practices, we still wouldn't have expunged the pervasive moral importance of our basic responsibility. It would still be apt for us to explain ourselves using reasons, even if nothing further turned on it.

You may say that I am guilty, here and more generally, of an equivocation. Let it be true that, as rational beings, we cannot but use reasons in the sense that we cannot but be guided by them. Surely it is quite another matter to claim that we cannot but use them again, after we have been guided by them, for the purpose of accounting for what we did? There are surely two distinct uses of reasons here, and two distinct abilities. Which of these abilities is our basic responsibility? Is it the ability to *have* justifications and excuses, or is it the ability to *offer* them?

We do not need to choose. It is one and the same ability, the ability known to the ancients as *logos*. Those who are able to use reasons are aptly disposed, and aptly expected, to use them for whatever they are there to be used for. And they are there to be used both for guidance and for explanation. Of course, the explanation itself is another action, and it also calls for guidance by reasons.

---

[14] I am here adapting the argument used by John Finnis in Finnis 1977.

The reasons that guide the act of self-explanation are not only the reasons that are mentioned in it—the ones that do the explaining—but also those that bear on whether the explanation should be given, and if so in what spirit, and to whom, and so on. No doubt there are occasions when one has no duty to offer any justifications and excuses. Sometimes, perhaps, one has a duty not to do so. And no doubt, even when duty-bound to do so, one is sometimes justified or excused in hesitating or refusing to offer one's justifications and excuses, such as they may be. Nevertheless, as a rational being, one is aptly disposed and aptly expected to offer them.

2 Consequential Responsibility

In a second sense—I call it 'consequential responsibility'—those who are responsible are those who are singled out to bear the adverse normative consequences of wrongful (or otherwise deficient) actions.[15] The consequences in question are normative in two ways. First, they are changes in someone's moral or legal (or otherwise normative) position. Second, they are effected by someone's violation of a norm (moral, legal, or otherwise). In other respects they are very varied. Someone may acquire a duty or permission to punish the responsible person or remonstrate with her or engage in other so-called 'blaming' responses. The responsible person herself may acquire a duty to make reparation or restitution, or to apologize or atone. She may lose a right to reparation or restitution from another. She may also acquire a duty to justify or excuse the action. Here we can already see a connection between basic responsibility and consequential responsibility. A duty to self-explain, to exercise one's ability as a basically responsible agent, may be among the normative consequences of a wrong one commits. In a way, as Lucas suggests, this is the most natural normative consequence of all, for it gives normative salience to an action that is already apt for human beings, by their nature, to engage in.

Both Hart and Feinberg prefer to talk of 'liabilities' where I talk of 'normative consequences'. Indeed Hart talks of 'liability-responsibility' rather than consequential responsibility. I find this both too narrow and too broad. Too narrow, because a liability in one person corresponds to a normative power in another.[16] Yet not every normative consequence of a wrong action involves the acquisition or exercise of a normative power. For example, while in some cases the normative consequence of *F*'s wrong action might be *G*'s acquiring a power to impose a duty to repair on *F*, in other cases the normative consequence is simply that

---

[15] The label 'consequential responsibility' is owed to Dworkin 2000, 287. Talk of consequential responsibility is sometimes extended, by analogy, to take in the welcome normative consequences of supererogatory (or otherwise admirable) actions. I will ignore this extension here.

[16] See Hohfeld 1989, 58–9.

F acquires a duty to repair without *G*'s having any power over the incidence of the duty. A case in the second class does not, strictly speaking, involve a liability, but it does involve a normative consequence. On the other hand, not all liabilities are normative consequences. My insurer, for example, may have a liability to pay for storm damage to my house. Paying for this damage may be the insurer's responsibility in another sense. Hart calls it 'role-responsibility' (Hart 1968, 212–14) and for Feinberg it is a kind of 'responsibility for the future' (Feinberg 1988b, 95–9). But this is not consequential responsibility. That is because the liability to pay is not a normative consequence of any norm-violation by anyone. The storm did no wrong and indeed was not capable of doing wrong (for it lacks basic responsibility). Would it be different if I were insured against vandalism rather than storm damage? Perhaps. It would depend, I think, on whether the insurer's liability is based on the fact that vandalism is a wrong, an action that violates a norm. Of course, my insurance policy is probably indeterminate on this score. Never mind that. What matters is that not every liability, whether legal or moral, involves adverse normative consequences in the sense that interests us here. In what follows I will treat Hart's and Feinberg's references to liabilities as if they were references to normative consequences. Indeed Hart and Feinberg make clear that this is what they have in mind, ie they admittedly use 'liability' in a stipulative sense.

So is being consequentially responsible just the same thing as being punishable, reproachable, bound to make amends, etc? Is the responsibility in each case to be identified with the normative consequence? Feinberg's treatment of what he calls 'retrospective responsibility' ('responsibility for the ϕ-ing' where the ϕ-ing is something already done) fragments into several sub-discussions, and sometimes, without realizing it, he ends up back at basic responsibility again, itself sometimes taking on some of the appearance of a liability. But here he seems to be talking more straightforwardly about consequential responsibility:

> To say of a person, after the fact, that he is responsible for something may mean... He is liable (properly subject) to some further response (overt blame, punishment civil suit, praise, reward, etc.) for it. (Feinberg 1988b, 110)

Here Feinberg treats the responsibility as entailing the liability. Hart, having previously endorsed much the same view (Hart 1968, 196), abandons it as oversimplified. Being responsible in the relevant sense does not entail being liable to certain responses, although the relevant ideas of responsibility and liability are 'very closely connected' (Hart 1967a, 350). What is the very close connection? To be liable-responsible, says Hart, is to meet 'a certain range of conditions' of liability—'mainly, but not exclusively, psychological' conditions—'it being assumed that all other conditions are satisfied' (Hart 1967a, 351). In extra-legal (or 'moral') contexts, says Hart, the relevant liability is usually an exposure to permissible blaming responses by others, also known as 'blameworthiness' (Hart 1968, 225). Some people indeed talk interchangeably of 'moral responsibility' and 'blameworthiness'. But to be morally responsible in the relevant sense is not to be blameworthy, says Hart. Rather, it is to meet 'a certain range of conditions' of blameworthiness. There are additional necessary conditions of blameworthiness which are not conditions of moral responsibility for the blameworthy act. That is true, Hart adds, even though we discuss the conditions of moral responsibility for the blameworthy act as conditions of moral responsibility only when we concede (at least for the sake of argument) that the other conditions of blameworthiness are met.

Hart's proposal certainly seems to be an improvement on Feinberg's. In the wake of some misadventure, one may intelligibly say 'I am responsible for that' or 'I take responsibility for that' in a way that already raises the spectre of normative consequences while leaving open (for further discussion) whether any normative consequences actually arise, and if so which ones (punishability? a duty to repair? a lost right to redress? etc). But then, we may ask, how is this consequential responsibility supposed to differ from basic responsibility, the possessor of which (according to Hart) also meets 'a certain range of conditions' of liability which are 'complex psychological characteristics'? Hart makes his list of (possible) conditions of consequential responsibility longer than his list of (actual) conditions of basic responsibility. He includes, for example, conditions of causal as well as psychological types. That is important, and I will return to it shortly. But Hart's main proposal for distinguishing basic responsibility from consequential responsibility is this. To talk of responsibility in the consequential sense is already necessarily to raise a question of blameworthiness or punishability or some other normative consequence. Whereas one may intelligibly talk of basic responsibility (Hart's 'capacity-responsibility') even 'where no particular question of blame or punishment is in issue' and 'simply to describe a person's psychological condition' (Hart 1968, 228).

We already know, from our discussion of basic responsibility, that this contrast is exaggerated. Basic responsibility is a moral status. While the law might not reflect it correctly in attaching normative consequences to actions, morality cannot but do so. So isn't it the case that, in sound moral thinking at least, basic responsibility and consequential responsibility tend to converge? Not quite. Here are some important differences between the two that emerge from our discussion of basic responsibility and that remain even once Hart's exaggeration is exposed.

(1) Being consequentially responsible is being in a certain kind of normative position for a certain kind of reason. Being basically responsible, by contrast, is having a certain kind of ability. In some cases, to be sure, it is part of one's normative position *qua* consequentially responsible that one is required or permitted to exercise one's ability *qua* basically responsible. The most natural normative consequence of wrongdoing, as I said, is that one acquires a duty to explain oneself by offering a justification or excuse for what one did. Often, indeed, this is the first normative consequence of wrongdoing, in the sense that one's exposure to certain other normative consequences of wrongdoing, such as punishment, depends on how well one performs one's duty to self-explain. Nevertheless the

duty to self-explain is not one's basic responsibility and is not entailed by it. The basically responsible have an ability that they are, as I said before, aptly expected to use. Indeed it is rationally defensible, all else being equal, that they use it. But it is quite another question whether they are required or permitted to use it, and in what circumstances, and addressing themselves to whom, and so on. These are questions of consequential rather than basic responsibility. A hallmark of the difference is that consequential responsibility may be responsibility *to* someone, such that one owes one's self-explanation to that person, or (put another way) that that person has a right to one's self-explanation.[17] Basic responsibility cannot be responsibility to someone, even though it can, *pace* Feinberg, be responsibility for something.

(2) Because consequential responsibility is imposed by a norm (by the moral or legal or other norm that attaches the normative consequence in question), the conditions of consequential responsibility may vary. Here I am thinking of the *material* as opposed to the *conceptual* conditions of consequential responsibility. Freedom of the will is often said to be a condition of moral responsibility, in the sense that nobody is consequentially responsible in morality (usually expressed as 'morally blameworthy') without it. This proposal strikes me as misguided in numerous ways. But put that aside for now. The point for now is that even if freedom of the will is a condition of consequential responsibility in morality, it is not a conceptual condition. Those who disagree about whether freedom of the will is required for moral responsibility are not thereby committed to disagreeing about the very concept of moral responsibility that is pertinent to their disagreement. One may agree on the conceptual conditions but disagree on the material conditions. This divide between material conditions and conceptual conditions can and must be drawn in respect of consequential responsibility, but it cannot be drawn in respect of basic responsibility. That is because the material conditions of basic responsibility are among the conceptual conditions of basic responsibility. This fact explains why Hart tries to analyse the concept of basic responsibility *exclusively* in terms of its material conditions, ie as a set of 'complex psychological characteristics of persons' without any built-in moral implications. That is a mistake, as we saw. But it is a mistake that reflects an insight. The material conditions of basic responsibility, unlike those of consequential responsibility, are conceptually determined and remain constant across all norms. That is one important way in which basic responsibility earns its name.

(3) The third difference is a consequence of the second. As already pointed out, basic responsibility cannot be assumed, imposed, assigned, transferred, excluded, etc, where this implies the exercise of some normative power over its incidence. The law, for example, cannot make one basically responsible when one is not, nor can it stop one from being basically responsible when one is. It can at best

---

[17] We sometimes reserve the word 'accountability' for that case. See Gardner 2007b, 194–200.

conjure up a fiction of one's basic responsibility, or lack of it, for certain purposes. Consequential responsibility, on the other hand, can be given or taken away or otherwise altered by the law, or by other authorities, without any hint of a fiction. It differs from basic responsibility in being incurred under and by virtue of a norm, viz a norm that attaches certain consequences, under certain conditions, to the violation of another norm. Such a consequence-attaching norm may in principle be created or revoked by an authority. By the same token such a norm may be created or revoked by promising, contracting, agreeing, and so on. So consequential responsibility, unlike basic responsibility, may be either self-imposed or other-imposed. Consider familiar utterances such as 'I hold you responsible', 'I accept responsibility', and 'I won't be held responsible'. When these refer to consequential responsibility, these are typically performative utterances which are intended to bring the world into line with themselves, to make themselves true by effecting some change of normative position. Whereas, when they refer to basic responsibility, the same utterances can only be interpreted as constative, intended to capture the truth that holds quite apart from the utterance.[18]

(4) The fourth difference is in turn a consequence of the third. As we saw already, one is only ever basically responsible for one's own actions (including, of course, one's own actions of contributing to the actions of others). This explains why, as Hart says, the expression 'he is responsible for his actions' is normally used to refer to basic responsibility (Hart 1968, 227). On the other hand, one may be consequentially responsible for the actions of others without contributing to those actions. This mode of consequential responsibility is known to the law as 'vicarious' responsibility. One acquires it by voluntary undertaking (promising, contracting, agreeing, or consenting to acquire it) or by entering into certain relationships or positions of which it is an incident (eg being an employer, being a parent, being a government minister). Because the identity of the responsible person in cases of consequential responsibility is not a foregone conclusion, talk of consequential responsibility, unlike talk of basic responsibility, performs a finger-pointing or allocative function. It answers a 'who?' question. It assumes (at least *arguendo*) that there are some adverse normative consequences to be borne by someone, and it answers the question of who is to bear them.[19]

This prompts a friendly reformulation of Hart's explanation of the concept of consequential responsibility. We may say: *A* is consequentially responsible if and only if, in the event of wrongdoing, some or all of the normative consequences of that wrongdoing will be *A*'s to bear. This reformulation allows us to see what unites the superficially miscellaneous 'certain range of conditions' that,

---

[18] I am borrowing John Searle's way of drawing the distinction (Searle 1989). Searle overcomes the destructive errors made by Austin in his original attempt to capture the distinction (see n 12 above).

[19] This yields a connection between consequential responsibility and justice, justice being the moral virtue of allocators. See Gardner 2000.

according to Hart, count as material conditions of consequential responsibility. Consider the material conditions under which one bears some specified norma- tive consequence of wrongdoing. Now subtract the fact that it was wrongdoing, and hence the material conditions of its being so. What are left are the material conditions of consequential responsibility (relative to that particular normative consequence). So the 'psychological' and 'causal' conditions that Hart mentions are material conditions of consequential responsibility only if they are not among the material conditions of the action's being wrong. This is an important restric- tion. Some but not all wrongs are causal wrongs (ie one does not commit them except by contributing, often in a specific way, to a certain result). Some but not all wrongs are intentional wrongs or advertent wrongs (ie one does not commit them unless one means to commit them or, as the case may be, unless one real- izes that one is committing them). Where wrongs of these types are concerned, certain 'causal' and 'psychological' conditions are not, *pace* Hart, material con- ditions of consequential responsibility for wrongdoing, because they belong to the material conditions of the wrongdoing itself. (Of course, some of them may still be material conditions of responsibility in some other sense. The causal conditions, for example, may be material conditions of what Hart calls 'causal responsibility', which is not under discussion here (Hart 1968, 214–15).)

If this is true, we have a puzzle. Hart relates consequential responsibility to basic responsibility in the following way. Of the conditions of basic responsibility, he writes:

These [also] constitute the most important criteria of moral liability-responsibility, though it is characteristic of most legal systems that they have given only tardy recogni- tion to all these capacities as criteria of legal responsibility. (Hart 1967a, 360)

So, for Hart, the conditions of basic responsibility figure among the material con- ditions ('criteria') of consequential responsibility, at least in morality. But haven't we just seen that this cannot quite be true? The material conditions of consequen- tial responsibility exclude the material conditions of wrongdoing. But don't the material conditions of wrongdoing include the conditions of basic responsibil- ity? One cannot commit a wrong unless one can violate a norm and one cannot violate a norm unless one is the kind of being—a basically responsible being— who can be guided by norms. Surely it follows that the material conditions of consequential responsibility also exclude the conditions of basic responsibility. This conclusion may seem counterintuitive. For it breaks an obvious link that one expects to find between the two senses of responsibility, viz that consequential responsibility depends upon basic responsibility.

Or does it? The possibility remains that basic responsibility is a material *precon-* dition, even though not a material condition, of consequential responsibility.[20]

---

[20] For a similar suggestion see Duff 1998. I also leave open the possibility that basic responsibil- ity is a precondition, rather than a condition, of wrongdoing.

I will call this 'the rudimentary link' between basic and consequential responsibility. What it means is that one must be basically responsible, or at least assumed to be basically responsible, for the question of one's consequential responsibility to arise in the first place. Only then do we move on to see whether the material conditions of consequential responsibility itself are satisfied.

Does the rudimentary link hold? It seems that it must. What is more, it is a conceptual link. For there to be wrongdoing that has normative consequences there must (conceptually) be a wrongdoer. And a wrongdoer, as we saw, must (conceptually) be a basically responsible agent. This simple answer, however, does not stay simple for long. Aren't there cases in which a fiction of basic responsibility may, with moral propriety, be sustained in the law (or in other institutional settings), so that the advertised precondition of consequential responsibility may be treated as satisfied when really it is not? And what about the fact that consequential responsibility, unlike basic responsibility, may be vicarious? Here F is the wrongdoer but G is consequentially responsible. Whose basic responsibility, F's or G's, is supposed to satisfy the advertised precondition in such a case?

These are troublesome questions. But they are questions about the justification of particular norms. These are not the questions that I want to emphasize for present purposes. Instead I want to focus on the implications of the rudimentary link for the way we think, more generally, about the moral importance of basic responsibility and consequential responsibility. A common thought is that the rudimentary link points to a way of explaining the moral importance of basic responsibility. The moral importance of basic responsibility stems from its role as a precondition of (morally defensible) consequential responsibility, which is morally important because of the independent moral importance of the various adverse normative consequences that fall within its scope. These consequences are morally important because of their unwelcomeness to the person who is subject to them. They threaten her interests. The explanation begins, in other words, with the interests that people have in not being punished, made to apologize, etc and works back from there to the moral importance of their basic responsibility. This I have elsewhere called the 'Hobbesian story' (Gardner 2007b, 179). It turns one's own responsibility, both consequential and (therefore) basic, into something to be *ceteris paribus* avoided, shirked, disclaimed, etc.

But one may equally reverse the whole explanation. One may equally argue: the moral importance of those adverse normative consequences that fall under the aegis of (morally defensible) consequential responsibility is, at least in part, owed to the fact that they have basic responsibility as a precondition of them. Think again about what it means to 'hold people responsible'. As I said, this turn of phrase may be interpreted performatively in relation to consequential responsibility, but only constatively in relation to basic responsibility. Yet notice that, even read in context, the turn of phrase is often ambiguous between these two very different interpretations. This ambiguity, it seems to me, is not obfuscating but revealing. It reflects the fact that one very powerful reason to hold someone consequentially responsible (performative 'hold') is that in the process one holds him basically responsible (constative 'hold'). One asserts *H*'s basic responsibility, in other words, by imposing consequential responsibility on *H*. This connects with the thought, sketched above, that human beings are defeasibly basically responsible. From this it follows that one treats *H* as a human being only if, in the absence of defeating conditions, one treats *H* as basically responsible. And that in turn yields a case for imposing consequential responsibility on *H* when *H* is indeed basically responsible, ie in the absence of defeating conditions. For imposing consequential responsibility on *H* is asserting *H*'s basic responsibility which is also affirming of *H*'s humanity. This is true, by the way, even if the consequential responsibility that one imposes on *H* is of a type, like the duty to repair or the duty to restitute, that is relatively unaffected by *H*'s justifications and excuses. The affirmation of *H*'s humanity does not lie in linking her consequential responsibility to her *success* in explaining herself (although that is sometimes required for independent reasons, as in the case of punishment and other blaming responses). Rather it lies in recognizing her *ability* to explain herself, her basic responsibility, by making her a candidate for consequential responsibility. This is possible, in turn, because the rudimentary link holds between basic and consequential responsibility. Here is what I elsewhere called the 'Aristotelian' story (Gardner 2007b, 179). It makes one's own responsibility, both basic and (therefore) consequential, into something to be prized, asserted, claimed, etc.

I still tend to think, as I did when I first applied these labels, that both stories are sound but that the Hobbesian story has enjoyed an ascendancy in modern thought that has been too much at the expense of the Aristotelian story. This, I think, is also Lucas's complaint. Feinberg and Hart are both, in their different ways, apt targets for the complaint. We already know that Feinberg gives a logical priority to consequential responsibility. He explains basic responsibility as a competence to fall under norms, including moral norms, of consequential responsibility. This points to consequential responsibility as the source of basic responsibility's moral importance. For any competence takes its moral importance from the norms that it is a competence to fall under. The more morally important the norms, the more morally important the competence. Hart, of course, does not fall into the same trap in the same way, for he does not understand basic responsibility as a competence. Yet he falls into the same trap in a different way. He understands basic responsibility to be a composite ability (correct) that is not in itself a moral status (incorrect). Since for him it is not in itself a moral status, it takes such moral importance as it has from something else. From what? Hart's only suggestion is that it takes its moral importance from the fact that it is a material condition of consequential responsibility according to 'morality [as] at present understood' (Hart 1968, 230). So Hart, like Feinberg, helps to maintain the ascendancy of the Hobbesian story.

3 Two Varieties of Responsibility

I have restricted my attention to just two of the several philosophically interesting 'varieties of responsibility' (to borrow Hart's phrase). I have restricted my attention to basic responsibility and consequential responsibility. I have not asserted that basic responsibility is logically the more basic of the two, in the sense that one cannot grasp the nature of consequential responsibility except in terms of it. I have merely rejected the opposite view as set out by Feinberg. Nor I have I argued that basic responsibility is morally the more basic of the two, in the sense that the moral importance of consequential responsibility is entirely derived from that of basic responsibility. Rather, I have suggested that there is a two way street here. The Hobbesian story and the Aristotelian story both explain part of the truth. So why—you may want to be reminded—is basic responsibility called 'basic'? There is more than one explanation. But the main explanation is that so much in our moral lives—indeed everything that makes our lives moral lives—turns on our possession of it. We are moral agents only insofar as we are basically responsible. This is what makes the Hobbesian story of the importance of basic responsibility more shallow than the Aristotelian. For it reduces to a specialized role in selecting people to bear adverse normative consequences something which, properly understood, goes to the very heart of all distinctively human life and experience.

PART III

CAUSATION IN THE LAW

8

Some Reflections on Hart and Honoré, *Causation in the Law*[1]

Judith Jarvis Thomson

1. It is a great book, nothing less. I am going to say something at the end about what marks it as a great book, but what I want to focus on is what has happened since its appearance to one of its most important theses.

Hart and Honoré—henceforth H&H—recommended that we opt for a certain formula governing what it comes to for a thing x to be what they called a 'causally relevant factor' in the coming about of a thing y. They said that for x to have caused y, more is required of x than that it have been a causally relevant factor in the coming about of y; I will comment on that idea later. For the time being, however, I will take H&H to have had causing in mind, not merely being a causally relevant factor. Interpreting their formula in a currently familiar way, the analysis of causing that it yields is attractive, and I take it to have friends among legal theorists nowadays. I am therefore going to draw attention to serious difficulties for it that philosophers have drawn attention to, difficulties in virtue of which they reject it.

But first, three preliminaries.

2. *First Preliminary*

Like many legal theorists, H&H used the words 'necessary' and 'sufficient' in discussing causation, and those terms are ambiguous: we just do not know what people are telling us about causation when they use those words unless they explicitly, or their texts implicitly, disambiguate.

Let 'x', 'y', and 'z' range over whatever causes and gets caused. Events, presumably; presumably states of affairs too. We say that events *occur* whereas states of affairs *obtain*, but for brevity, I will say of entities of both kinds that they do or do not *occur*.

And now: under what conditions does x cause y? Lawyers traditionally said the following words:

(Necessary Condition Formula)   x caused y just in case x was a necessary condition for y,

---

[1] Hart and Honoré 1959.

and they disambiguated—they made clear that what they meant to be offering us was the following analysis:

(Weak Necessary Condition Analysis)   x caused y just in case if x hadn't occurred, then y wouldn't have occurred.

They might have meant something stronger. There are several possibilities. Here is one—I stress that it is only one of several:

(Strong Necessary Condition Analysis)   x caused y just in case the proposition that x did not occur entails the proposition that y did not occur.

Of course nobody has ever thought *that* plausible. Let us assume throughout that Alfred threw a rock at Bert's window, and that his throwing his rock caused Bert's window to break. I am sure that nobody has ever thought that for that to be true is for it to be the case that the proposition that Alfred's rock-throwing didn't occur *entails* the proposition that Bert's window's breaking didn't occur. For it all too obviously might have been the case that Alfred's rock-throwing didn't occur but that Bert's window's breaking did occur all the same because Alice threw a rock at it instead.

So it is the Weak Necessary Condition Analysis that lawyers opted for. Alas, other lawyers found it easy to supply countercases. They drew attention to the possibility of overdetermination, that is, cases in which it is true of each of two things x and y, that it caused z. Philosophers have also found it easy to supply countercases: they typically focus on cases of what they call 'preemption'. Thus suppose that Alice not only might have been but actually was waiting in the wings, ready to throw her own rock at Bert's window if and only if Alfred's nerve failed him at the last moment. By hypothesis, Alfred's nerve didn't fail him, so Alice didn't throw her rock. Philosophers therefore say that Alfred's throwing his rock preempted Alice's throwing her rock. But although the window would have broken even if Alfred hadn't thrown a rock at it, his rock-throwing did cause the window to break.[2]

Having drawn attention to the fact that the Weak Necessary Condition Analysis won't do, H&H offered us something they thought better, and we will turn to it in section 5.

3. *Second Preliminary*
It isn't merely the word 'necessary' that is ambiguous: different legal theorists have meant different things by calling something *strongly* or only *weakly* necessary for

---

[2] David Lewis's analysis of causation is a sophisticated variant on the Weak Necessary Condition Analysis, and is capable of making room for some preemption cases—in particular, that of Alfred and Alice. See Lewis 1973a. Other preemption cases made trouble for it, however. A helpful discussion of the difficulties and of efforts to respond may be found in Collins, Hall, and Paul 2004a.

something else. I therefore want to bring out in what I hope is a perspicuous way my reason for labelling the two interpretations of the Necessary Condition Formula as I did.

My reason lies in a way of understanding the locutions I used that issued from the relatively recent development in philosophy of possible world semantics for modal logic. A philosopher may nowadays say that for the proposition that x did not occur to entail the proposition that y did not occur is for it to be the case that in all possible worlds in which x does not occur, y also does not occur. (In short, it just isn't possible for x to not occur without y's also not occurring.) That means that we can rewrite the Strong Necessary Condition Analysis as follows:

(Strong Necessary Condition Analysis*)   x caused y just in case in all possible worlds in which x does not occur, y also does not occur.

The development I refer to supplied the means by which to give—for the first time—a satisfactory account of what is asserted by people who assert counterfactual conditionals, such as sentences of the form:

If x hadn't occurred, then y wouldn't have occurred.[3]

According to that account, for an assertion of such a sentence to be true is for it to be the case that in the closest possible world in which x did not occur, y also did not occur. In other words, and roughly, 'If x hadn't occurred, then y wouldn't have occurred' is true just in case if you imagine a possible world as similar to our actual world as possible, compatibly with its being the case that x didn't occur in that world, then y also didn't occur in that world.[4] (I add explicitly, since I will rely on the point later, that if x did not occur in our actual world, then the closest possible world in which x did not occur is our own actual world itself.) Given that

---

[3] The account, widely accepted nowadays, is due to Stalnaker 1968 and Lewis 1973b. H&H report that many modern writers insist that 'the only factual element in the question whether a defendant's act is for legal purposes the cause of harm is whether or not the harm would have happened without the act' (Hart and Honoré 1959, 85). That confidence in the 'factuality' of counterfactuals might well surprise philosophers in the empiricist tradition, since until the appearance of the Stalnaker-Lewis account of counterfactuals, they typically regarded counterfactuals as deeply suspect: many took the view that counterfactuals have no truth-values.

[4] My summary of the account relies on the assumption that there is such a thing as *the* closest possible world in which x does not occur. There is no need to make so strong an assumption, and current friends of the account do not make it. They say instead: 'If x hadn't occurred, then y wouldn't have occurred' is true just in case there is a possible world in which x does not occur and y also does not occur that is closer to the actual world than any possible world in which x does not occur but y does occur. As David Lewis put the matter: 'If x hadn't occurred, then y wouldn't have occurred' is true just in case it takes less of a departure from actuality to make it the case that y does not occur given that x does not occur than it does to make it the case that y does occur given that x does not occur—see Lewis 1973a. But I abbreviate, since our purposes do not require that we be careful in this way.

account of counterfactual conditionals, we can say that what the Weak Necessary Condition Analysis says is:

(Weak Necessary Condition Analysis*)   x caused y just in case in the closest possible world in which x didn't occur, y also didn't occur.

And now it is clear in what way the Strong Necessary Condition Analysis is stronger than the Weak Necessary Condition Analysis. As you can see, the strong one entails but is not entailed by the weak one.

4. *Third Preliminary*

What I have in mind here is that it might have struck you to wonder why lawyers who reject not only the Strong Necessary Condition Analysis but also the Weak Necessary Condition Analysis haven't tried on for size a Sufficient Condition Analysis. To the best of my knowledge, there isn't any extended discussion of the possibility that you might have thought would strike a lawyer, namely that we should invert the Necessary Condition Sentence, and opt for:

(Sufficient Condition Formula)   x caused y just in case x was a sufficient condition for y,

meaning by that:

(Weak Sufficient Condition Analysis)   x caused y just in case if y hadn't occurred, then x wouldn't have occurred.

I offered you the weak thesis, rather than the analogous strong thesis:

(Strong Sufficient Condition Analysis)   x caused y just in case the proposition that y did not occur entails the proposition that x did not occur

because the strong one is so obviously not acceptable. We are supposing that Alfred's throwing a rock at Bert's window caused it to break, but it plainly isn't the case that the proposition that Bert's window's breaking did not occur entails the proposition that Alfred's rock-throwing did not occur. It wasn't, but might have been the case that Bert's window's breaking didn't occur, though Alfred's throwing a rock at it did occur. For example, it might have been the case that Annabel nobly jumped into the path of the rock, deflecting it away from Bert's window.

But then why not opt for the Weak Sufficient Condition Analysis? There are objections to it from Annabel that are first cousins of the objection to the Weak Necessary Condition Analysis from Alice. Suppose that Annabel not only might have jumped into the path of the rock but was prepared to, and would have—but for the fact that she noticed a butterfly, which distracted her. Then if Alfred had firmly committed himself to throwing his rock, it is at least as plausible to say

(1) If Bert's window's breaking hadn't occurred, then Alfred's rock-throwing would have occurred but Annabel's noticing the butterfly wouldn't have occurred

as it is to say

(2) If Bert's window's breaking hadn't occurred, then Alfred's rock-throwing wouldn't have occurred.

But there is a second, and more interesting, objection to the Weak Sufficient Condition Analysis. Accepting the Weak *Necessary* Condition Analysis commits us to accepting that the likes of

(3) If Alfred's rock-throwing hadn't occurred, then Bert's window's breaking wouldn't have occurred

might well be true. If Alice was waiting in the wings, and would have thrown a rock if Alfred hadn't, then (3) isn't in fact true. But it might have been true. What (3) tells us is that if a certain event hadn't occurred, then the world future to that event would have been different from what it actually was—and we often say such things, often truly.

Accepting the Weak *Sufficient* Condition Analysis commits us to accepting that the likes of (1) and (2) might well be true. But there is something odd about them. What they tell us is that if a certain event hadn't occurred, then the world prior to that event would have been different from what it actually was. David Lewis therefore calls (1) and (2) *backtracking* counterfactuals.[5]

Lewis says that we standardly view the future as dependent on the present. Thus we take it that whether or not Alfred now throws a rock at a window affects what will happen later—in particular, whether the window will break. We do not standardly view the past as dependent on the present. Thus we do not take it that whether or not a window now breaks affects what did happen earlier—in particular, whether a person did throw a rock at it, or whether a person did notice a butterfly. We think of the future as open, the past as fixed. And that we think this explains why—special contexts apart—saying (1) and (2) is saying something odd.

Indeed, I suspect that it is not because of possibilities like that of Annabel that lawyers haven't opted for the Weak Sufficient Condition Analysis: rather it is because of the oddity of backtracking counterfactuals such as (1) and (2) that opting for that analysis would commit them to the possible truth of.

In any case, lawyers haven't opted for the Weak Sufficient Condition Analysis, so let us turn now to H&H.

5. What H&H said was the words: x caused y just in case '[x] is one of a set of conditions jointly sufficient for the production of the consequence [y]: [x] is necessary because it is required to complete this set.' (Hart and Honoré 1959, 106). Thus, as I'll put it:

(Necessary/Sufficient Condition Formula)   x caused y just in case x was a necessary member of a set of things that were jointly sufficient for y.

---

[5] See Lewis 1973a and 1979.

But of course it should be clear by now that the words 'necessary' and 'sufficient' need disambiguation if we are to have an analysis before us. It is the single most important point of this paper that if a legal theorist (or anyone else) offers us an analysis of causation by use of those words, then we simply do not know what analysis he is offering us unless he tells us what he means by them.

The currently most familiar way of interpreting the words yields an analysis that is a version of what JL Mackie later called an INUS condition, what Jonathan Bennett still later called an NS condition, and if I have understood him, Richard Wright calls a NESS condition.[6]

Laying it out requires that we begin with a bit of ontology. As most commonly understood nowadays, the analysis is an analysis of the conditions under which one fact causes another fact. We don't normally think of *facts* as entering into causal relations with each other: we normally think it is events and states of affairs that do. Let us bypass the difficulty that arises here. Suppose that the analysis yields that the fact that Alfred threw a rock at Bert's window caused the fact that Bert's window broke. Then we can go on to say that the event that consisted in Alfred's rock-throwing caused the event that consisted in the window's breaking—which is what I invited you to assume at the outset.

Let us say, moreover, that facts correspond one-to-one with true propositions: thus for every fact F there is a unique true proposition P_F that corresponds to it, and for every true proposition P_F there is a unique fact F that corresponds to it. And let us say, finally, that LAWS is the conjunction of all scientific laws.

So much for ontology. Here is the analysis:

(Fact/Entailment Necessary/ Sufficient Condition Analysis)
   fact F caused fact G just in case P_F does not entail P_G, and P_G does not entail P_F, and P_F is a member of a set S of true propositions such that
   (i) the conjunction of LAWS with all of the members of S entails P_G, and
   (ii) the conjunction of LAWS with all of the members of S other than P_F does not entail P_G.[7]

Notice that there are no counterfactuals in the analysans here.

For example, consider Alfred and Bert's window. We are assuming that Alfred's rock-throwing caused Bert's window's breaking. What makes that true?

---

[6] Mackie 1974 and Bennett 1988. Wright's view is presented in a series of articles, most recently Wright 2001.

[7] I included the first two clauses for the following reason: friends of the idea at work here do not want to allow their analysis to yield that the fact that Charles is a bachelor caused, or was caused by, the fact that he is male. (An analogous constraint should have been imposed on the Weak Necessary Condition Analysis. No friend of that analysis wants to allow his analysis to yield that the event that consisted in Charles's eating both a banana and an apple caused, or was caused by, the event that consisted in his eating a banana.)

Jonathan Bennett would have us strengthen the analysans I supplied; I discuss the most important of his strengthenings below.

Well, suppose that Alfred's rock-throwing occurred at T, and that the following propositions are true:

(1) At T, Alfred threw a rock of weight α from place P toward place P* along path β with velocity γ,
(2) Bert's window was at place P* at T, and remained there for at least the time δ it would take a rock of weight α thrown from place P toward place P* along path β with velocity γ to reach place P*,
(3) Bert's window was made of glass of thickness ε,
(4) There was nothing along path β between times T and T+δ massive enough to deflect a rock moving along it of weight α moving with velocity γ.

Suppose also that LAWS has among its conjuncts:

(LAW-1)   If at T, a person throws a rock of weight α from place P toward place P* along path β with velocity γ, *and* a window is at place P* at T, and remains there for at least the time δ it would take a rock of weight α thrown from place P toward place P* along path β with velocity γ to reach place P*, *and* the window is made of glass of thickness ε, *and* there is nothing along path β between times T and T+δ massive enough to deflect a rock moving along it of weight α moving with velocity γ, then the window breaks at T+δ.

That's a funny-looking scientific law: there certainly isn't anything in physics that tells us about people, rocks, and windows. Still, we can suppose it is a low-level law, deducible from higher level laws.

Then it is plain that (i) the conjunction of LAWS with (1) through (4) entails that Bert's window broke at T+δ, and therefore entails that Bert's window broke.

Is that plain? It might be objected that further conditions have to be included in the antecedent of (LAW-1), and propositions added to our set that say that those further conditions are met, if (i) is to be true—as, for example, that the rock thrown was solid enough to not fall apart when thrown with velocity γ. Let us ignore this difficulty. Let us pretend that (LAW-1) *is* a law, and therefore that its conjunction with (1) through (4) *does* entail that Bert's window broke at T+δ.

We may surely suppose, finally, that (ii) the conjunction of LAWS with (2) through (4) does not entail that Bert's window broke. Our analysis therefore yields—as it should—that the fact that Alfred threw his rock caused the fact that Bert's window broke.

The analysis is attractive in several ways. First, it invites attention to the fact that if x caused y, then it is typically against a background of other events and states of affairs that it did. Alfred's rock-throwing caused Bert's window's breaking, but only in that Bert's window was in such and such a place, and was of thickness so and so, and so on.

Second, it copes very easily with certain preemptions that make trouble for the Weak Necessary Condition Analysis.[8] Consider Alice again, and suppose that she was in fact waiting in the wings, ready to throw her rock if and only if Alfred didn't throw his. Well, Alfred did throw his rock, so she didn't. But if he hadn't thrown his rock, she would have, and Bert's window would therefore have broken anyway, and the Weak Necessary Condition Analysis is therefore false. By contrast, a friend of the analysis we are looking at now has no trouble with Alice. For whether or not Alice was waiting in the wings, ready to throw if Alfred did not, makes no difference to whether or not (i) the conjunction of LAWS with (1) through (4) entails that Bert's window broke, and (ii) the conjunction of LAWS with (2) through (4) does not entail that Bert's window broke. Thus, on this analysis, whether or not Alice was waiting in the wings, ready to throw if Alfred did not, makes no difference to whether or not Alfred's rock-throwing caused Bert's window's breaking.

Third, the analysis makes room for causation by omissions and absences without ontological nervousness. Suppose the gardener, Jones, did not water the plants. We might well think it the case that Jones's not watering the plants caused their death. Was there such an event as his not watering the plants? Or should we say that his not watering the plants was a state of affairs? No matter. Friends of this analysis can point to what, on any view, there is, namely a fact to the effect that Jones did not water the plants, and they can ask whether the analysis yields that that fact caused the plants' death.[9]

Fourth, the analysis makes law-like connections between x and y crucial to its being the case that x caused y, and it is very plausible to think that they are.

It is therefore unfortunate that there are serious objections to the analysis. I will describe two of them. First, there are cases of preemption that make trouble for it. Here is an example. I assume that there are poisons for which there are no antidotes, and which are such that a physiologically normal person who drinks n

---

[8] Strevens (2007) brings out that this analysis is also safe against certain preemptions that make trouble for David Lewis's sophisticated variant on the Weak Necessary Condition Analysis. (I thank Stephen Yablo for drawing my attention to Strevens's article.) Strevens also brings out, however, that there are preemptions that do make trouble for this analysis, as well as other objections to it.

[9] Without *ontological* nervousness, but arguably not satisfactorily. If the plants died for lack of watering, then it was not only Jones who did not water them, Queen Elizabeth also did not water them. Are we prepared to accommodate the conclusion that the fact that she didn't water them caused their death?—for it is not at all clear how this analysis is to yield that Jones's not watering them caused their death without also yielding that Queen Elizabeth's not watering them caused their death.

I bypass this difficulty in the text below, however, partly because omissions make trouble for every analysis of causation, and partly because some people would say that the fact that Queen Elizabeth didn't water the plants did cause their death (as also did the fact that Jones didn't water them)—though it would typically be pragmatically out of order to say so, and though, since she was under no duty to water them, she is not appropriately held liable for their death.

I mention a different way of dealing with omissions in n 12 below.

ounces of them dies within fifteen minutes. Let us suppose that cyanide is among them. Then I take it that LAWS has among its conjuncts:

(LAW-2)   If at T, a physiologically normal person drinks n ounces of cyanide, then the person is dead by T+15.

(I stress that this is no less plausibly viewable as a law than LAW-1 is. Normal human physiology being what it is, it is not a mere happenstance truth that any physiologically normal person who drinks n ounces of cyanide dies within fifteen minutes: any physiologically normal person who does that *must* die within fifteen minutes.)

Suppose, then, that the time now is T+16, and that the following propositions are true:

(6)   At T, Charles was a physiologically normal person,
(7)   At T, Charles drank n ounces of cyanide.

The conjunction of LAW-2 with (6) and (7) entails that Charles died by T+15. I take it that there is no law such that the conjunction of it with (6) entails that Charles died by T+15. The analysis therefore yields that Charles's drinking the cyanide caused his being dead by T+15, and therefore caused his death. But we can suppose that it did not cause his death—for we can suppose that David shot Charles in the head at T+1, and that Charles died at T+2, thus before his drinking the cyanide had had time to cause his death. In short, we can suppose that David's shot preempted Charles's drinking the cyanide, and that *it*—not Charles's drinking the cyanide—caused Charles's death.

I will call that the preemption objection. There is a second objection, which I will call the entailment objection. It is easy to see what it is; many people have drawn attention to it. Consider the set of true propositions that we get if we replace (1) in our original set by both:

(1a)   Caesar crossed the Rubicon,

and

(1b)   Either Caesar didn't cross the Rubicon, or at T, Alfred threw a rock of weight α from place P toward place P* along path β with velocity γ.

If the conjunction of LAWS with (1) through (4) entails that Bert's window broke, then the conjunction of LAWS with the members of this revised set entails that Bert's window broke. It can be seen also that the conjunction of LAWS with the members of this set other than (1a) does not entail that Bert's window broke. The analysis therefore yields that Caesar's crossing the Rubicon caused Bert's window's breaking. That will hardly do!

6. Perhaps there is a way of emending the analysis so as to make it safe against those objections?

Here is a way of emending it that has been suggested, and that would make it safe against the entailment objection: require that the set S not contain any disjunctions. Alas, every proposition is expressible by a disjunctive sentence, and it is not clear what else could be thought to mark a proposition as a disjunction.

Here is another: require of the members of the set S of true propositions that they report facts that are causally relevant to the coming about of fact G. The fact that Caesar crossed the Rubicon was causally irrelevant to the coming about of the fact that Bert's window broke. So that example is not a countercase to the emended analysis.

Alternatively, require that LAWS have a conjunct whose antecedent lists only conditions that would be causally relevant to the coming about of fact G if they were met, and that the members of the set S of true propositions report only facts that meet those conditions. Since the fact that Caesar crossed the Rubicon was causally irrelevant to the coming about of fact G, we can suppose that even if the following is a law, namely

If Caesar crossed the Rubicon, *and* either Caesar didn't cross the Rubicon or at T, a person throws a rock of weight α from place P toward place P* along path β with velocity γ, *and* a window is at place P* at T, and remains there...*and*...*and*..., then the window breaks at T+δ,

it does not meet the requirement. So (again) that example is not a countercase to the emended analysis.

Now I am sure that the fact that Caesar crossed the Rubicon was causally irrelevant to the fact that Bert's window broke. But what is supposed to mark it as having been causally irrelevant?

The analysis we were originally offered is an analysis of causation in non-causal terms. What emending it in either of those two ways does is to weaken it: the results are analyses of 'causes' in terms of 'causally relevant fact'. That is no ground for thinking that the results are false, but only a ground for thinking they tell us less than we wanted to know. Moreover, we should notice that our ability to bring the results to bear on an example rests all too heavily on our ability to find out whether one fact is causally relevant to another. Once we have found out that the fact that Alfred threw his rock was causally relevant to the fact that the window broke, whereas the fact that Caesar crossed the Rubicon was not, the emended analyses make it trivially easy to draw the conclusion that the one did, whereas the other did not, cause the fact of the window's breaking.

A similar objection can be made to a similar idea about how to make the analysis safe against the preemption objection. Thus it might be suggested that we should require that LAWS contain a conjunct that is a causal law, where a causal law is a conditional such that if there is a fact that makes its antecedent true, then that fact causes a fact that makes its consequent true. In particular, then,

(LAW-2)   If at T, a physiologically normal person drinks n ounces of cyanide, then the person is dead by T+15 is not a causal law, since a physiologically normal person can drink n ounces of cyanide and that not cause there to be a fact that makes its consequent true. So that example is not a countercase to the emended analysis. But this emendation is even more obviously unhelpful. The result is an analysis of 'causes' in terms of 'causal law', supplemented by a definition of 'causal law' in terms of 'causes'.

7. An idea that all but suggests itself by way of response to the preemption objection is that what is missing in the analysis is a requirement that there be a causal route from the (putative) cause to the (putative) effect. When Charles drank the cyanide, a process got under way in him. But that process was interrupted: it failed to reach its terminus in Charles's death only because David's shot started a second process, and this second process reached Charles's death faster.

Indeed, LAW-2 is a law *because* a physiologically normal person's drinking cyanide starts a process that—if uninterrupted—ends in death within fifteen minutes. Similarly, what makes LAW-1 *be* a law is that a rock-throwing that has the features mentioned in its antecedent starts a process that ends in the window's breaking δ minutes later. It is a very attractive idea that if two past events, x and y, were discrete, then x caused y only if there is an answer to the question *how* x caused y, and that the answer to that question has to lie in x's having started a process that ended in y.

Shall we say that x caused y just in case x started a process that ended in y? That needs precisification, for not just any sequence of events will do. So shall we say that x caused y just in case x started a causal process that ended in y? But that again is not an analysis of causation in non-causal terms.

Jonathan Bennett suggested that we can capture the idea at work here in the following way. Let us say that the relation between fact F and fact G analysed by the Fact/Entailment Necessary/Sufficient Condition Analysis is not causation, but is instead the relation NS. Thus we are to say that

fact F has NS to fact G just in case P_F does not entail P_G, and P_G does not entail P_F, and P_F is a member of a set S of true propositions such that
(i) the conjunction of LAWS with all of the members of S entails P_G, and
(ii) the conjunction of LAWS with all of the members of S other than P_F does not entail P_G.

Then we are to say:

fact F caused fact G just in case for every time t_j between the time to which F pertains and the time to which G pertains, there is a fact f_j pertaining to t_j such that f_j belongs to a temporally ordered sequence of facts, running from F to G, each of which has NS to the next.[10]

---

[10] Bennett 1988, 46. Bennett says that his emendation is adapted from Lewis's procedure for emending the Weak Necessary Condition Analysis in such a way as to make the result safe from examples of preemption such as that of Alfred and Alice—see n 2 above.

(I leave it to intuition, as does Bennett, what counts as a fact 'pertaining' to a time.)

This emendation goes half way to making the resulting analysis safe against the preemption objection issuing from the case of Charles and David. By hypothesis, the time now is T+16, and: Charles drank n ounces of cyanide at T, David shot Charles in the head at T+1, and Charles died at T+2, before the cyanide had had time to cause Charles's death. So let F be the fact that at T, Charles drank n ounces of cyanide, and G be the fact that Charles died at T+2. Did F cause G? I take it that the emended analysis (rightly) yields that it did not. For by hypothesis, the cyanide had not had time to cause Charles's death by T+2. So consider a temporally ordered sequence of facts running from F toward G, each of which has NS to the next. I take it we can assume that however close in time we get to T+2, there is no fact f_j in the sequence such that the conjunction of P_{f_j} with a law entails that Charles *died at T+2*—thus no fact in the sequence has NS to G.

But the emendation only goes half way. Let F (again) be the fact that at T, Charles drank n ounces of cyanide, but now let G^* be the fact that Charles died. (Charles has already died, since by hypothesis, the time now is T+16.)

And consider a temporally ordered sequence of facts running from F toward G^*, each of which has NS to the next. Cyanide being by hypothesis a poison for which there is no antidote, and for which LAW-2 is true, we may well suppose that for every fact f_j in the sequence, the conjunction of P_{f_j} with a law entails that Charles *died by T+15*, and therefore that Charles *died*—thus every fact in the sequence has NS to G^*.

The trouble for this emendation issues from its being facts whose causal relations we are analysing. The event that consisted in Charles's dying at T+2 is, on any plausible view of event-identity, identical with the event that consisted in Charles's dying. But following Bennett, it is facts that we are dealing with, and the fact that Charles died at T+2 isn't, on any plausible view of fact-identity, identical with the fact that Charles died.

We should notice, moreover, that even if the emendation Bennett recommends did result in an analysis that is safe against the preemption objection issuing from the case of Charles and David, the result is not safe against the second objection I drew attention to, namely the entailment objection.

I repeat, however, that the idea that motivated Bennett's emendation remains very attractive. It really is plausible to think that if two past events, x and y, were discrete, then x caused y only if there is an answer to the question *how* x caused y, and that the answer to that question has to lie in x's having started a process—a causal process—that ended in y. But it remains an open question how that idea is to be analysed.

8. Perhaps there is some other analysis that provides the benefits of the one we looked at in the preceding sections but without its defects?

Perhaps we should reinterpret

(Necessary/Sufficient Condition Formula)   x caused y just in case x was a necessary member of a set of things that were jointly sufficient for y

as governing events and states of affairs, and 'necessary' and 'sufficient' in terms of counterfactuals in accord with the Weak Necessary Condition Analysis and Weak Sufficient Condition Analysis? I don't believe that anyone has ever been tempted by this idea, but it might just barely be worth looking at what happens if we accept it.

Thus we might try analysing out 'necessary' by way of the following first step:

x caused y just in case x and y are discrete, and x is a member of a set S of things such that
(i*)   the members of S were sufficient for y, and
(ii*) if x hadn't occurred but the other members of S had occurred, then those other members of S would not have been sufficient for y.

And then, analysing out 'sufficient' by way of the following second step:

x caused y just in case x and y are discrete, and x is a member of a set S of things such that
(i)   if y hadn't occurred, then at least one member of S wouldn't have occurred, and
(ii) if x hadn't occurred but the other members of S had occurred, then it would not be the case that: if y hadn't occurred, then at least one of those other members of S wouldn't have occurred.

Condition (i) is easy enough to understand. Let @ be the actual world. Let w_1 be the world closest to @ in which y does not occur. Then (i) is true just in case at least one member of S doesn't occur in w_1. But (ii) is hard to understand, since it contains the negation of a counterfactual embedded in a counterfactual. Let w_2 be the world closest to @ in which x doesn't occur but the other members of S do occur. Let w_3 be the world closest to w_2 in which y doesn't occur. Then (ii) is true just in case it is *not* the case that: at least one of the members of S other than x doesn't occur in w_3. Alternatively put, (ii) is true just in case all of the members of S other than x do occur in w_3.

It should be noticed that you cannot accept this analysis of causation unless you are willing to accept that backtracking counterfactuals can be true, for interpreting 'sufficient' in accord with the Weak Sufficient Condition Analysis commits you to them. On some views, that is a conclusive ground for rejecting it.

But suppose you are prepared to accept that backtracking counterfactuals can be true? Well, then, consider an example. Suppose that in the actual world, @, Alfred threw a rock at Bert's window, and caused it to break. Anne then threw another rock at Bert's window, which didn't break the window again: her rock instead passed right through the hole in the window made by Alfred's rock. I add that Alfred had been of two minds about whether to throw his rock, and had finally decided it would on balance be best to throw it, which he did; Anne, by contrast, firmly intended to throw her rock if and only if Alfred threw his. I add finally that if neither Alfred nor Anne had thrown a rock at Bert's window, then it would not have broken.

The analysis before us yields that Anne's throwing her rock caused the window to break—which is, by hypothesis, false. For let S be the set of things whose members are the following two events that occurred in @:

(1) Anne's throwing a rock at Bert's window.
(2) Caesar's crossing of the Rubicon.

The fact that (1) and (2) occurred doesn't entail that the window broke. Again, the conjunction of LAWS with the propositions that (1) occurred and that (2) occurred doesn't entail that the window broke. But that is irrelevant. It is counterfactuals that we are to rely on here.

Very well, we can suppose that condition (i) is met for this set S, for we can suppose that in the world closest to @ in which the window didn't break, namely w_1, Alfred decided not to throw his rock, and did not, and therefore Anne did not throw hers. So (1) didn't occur in w_1, so at least one member of S didn't occur in w_1.

Similarly, we can suppose that condition (ii) is met. For let w_2 be the world closest to @ in which Anne didn't throw her rock but Caesar did cross the Rubicon. Given Anne's firm intention, we can suppose that Alfred also did not throw his rock in w_2, so we can suppose that the window did not break in w_2. Let w_3 be the world closest to w_2 in which the window did not break. If w_2 is a world in which the window did not break, and w_3 is the world closest to w_2 in which the window did not break, then $w_3 = w_2$. But in w_3, the member of S other than Anne's throw—namely Caesar's crossing of the Rubicon—did occur.

It follows that Anne's throwing her rock caused the window to break.

It is of course the availability of backtracking counterfactuals that makes this refutation of the analysis possible. But then, as I said, it is only if backtracking counterfactuals are available that one can accept the analysis in the first place.

9. In section 2, I drew attention to the familiar fact that the simpler counterfactual analysis we looked at first, namely

(Weak Necessary Condition Analysis)   x caused y just in case if x hadn't occurred, then y wouldn't have occurred,

did not work. Let us look more closely now at the reason why it doesn't work.

In an article published in 1995, and entitled 'Necessary and Sufficient Conditions in Tort Law', Tony Honoré may (I think) be interpreted as arguing for the Fact/Entailment Necessary/Sufficient Condition Analysis. But counterfactuals put in an appearance along the way. Honoré says:

Suppose we want to test the assertion that Churchill kept Britain in the war in 1940. Was the fact that he was Prime Minister the cause of Britain remaining in the war?

He points out that if Churchill hadn't been Prime Minister, someone else would have been, and he goes on:

we must then ask whether that person would have wanted and been able to convince Parliament and the British people to continue the war. The causal statement about Churchill implicitly contrasts him with this hypothetical substitute...[who] might or might not have kept Britain in the war.

And he adds that if

someone other than Churchill had been in office, his colleagues would have been less afraid of contradicting him, and this must be taken into account in answering the historical question about 1940. (Honoré 1995, 104)

The idea Honoré is moved by here certainly appears to be the Weak Necessary Condition Analysis—which Honoré in 1995 (like Hart and Honoré in 1959) explicitly rejects.

But I think it was entirely reasonable on Honoré's part to take it that a person who asks that historical question about 1940 may want to know something for the answer to which arriving at a counterfactual is required. For what the person wants to know may well be whether Britain's remaining in the war depended on Churchill's being Prime Minister. Answering *that* question does require finding out what would have happened had Churchill not been Prime Minister.

Ned Hall points out that there are two questions that we might ask about the relation between x and y. On the one hand, there is the question whether x *produced* y; on the other hand, there is the question whether y *depended on* x (Hall 2004). That these are not the same emerges clearly the moment our attention is drawn to them. Suppose there is a key such that if anyone turns it, he or she will thereby start Donald's car. Carl and Carol both reached for the key, but Carl got to it first. Then his turning the key produced the car's starting; but the car's starting didn't depend on his turning the key, since if his turning the key hadn't occurred, Carol would have turned it. In short, 'x produced y' does not entail 'y was dependent on x'.

Hall also claims that 'y was dependent on x' does not entail 'x produced y'. Assume, for the purpose of a *reductio*, that 'y was dependent on x' *does* entail 'x produced y'. And now suppose that Alix learned that Alfred planned to throw a rock at Bert's window, and that she therefore raced out to stop him. Let x be her racing out to stop Alfred from throwing his rock at Bert's window. Suppose that if she had reached Alfred, she would have stopped him and the window wouldn't have broken. On the way, however, she tripped and fell, and therefore wasn't able to reach Alfred. So Alfred—unaware of Alix, whose fall occurred some blocks away—threw his rock, thereby breaking the window. Let y be the window's breaking. We can say that y depended on Alix's fall (since y wouldn't have occurred if she hadn't fallen); so given our assumption, 'her fall produced y' is true. We can also say that Alix's fall depended on x (since her fall wouldn't have occurred if she hadn't raced out to stop Alfred from throwing his rock); so given our assumption, 'x produced her fall' is true. So both of the following are true: 'her fall produced y' and 'x produced her fall'. But, says Hall, producing is surely transitive. It follows that x produced y. That is, Alix's racing out to stop Alfred from throwing his rock produced the window's breaking. But, says Hall, that conclusion is 'just silly'. And I take it that we should agree. If we do, we have to reject the assumption we made for the purpose of a *reductio*: we have to agree that 'y was dependent on x' does *not* entail 'x produced y'.

Hall calls cases like that one 'double prevention' cases: here x (Alix's racing out to stop Alfred) would have prevented y (the window's breaking), if not for its having produced an event (Alix's fall), which prevented it from preventing y.

I said I take it that we should agree with Hall that it is just silly to conclude that x produced y. But it is worth mention that not everyone agrees: on some views, x did produce y, though it would typically be pragmatically odd to say so. Again, not everyone agrees that production is transitive: on some views, the existence of double prevention is among the grounds for rejecting the idea that production is transitive. For my own part, I share Hall's intuitions on those matters. But as I know of no arguments for them, I leave it open to you to reject them.

Hall concludes, in any case, that there are two concepts of 'causation': one is dependence, and the other is production. Once we have had our attention drawn to the difference between dependence and production, I think we are likely to prefer the idea that causation is just production, dependence being something quite different. No matter. Hall is surely right, anyway, in saying that the question whether x produced y is not the same as the question whether y depended on x—and that the answer to the latter is fixed by whether y would have occurred if x had not, whereas the answer to the former is not.

Then what does fix the answer to the question whether x produced y? I return to that question shortly. Let us first return to Honoré's historical question. A person who asks it may want to know what events Churchill's being Prime Minister produced, and in particular, whether his being Prime Minister produced Britain's remaining in the war. But as I said, another person who asks it may well want to know, instead, whether Britain's remaining in the war depended on Churchill's being Prime Minister—thus whether Britain would have remained in the war even if Churchill had not been Prime Minister. (A third person may, of course, want to know both.) It is the second person that Honoré plainly had in mind.

In light of the difference between those two questions, one might wonder why it seemed to so many lawyers an attractive idea that x caused y just in case y would not have occurred if x had not occurred—thus an attractive idea that x caused y just in case y depended on x. Why dependence? Why not production? Perhaps because it was (and remains!) hard to see what production could consist in if it does not consist in dependence? Perhaps, instead, out of the thought that blame and praise attach specially to dependence?—thus, for example, that a person deserves the more praise, and another person the more blame, if the outcomes of their acts are not, or are not merely, produced by their acts but dependent on their acts? I doubt that that is everywhere true. In any case, I leave the question open.

For brevity, and because it seems to me intuitively right, I from here on assume that there is just the one concept 'causation', and that it just is 'production'.

10. What does fix the answer to the question whether x produced y, or as I now say, the question whether x caused y? There are counterfactual analyses of causation that are more sophisticated than the Weak Necessary Condition Analysis, and more plausible than the one we extracted in section 8 from the Necessary/Sufficient Condition Formula by use of the interpretations of 'necessary' and 'sufficient' supplied by the Weak Necessary Condition Analysis and the Weak Sufficient Condition Analysis. There also have been efforts to analyse causation that are not counterfactual analyses; these include analyses that are in the spirit of the Fact/Entailment Necessary/Sufficient Condition Analysis. But it's a jungle out there! There is no analysis that is regarded as satisfactory by a substantial number of philosophers.

Moreover, some philosophers believe that there is no such thing as an analysis of causation in non-causal terms, thus that while one causal term may be analysable into another or others—as, for example, 'caused' in terms of 'causal relevance' or 'causal law' or 'causal process'—the concept 'causation' is itself primitive.[11]

Should lawyers be troubled by the fact that no satisfactory analysis of causation in non-causal terms is to be found in the literature of philosophy?

H&H said at the beginning of *Causation in the Law* that their first objective was to 'identify the sources of the uncertainties and confusions which continue to surround the legal use of causal language in spite of a vast juristic literature dedicated to its clarification'. (Hart and Honoré 1959, 1). It was surely clear to most lawyers by the time of H&H's writing that great uncertainty and confusion had issued from the pressure lawyers had felt under to have all common law constraints on liability—even those that issue from normative considerations of justice or policy—turn out to be constraints on causality. The outcome of that pressure was the appearance on the scene of the likes of 'proximate cause' and 'legal cause', and thereby to deep obscurities in the reasoning that had to be conducted in the courtroom.

By way of reaction, many lawyers came to the view that the question whether a person's act caused a harm should be sharply distinguished from the question whether the law requires him to be held liable for a harm he causes, if he does. So far so good. But on their view, it should be made clear that the sole causal question is whether the person's act or omission meets the requirement expressed

---

[11] A helpful brief summary of the arguments for and against this idea may be found in Schaffer 2007.

in the Weak Necessary Condition Analysis. They say that that much is empirical; they say that the rest is normative.

It is *these* lawyers who were H&H's primary targets in *Causation in the Law.* H&H wished to show that there is more to causation than is expressed in the Weak Necessary Condition Analysis: more in the reasonings of the courts, and more in the common sense reasonings of the man in the street. There is room for dispute about whether causation is limited in the way H&H say it is. But that there is as much to it as they say there is seems to me to be unarguable. They made their point, in detail and beautifully.

Two questions remain, however. First, is causation limited in the way H&H say it is? And second, what should lawyers conclude from the fact that we lack a satisfactory analysis of causation, and that we are not likely to obtain one in the near future?

11. I said that what H&H said was the words: x caused y just in case '[x] is one of a set of conditions jointly sufficient for the production of the consequence [y]: [x] is necessary because it is required to complete this set.' Thus, as I put it:

(Necessary/Sufficient Condition Formula)   x caused y just in case x was a necessary member of a set of things that were jointly sufficient for y.

But that is not quite right. What they said was, rather, that x was a *causally relevant factor* in the coming about of y just in case '[x] is one of a set of conditions jointly sufficient for the production of the consequence [y]: [x] is necessary because it is required to complete this set'. Thus what they said was:

(Necessary/Sufficient Condition Formula*)   x was a causally relevant factor in the coming about of y just in case x was a necessary member of a set of things that were jointly sufficient for y.

Now on their view, x caused y only if x was a causally relevant factor in the coming about of y, but on their view, more is required for x to have caused y than that x have been a causally relevant factor in the coming about of y. The more they said is required is this: it must not have been the case that y followed on x only because of the presence of some third factor, which was either (i) an abnormal event, or (ii) a voluntary act of some person other than the agent of x.

Here is one of H&H's examples. 'A hits B who falls to the ground stunned and bruised by the blow; at that moment a tree crashes to the ground and kills B.' (Hart and Honoré 1959, 73). Let x be A's hitting B. Let y be B's death. On any plausible interpretation of the (Necessary/Sufficient Condition Formula*), x was a causally relevant factor in the coming about of y. But, H&H go on to say, 'A has certainly caused B's bruises but not his death...' Thus x did not cause y. Why not? There was a third factor, α, the fall of the tree, such that y would not have followed x if α had not occurred at a time at which B was under the tree, but also such that it was a coincidence that α occurred at a time at which B was under the tree—thus α was, for these purposes, (i) an abnormal event.

Here is a variant on that example. A hits B who falls to the ground stunned and bruised by the blow. At that moment, C comes along, and hating B, takes advantage of his opportunity: he knocks a tree over onto B, thereby killing B. Let x again be A's hitting B, and y be B's death. On any plausible interpretation of the (Necessary/Sufficient Condition Formula*), x was a causally relevant factor in the coming about of y in this variant just as it was in the example H&H gave us. But here too H&H would say 'A has certainly caused B's bruises but not his death . . .' Thus x did not cause y. Why not? There was a third factor, β, C's knocking the tree over, such that y would not have followed x if β had not occurred at a time at which B was under the tree; but here the third factor was (ii) a voluntary act of some person other than the agent of x.

H&H supply a considerable amount of evidence to the effect that courts would not impose liability on A for B's death in either of these two examples, the original or the variant on it. (B's bruises are one thing, his death quite another.) And H&H say that this would be right, not merely because it would be unjust to impose liability on A for B's death, but because A's hitting B didn't really cause B's death.

H&H say 'it is the plain man's notions of causation (and not the philosopher's or the scientist's) with which the law is concerned . . .' (Hart and Honoré 1959, 1). And I take them to think that if these examples were put to the plain man, he would agree that A's hitting B didn't really cause B's death.

I strongly suspect that they are right about the plain man: the plain man would say that while A's hitting B was a bad business, it didn't really cause B's death in either of those two examples.

There is room for doubt here, however. What exactly is the significance of the plain man's agreeing? For it is very plausible to think that the plain man's thought about causation is drenched in normativity. When we want to know what caused a bad outcome, we typically want to know this because we want to know what was to blame for it. And A's hitting B wasn't to blame for B's death in either of the two examples. Perhaps it is *that* thought that is responsible for the plain man's agreeing. If so, the plain man is committed to something highly implausible—and when we show him that he is, he may be expected to withdraw agreement. (The plain man's intuitions are rather more malleable than they are sometimes thought to be.)

For let us go back to the courts. H&H say that 'an extraordinary conjunction of events, if intended or designed, does not negative causal connexion' (Hart and Honoré 1959, 159). For example, if a defendant 'binds his victim and leaves him on the pavement at a place where he has reason to suppose a heavy tree will fall half an hour later, the victim's death from the fall of the tree is no coincidence'. They add that the same applies to human interventions. 'If the accused persuades his victim to sleep in a house to which he knows a third party will set fire that night, he is presumably guilty of murder if the victim dies in the fire.'

So let us return to our two examples. Here are variants on them; I'll call them the Design Variants. *First Design Variant.* A went for a walk with B, and hit him when they reached a place directly under a tree that A had good reason to believe would soon fall, and indeed, hit B precisely in order that B be under the tree when it fell. Then, I take it, the courts would impose liability on A for B's death, and H&H would say that this would be right, not merely because it would not be unjust to impose liability on A for B's death, but because A's hitting B did cause B's death. And I am sure that the plain man would agree: given A's designs, A's hitting B was to blame for B's death, and did cause it.

Second Design Variant. A knew that C wanted B dead, and was waiting only for lack of opportunity to get at him. A went for a walk with B near where C walks every afternoon. Having caught sight of C standing next to an old tree that he knew could easily be toppled onto B, and having seen that C saw them approach the tree, A hit B. Indeed, he hit B precisely in order that B fall to the ground under the tree, stunned and bruised by the blow, giving C his opportunity to topple the tree onto him. Then, I take it, the courts would impose liability on A for B's death, and H&H would say that this would be right, not merely because it would not be unjust to impose liability on A for B's death, but because A's hitting B did cause B's death. I am sure that the plain man would agree: given A's designs, A's hitting B was to blame for B's death, and did cause it. (Of course C's toppling the tree onto B was also to blame for B's death, and it too caused it.)

The following conclusion now emerges: the question whether A's hitting B caused his death turns on what A had good reason to believe, or knew, and what his intention was in hitting B. Given one epistemic state and intention, A's hitting B did not cause B's death; given a different epistemic state and intention, A's hitting B did cause B's death. But that *cannot* be right. A's epistemic state and his intention, do have a bearing on whether A's hitting B was to blame for B's death. But it cannot be thought that a difference in A's epistemic state and intention fixes that in the one case A's hitting B caused B's death whereas in the other case it did not—for whether A's hitting B caused B's death turns on what the world is like and not on what A does or doesn't believe or want it to be like.

We certainly cannot say that whether a thing's moving in a certain way caused a later event turns on whether the thing that moved in that way was a human being or a robot.

Did A's hitting B cause B's death in the Design Variants? I should think it plainly did. But then A's hitting B also caused B's death in the two original examples. And if the courts were to decline to impose liability on A in the two original examples, then that decision could not be justified by appeal to its having been the case that A's hitting B did not cause B's death in those examples, for that wasn't the case. I think that when the plain man is shown that he has committed himself to a conclusion that cannot be true, he may *now* be expected to concede that while A's hitting B is not to blame for B's death in the two original examples, that does not show that it didn't cause B's death.

12. Should lawyers be troubled by the fact that no satisfactory analysis of causation in non-causal terms is to be found in the literature of philosophy?

A persistent source of worry seems to be that if we lack an analysis of causation in non-causal terms then we are left with nothing but our intuitions about whether such and such caused so and so. And while philosophers might feel comfortable about that prospect, sitting in their studies, the courts need to settle causal disputes, and indeed, to give rationales for their decisions. Moreover, the image of the courts' simply relying on intuition is anything but conducive to a sense that the institution operates justly.

However we aren't left with nothing but intuitions about whether such and such caused so and so. We have a considerable amount of general knowledge about causation, none of which rises to the level of an analysis, but much of which bears on the causal question.

We know, for example, that if x and y were discrete events, then there is a non-normative empirical question whether x caused y. Whether A's act, and thus A himself, is to blame for B's being harmed, or, more generally, whether A should be held liable for B's being harmed just does not settle whether A's act caused B's being harmed.[12]

We also know that the Weak Necessary Condition Analysis won't do: that is because we know there are countercases to it. On the other hand, we know that very often (though if Ned Hall is right, *only* very often) where it is true that if x had not occurred, then y would not have occurred, x did cause y.

We also know that where x caused y, it typically did so only against a background of other events and states of affairs. This is explicitly, and therefore helpfully,

---

[12] I am sure that it was because of the pressure I mentioned earlier to have a person held liable for a harm only if he caused it that lawyers have thought it essential to be able to say that acts of omission can cause things. For example, we want to be able to hold the gardener liable for the death of the plants where it was his duty to water them but he didn't. And what lawyers traditionally said allowed them to have that acts of omission can cause things, for the Weak Necessary Condition Analysis happily accommodates that claim. After all, it may be true that the plants would not have died if the gardener had watered them, and that analysis therefore yields that his act of omission did cause their death.

But if all the plants needed for life was water, then they would not have died if Queen Elizabeth had watered them. This forces a choice on us: (i) accept that her act of omission also caused their death, but impose liability only on the gardener, or (ii) find a different ground for attributing causality to his act of omission that does not spill over onto hers. (ii) is a particularly unattractive option if what marks him as appropriately held liable is that he was under a duty to water them whereas she was not. For if we take *that* to fix that he caused their death while she did not, then the causal attribution we make is normative.

I am also sure that it is a lost cause (if you will pardon the expression), but it would probably have been a better option to distinguish as Ned Hall does between dependence and production—and to say that the death of the plants depended on the gardener's not watering them, and on Queen Elizabeth's not watering them, and on yours and mine, but was not produced by his or hers or yours or mine, and then to hold him alone liable for their death on the ground that he alone was under a duty to water them.

Hall argues in a forthcoming book that omissions do not cause things (in the sense of producing them). In Thomson 2003, I tried to make out that they do: that they cause things in the way in which states of affairs do. But the case I made there seems to me now to have been unsatisfactory.

brought to our attention by the Fact/Entailment Necessary/Sufficient Condition Analysis. It is worth noticing, however, that this consideration was already built into the Weak Necessary Condition Analysis in that what that analysis invites us to attend to is what happens in the closest possible world in which x does not occur.

We also know that where x caused y, there was a causal process started by x and ending in y. In some cases, the process is short. If Alfred hits Bert's window with a hammer, then there is a causal process that goes from the hammer's contact with the window to the breaking, and we take it that a physicist could explain to us how pressure on something fragile causes it to break. In other cases, the process is lengthy. Suppose Alfred throws a rock in Boston and some time later, a window breaks in Bert's house in New York. If we think that the one event caused the other, that presumably isn't because we have in mind that there is a law-like connection between those events. What we have in mind is that there was a lengthy, complex causal process that took place. (Perhaps Alfred's rock landed in a frying pan, which caused some hot fat to splatter onto a sensitive electrical device, which caused a circuit to close, which caused a rocket to launch, which caused...) We think that it is between the steps in this process that law-like connections hold. And they do, if the one event caused the other by that route.

I have listed here only bits of general knowledge that I mentioned in the preceding sections; there are any number of others.

I said that we *know* these things. What warrants that claim? Partly our knowledge of the interconnections among causal concepts, as, for example, between 'causes' and 'causal process'. Partly our past experience of ways in which one can bring about this or that outcome by doing this or that: we learn over the years that if you want to bring about an outcome of kind K, then if you act in such and such a way, then an outcome of that kind *will* come about.

Ultimately, of course, it all rests on intuition. But intuition can become more sensitive with experience, and intuitions can be organized into general principles by use of which we can predict still further intuitions. That is how it works elsewhere in our intellectual life. In case it hasn't been noticed by lawyers, the concept 'causation' is not the only concept central to our thinking that we have no analysis for. There is 'justice', for example. And 'justification' and 'knowledge' and 'consciousness'. Here too our reasoning is the better according as our intuitions are more sensitive and more productively organized.

The best way for lawyers to acquire general knowledge about causation is to study discussions of cases—actual and hypothetical—in which a perceptive author generalizes. H&H, for a splendid example. *Causation in the Law* isn't the last word on causation in the law, but every route that gets past it travels through it.[13]

---

[13] I thank Mahrad Almotahari, Tom Dougherty, Catherine Elgin, Adam Hosein, and Seth Yalcin for comments on an earlier draft.

9

The Nightmare and the Noble Dream:
Hart and Honoré on Causation
and Responsibility

Richard W Wright

When, as a beginning academic, I told a colleague that I had begun reading Herbert Hart and Tony Honoré's treatise, *Causation in the Law* (1959), he exclaimed, 'Don't! You'll never get out of it!' He was right. I was intrigued and captivated by their discussions of the complexities of the fundamental concepts of causation and responsibility, which have been a primary focus of my work ever since. In their treatise, Hart and Honoré advanced the separate discussions of these concepts in the legal and philosophical literature by combining insightful philosophical analysis with a detailed discussion of the case law. They introduced philosophers to legal puzzles of causal overdetermination that the philosophical literature had hardly addressed or even recognized, set forth a novel philosophically grounded test for resolving those puzzles, and proposed a set of 'causal' principles, deeply embedded in ordinary thought, for identifying causes and attributing legal responsibility.

The major accomplishments of the treatise are the first two items: the introduction of philosophers to the puzzles of causal overdetermination and the setting forth of a novel philosophically grounded test for resolving those puzzles. I have written extensively about these accomplishments elsewhere (Wright 1985, 1788–803; Wright 1988, 1018–39; Wright 2001, 1101–31; Wright 2007). I want to focus here on the third item, the attempt to set forth a set of causal principles, deeply embedded in ordinary thought, for identifying causes and attributing legal responsibility. I agree with Hart and Honoré that there are basic principles for attributing legal responsibility that are not based on contingent policy or expediency; indeed, I believe that there are more of those principles than the superseding cause principles upon which they focus (Wright 2003). However, I strongly disagree with treating these principles, insofar as they encompass more than the fact of natural causation, as principles of causation rather than as non-causal principles of just attribution of legal responsibility. Hart and Honoré's treating their principles as principles of causation distorted their elaboration of the principles of attributable responsibility and has contributed to continued confusion about, rather than clarification of, the concept of causation and its relation to moral and legal responsibility.

1 The Nightmare and the Noble Dream[1]

Hart and Honoré's attempt to treat the normative principles for attributing legal responsibility as principles of causation is at first glance quite puzzling, given the remarkable contradiction between that attempt and the strict positivist theory of law that Hart was simultaneously engaged in elaborating and defending. During the same period that *Causation in the Law* was being written, Hart was writing his famous defences of legal positivism, which defended legal positivism in its strictest form. Despite his protestations to the contrary, Hart initially was not merely a legal positivist, who insisted that there is no necessary connection between law and morality, but also a legal formalist. He insisted that the existing law consists solely of the core of plain or settled meaning of explicitly stated legal rules, which are applied deductively[2] to resolve the great majority of legal disputes, and that for cases not falling within the core of settled meaning there is no existing law that constrains judicial decision-making. Judges instead should decide such cases by making new law to achieve what each judge deems to be the most socially advantageous result (Hart 1958, 606–15, 627–9; Hart 1961, 119–32, 150, 200–1).

Yet, in *Causation in the Law*, Hart and Honoré are committed to elaborating a set of principles for attributing moral and legal responsibility that they insist are not 'inventions of the law' or based on 'expediency, justice, or social policy', but rather are 'common-sense principles of causation' that are 'part of the ordinary man's stock of general notions' and involve questions of fact rather than questions of policy, 'similar to the conventional view of the law's use of other highly general notions such as those of temporal or spatial location' (Hart & Honoré 1985, 91–2). They assert that these causal principles 'have very deep roots in all our thinking and in common ideas of when it is just or fair to punish or exact compensation' (Hart & Honoré 1985, 1):

[W]henever we are concerned with [tracing connections between human actions and events], whether for the purpose of explaining a puzzling occurrence, assessing responsibility, or giving an intelligible historical narrative, we employ a set of concepts restricting

---

[1] As I do here, in her insightful intellectual biography Nicola Lacey (2004) borrows the phrase that Hart applied to those critical of his theories and applies it to Hart himself, although she uses it in a different sense than I or Hart, to encapsulate Hart's life-long psychological turmoil as his intellectual ambitions and emotional hopes were constantly beset with anxieties and doubts.

[2] For cases in the core of settled meaning, 'subsumption and the drawing of a syllogistic conclusion...characterize the nerve of the reasoning involved in determining what is the right thing to do' (Hart 1961, 123–4).

in various ways what counts as a consequence. These restrictions colour *all* our thinking in causal terms; when we find them in the law we are not finding something invented by or peculiar to the law, though of course it is for the law to say when and how far it will use them and, where they are vague, to supplement them. (Hart & Honoré 1985, 70)

Hart and Honoré seem to treat instances of humans' 'causing harm' as defined by these principles as sufficient grounds for attributing moral responsibility (Hart & Honoré 1985, 63–7) and as prima facie sufficient grounds for attributing legal responsibility, which are overridden only by consideration of adverse 'social consequences':

Usually in discussion of the law…to say that someone is responsible for some harm means that in accordance with legal rules…it is at least permissible, if not mandatory, to…punish or exact compensation from him.…[D]oing or causing harm constitutes not only the most usual but the primary type of ground for holding persons responsible in [this] sense. (Hart & Honoré 1985, 65)

[I]n both law and morals the various forms of causal connection between act or omission and harm are the most obvious and least disputable reasons for holding anyone responsible. Yet, in order to understand the extent to which the causal notions of ordinary thought are used in the law, we must bear in mind the many factors which must differentiate moral from legal responsibility in spite of their partial correspondence. The law is not only not bound to follow the patterns of moral attribution of responsibility, but, even when it does, it must take into account, in a way in which the private moral judgment need not and does not, the general social consequences which are attached to its judgments of responsibility.… The use of the legal sanctions of imprisonment, or enforced monetary compensation against individuals, has such formidable repercussions on the general life of society that the fact that the individuals have a type of [causal] connection with harm which is adequate for moral censure or claims for compensation is only *one* of the factors which the law must consider. (Hart & Honoré 1985, 66).

Given the fundamental and pervasive role of causation in the law, Hart and Honoré contradict the basic tenet of legal positivism—the lack of any necessary connection between law and morality—by insisting that their principles of attributable moral and (prima facie) legal responsibility are factual principles of causation deeply embedded in human thought.

What accounts for this remarkable contradiction? I believe that it was generated by Hart's attempt, in both *Causation in the Law* and his writings on legal positivism, to defend law and legal reasoning against the rule scepticism and legal nihilism that he attributed to the American legal realists. The legal realists rejected the formalist conception of law as a system of explicitly stated rules that are deductively applied by judges in particular cases. They insisted that legal adjudication inevitably requires explicit or implicit resort to underlying principles or purposes. The extreme legal realists argued that such resort opens the door to unconstrained judicial discretion and thus to legal nihilism. Moderate legal realists such as Karl Llewellyn—whom Hart initially misdescribed as a legal nihilist (Hart 1961, 130)—believed that through careful analysis of actual case results one could ascertain the often unarticulated real rules and their underlying purposes and principles, which constitute the actual law that guides and constrains judicial decision making (Llewellyn 1951, ix–xi, 2–5, 12–15, 40–4, 69–76, 81, 88, 91–2, 187– 90; Twining 1973).

Hart initially rejected the argument, which he later described as a noble dream (Hart 1977), that the nightmare of legal nihilism could be avoided by resort to the purposes or principles that underlie legal rules and judicial decisions.[3] He accepted and repeated the extreme legal realists' argument that such resort leads to unconstrained judicial discretion and pervasive indeterminacy. However, he denied that such resort is inevitable or even frequent. Instead, in his initial writings he proposed his own noble dream: that the law consists of the core of plain or settled meaning of a system of explicitly articulated rules, which are applied deductively in the great majority of cases without any resort to underlying purposes, policies, or principles (Hart 1958, 607–15, 627–9; Hart 1961, 119–32, 150, 200–1).

Hart attempted to apply his own version of the noble dream in *Causation in the Law*. One of Hart and Honoré's two stated objectives in *Causation in the Law* is to rebut the claims of the 'causal minimalists' and causal nihilists. Their main target in both editions is the American legal realists, who generally were causal minimalists but a few of whom were causal nihilists. (By the time of the second edition the more extreme legal realists had been joined as causal nihilists by the legal economists and the critical legal scholars.) The causal minimalists insist that the only truly causal issue in any case is the purely empirical issue of whether the alleged cause actually contributed to the occurrence of the alleged effect, that this issue of empirical or natural causation is usually trivially satisfied, and that the courts' use of causal terminology to refer not only to the natural causation issue but also to the further issue of appropriate legal responsibility camouflages and distorts the multiplicity of policy issues that should and usually do govern legal responsibility. The causal nihilists assert that even the natural causation issue inevitably involves discretionary policy judgments regarding ultimate legal responsibility (Hart & Honoré 1985, xxxiv–xxxv, 3–5, 69, 88–90 & n 18, 95–108).

Hart and Honoré's other stated objective in *Causation in the Law* is to rebut the claims of the causal minimalists and causal nihilists by identifying and articulating, through analysis of ordinary language as employed in and outside the law, 'common sense' principles of causation embedded in ordinary thought that encompass not only the issue of natural causation but also attributions of legal responsibility (Hart & Honoré 1985, xxxiii–xxxiv, 1–3). At the time, Hart was a

---

[3] As a result of devastating criticisms of his formalist position by Lon Fuller (1958) and Ronald Dworkin (1967), Hart subsequently admitted that underlying purposes and principles are part of the existing law and guide and constrain proper adjudication in all cases, while however continuing to assert that the underlying purposes and principles might not be morally attractive and will not provide a determinate answer in every case (Hart 1983, 6–8; Hart 1994, 259–63, 274–5; Wright 1999, 266–9, 272–4).

recent and devout convert to J L Austin's 'ordinary language analysis' approach to philosophy (Lacey 2004, 132–47, 155–7). As Hart later explained, Austinian linguistic philosophy was based on 'a conviction that longstanding philosophical perplexities could often be resolved not by the deployment of some general theory but by sensitive piecemeal discrimination and characterization of the different ways, some reflecting different forms of human life, in which human language is used' (Hart 1983, 2).

Hart's primary motivation in co-authoring *Causation in the Law* presumably was the opportunity to apply ordinary language analysis to what is perhaps the most fundamental and pervasive element in law and legal obligation: causation. Yet anyone who has read more than a few judicial discussions of causation must despair when confronted with the morass of conclusory, unelaborated, extremely broad and imprecise assertions of the existence or non-existence of causation, whether natural or 'proximate', which often confuse the natural causation issue with the further issues of ultimate legal responsibility encompassed by 'legal' or 'proximate' causation. Indeed, when, during the year that he spent in America in 1956–1957, Hart was exposed to the American case law and the legal realist literature that laid bare this dismal state of affairs, he had serious doubts about continuing with the causation project, and he believed that if he did continue a major revision was required to try to deal with the legal realists' arguments and the case law that seemed to support their arguments.[4] When Hart returned from America, Honoré had to convince him to continue with the project (Lacey 2004, 210–11).

It is fortunate that Honoré convinced Hart to continue, since *Causation in the Law* contains much of great and lasting value, including its major breakthrough in analysing natural causation and its insistence on the existence of some basic principles of attributable responsibility. It is unfortunate that these major accomplishments are distorted and clouded by Hart's devotion during this period to legal formalism and the arid and fruitless philosophical technique of ordinary language analysis. One wonders how much clearer and stronger the book would have been if Honoré's jurisprudential views had prevailed and Hart had nonetheless remained committed to the project. Nicola Lacey reports that 'Tony Honoré...was aware that Herbert was worried by certain differences between the two of them, notably Tony Honoré's less whole-hearted espousal of linguistic philosophy and more Kantian approach.... [Hart] cavilled at a view which Tony Honoré had expressed, describing it as *"naturrechtlich"*' (Lacey 2004, 210).

---

[4] During his year at Harvard, Hart's 'regular exchanges [with Herbert Wechsler], as well as his reading of the vast American literature on proximate cause, convinced him that his and Tony Honoré's approach would have to be modified to take more seriously the "policy approach".... As a direct result of Herbert's encounter with Wechsler, the final version of *Causation in the Law* was reconstructed in terms of a debate with the policy approach' (Lacey 2004, 188). On his way back to England, Hart wrote in his notebook 'need to order book round the "policy approach"—*difficult*' (Lacey 2004, 208).

In the event, however, Hart was the dominant senior author, and there are only rare but interesting indications of their different views in the portions of the book for which each was primarily responsible.[5]

2 Attributing Responsibility: The Pathology of
Ordinary Language Analysis

Causation in the Law has been described as the 'pinnacle' of the Austinian school of ordinary language analysis (Lacey 2004, 215). As such, it may well have contributed to the rapid decline of that school. Ordinary language analysis is supposed to work by taking ordinary language use seriously and carefully dissecting it to reveal the significant philosophical distinctions behind different usages in different contexts (Lacey 2004, 134–5). I doubt that there is any corpus of language use less suitable for this type of analysis than cause talk, especially cause talk as employed in the law.

Hart and Honoré acknowledge that the causal language used by the courts is often 'unsatisfactory' (Hart & Honoré 1985, 5), and that 'courts discuss and decide [issues] in causal terminology so often with an accompanying cloud of metaphors' (Hart & Honoré 1985, 88). They agree that the very commonly used phrase, 'proximate cause', is misleading rather than enlightening, apart from its solely 'negative force as a reminder that, to demonstrate causal connection between events for legal purposes, it is not enough to show that one was a necessary condition (cause in fact) of the other' (Hart & Honoré 1985, 86–7). Indeed, despite their avowed commitment to taking ordinary language use seriously, they could only have viewed the morass of indiscriminating and metaphorical causal terminology in law as an obstacle to be overcome, rather than as a source of enlightenment regarding causal concepts or principles. As Nicola Lacey (2004, 217) notes, this sometimes becomes dramatically evident, as when they follow Mill in criticizing courts' common usage of the metaphor of active forces and the concomitant failure to recognize persistent states and omissions as causes (Hart & Honoré 1985, 16, 30–1, 38, 97), or when they summarily reject judges' explicit statements that the word 'proximate' in 'proximate causation' has nothing to do with the issue of causation but rather refers to considerations of convenience, public policy, or justice (Hart & Honoré 1985, 90–1).

More generally, Hart and Honoré note the ambiguous uses in ordinary language in and outside of the law of the terms 'cause' and 'responsible for', each of which is sometimes used merely to refer to the fact of natural causation but at

---

[5] Hart drafted the initial, philosophical chapters in Part I and the chapters on criminal law in Part II, while Honoré drafted the chapters on tort, contract, and evidence in Part II and the chapters on the continental theories of causation in Part III ('about which Herbert was dismissive') (Lacey 2004, 210–11).

other times to encompass also or instead the attribution of moral or legal responsibility (Hart & Honoré 1985, 65). This is especially true with the phrase 'the cause' rather than 'a cause', although even the latter phrase is often employed to refer not merely to natural causation but to the attribution of legal responsibility (Wright 1988, 1012–14). They acknowledge that in ordinary usage identification of something as a 'cause', rather than as a mere 'condition' or 'circumstance', depends on our 'practical interests', and that different people can and will give different answers in the same situation, depending on their particular practical interests and purposes (Hart & Honoré 1985, 35–7, 62). 'Plainly', they state, 'the distinction has... very much to do with the particular context and purpose for which a particular causal inquiry is made and answered' (Hart & Honoré 1985, 11). The generally acknowledged purpose of causal or other inquiries in law is justice (Wright 1999; Wright 2000)—or, according to some, efficiency—either of which contradicts Hart and Honoré's claim that their principles of attributable causation and responsibility are neither peculiar to the law nor based on 'expediency, justice, or social policy' (Hart & Honoré 1985, 91–2).

Nevertheless, Hart and Honoré persist in attempting to explain the distinction that is often drawn between 'causes' and mere 'conditions' as being based not on 'expediency, justice, or social policy', but rather on 'common-sense principles of causation' that are not 'inventions of the law' but rather 'part of the ordinary man's stock of general notions' (Hart & Honoré 1985, 11–13, 17–19, 26, 91–2). They state that '[a]s with every other empirical notion we can only hope to find a core of relatively well-settled common usage amid much that is fluctuating, optional, idiosyncratic, and vague' (Hart & Honoré 1985, 27). They admit to being unable to find any core of well-settled common usage for 'cause', but they argue:

It is fatally easy... to make the transition from the exhilarating discovery that complex words like 'cause' cannot be simply defined and have no 'one true meaning' to the mistaken conclusion that they have no meaning worth bothering about at all, but are used as a mere disguise for arbitrary decision or judicial policy. This is a blinding error.... The proper inference from the fact that no common property can be found in all cases where causal language is used is that some more complex principle or set of principles may guide, though not dictate its use. (Hart & Honoré 1985, 3)

They make only a couple of very brief, cursory attempts to suggest distinctions between different ordinary causal expressions, which, however, do not result in the identification of any causal principles; moreover, they acknowledge that these causal expressions usually can be and are used interchangeably (Hart & Honoré 1985, 27–8, 87). Without engaging in any ordinary language analysis, they simply assert that there are three different but related causal concepts or principles latent in ordinary thought by which 'causes' are distinguished from 'mere circumstances or conditions' (Hart & Honoré 1985, 28):

The first of these has a claim to be the central concept: it is that of a contingency, usually a human intervention, which initiates a series of physical changes, which exemplify general connections between types of events, and its features are best seen in the simplest cases of all where a human being manipulates things in order to bring about intended change. Here the language of 'cause and effect' sits most happily; and in the light of this simple case the complex imagery and metaphors associated with causes can be understood, and, with them, the distinctions drawn in more complex cases between voluntary interventions and abnormal events as 'causes' and other events as 'mere conditions'.

To be distinguished from this central case is the concept of one man by word or deeds providing another with a reason for doing something. Here there is not even an approximation, as there is in the first case, to the model of 'regular sequence' which since Hume has been accepted as the essence of causal connection. This concept is often required for the analysis of the notion of one man's 'causing' or 'making' another act and many other relationships (such as 'inducing' and 'enticing') between human actions.

Thirdly, the idea that the provision of an opportunity, commonly exploited for good or evil, may rank as the cause of the upshot when the opportunity is actually exploited is very important in both law and history. (Hart & Honoré 1985, 2)

Paradoxically, Hart and Honoré identify as the 'most obvious and fundamental case of all' for the attribution of causation and responsibility, by analogy to which all other causal usages and concepts are supposedly explained, situations 'which we do not ordinarily describe in causal language at all but by the simple transitive verbs of action', such as 'push, pull, bend, twist, break, injure', or simply 'he did it' (Hart & Honoré 1985, 28, 73). Their focus is not on the language used, but rather on the fact of a deliberate human intervention that 'makes a difference' from the normal course of events (Hart & Honoré 1985, 29). They then engage in some sleight of hand by applying the idea of a 'difference from the normal course of events' to the condition identified as the cause as well as to the effect, in order to treat 'abnormal' conditions, whether or not they involve human conduct, as supposedly apt analogies to deliberate interventions, even though deliberate interventions need not and indeed usually do not themselves constitute a difference from the normal course of events:

Analogies with the interference by human beings with the natural course of events in part control, even in cases where there literally is no human intervention, what is to be identified as the cause of some occurrence; the cause, though not a literal intervention, is a *difference* from the normal course which accounts for the difference in outcome. (Hart & Honoré 1985, 29)

Through this route, rather than through any ordinary language analysis, Hart and Honoré arrive at their proposed principles for distinguishing 'causes' from mere 'conditions':

[I]n distinguishing between causes and conditions two contrasts are of prime importance. These are the contrasts between what is abnormal and what is normal in relation to any given thing or subject matter, and between a free deliberate human action [intended to produce the effect that occurred] and all other conditions. The notions in this pair of contrasts lie at the root of most of the metaphors which cluster around the notion of a cause and must be used in any literal discussion of the facts which [the metaphors] obscure. (Hart & Honoré 1985, 33)

These supposed causal principles are not supported by the ordinary use of causal language. Although 'what is abnormal in relation to any given thing or subject matter' may often be identified as the 'cause', so may what is normal: for example, a person's smoking causing cancer (Hart & Honoré 1985, 70), a battery's running out of power causing electronic equipment to quit working, a normal for the area drought causing the browning of the vegetation or the failure of crops, a predator animal's attacking another animal causing the death of that animal, the sunlight's streaming into a window causing a person to wake up, a person's working hard causing her to become tired, and a person's becoming tired or bored causing her to fall asleep in class or while reading this essay.

Moreover, while these 'causal' principles are supposed to be general and factual in nature rather than being dependent on purposes or considerations of expediency, justice, or social policy, Hart and Honoré admit that what is deemed 'abnormal' and hence a 'cause' in a particular situation often (always?) depends on the interests and purposes of the person making the causal statement (Hart & Honoré 1985, 35–7, 62), and that '[i]n relation to human conduct...the notion of what is "natural" is strongly influenced by moral and legal standards of proper conduct, though weight is also given to the fact that certain conduct is usual or ordinary for a human being' (Hart & Honoré 1985, 183).

Similarly, although they admit that in common usage the term 'voluntary' often has a much less restricted meaning, they state that human conduct was 'voluntary' or 'fully voluntary' and hence a 'cause' only if it was a free, deliberate, and informed act or omission, intended to bring about what in fact happened, in the manner in which it happened. A human intervention was not 'voluntary' if the consequence was not intended, or not 'fully voluntary' even if it was intended if the intervention occurred as a result of mistake, ignorance, coercion, duress, the pressure of moral or legal obligation, or a choice of the lesser of two evils (Hart & Honoré 1985, 41–2, 75–7, 136 n 18, 138 & n 40), or if it was a reasonable action taken to defend persons or property against reasonably perceived perils, to safeguard legal rights or interests, or to rescue others (Hart & Honoré 1985, 142–62). They admit that their voluntary intervention criterion calls for policy judgments on matters of degree and reasonableness, and that many of the circumstances which are treated as rendering even deliberate conduct 'nonvoluntary' correspond to the recognized moral and legal grounds for justifying or excusing harmful behaviour (Hart & Honoré 1985, 76–7, 138). Overall, their voluntary intervention criterion simply incompletely describes one of the principal recognized types of criminal or tortious conduct: intentional, unjustified, and unexcused infliction of injury.

Indeed, without their seeming to realize that they have done so, their attempt to develop 'causal' principles that encompass not only natural causation but also attributable responsibility, in a way that enables only one or a few causal conditions to be treated as 'the' or 'a' cause, leads them to incorporate within their 'causal' principles not only the issues of natural causation and so-called 'proximate' causation, but also the wrongful conduct issue. Under their 'causal' principles, human action cannot be a 'cause' unless it is 'voluntary' or 'abnormal'. Conduct is not 'voluntary' unless it is intentional, unjustified, and unexcused. While conduct could be 'abnormal' without being negligent (but not vice versa—Hart & Honoré 1985, 135 n 15), generally conduct that is abnormal—ie, departs from what is normal and expected—will be negligent. Thus, it is not surprising that, with rare exceptions, they refer to a causal connection between conduct (acts, omissions) and harm, rather than a causal connection between wrongful, criminal, tortious, intentional, or negligent conduct and harm,[6] even when talking about causal issues in the law (Hart & Honoré 1985, 84–6). The wrongfulness of the conduct is already built into their 'voluntary' and 'abnormal' criteria for a condition to be a cause. Thus, despite appearances, there is little if any room for strict liability. Certainly not for strict liability for ultrahazardous activities, since the normal, indeed inherent characteristic of those activities is their ultrahazardous nature.

Hart and Honoré are aware of, and struggle with, another awkward result of their attempt to have their 'causal' principles encompass attributable responsibility and thereby distinguish the 'cause' from 'mere conditions':

[A difficulty arises when] among the conditions required to account for the harm which has occurred, there is found in addition to the defendant's action a factor (usually a human action or some striking natural phenomenon) which itself has some of the characteristics by which common sense distinguishes causes from mere conditions; so that there seems as much reason to attribute the harm to this third factor as to the defendant's action. (Hart & Honoré 1985, 24)

As Hart and Honoré recognize, their 'causal' principles should be consistently applied whether one is looking at the cause-consequence relation from the tail end, as in causal explanation, or from the front end, as in attribution of responsibility (Hart & Honoré 1985, 22–3, 68, 70). They therefore state that the same criteria of 'voluntary' conduct and 'abnormal' contingencies delimit both ends of the cause-consequence relation:

[I]f we find, on attempting to trace by stages a causal connection, that these factors include voluntary interferences, or independent abnormal contingencies, this brings into question our right to designate the earlier factor as *the* cause, for this expression is used of something which, with the co-operation only of factors that rank as mere conditions and not themselves as causes, is sufficient to 'produce' the effect.... This displacement of one event from the position of 'the cause' by other events, which have also the characteristics by which common sense distinguishes causes from mere conditions, is of crucial importance...when causal connection is the basis of the attribution of responsibility. (Hart & Honoré 1985, 49–50. Also see xlviii–xlix, lxxviii–lxxix, 5, 71, 73, 130–1, 133, 135).

---

[6] See, eg, the quotes in Part 1 of this essay.

Yet, such symmetry at the front (wrongful conduct) end and the tail (attributable responsibility) end of the 'causal connection' is inconsistent with the actual law. For example, in tort law broader notions of 'voluntary' and 'abnormal' are required for the tortious conduct analysis than for the attributable responsibility analysis. In the attributable responsibility analysis, narrow definitions are needed to avoid cutting off the defendant's liability because of subsequent (a) intentional ('voluntary') interventions by the plaintiff or others that were justified or done in ignorance of the circumstances or the possible consequences, or (b) negligent ('abnormal') conduct by others that was 'routine' rather than 'highly unusual'. In the tortious conduct analysis, on the other hand, broader definitions are needed: the defendant's intentional ('voluntary') intervention often may be treated as tortious despite ignorance, mistake, or necessity, and his negligent ('abnormal') conduct will be treated as tortious whether it is 'routine' or 'highly unusual'.

Hart and Honoré recognize and try to adjust for some of these differences, without any acknowledgment of the resulting inconsistent employment of their 'causal' criteria. In their attributable responsibility analysis, a subsequent contingency will not be considered sufficiently abnormal to negative causal connection unless it is grossly negligent or extraordinary or is a coincidence (an abnormal conjunction of events) (Hart & Honoré 1985, 50, 77–81, 162–6, 184–5), and, in the second but not the first edition, they do not require that the intervening conduct be intended to produce the harmful result, but rather only that it be intended to exploit the situation created by the defendant (Hart & Honoré 1985, 136 & n 23).

Hart and Honoré have the greatest difficulty with the many cases in which a defendant is held liable for some harmful consequence despite the subsequent deliberate intervention of another person. The difficulty stems from their belief that, despite contrary statements in ordinary language, human conduct cannot be caused. They therefore treat such deliberate interventions, when 'fully voluntary', as the 'paradigm' instances of contingencies that negative causal connection by any prior conduct or event under their primary, 'central case' concept of causation, and they create two additional categories of causal connection, which they acknowledge are not distinguished from each other or from their 'central case' by the courts, to accommodate liability in such cases. These two additional categories encompass the intentional provision of another with reasons or means for doing harm or negligently or intentionally providing another with the opportunity to do harm, which they prefer to describe as situations that do not involve 'causing' harm but rather 'inducing' or 'occasioning' harm. They treat liability in such cases as being based on non-causal 'harm within the risk' policies that extend liability beyond liability justified by their basic causal principles, but which do not limit liability justified by those principles (Hart & Honoré 1985, 6–7, 42–3, 51–2, 57–61, 71, 76–7, 81–3, 133–4, 186–7, 439).

3 The Road Not Taken

Hart and Honoré's attempt to combat legal nihilism and causal minimalism by using ordinary language analysis to derive basic principles of responsibility was doomed from the start. Their objective was worthy, but their chosen means was not. They had to ignore or even reject the courts' unhelpful causal language when fashioning their principles, yet the attempt to structure those principles as factual, causal principles severely confined and distorted their analysis. They themselves admit that their 'common sense principles' are not very helpful except in the most simple cases and do not fit many cases (Hart & Honoré 1985, 68, 91–2, 131). Their principles have not been adopted by the courts, who unfortunately instead, when faced with difficult issues of causation and attributable responsibility, have often taken up Hart and Honoré's invocation of 'common sense' without feeling any need to elaborate its content.

In the preface to the second edition of *Causation in the Law*, Hart and Honoré note the decline of ordinary language philosophy and the 'pathological aspect' of ordinary language and legal discourse, with its varied and inconsistent use of 'obscure' and 'bewildering' causal metaphors, while weakly claiming 'that the method we chose remains viable and that the analysis we propounded by the use of it is still, in its main lines, tenable' (Hart & Honoré 1985, xxxiii–xxxiv). They could hardly claim otherwise without a wholesale revision of the entire treatise. A different and franker perspective on the method that they purportedly adopted in *Causation in the Law* was provided by Hart a couple of years earlier, in the preface to his *Essays in Jurisprudence and Philosophy*, where he admitted the errors in his initial formalistic conception of law and his 'early invocation in jurisprudence of linguistic philosophy' (Hart 1983, 5). In a statement that seems especially applicable to the 'partly overlapping concepts' of causation and responsibility, he acknowledged that

[t]he methods of linguistic philosophy which are neutral between moral and political principles and silent about different points of view which might endow one feature rather than another of legal phenomena with significance . . . are not suitable for resolving or clarifying those controversies which arise, as many of the central problems of legal philosophy do, from the divergence between partly overlapping concepts reflecting a divergence of basic points of view or values or background theory, or which arise from conflict or incompleteness of legal rules. (Hart 1983, 6)

There is an alternative route that Hart and Honoré could have taken to achieve their basic objective in *Causation in the Law*, of which they were well aware (Hart & Honoré 1985, 105–7) but which they were prevented from taking by their (or at least Hart's) commitment to ordinary language philosophy and thus to cause talk. Their basic objective was to combat legal nihilism and causal minimalism or, worse, causal nihilism. The alternative route toward accomplishing that objective would have been to follow the legal realists in clearly separating the issue of natural causation from the non-causal issue of attributable responsibility but to depart from the legal realists by articulating a comprehensive test of natural causation and justice-based general principles of attributable responsibility.

Hart and Honoré cleared away much of the debris along the first portion of this route by their articulation, in *Causation in the Law*, of the NESS (necessary element of a sufficient set) test of natural causation, which undercut the claims of the causal nihilists by providing, for the first time, a comprehensive test of natural causation capable of correctly resolving the causation issue in situations involving causal overdetermination (Hart & Honoré 1985, 112–13; Wright 1988, 1018–39; Wright 2007). Although they did not clearly realize it, they also undercut the claims of the causal minimalists—that the natural causation issue is minimally significant because it is trivially satisfied—not only by their articulation of the NESS test but also by their recognition that the causal inquiry should be focused on the wrongful aspect of a defendant's conduct rather than on the defendant's conduct as a whole (Hart & Honoré 1985, 115–20; Wright 1985, 1759–74).

However, Hart and Honoré took the wrong turn when they insisted that the principles of attributable responsibility should be treated as causal rather than non-causal principles. They seem to assume that in order to avoid ad hoc, policy-driven determinations of attributable responsibility, the principles of attributable responsibility (beyond the basic natural causation principle) must be 'causal' principles, and that principles of attributable responsibility based on justice would be as unprincipled and ad hoc as those based on 'expediency' or 'social policies'. But neither of these assumptions is valid. The 'harm within the risk' principle that they discuss and acknowledge is much more general and principled than the 'first burnt building only' rule that they repeatedly cite as an example of policy-driven determinations of attributable responsibility (Hart & Honoré 1985, 89–94). Might not something like it (a 'harm results from the risk' principle), as well as a superseding cause principle somewhat like their 'causal' principles of attributable responsibility, be non-exclusive non-causal principles of attributable responsibility that 'have very deep roots in all our thinking and in common ideas of when it is just or fair to punish or exact compensation'? I have so argued (Wright 2003).

PART IV

JUSTICE

10

Fairness, Needs, and Desert[1]

Brad Hooker

1 Introduction

A man whom I never met but for whom I have immense admiration is H.L.A. Hart. For the quality of his publications and the political causes he supported, he has been one of my heroes. Thus I am deeply honored to be contributing an essay to this memorial volume.

Hart's contribution to the festschrift for Isaiah Berlin attacked the theories of rights developed by Robert Nozick and Ronald Dworkin (Hart 1979). In that paper, Hart noted that the then fashionable idea that rights theories would be able to succeed where 'unreconstructed utilitarianism' was bound to fail grew out of prominent criticisms of utilitarianism, such as that utilitarianism failed to take seriously the separateness of persons. Nozick proposed that only his libertarian rights theory did justice to the separateness of persons. Another prominent criticism of utilitarianism mentioned by Hart is that utilitarianism cares only about how much utility results, and not at all about how equal the distribution of utility is.

---

[1] This paper was written while I held a Research Readership from the British Academy for Humanities and Social Sciences. I am grateful for that support. The paper benefited from outings at the following universities: Reading, Cambridge, Oxford, Cork, Virginia, Glasgow, York, Leeds, Heythrop College London, and of course at the 'The Legacy of H. L. A. Hart: Legal, Moral & Political Philosophy' Symposium in Cambridge. Jonathan Dancy, David Miller, Serena Olsaretti, and Anne Raustol provided me with written comments on drafts of the paper, and these comments resulted in significant improvements. Also helpful were comments on the paper from Timo Airaksinen, David Bain, Ana Barandalla Ajona, Simon Blackburn, Michael Brady, Talbot Brewer, Chris Brooke, Vittorio Bufacchi, Adam Carter, Alan Carter, Paula Casal, Desmond Clarke, Nat Coleman, John Cottingham, Jonathan Dancy, Katherine Eddy, Brian Feltham, Craig French, Max de Gaynesford, Bernard Gert, Hanjo Glock, Vinit Haksar, Jonathan Harrison, Jane Heal, Kent Hurtig, Dudley Knowles, Matthew Kramer, Hallvard Lillehammer, Loren Lomasky, Joachim Lyon, Andrew Mason (Edinburgh), Elinor Mason, Fiona Macpherson, David McCarthy, Conor McHugh, Cheryl Misak, Kieren Oberman, David Oderberg, Max Pensky, Martin Peterson, Mike Ridge, Adam Rieger, Ben Saunders, Rebecca Stangl, Philip Stratton-Lake, Adam Swift, John Tasioulas, Andrew Williams, and Jonathan Wolff.

My paper is directly about distribution, and not directly about rights. Admittedly, discussions of the distribution of welfare or resources take various stands on rights. For example, we might support various possible redistributive programmes without going quite so far as to claim that the *beneficiaries* have *rights* to the benefits those programmes would provide to them. Nevertheless, if we support such redistributive programmes, we presumably deny that those *from* whom wealth or other goods are to be taken have an overriding moral right to what is to be taken. For if they did have an overriding moral right to those goods, then taking those goods away from them for redistribution cannot be morally permissible. So my paper must presume that those *from* whom wealth or other goods might be redistributed do not have an overriding moral right to those goods.

I turn now to the objection that utilitarianism can endorse even extreme inequality if this is what maximizes utility. But wait: is inequality necessarily bad? Wouldn't *equality* be *bad* where equality would be unfair or unjust? Shouldn't we think that equality is essential only where fairness or justice demands (or at least permits) it?

Allow me to pause for a moment to comment on the relation of fairness to justice. Hart (1994, 158) wrote, 'The distinctive features of justice and their special connection with law begin to emerge if it is observed that most of the criticisms made in terms of just and unjust could almost equally well be conveyed by the words "fair" and "unfair".' For much of this paper, I will assume that fairness is an important part of justice—and the part of justice with which I will be concerned. I do not claim that fairness is all of justice. I am willing to accept that justice requires people to have the legal rights they ought to have, including non-welfare rights as well as welfare rights. Fairness may or may not support certain welfare rights, but I admit that it may well not insist upon various non-welfare rights. Again, I think Hart suggested this: 'while making no unfair discriminations they [the laws] might fail altogether to provide a remedy for certain types of injury inflicted by one person on another, even though morally compensation would be thought due. In this matter the laws might be unjust while treating all alike' (Hart 1994, 164).

So, then, what does fairness demand? One kind of fairness consists in the equal application of rules, or, as it is sometimes put, the same rules being applied to everyone. This kind of fairness is often called formal fairness. Hart wrote that justice's 'leading precept' is 'often formulated as "treat like cases alike"; though we need to add to the latter "and treat different cases differently" '.[2]

But as Hart implied with his example about a system of rules lacking a remedy for certain types of injury inflicted by one person on another, there is more to fairness than formal fairness. To borrow another example from Hart (1994, 160), suppose some society had a rule that red-haired murderers were to be punished by thirty years in prison whereas murderers with other hair colours were to be

---

[2] Hart 1994, 159. See also ibid, 206.

punished by sixty years in prison. Even if that rule were rigorously and equally applied to everyone, the arrangement would hardly be fair.

Rules need to be not only equally applied but also fair in their content. To be fair, rules must not make distinctions where none are relevant—like the distinction between red-haired people and people without red hair. So, what distinctions *are* relevant to fairness?

This paper will discuss two of the distinctions often thought to be relevant to fairness. One distinction under consideration here is between benefits that *satisfy some need* and benefits that *do not satisfy any need*. The other distinction under consideration here is between *deserved* benefits and *undeserved* benefits. (I do not mean to suggest that the only distinctions to which rules have to be sensitive in order to be fair are distinctions concerning need and desert. But these are the ones on which this paper is focused.)

2 Needs Contrasted with Desires

Before I start raising problems for the idea of needs, let me try to articulate some of its attractions.

Insofar as needs play (or purport to play) a central role in moral and political thought, the needs in question are thought to be much *less optional*, much *more tightly restricted*, than merely whatever means to whatever ends. Obviously, there is a more general instrumental meaning of '*y* needs *x*'. In this more general instrumental sense of 'needs', *y* needs *x* whenever *x* is a necessary means to some further state of *y*. The more general instrumental sense of 'need' often carries no moral weight whatsoever, because the end for which the means is 'needed' might be trivial or even evil.

In order to make sense of the contemporary discussion of needs, we must juxtapose what people need with the more general instrumental sense of 'need'. We must also juxtapose what people need with whatever would help people fulfil their desires. For example, David Wiggins (1991, 17, 43) juxtaposes objective needs with merely subjective desires, as does David Miller (1999, 209, 211, 222–3).

Were the contrast between objective needs and subjective desires truly exclusive, there would be a great deal to be said for thinking that moral and political thinking should prioritize the narrower category of need-satisfaction rather than the broader category of desire-fulfilment. But to reject needs as a focus of moral and political concern is not necessarily to endorse having as the focus the fulfilment of people's desires. Some might propose that the focus should be on ideals other than welfare. Others might propose that, though the focus should be welfare, welfare is not best understood exclusively in terms of items so variable as people's desires or feelings. For example, there are so-called objective list theories of welfare.³ Those who hold this view might think that the foundational principle of moral and political thought should be concerned with welfare promotion, where welfare is best understood as a mix of ingredients that are the same for everyone. This view can acknowledge relevant variation between individuals, but the view would hold that the variation is in the proportions, not in the basic ingredients.

3 Need-satisfaction Contrasted with Equality

Before I consider some proposals about exactly what the criterion of need is, let me rely on a rough and intuitive sense of need in order to compare the aim of need-satisfaction with the aim of *equalizing resources*. Those who have least are, at least typically if not necessarily, the most needy. If pursuing need-satisfaction entails trying first to aid the most needy, then pursuing need-satisfaction will typically reduce inequality of resources.

However, pursuing equality of resources can require much more than satisfying needs, at least in circumstances where there are more than enough resources available to satisfy everyone's needs (Feinberg 1973, 109, 117, 119; Wiggins 1991, 28, 36). In this sense, a requirement on society to make sure all have as much as they need will typically require less redistribution than a requirement to establish or maintain equality of resources (and less than a requirement to maximize utility).

There are cases where the only way to achieve equality of resources is to level *down*. The goal of maximally satisfying needs contrasts here with the goal of equalizing resources. Equalizing resources can, and satisfying needs cannot, necessitate levelling down.

Actually, we might distinguish two kinds of case. In one, the only way to equalize resources is to take away some of those held by the better off when for some reason the taken away resources cannot be distributed to anyone else. This is what levelling down usually means. The other kind of case is one where the only way to equalize resources is to prevent some people from getting a resource that only they could get. Let us use the expression 'wasting resources' to refer to this kind of case (Raz 1986, 227). A question I'll come back to is whether there is always something undesirable in levelling down or wasting resources.

Arguably, there are cases where equalizing resources would not even give everyone what they need, precisely because some people need much more than others. For example, an able-bodied person needs socks and shoes; someone with no legs and only one arm needs a wheelchair, which is more expensive than socks

³ The now classic formulation of objective list accounts of welfare appears in Parfit 1984, Appendix I. Another especially good discussion appears in Crisp 1997, ch 3.

and shoes. In a particularly bad situation, equalizing resources might result in each person's getting less than he or she needs.

Many of the same points go through if we compare the goal of *equalizing welfare* with the goal of need-satisfaction. Where there are more than enough resources available to satisfy everyone's needs, satisfying everyone's needs might stop short of equalizing welfare. Equalizing welfare would require, at least in developed economies, much more redistribution than satisfying needs would require. And, there are cases where the only way to achieve equality of welfare is to level down or to waste benefits. (Here I'm using the term 'waste benefits' in a way parallel to my earlier use of 'waste resources'.) In contrast, satisfying needs cannot necessitate leveling down or wasting benefits.

4 Defining 'Need' in Terms of 'Harm'

Elizabeth Anscombe wrote, 'To say that [an organism] needs that environment is not to say, eg that you want it to have that environment, but that it won't flourish unless it has it.'[4] Feinberg switched from explicating needs in terms of necessary means to *flourishing* to explicating them in terms of *harm*. Feinberg (1973, 111) wrote, 'In a general sense, to say that S needs X is to say simply that if he doesn't have X he will be harmed.' David Wiggins called this sense of need, the 'absolute' sense. Wiggins (1991, 10) influentially explicated 'I need [absolutely] to have x' ... [as] 'It is necessary, things being what they actually are, that if I avoid being harmed then I have x.'

Wiggins points out some complexities that deserve mention. One is that what constitutes flourishing and harm may be not only controversial but also essentially contestable and 'to some extent relative to people's conceptions of suffering, wretchedness and harm' (Wiggins 1991, 11; cf ibid, 322). I will come back to debates about what constitutes harm.

Another complexity he mentions is that need is relative to the possibilities at the time. A claim about y's non-instrumental need implies that there exists a possible future in which y has at least some minimal degree of flourishing:

[I]f y non-instrumentally needs x at t under circumstances c, then there *exists* some alternative future in which y does flourish to some however minimal extent. (When I am utterly doomed however the future is realistically envisaged, then I can begin to lose some of my ordinary needs...) (Wiggins 1991, 13)

Wiggins's reference to alternative possibilities suggests his account of harm includes what I shall later discuss as the counterfactual account.

Wiggins puts a moral rider on needs. In his analysis, I cannot need something the provision of which involves 'morally (or otherwise) unacceptable acts

---

[4] Anscombe 1958, 7. Cf Hart 1994, 190–2.

or interventions in the arrangements of particular human lives or society or whatever' (Wiggins 1991, 12). I can see why he wants this rider. He wants an analysis of needs such that they turn out to be morally compelling. Needs could not be morally compelling if satisfying them involves morally unacceptable acts. Still, if what we want is first an analysis of the ordinary-language use of the term 'needs' and only then an evaluation of the moral force of needs so construed, Wiggins's account seems to me faulty here. As we ordinarily use the term 'needs', morally unacceptable acts are sometimes the only possible way of preventing harm to someone. It is false that morality's forbidding your getting x entails that you don't need x.

In any case, a few pages later, Wiggins (1991, 14) writes,

The thought we have now arrived at is that a person needs x [absolutely] if and only if, whatever morally and socially acceptable variation it is (economically, technologically, politically, historically...*etc.*) possible to envisage occurring within the relevant time-span, he will be harmed if he goes without x.

5 Defining 'Harm' for the Purposes of the Need Principle

If y's needs are defined as things without which y would be harmed, we need to ask how harm is to be defined. There seem to me four possible understandings of 'harm':

(i) Harm could be understood as a *reduction* in welfare, such that y is harmed if and only if y's welfare is less than it was right before the harm.

(ii) Harm could be understood in a counterfactual way: an event e harmed y if and only if e's not occurring would have left y better off than y was in fact left because of e's occurrence.[5]

(iii) Harm could be understood in a *highly moralized way*, as in y is harmed if and only if y is wronged.

(iv) Harm could be defined in terms of reduction in welfare below a certain threshold, eg, the threshold for a decent human life.

First consider (i), the view that harm is a *reduction* in welfare, a reduction from an immediately prior higher level of welfare. (i) is perhaps the most common understanding of the concept of harm. But (i) seems to be inappropriate for combination with the definition of needs in terms of harms. I have three arguments for the conclusion that this combination is unappealing.

One argument is as follows. Needs are to be at least roughly the same for everyone, or at least everyone within some society. But what Bill Gates must have in

---

[5] This is a *very* rough statement of the counterfactual understanding of harm. For discussions of the counterfactual understanding of harm, see Feinberg 1992, 7–11; and Greene, unpublished.

order to prevent reductions in his welfare is vastly greater than what I must have in order to prevent reductions in my welfare. So consider this *reductio*:

Premise 1:   Needs are what a person must have to avoid being harmed.
Premise 2:   Harm is reduction from an immediately prior higher level of welfare.
Conclusion 1: Needs are what a person must have in order to avoid reduction from an immediately prior higher level of welfare.
Premise 3:   There is huge variation in the welfare levels, even within a single society.
Conclusion 2: Even within a single society, there is huge variation in needs, in line with the variation in levels of welfare

Conclusion 2 will be unattractive to needs theorists and is anyway implausible.

How could we avoid conclusion 2? Not by trying to deny the undeniable truth that there is huge variation in the welfare levels of people, even within a single society (premise 3). To avoid conclusion 2, we should instead either deny the definition of needs as necessary means to avoiding harm (premise 1) or deny the definition of harm as a reduction in welfare from an immediately prior level (premise 2).

Here is my second argument against defining needs as necessary means to avoiding reductions in welfare: there are plenty of reductions in welfare that don't involve needs. Suppose Bill Gates has vastly more than he needs, both materially and otherwise. Then he loses one of his most loved friends. His welfare is thus reduced. But this reduction in no way takes him below the threshold of need satisfaction. So, if harm is understood as reduction in welfare, then being harmed is not a sufficient condition for having unmet needs.

My third argument against defining needs as necessary means to avoiding reductions in welfare is that the suggestion that someone should be given what he needs is often *not* about preventing *reductions* in his welfare. It is instead about making him better off than he is now and would otherwise remain. Someone already very badly off—for example, someone chronically malnourished and afflicted by an unpleasant but not progressive sickness—might well *need* more calories and more medicine. But this is not to prevent his going downhill from here, but rather to improve his position. If harm is understood as reduction in welfare, there can be need satisfaction that does not prevent harm. In other words, if harm is understood as *reduction* in welfare, then avoiding harm is not a necessary condition for satisfying need.

Hence, if harm is understood as reduction in welfare, then being under threat of harm is neither a necessary nor sufficient condition for being in need. For the purposes of specifying a sense of harm appropriate for Wiggins's account of needs, harm cannot plausibly be understood as reduction in welfare.

Having rejected the idea that need should be defined in terms of harm where harm is defined as reduction of welfare, let us turn to the counterfactual account of harm: an event *e* harmed *y* if and only if *e*'s not occurring would have left *y* better off than *y* was left because of *e*'s occurrence. Suppose I'm tied to a stake about to be burned alive. The only way you can stop me from experiencing this horrible end is to shoot me dead. You do this to prevent my suffering. Now, on the counterfactual account, you didn't harm me. For if I hadn't been shot, I would have been worse off, dying only a little later but after the most acute physical agony.

I believe that, in very many jurisdictions, the counterfactual account of harm is not accepted in *law*. Nevertheless, I think it has some *moral* grip on us. Suppose someone shoots me dead right before the fire reaches me, or destroys my diaries before the cops get their hands on them, or steals my intoxicants just before my camping trip. If shooting me saved me from burning to death, if destroying my diary prevented my arrest, if stealing my intoxicants forced me to undergo the detoxification that saves my life, then we feel some pressure to say that I am benefited rather than harmed.

But even if the counterfactual account of harm is acceptable for moral evaluation, it won't fit with an analysis of need in terms of avoiding harm. Consider this argument:

Premise 1:   A person y needs x if and only if y must have x to avoid harm.

Premise 2: y's not getting x harms y if and only if y's not getting x leaves y worse off than y would be left if y got x.

Conclusion 1:   Needs are what a person must have in order to avoid being left worse off than she or he would have been if she or he had gotten the needed items.

Premise 3:   Even within a single society, because of the huge variation in levels of welfare, there is huge variation in what a person must have in order to avoid being left worse off than he or she would have been.

Conclusion 2:   Even within a single society, there is huge variation in needs, in line with the variation in levels of welfare.

Again, conclusion 2 will be unattractive to needs theorists and is anyway implausible. And again, premise 3 is undeniable. So the problem must be in premise 1 (understanding needs in terms of avoiding harms) or premise 2 (understanding harms in the counterfactual way).

I am confident that no needs theorist who reflects carefully would accept the counterfactual account of harm. Suppose we favour redistributive taxation such that Bill Gates and other very rich people have a significant percentage of their wealth or income taken for spending on the very poor. Such programmes are of course regularly defended on the grounds that the very rich don't need all of their income or wealth and that the very poor need more resources than they currently have. But such thoughts are not compatible with defining 'need' as what is necessary to avoid harm, and then understanding 'harm' in the way the counterfactual account does. On the counterfactual account, redistribution from rich to poor *does* harm the rich, or at least many of them, since without the redistribution they would be better off.

Now suppose that harm is understood in a *moralized way*. For example, it might be held that whenever y is wronged, y must be harmed. But this is very implausible. I wrong you if I fail to keep my promise to you, but sometimes not keeping promises to someone does not harm, or perhaps even benefits, that person. So now consider another moralized understanding of harm: whenever *y* is harmed, *y* is wronged. This view is even more obviously implausible. We are sometimes harmed by acts of nature, but they do not wrong us.

So I have now argued against the moralized conceptions of harm, and against combining the idea that needs are whatever one must have to avoid harm with either the counterfactual account of harm or the idea that harm is a reduction in welfare.

What remains is (iv), the view that harm is defined in terms of reduction in welfare below a certain threshold (for example, the threshold for a decent human life). I agree that, if harm is defined this way and needs are defined in terms of what is necessary to avoid harm, the category of needs would not be too wide. And I agree the most plausible conception of needs points to some threshold.

However, there are two objections to this approach. First, the concept 'harm' gets only a technical, stipulated sense within the formula 'needs are what you must have to avoid being harmed and being harmed consists in being below a threshold'. In the ordinary language sense of 'harm', it is false that something harms you only if it reduces you to a level below some threshold.

Secondly, if needs are defined in terms of harm and harm in terms of a threshold, then the concept of harm is actually doing no work. Really, in this conception, needs are defined in terms of the threshold. On balance, I think defining needs *directly* in terms of a threshold—by omitting an otiose reference to harm—is clearer and more promising. To that more direct approach, I now turn.

6 Three Alternative Possible Criteria of Need

David Miller can be taken as an exemplar of the more direct approach. He distinguishes three alternative possible criteria of need.

One criterion that Miller identifies refers to 'biological or quasi-biological facts' about what someone must have to survive and function (Miller 1999, 207). These are going to be facts about water, nutrition, warmth, and the like. If needs are limited to the amount of water, nutrition, warmth, and the like that people need to survive for some limited period, then satisfying people's needs is quite undemanding, at least in most modern economies (Miller 1999, 208).

However, as Miller objects, how should we determine the span of life the shortening of which gives people less than they need? What you need for a healthy life for the next twelve months might be shelter plus only 1460 pints of clean water and 730,000 calories, spread out fairly evenly over the time period. But, if you are now, say, 60, then what you need to live the next 30 years in good health might be not only shelter, 21,900,000 calories, and 43,800 pints of clean water, but also medical breakthroughs in combating cancer, heart disease, osteoporosis, Alzheimer's disease, etc. And why stop at only 30 more years?

Wiggins's account was:

You need *x* if and only if, without *x*, you can't avoid harm.

As Miller suggests, Wiggins's account was incomplete. It should have been:

You need *x* if and only if, without *x*, you can't avoid harm during the next *n* amount of time.

In response to this objection, some people have said to me that the length of time that humans *need* has been and will remain but 'three score and ten' years. The idea is that, no matter what the varying statistics about life expectancy, there is a normative idea that can be put as: 'we *need* to live long enough to see our grandchildren; we *don't* need to live long enough to see our great-grandchildren'.

In response, I of course agree that life extended *beyond* our capacity to be productive and our capacity to enjoy life is *not* what we need. But, insofar as I can make sense of the concept of need, I think it a gross failure of imagination and ambition to draw the line at three score and ten. Advances in medical technology offer the extension of healthy, alert years. Advances in communication technology give people the ability to find out about the world via the web and to talk to the world via email, even as their actual mobility reduces with age. As long as a pleasant, intellectually active, socially interactive life is possible, I cannot see why anyone's 'needs' expire at 70 years, or at 100 years, or at 150 years.

Here needs theorists face a dilemma. One horn is to insist on a line at something like 'three score and ten', in which case needs remain limited, but at the cost of a seemingly arbitrary (and mean) limit on needs. The other horn is to admit that the span of life the shortening of which gives people less than they need is very long, perhaps indefinitely so. In this case, needs are voracious (think of the cost of medical research), even to the point of being practically unending. Once the concept of needs is expanded to include vaccines and cures for every malady that threatens physical or mental health, the principle that needs must be satisfied threatens to be virtually insatiable. Much of the advantage (concerning demandingness) that the needs principle had over utilitarian and egalitarian principles has been lost. So neither horn of this dilemma provides a comfortable position for needs theorists.

Miller's second possible criterion of needs specifies that needs are the necessary means to the achievement of people's subjective aims and ambitions. However, here are just a few of the many compelling objections to having this be the criterion. There will be too much variation on this criterion of needs, since subjective aims and ambitions vary considerably. Furthermore, if needs are just whatever is necessary to the achievement of subjective aims and ambitions, then, since new aims and ambitions spring up when old ones are satisfied, the principle that needs should be met won't be satiable.

Miller's own reason for rejecting the criterion of needs in terms of subjective aims and ambitions is that people should be responsible for their subjective aims and ambitions (Miller 1999, 209). As he puts the idea, one's subjective aims and ambitions should not impose duties on others unless others *validate* one's aims and ambitions as being essential elements of a 'decent human life'.

This brings us to Miller's third possible criterion of needs, according to which *y* needs *x* if and only if *y* must have *x* in order to have a minimally decent life according to society's beliefs about what constitutes a minimally decent human life. Note, these beliefs are shared ones about a *minimally decent* life; they are not beliefs about *average* standard of living (Miller 1999, 212, 319 n 23, n 25). The average standard of living in a society might be above or below what that society thinks is minimally decent.

I think those who focus on needs have their hearts in the right place. They are concerned about the needy, an excellent focus of practical concern (as long as the worst off are the neediest). But, on balance, the reason not to put too much philosophical weight on the concept of need seems to me compelling, as I will now explain.

What counts as a need is especially contestable and indeterminate. Admittedly, ethics cannot do without concepts that are contestable and indeterminate. Still, the concept *need* is *especially* contestable and indeterminate (see the discussion above about how many healthy years of life one 'needs'). We should avoid making personal and social decisions turn on such problematic concepts, if we can do so without implausible implications.

7 Weighted Prioritarianism Instead of a Needs Principle

I have already indicated why I think strict equality of resources and equality of welfare are unattractive ideals. Those ideals can insist upon levelling down and the waste of resources and benefits. I noted that a needs principle can often call for *redistribution* for the sake of the worse off, *without* ever having to insist upon the *levelling down* or the waste of resources and benefits. But I have just pressed an objection against the needs principle—namely that the concept of need is too contestable and indeterminate. That objection seems to me enough to condemn the needs principle as long as there is some other principle that captures much of what was appealing about the needs principle without also being subject to the same forceful objection.

Consider what has come to be called weighted prioritarianism, the view that benefits or harms to the worse off matter somewhat more than the same size benefits or harms to the better off. Weighted prioritarianism, unlike absolute (or 'strict', or 'lexical') prioritarianism, does not give strict priority to the worse off. According to weighted prioritarianism, a benefit to a better-off person can be preferable to a benefit to a worse-off person if the benefit to the better-off person is sufficiently larger. Most forms of weighted prioritarianism are also aggregative, in the sense that a benefit to a worse-off person can be outweighed by many better-off people's each getting smaller benefits.[6]

---

[6] For the attractions of but also problems with non-aggregative weighted prioritarianism, see Fleurbaey, Tungodden, and Vallentyne 2009 (forthcoming).

8 Non-needs-based Threshold View

Roger Crisp rejects weighted prioritarianism because of cases where there are very few badly off and many better off (Crisp 2006, ch 6). Consider a choice between giving a fairly small benefit to each of a small number of badly off and giving a larger benefit to each of a larger number of better off. Since the benefit to the better off would be greater in size per beneficiary and would go to a larger number of people, even weighted prioritarianism, which weights the benefits to a worse-off person somewhat more heavily than the same size benefits to a better-off person, could favour choosing the benefits for the better off rather than the benefits for the worse off. Crisp takes such cases to be objections to weighted prioritarianism.

I don't share his reaction. If the number of potential better-off beneficiaries is the same as the number of worse-off beneficiaries but the benefit per person is much larger for the better off, or if the size of the benefits per person are the same but the number of better off is much larger, then I do think the benefits should go to the better off.

Even in cases where the benefit per person to the better off is smaller than the benefit per person to the worse off, aggregative weighted prioritarianism will endorse the benefits going to the better off as long as two conditions are filled. One is that the number of better off is sufficiently greater than the number of worse off. This is the aggregative element coming into play. The other condition is that the benefits in question are of 'continuous value'. Two kinds of benefit are of continuous value if and only if enough of one kind can outweigh a little of the other kind.

To be sure, such examples show how weighted prioritarianism can work against equality of distribution where waste of resources or benefits is in question. So weighted prioritarianism can work against equality of distribution not only in the levelling down cases I earlier mentioned but also in these cases Crisp describes. But these seem to me to be cases where weighted prioritarianism gets the right answer and any stronger egalitarianism gets the wrong answer.

Crisp himself rejects weighted prioritarianism in favour of a threshold 'above which priority does not count, but below which it does...'. Crisp (2006, 158) distinguishes his threshold view from the need-satisfaction principle:

[O]n any plausible distinction between needs and other components of welfare, needs give out before [appropriate] special concern. Imagine a society which includes among a large number of very wealthy and flourishing individuals a group which is very poor but whose basic and indeed non-basic needs are met. Concern for the badly off speaks in favour of at least some transfers from the rich to the poor, even if the poor use any resources gained to purchase goods which they could not be said to need.

Though the need-satisfaction principle and Crisp's threshold view are distinct, they do have much in common—both strengths and weaknesses.

One strength they share is conformity with common opinion. Miller reports that empirical studies reveal that most people's view of justice is that, once everyone has reached a certain level of basic provision, the appropriate thing to do is to stop giving special weight to benefits for the worse off and instead focus on maximizing average income (Miller 1999, ch 2). Miller seems to think that theories of justice lose plausibility insofar as they depart from the views of the common person.

A point against according those studies much weight is that the studies on which Miller focused were ones that framed the choices in terms of material goods, and especially money, not in terms of welfare. Now, the diminishing marginal utility of resources gives even utilitarians reasons to favour some level of universal provision of resources, and then to give equality of resources far less importance. Everyone *needs* at least a minimal amount of water, food, shelter, and education in order to be comfortable, secure, and knowledgeable enough to develop and achieve aims beyond survival. But once everyone has the resources for a long and healthy life, there is far less utilitarian reason for equalizing resources.

One advantage that prioritarianism has over a need-satisfaction principle is that prioritarianism does not have to draw a line between needs and non-needs. All prioritarianism has to do is determine who is worse off, and this seems much easier than determining whether y's getting x is something that y needs or merely something that would benefit y. Prioritarianism has precisely the same advantage over Crisp's non-needs-based threshold account. Crisp needs to defend a line; prioritarianism has no line to defend.

9 Weighted Prioritarianism and Comparative Unfairness

Feinberg (1973, 98–102; 1980) distinguished between comparative and non-comparative justice. Suppose you and I are each guilty of stealing an apple, and we are each punished by a lifetime of torment followed by a painful death. This is an example of non-comparative injustice. Hart's example above of a legal system with no legal remedy for an injury that people may inflict on others is another illustration of non-comparative injustice. Comparative injustice or unfairness is simpler. If you and I are equally deserving but you get less prizes or rewards or other goods than I do, then there has been a comparative injustice.

Using the concept of comparative injustice, Miller puts forward an argument against weighted prioritarianism. His example is, 'A, B, C, and D are each at minus 10, and the only possibility open to us is to raise D to minus 5 or leave things as they are' (Miller 1999, 225). One of the major points of prioritarianism is to mandate that the good be given to the available recipients in such cases. Miller and other writers present such cases as conflicts between non-comparative justice (each should be given exactly what he is due) and comparative justice (no one should get more than another unless he needs or deserves more). Miller thinks that at least in some such conflict cases weighted prioritarianism gets the wrong result, because the result that the prioritarian favours will always contain *comparative* unfairness (since D didn't need or deserve the benefit any more than A, B, or C did). Miller and these other writers think it is sometimes better for everyone to go without than it is for only some to benefit though they are no more needy or deserving than others who don't benefit (Miller 1999, 220, 225).

In reply, let me say how I reject the very description of the example. Miller specifies that each of A, B, C, and D are equally needy and equally deserving. Let me set aside desert until later in this paper, since I have not yet started to discuss it. As for the question of these four people's needs, I've argued that we should focus on how badly off people are instead of how needy they are. Suppose that part of my argument was successful. Then we should re-describe Miller's example so that A, B, C, and D are equally badly off. Again, suppose a benefit can be given to one of them, specifically D, but to no other. Is it unfair that this benefit go to D, making him or her better off than the other three?

We might think that there is comparative unfairness whenever one person ends up better off than another *without justification*. As Hart and many others have noted, fairness requires not only that irrelevant differences between people be ignored but also that relevant differences between people not be ignored. And then the question is whether the fact that you could benefit D but not A, B, or C is a relevant difference between D and the others. If it is a relevant difference, then fairness provides no objection to benefiting D. Miller's counter-example to weighted prioritarianism seems to me to trade not only on the idea that A, B, C, and D are equally *needy* and *deserving* but also on the idea that *these facts are the only ones relevant to fairness in this context*. In contrast, I contend that the fact that D is the only one you could help is also relevant to fairness.

What many pluralists would say about Miller's example is that, although giving D the benefit would result in some comparative unfairness, this is a case where more than one principle comes into play. They might go on to say that giving D the benefit would be best all things considered because the comparative unfairness would be outweighed by the increase in need satisfaction (D would be getting more of what he needs, even if the others are not). Or they might hold that giving D the benefit would be best all things considered because the comparative unfairness would be outweighed by the increase in non-comparative fairness (D would be getting what he deserves, even if the others are not). Or they might hold that it would be best all things considered simply because the increase in utility is enough to outweigh the comparative unfairness. But, if I am correct that the fact that D is the only one you could help is also relevant to fairness, then perhaps this is not a case where fairness is outweighed by another principle.[7]

---

[7] This paragraph and the previous one owe much to Serena Olsaretti for discussion.

Of course weighted prioritarianism (which makes no reference to the concept of desert) can conflict with principles of desert. That point has no bearing on the contention that weighted prioritarianism is superior to the needs principle. I will return to the relation of weighted prioritarianism to desert after I have contrasted the main views about the place of desert in moral and political philosophy.

10 Desert Basics

The term 'deserve' seems to have a narrow and a wide sense, corresponding to a narrow and a wide view about what the desert-basis can be. On the narrow sense of desert, the desert-basis must be the *deserver's intentional activity or performance* at a time or over time *in the past*. Sometimes the term 'deserve' is used in a wider way. Some people say that everyone *deserves* equal concern and respect. Some people say that the worse off *deserve* greater attention. In this wide sense of 'deserve', to say that you deserve something is to say that you ought to get it, whether or not you have actually done anything in the past to ground this desert.

In so far as fairness is supposed to be based at least partly in desert, it is narrow desert that is in play, not wide desert. Propositions about what people deserve in the wide sense do not indicate why they should be treated in a certain way; these propositions simply record that people should be treated in this way. Propositions about what people deserve in the narrow sense do indicate why people should be treated in a certain way, namely because of facts about their past intentional activity.

11 The Relationship between Desert and Need-satisfaction

If we focus on the primary sense of desert as tied to the past intentional activity or performance of the deserver, we are taking past intentional activity or performance to be the desert-basis. If we go down this route, then we cannot take *need* to be a desert-basis. Need is a forward-looking rather than backward-looking concept, and need is not restricted to *intentional* activity or performance. Thus, there is no conceptual guarantee that desert and need cannot conflict. In fact, of course, they often do conflict.

12 Desert, Pre-institutional or Institutional?

As John Rawls (1971, §§ 17 and 48) argued, the institutional account of desert understands desert as the *product* of *just* institutions, *not* as a restriction on what counts as just institutions. This institutional account of desert is common ground between utilitarians, Rawls, and weighted prioritarians.

The idea that desert is an institutional concept does not deny that institutions can be too evil to generate deserts. Typically, the idea is that only those institutions that meet some standard of justice can generate desert claims (where this standard of justice does not itself invoke desert).

The opposition to the institutional account of desert takes the form of commitment to a pre-institutional concept of desert. This pre-institutional account does not deny that institutions are regularly relevant to desert, and that many desert claims make no sense outside of an institutional context (Miller 1999, 138–9). You deserve promotion to a higher rank only if there are various institutions making up the profession and its aims. What makes the pre-institutional account distinctive is its insistence that there are some principles of desert that are 'pre-institutional', ie, whose legitimacy is prior to the justification of institutions. According to the pre-institutional account, some principles of desert operate as restrictions on what can be a just institution or practice.

If desert turns out to be purely an institutional concept, in the way that utilitarians, Rawls, and weighted prioritarians think, then desert is not morally fundamental. What are fundamental are the considerations that shape the moral and other practices we *should* have, and these considerations don't include desert.[8]

I offer the picture below to clarify the debate.

Rival principles for picking rules/institutions	→	Rules of Morality & Social Institutions	→	Institutional Desert
U Pick rules & institutions that maximize expected utility. Or R Pick rules & institutions that maximize the minimum. Or P Pick rules & institutions that maximize expected value in weighted prioritarian terms. Or D From the possible rules & institutions that respect pre-institutional desert, use the best of U, R, P, or…to select rules & institutions.		1 Don't kill or hurt others. 2 Don't take or harm others' property. 3 Don't break your promises. 4 Don't lie. 5 In allocating your own time, effort & other resources, give extra weight to special connections—eg, family, friends, & benefactors. 6 Do good generally, especially for the worse off. 7 People are morally free to make whatever agreements are compatible with the above. So markets will shape pay rates.		Moral rules & social institutions are the framework for institutional desert. Thus, praise those who are especially good at following rules 1–6, punish those who break any of 1–4, and pay according to valid agreements.

In the table above, utilitarians espouse U, Rawlsians R, and weighted prioritarians P. None of these views holds that desert should be mentioned in the left column (in other words, in the correct first principle). Those like Miller who believe in

---

[8] A helpful discussion of desert as a 'parasitic' notion appears in Olsaretti 2003, 196–7.

pre-institutional desert reject U, R, P, and any other similar first principle that fails to mention pre-institutional desert. Miller and others who believe in pre-institutional desert espouse D.

Here is Miller's argument for pre-institutional desert. Imagine that rules are assessed in terms of whether they would maximize the position of the worst off, or maximize utility, or satisfy whatever other non-desert principle. Suppose that the rules that satisfy this test are ones that would pay men more for biscuit-packing than they would pay women for the same work. Given the situation as described, justice and fairness cannot oppose this differential pay scheme unless desert is not purely a matter of what rules and institutions the non-desert principle mandates (Miller 1999, 141). Desert requires equal pay for equal work, and this principle is prior to any institutions or practices or rules endorsed by some other principle. This suggests principle D in the left-hand column of the above table.

I accept that the principle of equal pay for equal work has had many beneficial effects. But I cannot believe it is as fundamental as Miller suggests. Think of cases where equal pay for equal work would rightly be compromised, and where no injustice seems to be done. Suppose universities need to recruit more women lecturers, and suppose that women candidates are in short supply. In such circumstances, many universities might have to pay women lecturers more than men, because the relative demand for women lecturers is higher. I cannot believe this is unjust, any more than the workings of supply and demand more generally are.

Now what one might say is that in the circumstances described women lecturers really would be doing more than men, since the women would be in effect helping with gender diversity. But once this sort of thing is allowed into the 'equal pay for equal work' principle, that principle loses its bite.

Miller has another example illustrating that desert is a pre-institutional concept. He writes, 'desert requires that superior performance attracts superior recognition in whatever form the institutions mandate.... [I]f people are paid for work of this kind [as opposed to having their performance recognized in some other way, such as prizes or honours], then those whose productivity is higher deserve, *ceteris paribus*, higher pay (something, once again, that Rawls's difference principles do not necessarily require)' (Miller 1999, 141). More generally,

If there are performances that are socially valued, then those who undertake them do have deserts, albeit rather vague ones, prior to the establishment of institutions. They deserve recognition or reward *in some form* even though the form may legitimately vary a good deal from place to place. If a society simply refuses to show its appreciation of voluntary activities that are valuable by its own standards, then its institutions are less than just. (Miller 1999, 142)

But is it conceptually possible that a society could value a certain kind of performance and yet recognize the valued performance in no way at all—not even by admiring it? Admittedly, for some reason, a society could value a certain kind of performance and yet neither *publicly* reward nor even *outwardly express* admiration for the valued performance. Perhaps the society keeps its admiration to itself, so to speak, for fear of making those who perform well big-headed. Must this be an unjust practice in the way Miller suggests? I cannot believe that it must be so.

I have thus concluded that Miller's two examples of pre-institutional desert are not compelling. There might, however, be better examples of pre-institutional desert. So I am open-minded but not yet persuaded that there is pre-institutional desert.

13 Desert on a Different Level than Weighted Prioritarianism

Suppose that desert is a purely institutional concept. Then desert plays no role in the first column, which is where weighted prioritarianism plays its most important role. However, desert and weighted prioritarianism can run into one another at a different, derived level, since one of the rules of morality chosen by weighted prioritarianism will itself be a *pro tanto* duty to do good for others, especially the worse off. See rule 6 below:

Principle for picking rules & institutions	→	Rules of Morality & Social Institutions	→	Institutional Desert
Pick rules & institutions that maximize expected value in weighted prioritarian terms.		1 Don't kill or hurt others. 2 Don't take or harm others' property. 3 Don't break your promises. 4 Don't lie. 5 In allocating your own time, effort & other resources, give extra weight to special connections—family, friends, & benefactors. 6 Do good generally, especially for the worse off. 7 People are morally free to make whatever agreements are compatible with the above. So agreements will determine pay rates.		Praise those who are especially good at following rules 1–6, punish those who break any of 1–4, and pay according to valid agreements.

In this picture, weighted prioritarianism appears in the first column as the principle for selecting rules and institutions. It also has a place in the second column as a rule thus selected (rule 6 above). Rules about desert are primarily in the third column, but the second column's rule 7 suggests that agreements will determine some kinds of desert.

The above picture does not deny instances of conflict between respecting desert and other requirements. More specifically, rules and institutions selected on weighted prioritarian grounds will frequently result in situations where appropriate praise, punishment, or pay will not have the best outcome in weighted prioritarian terms. But weighted prioritarianism is outrageously implausible unless it is either *merely one of multiple first principles to be balanced against one another at the same level*, or *the only first principle but in a multi-level theory*, where other considerations can be dominant at the derived levels. In short, any plausible form of weighted prioritarianism will have to accept that sometimes other kinds of considerations determine what, on balance, should be done.

Conclusions

Talk of needs can be a way of expressing appropriate concern for the worst off. But what seems to me pivotal is who the worst off are and how to help them, not whether their lives are above or below some line of need or some other threshold.

I attacked two of David Miller's arguments for pre-institutional desert. I also defended weighted prioritarianism against Miller's objection that, because weighted prioritarianism can conflict with desert, it can lead to comparative injustice. Part of my defence involved the idea that desert and extra concern for the worse off can come in at different levels of injunction. But I admit that, when desert and concern for the worse off come into direct conflict, desert can be the more important consideration.

11

The Basic Liberties

Philip Pettit

We have two ways of talking about liberty or freedom, one in the singular, the other in the plural. We concern ourselves in the singular mode with how far someone is free to do or not to do certain things, or with how far someone is a free person or not a free person. But, equally, we concern ourselves with the plural question as to how far the person enjoys the liberties that we take to be important or basic. What are those plural liberties, however? What does it take for something to count as a basic liberty?

The usual approach to this question is to give a list of some presumptive basic liberties—say, those of thought, speech, and association—and then to add a gestural 'and so on'. My aim in this paper is to do a little better in elaborating a conception of the sorts of liberties at which the 'and so on' gestures. I argue that the basic liberties can be usefully identified as the liberties required for living the life of a free person or citizen and I spell out that requirement in three constraints, which I describe as feasible extension, personal significance and equal co-enjoyment.

There are many candidate sets of basic liberties that might be proposed for protection, whether in general or for a particular society. The claim that I defend is that in order to count as a set of basic liberties, the types of choice protected under any proposal should be capable of being equally enjoyed at the same time by everyone (equal co-enjoyment), should be important in the life of normal human beings (personal significance), and should not be unnecessarily restricted: they should be as extensive as the other constraints allow (feasible extension).

The aim of the paper being quite limited, I abstract from many important issues. I do not provide an argument for why it is important that some set of basic liberties be protected, nor do I rate the importance of such protection against other social goals. I say nothing on how far it should be a requirement of democracy that certain sorts of liberties are entrenched—whether constitutionally or otherwise—and how far democratic process should be allowed to vary the specification and protection of basic liberties. And I do not rank the different candidate sets of basic liberties—the different sets that satisfy my three constraints—in relation to one other. These candidate sets will vary in how they invoke co-ordinating rules to specify the liberties—this variation will be illustrated later—in how they trade off different liberties against one another, in how they trade off the quantity of choices protected against the quality of protection provided, and in how many liberties they actually include.

My own interest in the basic liberties stems from the place that I think they must be given in a republican conception of freedom and government. But the basic liberties are invoked at some point in almost every political theory, so that the topic should be of interest to others also. It should be of particular interest for those who follow John Rawls (1971) in thinking that a first requirement of justice is the institution of a system of basic liberties to which everyone has equal access. H.L.A. Hart (1973) provided an extended analysis of the difficulties facing this Rawlsian claim and his essay will figure prominently in my discussion. Hart brought to light a daunting range of difficulties in the Rawlsian idea. And in the course of doing that he marshalled a number of important observations. My account of the basic liberties is deeply shaped by these, for they identify the rocks that any theory of the basic liberties has to navigate around.

1 From Republican Theory to the Basic Liberties

The key republican idea is that a person or citizen will be free to the extent that suitable choices are suitably protected and empowered. The suitable-choices clause means that it will not be enough for the person to have any old choices protected—say, those that have no significance for anyone or even those that harm others. And the suitable-protection clause implies that it will not be enough for the person to have those choices protected by being enabled to appease or buy off would-be offenders, for example, to take evasive action, or to call on some mafia friends.

The republican theory of suitable protection emphasizes the need to guard against domination, not just interference. You will enjoy suitable protection in a particular choice just to the extent that other individuals or groups do not have access to means of non-deliberative control over that choice. Others may be able to deliberate with you on the basis of sincere, take-it-or-leave-it reasons and influence what you do. But they should not be allowed a power of interfering with the choice, without exposing themselves to an inhibiting risk of punishment; they should not be able to block, burden, or deceptively redirect the choice with any degree of impunity. In short, they should not have 'dominating control' over what you choose.

Dominating control is not equivalent, it should be noticed, to interference. One the one hand, people may have dominating control in a choice you make, yet not actually interfere with you; they may invigilate what you do and only resort to obstruction, coercion, or deception when such interference is necessary to get you to do as they wish. And, on the other hand, people may interfere in your choice and yet not have dominating control; their interference may be subject to your check or counter-control. The protected, free choice is the choice that evades dominating control, then, but not necessarily the choice that escapes interference (Pettit 1997; Skinner 1998; Pettit 2008b; Pettit 2008a)

To have a theory of suitable protection is not yet to have a theory as to what choices are suitable for protection. I assume that the set of choices to be protected in any society will have to be choices of the kind that we might expect any free person or citizen to be able to exercise; they will have to be choices that can define the 'freeman' of traditional republican discourse (Skinner 2006; Pettit 2007). I call such a set of choices basic liberties. No free citizenship without enjoyment of a suitable set of basic liberties, in this sense, and no enjoyment of such a set of basic liberties without free citizenship. The free person or *liber* is the citizen or *civis* who is fully incorporated into a framework that guards those basic liberties against the control of others. In that sense, to give the equation a Roman cast, 'full *libertas* is coterminous with *civitas*' (Wirszubski 1968, 3).

Linking the basic liberties with the ability to enjoy the life of a free citizen has a natural appeal for anyone who affiliates with the long republican tradition but it should make sense within a variety of other approaches too. The linkage is useful, as we shall see, because it enables us to spell out three specific constraints that we might expect any candidate set of basic liberties to satisfy.

2 Introducing the Basic Liberties

The question of how to identify the basic liberties is remarkably neglected in the literature. The only prominent discussions are in Rawls's work and in the essay by H.L.A. Hart (1973) on Rawls's view of liberty. Rawls argued, in an early formulation of his theory, that the first requirement of justice, one with priority over any other demand on the basic structure of a society, is that everyone should have 'an equal right to the most extensive liberty compatible with a like liberty for all' (Rawls 1958). This may have seemed to rule out private property, since the restrictions on the property-less might outweigh the liberties of the propertied (Hart 1973, 538). Perhaps for that reason, he later moved on to a formulation involving liberties, not liberty. 'Each person is to have an equal right to the most extensive total system of equal basic liberties compatible with a similar system for all' (Rawls 1971, 302; see also 1993; 2001).

By all accounts, the basic liberties are choices, each of which is distinguished by a particular, significant option. Thus, to follow a rough enumeration suggested by Rawls, there is the liberty of judging as one thinks best; speaking one's mind; associating with others; holding private property; casting a vote; and putting oneself forward for office (Rawls 1971, 61).

People will possess such liberties to the extent that they have the wherewithal to be able to access the distinguishing option, or not, as they choose. This means that they must be protected against the uninvited control of others over what they say, where they associate, what they own, or how they vote. These liberties will be more valuable for bearers to the extent that their resources do not just provide the basic wherewithal required but make it possible to exercise the liberties more frequently, more widely, or more easily. Further resources may enable people to speak on the media, for example, not merely in private; give them a larger network for making contacts with others; provide a wider range of things to own; or just make it easier to go and vote. Although such differences in resources affect the value of the liberties, the idea is that the possession of the liberties does not increase with such access to further resources (Rawls 1971, 204). While those resources enable people to exercise the choices at less and less cost or over a wider and wider range, they do not necessarily mean that those with greater resources possess the liberties in a higher degree than those with fewer (Pettit 1997, 75–6).[1]

All of this serves to introduce basic liberties but not to make the category particularly precise. In this paper I rely on three constraints in order to determine more exactly the sets of liberties that should count as candidates for the status of basic liberties. The three constraints are justified by reference to the association between the basic liberties and being able to live the life of the free citizen. Two can be stated quite briefly but discussion of the third will take up most of the paper.

3 The Constraint of Feasible Extension

If the basic liberties are to be required for free citizenship, then a first constraint is that they should be as numerous as possible, subject to the satisfaction of the other constraints that I go on to discuss. The other constraints, as interpreted in a given society, will constitute a bar that choice-types have to pass there, if they are to count as basic liberties that ought to be protected. The constraint of feasible extension holds that, consistently with the other liberties established in any proposal, further liberties that pass that bar also deserve to count as basic liberties and should be suitably protected in the society.

Suppose that the society protects certain liberties that count as basic by other constraints but that it does not do optimally in this respect: there are further liberties that it might equally protect, consistently with those constraints, and

---

[1] On the republican approach, there will be limits on the poverty or inequality of resources that is tolerable, since a certain level of deprivation or imbalance will make in itself for dominating control; it will reduce the costs of interference to the strong and so give them a controlling power of interference in the lives of the less well off (Pettit 1997; 2006; 2008). But still the distinction remains in place between having a liberty and having the resources to maximize its value. Possession of the liberty will not vary in degree with the addition of resources beyond those that are required to avoid domination by others and—if this makes for a distinct requirement—for having suitable access to the choice involved. One recent theorist who rejects this approach is Kramer (2003); see too (Van Parijs 1995).

doesn't. The members of that society would not count as fully free, on any plausible reckoning; the missing but unimplemented liberties would testify to their deprivation. If we associate the basic liberties with the life of free citizens, therefore, then we have to say that the liberties provided must be as rich as possible, consistently with the other constraints.

Consider a society in which choice-types 1 to N count as basic liberties by other constraints and are suitably protected. And suppose that choice-types N+1 and N+2 satisfy those same constraints, are consistent with the established liberties, but are not protected. The constraint of feasible extension says that they ought equally to count as basic liberties and to be protected. The class of basic liberties is closed under such extension.

The fact that this constraint comes into play only in the wake of other constraints means that it has a Paretian profile. The Pareto principle says, roughly, that if there are some people who can be given a benefit without depriving those who enjoy the benefit already, then that is what should be done. The constraint of feasible extension says, in loose parallel, that if there are some choice-types that can be protected as basic liberties without denying that status to those choice-types that have it already, then that is the path that should be taken.

The Paretian profile is important, because it means that the constraint does not rely on the controversial idea that the basic liberties should be identified with a view to ensuring that there is as much liberty—liberty in the abstract—as possible. Hart (1973, 543–5) understood Rawls to be committed to that controversial idea in arguing for 'the most extensive total system of equal basic liberties', and he argues from considerations that I rehearse later that the idea does not make sense (see O'Neill 1979–80).[2] But Rawls would certainly have endorsed the weaker Paretian idea and there is nothing in Hart to suggest that he would not have been happy to take the same line.

The Paretian idea is weak enough to be fully persuasive. But is it too weak? Why not replace it with the somewhat stronger idea that even when there is some cost to those choices that already have the status of basic liberties, still it may be reasonable to extend the liberties at that cost? I think that such a trade-off will often be perfectly reasonable and I allow for it, though only indirectly, within the approach taken here.

Suppose that choice-types 1 to N cannot be extended in the manner required but that if we vary them slightly—if we replace them by choice-types 1* to N*—then we can add choice-types N+1* and N+2*. To say that it may be reasonable to make the trade-off suggested is just to say that it may be reasonable to prefer to give the status of basic liberties to the larger, starred set of choices than to the smaller, unstarred set. The constraint of feasible extension does not rule out

---

[2] I came to appreciate this point fully only as a result of an exchange with Onora O'Neill. Her paper on the topic (O'Neill 1979–80), which itself builds on Hart's essay on Rawls, is the classic source on the difficulties generated by the Rawlsian idea that the notion of maximum abstract liberty is well defined.

such a preference. It merely says that no set of choice-types can be a candidate set of basic liberties if it is unnecessarily restricted. The 1 to N set may be a candidate set, if it cannot be extended further, and the 1* to N+2* set will be a candidate set on just the same grounds. All that the constraint does is to rule out the 1* to N* set. This set is unnecessarily restricted and in breach of the constraint of feasible extension.

4 The Constraint of Personal Significance

A second constraint is supported even more directly by the association between free citizenship and the basic liberties. It says that the types of choices that count as basic liberties should have personal significance for people; they should have the sort of significance that would make them important in the lives of free citizens. Specifically, since the basic liberties are not custom-made to individual, idiosyncratic taste, they should have personal significance for their bearers, by society-wide criteria.

There may be some variation between societies in the criteria of personal significance but on any plausible account this second constraint means that the basic liberties must be relatively distal and relatively general. They must be relatively distal in the sense of not just involving choices over how to move one's tongue or hands or body, without any guarantee as to what this will achieve in the world. One must be free to speak, not merely to make noise, and one must be free to speak to others, not merely to oneself. The basic liberties must be relatively general in the sense of not just involving choices between tightly specified options. One must be free to speak on more or less any topic to others, not merely on whether the weather has improved, and one must be free to speak to others in general, not merely to designated interlocutors.

No liberties can count as basic liberties, according to the second constraint, unless they are intuitively significant in the life of the free citizen. And excessively proximal or specific liberties can clearly fail to have such significance. In order to have the distal, general freedom to speak to others on any topic, I must have the specific freedom to speak about the weather and the proximal freedom to open my mouth. But the more specific and proximal freedoms need not be important as such in my personal life; their importance will turn on the importance of the more distal and general freedom that they can serve. Hence it is the latter freedom that ought to count as a matter of basic liberty.[3]

---

[3] There is a background issue as to how distal or indeed general an action can count as an option—as something that can be just chosen or enacted—by an agent. One suggestion might be that I can choose to enact an action, A, only if 'A' describes what is to be done in such a way that its realization is logically guaranteed by my trying to enact it. And that might suggest that while I can choose to open my mouth or perhaps speak, for example, I cannot choose to speak to someone else; I have to depend on the logically contingent fact that the person will not disappear or die before my

The second constraint does not say that all personally significant types of choice should count as basic liberties but that only personally significant types should do so. The idea is that a type of choice will only get to be considered as a candidate for a basic liberty insofar as it has personal significance in people's lives, by society-wide criteria. It is perfectly possible that some personally significant types of choice will fail to meet other constraints for counting as basic liberties; in particular, they may fail to meet some versions of the third constraint that I go on to discuss in a moment.

This second constraint, like the first, fits with the approach taken by Rawls and endorsed by Hart. That they each endorse the constraint shows up in a shared assumption about the sorts of choices that illustrate the category of basic liberties; they assume that these will be the choices traditionally associated with freedom of speech, freedom of association, and the like. Neither suggests that we might go to more proximal or specific choice-types in identifying basic liberties.

The third constraint on basic liberties that the linkage with free citizenship supports is the constraint of equal co-enjoyment and it will be the topic of the rest of this paper. This is the most important constraint of all and is indirectly at the heart of the concerns that Hart raises about the Rawlsian approach. While both of them give importance to the constraint, broadly conceived, Hart obviously feels that Rawls does not take sufficient account of the demands it imposes. The discussion to follow broadly supports Hart's side.

5 The Constraint of Equal Co-enjoyment

According to the constraint of equal co-enjoyment, no type of choice can constitute a basic liberty unless it is a choice that all of those who count as the full members or citizens of a society can co-enjoy equally: that is, can enjoy equally at one and the same time, however tightly or loosely same time is determined. We may ascribe a certain freedom of choice to someone without any suggestion that that is a degree or form of liberty that others can co-enjoy in equal measure; it may be a sort of freedom that is available only to the few. But talk of a basic liberty does suggest that it must be equally and simultaneously accessible to all. Otherwise it is hard to see why we should treat it as a liberty that marks out all free citizens.

The equal co-enjoyment constraint may impose different sets of requirements, of course, depending on how inclusive is the category of full members or citizens who

words reach them. But this can't be right, since I have to depend on logically contingent facts even to succeed in opening my mouth. For the record, I hold that any action description identifies an option if things are actually such at the time of action that the agent can make the description true; that they are such does not need to be logically guaranteed. An action description will identify an option in a way that engages with the agent's deliberation, of course, only if the further condition is fulfilled that the agent takes the description to be one that he or she can realize. I assume here that the basic liberties will naturally be capable of meeting that further condition.

are to enjoy the liberty equally. Were the citizens restricted to mainstream, propertied males, for example, then certain liberties might count as basic that would not pass the equal co-enjoyment test under other less restrictive conceptions; they could not be made simultaneously available to a wider category of individuals. Thus the *Magna Carta*—the Great Charter of the Liberties of Englishmen (Hobbes 1990, 37)—did not give liberties such that women, or indeed all men, could equally co-enjoy each. In my argument here, I shall assume that any normatively tolerable society will have to be maximally inclusive in its demarcation of full members or citizens and that these will certainly include native or naturalized members of the society who are adult and able, by intuitive criteria of adulthood and ability. Under that assumption, the equal co-enjoyment constraint means that any account of the basic liberties will have to identify choice-types such that all full members of an inclusive society can enjoy each of them equally at one and the same time.

When Rawls formulates his principle governing the liberties, he stipulates that each is to have the same right to a 'system of equal liberties compatible with a similar system of liberty for all'. Let his stipulation be satisfied and, at least under natural interpretations, the equal co-enjoyment constraint will be satisfied too. Each of the parties will be able to enjoy any of the relevant liberties equally with others, and do so at the same time that others enjoy it. The parties will be able to co-enjoy the liberty equally, as I have been putting it.

Rawls's stipulation is stronger than the constraint of equal co-enjoyment. It suggests that not only should each basic liberty be co-enjoyable equally by all; in addition, each basic liberty should be capable of being enjoyed equally by all at the same time that other basic liberties are enjoyed equally by all. But for our purposes there is no need to introduce this stronger requirement. Suppose that a set of basic liberties is consistent, as ideally it ought to be. Suppose, in other words, that the exercise of one liberty in the set is guaranteed not to compromise the exercise of any another. Given that each liberty in the set is to be co-enjoyable equally by all, consistency among the liberties will ensure, in itself, that the Rawlsian condition is also satisfied.[4]

Let us agree, then, that besides feasible extension and personal significance, equal co-enjoyment is a constraint on the basic liberties. No type of choice is a candidate for being cast as a basic liberty, unless it is capable of being equally co-enjoyed by all. But it turns out that the equal co-enjoyment constraint can be understood in different ways, with different effects; it devolves into a

---

[4] At any time, the set of basic liberties established in a society is almost certain to involve hidden inconsistencies, as constitutional and legal history illustrates (Zucca 2007). These inconsistencies are likely to become visible sooner or later, however, and to raise questions for the local democratic process. And if things go well, they will be resolved by the courts or the legislature, or by resort to referendum. Consistency may not be something we can assume at any point in time, then, but over time it serves as a regulative ideal in the process of articulating the basic liberties (Dietrich and List forthcoming).

number of more specific constraints or conditions. In the remainder of the paper, I shall explore three sets of conditions it supports, I shall look at how far each is supported by the association with the idea of the free citizen, and I shall ask about its implications for the organization of a society.

6 Two Sources of Ambiguity

The equal enjoyment constraint holds that if any liberty, say the liberty to X or not to X, is to count as basic then it must be possible for all the citizens of a society to co-enjoy that liberty equally. In particular, it must be possible for them equally to co-enjoy freedom in relation to the option, say X-ing, that makes the choice significant and distinctive.[5] But there are two obvious sources of ambiguity in this formulation. The first bears on what it means to co-enjoy a liberty, the second on the sort of possibility involved. As those ambiguities are resolved in favour of more demanding construals, the category of basic liberties gets to be more and more restricted in scope.

In order to introduce the first ambiguity, consider what we might mean when we say that someone enjoys the freedom to X, where this is the option that gives significance to the choice. We might mean that the person enjoys the opportunity to X or, more strongly, that the person enjoys the action of X-ing or, more strongly still, that the person enjoys the benefit associated with X-ing. The person may enjoy the opportunity to X without managing to perform the X-action, but not vice versa. And the person may enjoy the action of X-ing, without actually enjoying the associated benefit, but not vice versa. The gap between opportunity and action comes about because the opportunity ensures only that the agent can try to X, not that the agent can actually do so. The gap between action and benefit comes about because the agent may X in circumstances that undermine the benefit associated with X-ing.

The ambiguity in what it means to enjoy freedom in regard to an X-choice— specifically, in regard to X-ing—generates a corresponding ambiguity in what it might mean for people equally to co-enjoy the associated freedom or liberty. It may mean that they equally co-enjoy the opportunity to X, or equally co-enjoy the action of X-ing, or equally co-enjoy the benefit of X-ing. That is the first of the two ambiguities that affects the interpretation of the co-enjoyment constraint on the basic liberties.[6]

---

[5] If there is more than one option that confers significance on the choice, then the argument that follows can be adapted to cover that possibility.

[6] For all that the present argument supposes, the equal opportunity to choose X may mean the equal legal opportunity to make that choice, or the equal real-world probability of making that choice. In either case, it will be true that to have the opportunity is to be able to exercise choice as between trying to X and trying not to X.

The second ambiguity is of a kind that is familiar from other contexts. The equal enjoyment constraint might mean that it must be logically or metaphysically possible for all the members of the society to co-enjoy the liberty equally. Or it might mean, more demandingly, that it must also be physically possible—possible in standard physical conditions, under actual physical laws—for all the members to co-enjoy it equally.

The following matrix identifies the different ways in which the ambiguities may be resolved and the constraint imposed. The stronger versions are towards the right and towards the bottom. They identify choices that are equally co-enjoyable in physical conditions, not just logically, and that are equally co-enjoyable in all three respects: that is, in regard to opportunity, action, and benefit.[7]

People can co-enjoy equally	as a logical possibility	or also as a physical
the opportunity to X;	1	2
the action of X-ing;	3	4
the benefit of X-ing.	5	6

7 The Top-row Conditions

It would be highly implausible to say that an X-choice is a matter of basic liberty, although it is not possible for people to co-enjoy equally even the opportunity to X. We could scarcely regard the liberty as the mark of a free citizen—a mark shared by each citizen in a body of equally free citizens—if it did not satisfy that minimal possibility condition.

It may not be possible for people to co-enjoy equally the opportunity to X as a result either of logical or of physical constraints. If it is logically impossible for each to have that opportunity equally, then the box 1 condition will rule out the X-choice as a candidate for a basic liberty. If it is physically impossible for each to have an equal opportunity to X—if it is impossible under contextually standard physical conditions—then the box 2 condition will rule out the X-choice.

What sorts of choices do the top-row conditions rule out as basic liberties? The most salient category is the sort of choice that engages one member of the population in particular and that gives that person or the associates of that person a better opportunity to choose the significant option than others can possibly enjoy. We may describe these sorts of choices as particularized, because of their

---

[7] Hart's interrogation of the Rawlsian principle takes the form of a series of questions that accumulate to support the following suggestion: that it will be desirable to establish a system of basic liberties—and in particular the most extensive version of such a system—only to the extent that the equal co-enjoyment constraint is interpreted more strongly and the basic liberties are construed more narrowly. He thinks that this raises problems for Rawls but those difficulties need not concern us in the present context. Our interest is in giving a plausible account of the basic liberties that we might want a society to establish, not in seeing where Rawls's claims are unsupported or indeterminate or even, as Hart (1973, 547) once suggests, unintelligible.

association with particular people. An example will be provided by any choice in which the significant option refers by name to a particular person, A, as in getting A to do something or enabling A to enjoy some benefit or helping out A's friends.[8]

It will be logically impossible for people to co-enjoy equally the opportunity to make some particularized choices, and physically impossible for them to co-enjoy equally the opportunity to make others. Thus it is logically impossible for everyone to co-enjoy an equal opportunity to decide the mind of a particular person, A, on some issue; as a matter of logic, only that very person can make up A's mind. And so it cannot be a basic liberty for each that he or she make up A's mind on any issue or issues. Again, it is physically impossible in our sense for everyone to co-enjoy an equal chance of exploring friendship with A; there is an inescapable, if contingent, limit on how many people A can know and can contemplate as possible friends. And so it cannot be a basic liberty for each that he or she pursue friendship with A.

Such particularized choices are not candidates, then, for basic liberties. Looking ahead, they will also fail the conditions associated with the second row and third row in our matrix, since not everyone will be able equally to co-enjoy the choice of the distinguishing option and not everyone will be able equally to co-enjoy the benefit of the option. But the important point to notice is that they will fail even the conditions associated with the first row. Not everyone will be able equally to enjoy the opportunity to choose that option, let alone the choice itself or the associated benefit.

8 The Impact of the Top-row Conditions

How should we react to this first set of conditions on those choices that can count as basic liberties? The obvious response is to say that while various particularized choices cannot plausibly be matters of basic liberty, this is not the case for corresponding relativized choices: specifically, for corresponding agent-relative choices.

Take the choice of making up A's mind on some question. It is certainly true that not everyone can equally co-enjoy the opportunity to make up A's mind. But what remains true is that for each person, V, that person may have the opportunity to make up their mind—that is, V's mind—that is equal to the opportunity that any other person, W, has to make up their mind—that is, W's mind. With the agent-relative as distinct from the agent-particular choice, each can enjoy an equal opportunity to exercise it.

---

[8] My discussion in this and the following section was heavily influenced by exchanges with Ian Carter and Serena Olsaretti.

Again, take the choice of exploring friendship with someone. It is certainly true that not everyone can enjoy an equal opportunity to explore friendship with a given person. But nonetheless everyone—or at least everyone in society—can enjoy an equal opportunity to explore friendship with one or another person within their circle of acquaintances. The agent-relative choice can be a matter of basic liberty, then, where it is impossible to give the agent-particular choice that status.

It should come as no surprise that particularized choices are not matters of basic liberty but corresponding agent-relative choices are. Many of the basic liberties that figure in the standard list—the sort of list that is taken for granted, for example, by Rawls and Hart—are of the agent-relative kind. They include the liberty of forming your own views, for example, speaking your mind, following your conscience, and associating with those who will have you.

9 The Middle-row Conditions

The conditions in boxes 3 and 4 rule against X-choices such that not everyone in the society can simultaneously perform the X-action, even if the choice is non-particular and everyone can have an equal opportunity to do so.[9] Whether one person is able to perform that action will depend on its not being the case that all others—perhaps even some others—are performing it at the relevantly same time. The association between the basic liberties and the idea of the free citizen argues strongly in favor of ruling out such options. There would be a real paradox in claiming that the X-choice was a basic liberty in the society, suitably protected by public institutions, if there was no physical or even logical possibility that everyone might X together. It would mean that the status of free citizenship that is linked to the enjoyment of the basic liberties would not be a status that all could simultaneously assert.

Suppose, then, that the X-choice can be a basic liberty only if it is logically possible for people to co-enjoy the action of X-ing. Does this box 3 condition put a substantial restriction on the candidates for basic liberties? Yes, it does. Let X-ing be the action of controlling the choices of others, where it may be assumed that if I control your choices, you can't control mine; mutual control is no control (Pettit 2008). Or let it be the action of surpassing others—as distinct from trying to surpass others—where it is manifest that not everyone can surpass others; not everyone can be first or even above average. Let it even be the rather trivial action

---

[9] A choice will be non-particular if it is agent-relative, as we have seen. But it will also be non-particular if, as in many possible cases, it is agent-neutral and does not involve reference to any particular agents in the options.

of staying out later than others (O'Neill 1979–80, 49). The box 3 condition would say that the freedom to exercise choices over such actions cannot be basic liberties, since it is not logically possible for people to co-enjoy those actions; they cannot each control others—certainly not all others; they cannot each surpass others—certainly not in the same respect; and they cannot each stay out later than others (O'Neill 1979–80, 49).[10]

Box 4 introduces a condition that would make the category of basic liberties even more restrictive. For it would rule out cases of X-ing where it may be logically possible for everyone to co-enjoy the performance of that action but it is physically impossible for them to do so. The farmer and the cowboy may be friends, in the words of the song, if there is country enough for them each to find land that they can use as they wish; the farmer will fence in one region, the cowboy let cattle roam in another. But if there is only so much land to go around, then under that condition of scarcity it will be impossible for them each to use the land as they wish. Put this condition in place and the freedom to use land to one's personal taste cannot be a basic liberty.

In his discussion of Rawls, Hart focuses on competitive actions of the kind that these middle-row conditions—in particular, the condition in box 4—would rule out. In the words of an earlier paper, such actions are paradigmatically illustrated by options where 'owing to scarcity, one man's satisfaction causes another's frustration' (Hart 1955, 175). The choices that the box 3 condition would banish from the category of basic liberties involve necessarily competitive options: actions such that it is logically impossible for everyone to succeed in bringing them off. The options that the box 4 condition would banish involve contingently competitive options: actions that it is impossible in standard physical circumstances, such as the circumstance of scarce land, for everyone to realize.

Hart uses the unrestricted use of land to illustrate the fact that there are some liberties that cannot be simultaneously exercised by all; there would be physically inevitable conflicts among people who sought to exercise that liberty at once (Hart 1973, 546–7). Another example, as he suggests, would be the action of travelling by one's preferred mode of transport, since there would be a similar 'conflict between pedestrians' freedom of movement and the rights of automobiles' (Hart 1973, 546, n 49). And another might be the action of withdrawing one's money from a bank; let everyone try to do that and the institution will break down. Further examples can readily be imagined. Thus an interesting class of illustrations might be derived from G A Cohen's (1979) case, where everyone in a room is free to leave by the doorway, provided that others are not attempting to do so at the same time.

---

[10] This sort of constraint is close to the constraint of compossibility that Hillel Steiner (1994) imposes on basic rights. For related discussions see Carter 1999; Kramer 2003.

10 The Impact of the Middle-row Conditions

Suppose we go along with these anti-competitive conditions. What do we do then? Do we say that use of land or mode of transport, for example, is not an area in which people can have a basic liberty protected? In that case there might be an anarchic free-for-all where the spoils go to the victor. Or there might be a system of central rationing under which people have to live with whatever they are centrally allocated in the way of permits for land-use or transport.

Neither of these alternatives is very attractive but that need not be of concern, for there is a third, more appealing possibility. This would require a society to take two steps: first, to introduce rules of coordination that would eliminate the problem of competition in the use of land or transport or whatever; and then, second, to protect a suitable rule-dependent choice in the manner of a basic liberty. Set up common rules of ownership, for example, and it will be possible for everyone at once to own and use land or any other commodity according to those rules. And then the basic liberty of owning and using property according to those rules can be given suitable protection. Set up rules of the road and it will be possible for everyone at once to use his or her preferred mode of transport; drivers will take one route, pedestrians another. And so, again, a corresponding basic liberty can also be protected in this area: the liberty of travelling under the rules of the road by whatever means one prefers.

This regulatory or coordinating initiative would enable a society to avoid the anarchist or centralist alternatives and introduce instead certain rule-dependent basic liberties. Parallel initiatives could be used to allay a vast array of similar problems. The rules governing banking can make it possible for people to have regulated or coordinated access to their funds. And any rules that coordinate access to something that cannot be accessed at once by all—this, on the model of exit from a crowded room—can make it possible for people to have a basic, protected liberty in the exercise of the rule-dependent choice.

Should a society identify and protect rule-dependent basic liberties rather than going the anarchist or centralist route? The constraint of feasible extension suggests that it should. Take two societies that do equally well in protecting certain basic liberties such as the liberty to speak your mind, associate with those who welcome your association, or reside where you will in the available territory. Now suppose that, consistently with the constraints of personal significance and equal co-enjoyment, one society introduces rules whereby the stock of protected liberties is increased but that the other does not do so. In that case, the principle of feasible extension argues in favor of the first society. The second society does not protect the basic liberties of its members, only an unnecessarily restricted subset of those liberties.

In every case where they serve to extend the stock of basic liberties, then, rules of coordination are desirable on grounds of liberty alone. They are supported by the principle of feasible extension, which is itself supported by the association between the idea of basic liberties and the image of the free citizen. To make this point is to go along with Rawls (1971), when he suggests that a case can be made on the grounds of liberty for having a system of liberties that includes the freedom to own personal property under the local rules of ownership. But the case made here does not depend on the notion that introducing such a freedom would increase liberty in the abstract, as the Rawlsian argument seems to do; as mentioned earlier, the principle of feasible extension is Paretian in character and does not rely on any such idea. Still, the line taken is in the spirit of Rawls and runs against Hart's suggestion that introducing rule-dependent basic liberties can only be justified on broadly utilitarian grounds (Hart 1973, 547).

But it is one thing to say that the cause of the basic liberties—the cause associated with the idea of the free citizen—argues for introducing rule-dependent basic liberties. It is another thing to argue that this or that set of rules is the best one to put in place in any domain. How is the decision to be made between the different systems of rules that might govern ownership or travel or indeed any similar area of choice?

It should be clear from within the viewpoint defended here that no rules will be appropriate that compromise the project of providing suitable protection for personally significant liberties that every member of the society is to be able to co-enjoy equally. Suppose that suitable protection is identified with robust protection against the dominating control of others, as on the republican approach. It will be important, then, not to introduce rules that give such wide discretion to public officials that protection against those very officials is compromised. And, perhaps even more strikingly, it will be important not to introduce rules—say, rules of ownership—that enable some individuals to gain such economic power that they are bound to dominate others in certain domains. This may require supporting limits on wealth or inequality or restricting the comparative advantages—say, advantages of education or publicity—that money can buy.

But this restriction on suitable rules for establishing rule-dependent basic liberties may well leave various candidate systems of rules in play. And how then should we want the choice to be made between those systems? How should we decide between the different rule-dependent basic liberties that the rival systems would establish?

This, plausibly, should be a matter for democratic process to resolve. In that process it will be perfectly legitimate to introduce values other than liberty, including the utilitarian considerations that Hart supports, in favour of one system of rules rather than others. Among the values that may legitimately be taken into account is the value of having a system that fits with the received culture of the society. Thus there need not be one system of rules, and one set of rule-dependent basic liberties, that is the right one for every society. There may be a permissible degree of cultural relativity in the liberties that should be established across different societies.[11]

11 The Bottom-row Conditions

The conditions in boxes 5 and 6 rule against the sort of choice involving an option such that if everyone chooses it, then the benefit associated with the option is undermined or diminished. The benefit that makes such an option attractive for the person who does not think everyone will go the same way ceases to provide support at the point where all or perhaps just some others opt for the same path. There may or may not be a distinct reason at that juncture for an individual to stick with the option—more on this in a moment—but that will be a different reason from the consideration that made it attractive in the first place.

The association with the free citizen argues for imposing these conditions, as it does for imposing the other conditions associated with the equal co-enjoyment constraint and the earlier constraints of feasible extension and personal significance. If the types of choice that should be protected as basic liberties are to be associated with the status of free citizenship, then it would be strange to allow them to include liberties such that people will frustrate one another by exercising them; in particular, will frustrate one another to the extent of depriving the choice of its original appeal. There is an intuitive case against allowing basic liberties to include such collectively self-defeating or counter-productive choices.

Hart directs attention to our bottom-row conditions with the simple example of speaking to a large group (Hart 1973, 543). Let everyone enjoy the liberty of addressing a group at will. It will be logically and physically possible for them each to address the group at the same time, so that that liberty would pass the top-row, anti-particularized conditions and the middle-row, anti-competitive conditions. But still we might pause over thinking that this liberty should be established and protected in the manner of a basic liberty. For if every member of a group speaks to the assembly at one and the same time, no one will be heard. And so it will be physically if not logically impossible that they should equally co-enjoy the benefit of their speaking to the group. The point of the activity in which the liberty is protected will be undermined in the event that everyone pursues the activity at once.

This sort of example stands in for a wide spectrum of cases. In these cases the type of choice under consideration as a candidate for a basic liberty involves an option that can be chosen at once by all. But let the option be chosen by all and,

---

[11] This is not inconsistent with the argument, which I have advanced elsewhere (Pettit 1997, 2008), that the judgment as to whether a given choice is relatively dominated or non-dominated, unfree or free, is fixed independently of any value commitments. The notion of freedom as non-domination is not moralized, though the issue as to which choices should be protected from domination may be.

whether as a matter of logical or physical necessity, no one is going to be able to enjoy the benefit that gave the option its original point and attraction. The problem arises, in Hart's words, from the fact that to protect the choice of a certain option as a basic liberty 'necessarily does two things: first, it confers on individuals the advantage of that liberty, but secondly, it exposes them to whatever disadvantages the practice of that liberty by others may entail for them' (Hart 1973, 550). More specifically, the problem is that the practice of that liberty by all may mean that its exercise loses its original point from everyone's perspective.[12]

In every case where the bottom-row conditions apply, then, there is an option that can be protected for all, there is a more or less obvious benefit that the choice of the option promises each, and that benefit is undermined in the circumstance where all or perhaps just some others simultaneously choose the option. Everyone would want to pursue the activity protected were no one else to do so but everyone would prefer the scenario where no one pursues it to that where all do. Everyone would like to address the group but everyone would prefer that no one speak than that all should do so at once; in that case, each would waste effort to no good effect. The exercise of the activity in question may be individually attractive but its exercise by all is self-defeating or at least counter-productive (Parfit 1984, Part 1).

Presumptive examples of choice-types where the bottom-row constraints apply are provided by cases that are familiar from the literature on predicaments where the individual choice of a certain option is attractive for each but the aggregate result of everyone taking that choice makes each worse off. Every householder in a neighbourhood may wish to have the liberty to extend or decorate their house just as they will but if every householder does this, then by their own aesthetic standards they may end up living in a truly ugly public space. Everyone may wish to be able to pry and report on anyone else's private affairs but if everyone does this, they may each live in a society that all abhor. Everyone may wish to have the liberty to own a gun but if everyone owns a gun then, the arms industry apart, no one is likely to be defensively better off.

As in the case of speaking to the group, the claims that give these examples a presumptive connection with the bottom-row conditions are: first, that everyone has a reason to pursue the activity if no one else does; and second, that everyone prefers that no one pursue it to everyone's pursuing it. But it is worth noting that in some of these cases, unlike the group case, a third clause is satisfied too: everyone may have a reason—a new reason—to pursue the activity if others all do so. Setting virtue aside, no one will relish being the only person without a gun in a gun-toting society, or being the only person without the licence to gossip in a

---

[12] Hart is concerned about any disadvantages that the general practice of the liberty may occasion, not just about the more specific disadvantage on which I focus: that exercising the choice in question loses its point for each. Thus he speaks of the possibility that the general practice of the liberty may involve 'harm or loss of amenities or other elements of real utility'—for example, 'pain and suffering and distress' (Hart 1973, 548).

gossipy society. This makes these particular examples into cases of a broadly free-riding character.[13] In these cases everyone has a reason for pursuing the activity even if all others do—they will not want to be made a sucker, as it is sometimes said—but that reason is not the consideration that originally gave the choice its appeal.

12 The Impact of the Bottom-row Conditions

Where does this leave us? What are we to say at a general level about how these bottom-row conditions should impact on the basic liberties to be recognized within a polity?

There are certainly some cases, such as that of speaking to a group, where it seems like the merest common sense to deny the status of a basic liberty to the unregulated choice. In this type of case the required line will be, not to give up altogether on establishing a basic liberty to speak to a group, but to put rules in place that allow us to define a more restricted option—say, speaking under Robert's rules of order—that can satisfy the bottom-row conditions and figure as a basic liberty. This line will be attractive from our point of view, because it will increase the number of basic liberties available, as required by the principle of feasible extension. The case is relatively straightforward because the idea of speaking to a group when everybody else is speaking too has absolutely no value or appeal.

Hart (1973, 543) supports this line, and recognizes that it makes sense in Rawlsian terms, not just in utilitarian (see too Rawls 1971, 203). Thus he recommends 'the introduction of rules of order in debate, which restrict the liberty to speak when we please. Without this restriction the liberty to say and advocate what we please would be grossly hampered and made less valuable to us.' Let the rules be introduced and it will be a basic liberty to address a group according to the rules, but not to address the group when and as one likes.

The suggestion supported by this example is that just as we accommodate the middle-row conditions against competition by introducing rule-dependent basic liberties, and giving them suitable protection, so we should accommodate the bottom-row conditions against counter-productivity by parallel measures. The case for the introduction of rule-dependent basic liberties will be that the stock of protected liberties can thereby be increased, as required by the constraint of feasible extension. And the choice among possible systems of rules will be dictated both by the requirements of suitable protection and by recourse to other values, including the value of fitting well with local mores.

Are there many cases as straightforward as the case of speaking to a group? It may seem not. In other cases, there may be ground for arguing that the choice

---

[13] On free riding problems and multi-lateral prisoner's dilemmas, see Pettit 1986.

retains its original point in the case where everyone makes it, so that it is not really subject to the aggregate, counter-productive effect. Thus, some rugged individualists may deny that as a matter of fact the defensive point in having a gun is undermined if everyone comes to have a gun. Or they may not agree that its original point was purely defensive; they may give the activity an expressive significance. Other more communitarian types may take a different view, as Hart insists. 'Other persons would not pay this price for unrestricted liberty in these matters, since, given their temperament, they would value the protections afforded by the restrictions higher than the unrestricted liberty' (Hart 1973, 549).

We may all agree, then, that the basic liberties should not be collectively counter-productive in the manner of the liberty to address a group as one likes. But that agreement will leave considerable room for divergence between the rugged individualist attitude and more communitarian views. Communitarians would argue for allowing householders to extend or decorate their houses but only under common rules of zoning, development, and heritage preservation. And they would argue for giving people the liberty to own guns but only subject to strict rules for the possession and use of firearms; these rules might make it impossible for many people to have access to guns. Rugged individualists would insist that such regulations are unnecessary, denying that the aggregative effect of everyone's making the relevant choice undermines the original point of the individual choice. They may hail diversity in house styles as attractive, and the universal possession of firearms as mutually inhibiting and individually protective.

Rugged individualists may pride themselves in such cases on not making the liberties under discussion rule-dependent. But in practice they are bound to agree—on grounds related to the bottom-row conditions—that there should be some rules, however minimal, to regulate certain extreme choices. They are almost certain to think that whatever the point of gun ownership, it is likely to be undermined if some are allowed short-range nuclear weapons and that whatever the point of renovating one's own home, it is in jeopardy if some are allowed to build skyscrapers next to suburban houses. Thus they too will argue for introducing rules to define and channel choices in these domains; that will be the way to extend liberties as far as possible, while respecting the bottom-row conditions. The debate between more individualist and more communitarian types will not bear on whether to have rule-dependent rather than rule-independent liberties in such areas, but rather on how restrictive the rules ought to be.

This means that here as in the case of the middle-row conditions, the crucial issue arises on the supposition that there will be some rules to regulate liberties. That issue bears on which system of rules to prefer in any area of choice. As in the earlier case, the answer will plausibly be resolved in democratic process. It may be determined in part by how well rival systems do in supporting the robust protection of liberties and in part by how well they serve independent values, including the value of fitting with the existing mores of the society. Thus the system of rules ought not to give government such discretion that people are exposed to domination from public officials; nor ought it to allow individuals or groups such power that domination is more likely on the private front. And the system of rules in any society, while it may be challenging in some respects, ought to have the minimal fit with social mores that is likely to be required for the system to prove resilient. Thus the appropriate rules may be subject to a degree of cultural variation.

13 In Conclusion

We began with the connection between the basic liberties and free citizenship, and then identified three constraints on the category of basic liberties that that connection supports: the constraints, respectively, of feasible extension, personal significance, and equal co-enjoyment. Many different sets of liberties satisfy these constraints, as we noted, and compete as candidates for being given the status of basic liberties. In each such set, the choices to be protected will satisfy our three constraints, being maximally extensive, personally significant, and capable of being equally co-enjoyed by all.

The co-enjoyment constraint is of particular importance, since it imposes three separate sets of conditions on basic liberties. The effect of those conditions is caught in the following variation on an earlier matrix.

People can co-enjoy equally	as a logical and physical possibility
the opportunity to X;	→ no agent-particular options
the action of X-ing;	→ no mutually competitive options
the benefit of X-ing;	→ no collectively counter-productive options

I hope that this discussion gives some guidance on what choices should count as candidates for basic liberties and, to return to a republican key, as choices that ought to be protected from the dominating control of others. I do not think that the sorts of choices to be supported under the approach taken will be a surprising set; if they were, that might be in itself a reason for concern. Thus the basic liberties will certainly include freedoms of thought and speech, association and assembly, the freedom to move around one's society and to own personal property, as well as the freedom to assume a part in public life, whether as voter, candidate, or critic. Let these basic liberties be protected in the manner that republican theory requires—protected against dominating control of any kind over the exercise of such choices—and people will be enabled to perform as equal citizens of the society.[14]

---

[14] Thus, to connect with another approach, they will share equally in the basic capabilities that are required for functioning in their society (Sen 1985; Nussbaum 1992). See (Pettit 2001).

There may be just one surprise in the list of basic liberties supported. This is that by our account, many liberties will have to be identified in a rule-dependent way, if they are to satisfy the middle-row and bottom-row conditions in the matrix. That necessity raises the question as to which system of rules ought to be established in any domain. I argued that although some freedom-related concerns may help to reduce the set of candidate systems, it may also be necessary to invoke other values to select between those candidates, including the value of installing a set of liberties that fits well with existing mores.

The selection of the particular rules to impose in defining the basic liberties will naturally be left to democratic practice. There are some basic liberties, or some types of basic liberty, such that no society that did not protect them would count as democratic; examples will certainly include freedom of speech and the freedom to take a part in public life. But given that a society does count as democratic on that basis, it is bound to have a degree of discretion in determining the detailed specification of the basic liberties it protects: that is, in fixing the rules whereby various liberties are specified and in resolving the trade-offs and related issues canvassed in the introduction. In every society there ought to be protection for the basic liberties, where these are defined in different ways for different societies. But it is not the case that there are basic liberties, defined on a universal, rule-independent basis, that ought to be protected in every society.[15]

---

[15] I am most grateful to Matthew Kramer and Kinch Hoeskstra, who gave me very useful comments on drafts of the paper, and to Ian Carter and Serena Olsaretti who raised helpful questions about the third constraint. The paper was presented at the British Academy Symposium on H.L.A. Hart in Cambridge, July 2007, and later at a law and philosophy workshop in Berkeley, and as the Max Kampleman Lecture in the Hebrew University, Jerusalem. I am in the debt of many participants at these events, most notably Matthew Adler, Bob Cooter, Peter Lipton, Susan Mendus, Onora O'Neill, Leif Wenar, and Lorenzo Zucca.

PART V
RIGHTS

12

Posthumous Rights*

Cécile Fabre

1 Introduction

One of H.L.A. Hart's important contributions to debates over rights is his articulation of the so-called Will Theory of rights. Not only do other Will theorists routinely refer to it; so do the theory's main opponents, who endorse the Interest Theory instead. Briefly put, according to the Will Theory of rights, X has a right against Y that Y φ if, and only if, X is able to waive, or demand, the performance by Y of his duty to φ, and if he is able to waive, or demand, remedies should Y fail to φ. According to the Interest Theory of rights, X has a right against Y that Y φ if Y's performance of his duty to φ preserves some interest(s) of X's. On the Interest Theory, it is not necessary for X to have a right that he be able to waive, or demand, the performance by Y of his duty.[1]

This particular point—whether the ability to exercise control over duty-bearers is a necessary condition for being a right-holder—is one of the main bones of contention between the two theories. Whereas Will theorists tend to charge Interest theorists with conferring rights on individuals who (they claim) simply cannot be coherently regarded as right-holders, Interest theorists criticize Will theorists

* I am very grateful to Matthew Kramer and Claire Grant for inviting me to present this paper in Cambridge at the British Academy Symposium on the legacy of H.L.A. Hart. Although ill health prevented me from attending the conference, their invitation gave me a much needed incentive to buckle down to the task of defending my long-held intuition that there cannot be posthumous rights. In addition, Kramer sent me written comments on an earlier draft which greatly helped me improve it. Finally, a version of this paper was presented at the Edinburgh Legal Theory Workshop. I am very thankful to all participants for a very stimulating discussion, as well as to Rowan Cruft, Katrin Flikschuh, and Leif Wenar for their written comments.

[1] For defences of the Interest Theory, see, eg, Raz 1986, McCormick 1977, Kramer 1998 and 2001. For defences of the Will Theory, see, eg, Hart 1955, Simmonds 1998, Steiner 1994, Sumner 1987, Wellman 1985 and 1995. For recent discussions of the debate between the two theories, see, eg, Cruft 2004, Kramer and Steiner 2007, Sreevenisan 2005, and Wenar 2005. For an account of rights which is committed neither to the Interest nor to the Will Theory, see Rainbolt 2006. On Rainbolt's view, 'a person has a right if and only if a feature of that person is a *reason* for others to have an obligation or impossibility' (xiii). As Rainbolt argues, rights so understood do not rule out posthumous or preconception rights as conceptually incoherent.

for illicitly ruling out the possibility that individuals such as children and the mentally ill might have rights. But whereas the Will Theory rules out the conferral of rights on those individuals by definitional fiat, the Interest Theory does not rule it in by stipulation: rather, it does so by providing a substantial account of the conditions which one must meet in order to be a right-holder.

Now, there are two broad reasons as to why X might not be in a position to waive or demand the performance by Y of his duty. On the one hand, X does not have the mental abilities to do so. On the other hand, X does not exist at the point at which the issue arises as to whether or not Y will, or will not, do his duty. Interestingly, in the dispute between the two theories, there is rather a lot on comatose individuals, the severely handicapped, and children. By contrast, there is comparatively little on non-existing people.[2]

In this paper, I shall argue that on the Interest Theory, the dead cannot have (moral) rights. I shall make my case in section 2, and deal with two objections in section 3.[3] If my argument is successful, it deprives the Interest Theory of one of its favourite weapons against the Will Theory in general, and H.L.A. Hart's account of it in particular.

A few remarks before I begin. First, I shall focus on moral, rather than legal, rights. Second, I shall not attempt to evaluate the Interest Theory as a plausible alternative to the Will Theory. Nor, in fact, shall I assess whether the fact that (if I am correct) it must deny the status of rights-holders to the dead counts decisively against it. My aim, thus, is in the main descriptive. Third, I shall assume that the dead do not exist. As some have noted, the mortalist assumption makes it difficult to account for a number of our practices with respect to the dead (Mulgan 1999, Gosseries 2003). However, it is too strongly entrenched in our common intuitions and discourses for me to jettison it here. In that sense, this paper can be read as an attempt to show that, notwithstanding arguments to the contrary, the mortalist assumption *is* incompatible with the view that there can be posthumous rights.

2 The Interest Theory and Posthumous Rights

The term 'posthumous rights' is ambiguous, denoting as it does either the claim 'the dead can have rights that certain states of affairs obtain' or the claim 'the living can have rights that certain states of affairs obtain once they are dead'.

---

[2] I do not mean to say that few pay attention to the rights of non-existing people; rather, I mean to say that participants in the debate between those two rival accounts of rights tend not to pay much attention to them. Hillel Steiner and Matthew Kramer are notable exceptions.

[3] In a separate paper, I argue that future generations can have rights, but in far fewer cases than might at first be thought (Fabre forthcoming). In other words, the cases of the dead and of future generations are somewhat distinct—*pace*, for example, Joel Feinberg and Matthew Kramer, whose views will be discussed in section 2 below, or A Baier, who invokes the notion of a transgenerational community as the basis for conferring rights on both the dead and future people (Baier 1980).

Accordingly, in order for there to be interest-based posthumous rights, it must be the case, either that the dead can have interests that certain states of affairs obtain, or that the living can have interests that certain states of affairs obtain once they are dead. Both claims suppose that the occurrence (or not) of certain states of affairs once people are dead can be harmful to them. In what follows, I argue that neither claim is sound.

Standardly, the degree to which an interest of X's is important enough to warrant the imposition of a duty on Y is a function of the degree to which X would be harmed if Y desisted from acting as required by the duty. Thus, what the Interest Theory requires, for the conferral of posthumous rights, is a plausible account of posthumous interests as well as a plausible account of posthumous harms.[4] If no such account can be provided, then there cannot be such a thing as a posthumous right (again, on that particular theory).

Now, any argument to the effect that interest-based posthumous rights (posthumous rights for short) are, or are not, a coherent notion must first offer an account of interests *tout court*. On some views, interests are defined purely objectively, as what is good for their bearers irrespective of the latter's wants or desires. On other views, interests are defined purely subjectively, as what their bearers want or desire. Others still claim that interests are defined purely objectively but include an interest in the satisfaction of one's desires.

Definitionally speaking, the Interest Theory of rights is neutral as between those various accounts of interests. Depending on which account is preferred, the Interest Theory posits that X has a right against Y that φ if not-φ would thwart X's objective good, or X's desires, to such an extent as to constitute a harm, *and* a harm such as to warrant holding Y under a duty to φ. By implication, then, the conferral of the status of a right-holder on some entity requires that the latter be capable of incurring some harm as a bearer of projects, wants, goals, and desires.

The foregoing points might give the impression that (as Feinberg would have it) it is a necessary and sufficient condition, for X to be harmed by some event E at time *t*, that E sets back X's (fundamental) interests at *t*. However, the requirement that E should set back X's (fundamental) interests, though necessary, is not sufficient for X to be harmed by E at *t*: in addition, or so I argue, it must be the case that E adversely affects X's experience at *t*. To see this, let us return to posthumous rights, and let us first examine the view that we can have rights once we are dead. In so far as rights protect interests, it is a necessary condition for us to have posthumous rights that we can have posthumous interests, interests, that is, which survive us and can be thwarted after we die. At first sight, that condition seems to be met. It does seem to make sense to say, for example, that if I devote my life to a given cause, I have an interest once dead in that cause not failing, and

---

[4] This does not in any way commit proponents of the theory who also believe that the dead can have rights to endorsing the thesis that they do have those rights. It might be that their interests are not important enough to hold some other person(s) under some duty.

that if it does fail, this particular interest of mine is thwarted even though I am dead. Similarly, it does seem to make sense to say that my interest in my children's flourishing survives my death, and that should my will, which provides for them, be nullified after I die, this particular interest of mine is thwarted even though I am dead. In both instances, it does seem to make sense to say that I am harmed, even though I am dead, by the failure of my cause or the nullification of my will.

And yet, further scrutiny casts doubts on the coherence of ascribing interests to the dead and, by implication, of regarding them as subject to a harm. For in order to do so, one must give an account of who the interest-bearer is. Clearly, it cannot be the corpse, or the ashes, of the deceased; and so it can only be the person who was and no longer is, or, as Feinberg puts it, the *antemortem* person (Feinberg, 1984, 89; Pitcher 1984; see also Gosseries 2003 and Waluchow 1986). However—to rehearse a familiar point—the *antemortem* person, in fact, is the person while she was alive, in short, the living under another name. The post-humous event does not affect any interest *of a dead person*. Put differently, that event does not cause the now-dead person to suffer a setback to her interests at the point at which third parties so act. In so far as the dead do not suffer a setback to their interests, and in so far as suffering such a setback is a necessary condition for being harmed, the dead cannot be harmed, from which it follows that they cannot have rights.

Suppose, for the sake of argument, that the dead can have (posthumous) interests, and thus that they do meet that necessary condition for being harmed by third parties. Should they suffer a setback to some important interest of theirs, is it enough, then, to say that they have been harmed? The issue, here, is whether the dead, understood not as a skeleton or a bunch of ashes, but as existing non-materially *and* nevertheless having interests, can be harmed. I do not believe that they can. To see this, let us identify a set of beings of which it is clear that they cannot be harmed, even though it is not wholly incoherent to ascribe interests to them; let us then distinguish them from beings of which it is clear that they can be harmed, and let us assess where the dead fit.[5] Now, I take it for granted that inanimate objects[6] cannot be harmed. Consider a damaged painting. We might say, not entirely implausibly, that it is in its interest not to be slashed. Should we decide to slash it, however, we would not thereby harm it, as it does not have the ability to experience what it is like to live in a damaged state. Likewise, we might be able to say that it is in the interest of a car not to be kicked around; but were we to kick it around, it would not be harmed in its physical integrity. Contrast those objects with Red, an adult human being, whom White subjects to a severe beating. The crucial difference between them—to point out the obvious—is that Red

---

[5] I follow M Kramer's strategy in Kramer 2001. As will be clear presently, though, my conclusions are radically different from his.

[6] As distinct from entities such as corporations which are inanimate as corporations but which are constituted by animate beings. Whether such entities can be harmed is an issue on which I need not take a stand here.

is, but the car is not, a subject of experiences. The reason in turn why Red, unlike the car, is harmed by the beating is precisely that the beating makes a difference (and an adverse one at that) to his experience. Contrast both objects and humans with the dead. Unlike a car, the latter belonged, whilst alive, to the human species. In this, they are importantly similar to Red. Unlike Red, however, and like a car, they do not have experiences. And if that—having experiences which can be affected—is what enables us to say that a car cannot, but that Red can, be harmed, then it does seem that the dead cannot be harmed. Generally put, in so far as, once dead, one no longer is a subject of experience, one's experience cannot be adversely affected by posthumous events—and this even if (*pace* my argument in the last paragraph) the dead can have interests.[7]

Let us now turn to the second sense of the term 'posthumous rights', whereby they are rights held by the living that certain states of affairs obtain once they are dead. Now, it clearly makes sense to say, of some people, that they *now* have an interest in their body remaining intact after they are dead. And it does seem, at first sight, that this interest can be protected by a right which they now have that their body not be desecrated—for example by necrophiliac acts—once they are dead. Likewise, when Blue promises to Green that he will burn all of Green's manuscripts after the latter's death, he can be interpreted as conferring on Green, *at the time he makes the promise*, the corresponding right, and thereby as putting himself at the time of the promise under a duty to do so *once Green is dead*. This, after all, is how we understand most promises. If I promise to you at noon that I will meet you for tea at 4pm, you now acquire a right that I do so, and I now place myself under a duty to do so.

However, it does not make sense to confer on the living rights that states of affairs obtain posthumously anymore than it does to confer rights on the dead. This is because the living cannot have such rights, while alive, unless they also have them once dead. For illustrative purposes, take the aforementioned case of a promise. It is true that you now have a right that I meet you at 4pm. But it is also true that you must still have that right, *at 4pm,* in order for me to be under a duty, *at 4pm,* to turn up then. If you have specifically released me from my promise at 3:50, or if you have double-booked yourself and undertaken at 1pm to meet someone else 30 miles away at 4pm, you do not have a right against me, at 4pm, that I meet you for tea at 4pm, and I am no longer under a duty to do so. Similar considerations apply, *mutatis mutandis*, to the case of the dead. Consider

---

[7] For an attempt to establish that the dead cannot have interests but that they can nevertheless be harmed, see Levenbook 1984 and 1985. Levenbook argues that if one conceives of harm as the suffering of a (considerable) loss, then the notion of posthumous harms (of harms, that is, which one incurs after one's death) makes sense. However, if one conceives of harm as a setback to interests, then that notion does not make sense, since at and after death, there is no longer an interest-bearer to speak of. I lack the space to scrutinize her argument here. But it pays to note that if Levenbook is correct, then there is no such thing as an interest-based posthumous right. It is also worth mentioning that it is not clear at all how a *dead person* can incur a loss even though they no longer have interests.

the claim that X now has a right against Y that his body not be desecrated posthumously. Y will fulfil his duty to X once X is dead: in fact, he can do so only once X is dead. Similarly, consider the claim that X now has a right that some insurance company pay out a life cover policy to his children in the event of his death. The company can fulfil its duty only once X is dead. In both cases, Y can be held under such a duty to act only if it is *still* the case that X, who is dead, has a right that he do so. As we saw above, however, one cannot have any such right once one is dead.

The foregoing argument implies that, in order for X to have posthumous rights against Y, whilst alive, in respect to posthumous states of affairs, it must be the case that Y harms X, once the latter is dead, by failing to fulfil his duty. But perhaps that is wrong. Perhaps, as Feinberg argues, the harm to X begins 'at the point, well before his death, when the person had invested so much in some post-dated outcome that it became one of his interests' (Feinberg 1984, 92). This will not do. If Feinberg is correct, X has a right, before he dies, that the insurance company pay up, since he has a strong *antemortem* interest in its doing precisely that. Suppose now that X takes out an insurance policy which will pay out a certain sum to his child should X become severely disabled. On Feinberg's view, X has a right, before he becomes disabled, that the insurance pay up, since he has a strong *pre-disability* interest in its doing precisely that. But this is odd, for it is only if and when he becomes disabled that the company will be called upon to fulfil its duty to X, and might default on it; accordingly it is only if and when X becomes disabled that the question of whether X is harmed, or benefited, by the company's conduct will arise. And if that is correct, then it is only when X dies that, in the life policy case, the question of whether X is harmed, or benefited, by the company's conduct will arise (Rainbolt 2006, 214 and Waluchow 1986, 230–32).

Note that although I have denied that the dead can be harmed, I have not denied that the insurance company sets back X's interest in his children's flourishing by failing to pay up; nor have I denied that third parties set back one's interest in bodily integrity if they subject one's body to necrophiliac acts. In fact, it is wholly plausible to say that, should those interests which we have whilst alive be thwarted once we are dead, our life overall (say of a parent concerned for her child's welfare) will be the worse for it. To say this, however, does not suffice to establish that *we* would be *harmed* if our plans were thwarted once we are dead. Put in general terms, the claim that someone is harmed, or benefited, by some event E, is not the same as the claim that his life goes badly or well as a result of E (Glannon 2001, Kagan 1994). To be sure, there must be some connection between them: it would be strange to think of someone's life as going well if that person were never benefited in anyway by sequences of events and/ or third parties' actions. Still, there are interstices, as it were, between those two claims, which do enable us to make sense of these two intuitions: that the dead are not harmed by posthumous events since the latter make no difference to their experience, and that there nevertheless might be something to regret about the occurrence of those events.[8]

My argument against the view that there can be interest-based posthumous rights appeals to the difficulties inherent in identifying the bearers of those rights and, more widely, in accounting for the sense in which one can be harmed posthumously. To some, however, this presents no difficulty at all. Thus, in his interesting discussion of this issue, Matthew Kramer argues that the dead can be right-holders to the extent that they still shape and influence the lives of the living (through the latter's memories of the dead, the actions which they take in respect of the dead, and so on). As he puts it, a dead individual 'endures not typically as an intact material being but as a multifaceted presence in the live of his contemporaries and successors' (Kramer 2001, 49–50. See also Sperling forthcoming, esp ch 1). On that view, it is the fact of the dead's enduring presence, and not their material properties, which is decisive to the conferral on them of the status of right-holder. Once one sees that, there is nothing mysterious in ascribing interests now to, say, Martin Luther King, anymore than there is anything mysterious in claiming that one now admires Martin Luther King.

However—and by way of reply—even if I can without linguistic or conceptual impropriety claim, here and now in 2008, to admire Martin Luther King, my (or anyone else's) admiration does not in any intelligible way benefit him. Nor, conversely, can he be harmed, here and now, by the allegations of marital infidelity which were made after his death.[9] Put generally, the fact that a long-dead individual endures in the lives of his successors is not enough to confer on him moral status. That individual must be the kind of being of whom it makes sense to say that it can be harmed, or benefited. As I have argued above, the dead are not that kind of beings.

Incidentally, that last point also disposes of another possible attempt to rescue rights-correlative posthumous duties. In his insightful account of rights, Carl Wellman argues that 'the rights of the living continue to impose duties even after the persons who possessed those rights have ceased to exist', even, that is, after those rights themselves cease to exist (Wellman 1995, 156).[10] Wellman's point appeals to the interesting thought that the duty-holding and the right-holding need not be contemporaneous. However, even if that is true, it must still be the case that, at the point at which Y fulfills, or defaults on, his duty to X, the latter

---

[8] For a failure to draw that distinction, see Lomasky 1987, 216.

[9] Our use of ordinary language does seem to suggest that claims such as 'I admire—now, in 2008—Martin Luther King' are unproblematic. But we might in fact be misusing ordinary language (Callahan 1987, 342–3). To put my point differently, even if it is true that Martin Luther King has, in 2008, the (relational) property of being admired by me, this is not enough to establish that there is a sense in which being admired by me (or, indeed, anyone else) benefits him, here and now, in 2008.

[10] Although Wellman endorses the Will Theory of rights, his point could conceivably be made by an Interest Theorist.

can be benefited, or harmed, by his action. This, in turn, requires that X be a subject of experiences—which he clearly is not once he is dead.

To recapitulate, the dead cannot be harmed; moreover, although the living can have, whilst alive, interests in respect of posthumous states of affairs, they cannot be harmed by the posthumous thwarting of those interests. Consequently, there cannot be such a thing as posthumous interest-based rights, in either of the two senses of the term 'posthumous rights' which were identified at the outset of this section.

3 Two Objections

The view I defend in this paper might be thought vulnerable to two objections. First, some might argue, it implies—implausibly—that what we do not, and never will, know cannot harm us while we are alive. Second, others might press, it has counterintuitive implications regarding the significance of death. I address each of those two objections in turn.

3.1 The Dead and the Wholly Ignorant

I have argued that one cannot be harmed at *t* by some event E unless the latter adversely affects one's experience at *t*. In so far as a posthumous event E does not make a difference to one's experience once one is dead, one cannot be harmed by it then, from which it follows that one cannot have a right then that E not happen. My argument against posthumous rights thus rests on an experiential account of harm, and as such is likely to invite the following objection: if one's experience must be affected by E in order for E to harm us, then it follows that what we do not, and shall never, know cannot harm us either. And yet, as Feinberg famously notes, we do not really believe that to be true: if someone spreads defamatory lies about me amongst people I love and respect, I am harmed, even if I do not, and will never, know about it, and will be unaffected by it. If that is the case, then, I can be harmed by posthumous defamatory allegations or by the posthumous destruction of the will in which I make ample provision for my children, even though I clearly do not, and never will, know about it (Feinberg 1984, 87 and 1974, McMahan 1989).

If one accepts that there cannot be posthumous harms (a point I now regard as granted), the objection could be met in two different ways. On the one hand, one could argue that the case of the dead and that of someone who will never know, or be affected, by defamatory allegations are indeed analogous, and draw the conclusion that, just as the dead are not harmed by defamatory allegations, then neither is the wholly ignorant person (Partridge 1981 and Glannon 2001). On the other hand, one could accept the claim that the living can be harmed, whilst alive, by events and actions which they do not, and never will, know about, and deny that their case is relevantly similar to that of the dead.

Those who are hostile to the notion of posthumous harms standardly go down the first route. In what follows, I offer a defence of the second strategy. At first sight, that is not a very promising avenue of inquiry: if one is harmed by some event at *t* only if that event adversely affects one's experience at *t*, then, in so far as one's experience is not affected by events we do not and will never know about, one cannot be harmed by those events. Or so might one suppose.

And yet, my account of harm does not commit me to the view that the living cannot be harmed by events which they will never know about. Note, first, that the claim that one is harmed by some event E at *t* if, and only if, E adversely affects one's experience at *t*, is not the same as the claim that one must experience either the event itself, or the setback to our interests which this event causes. Suppose (*Time Trial 1*) that A competes in the individual time-trial of a cycle race which he believes is run cleanly, and in which, if it is so run, he is the overwhelming favourite. A's goal is to win the race, and to win it cleanly. Unbeknownst to A, B takes performance-enhancing drugs before the trial, as a result of which he wins. A does not experience B's drug-taking, but he does experience a setback, that of losing the race. By contrast, suppose (*Time Trial 2*) that A, who does not know that B is taking drugs, believes throughout the race that he is winning (he knows that he is incomparably better than B at time-trials, but does not know that B, who started first, has run a better individual time-trial). A crosses the finishing line, falls off his bike, and sustains a head injury which sends him in a deep coma from which he never wakes up. A experiences neither B's drug-taking nor the setback of losing the race. I believe, however, that B's drug-taking does harm A.

For consider. There are different ways in which some event can affect, or make a difference, to one's experience. Most obviously, it can turn our experience from a good one (B does not take drugs and A wins) to a bad one (B takes drugs and A loses). It can also destroy our experience altogether (a point to which we will return below). Less obviously, but crucially for our purpose here, it can turn our experience of the world from one which is true to the world, to one which no longer fits with it. Suppose that I am in a room with a chair. I see that chair, in that room, at time *t*. Suppose now that, at time *t₁,* two things happen: the chair is removed from the room, and I take a hallucinogenic drug which makes me experience things as they were at time *t*. There is a sense in which my experience (understood as 'lived experience') has not been affected by the drug: I still see the chair. But there is another, important sense (understood as 'veridical', if you will) in which it has been affected, namely that, as it is no longer the case that there is a chair in the room, I no longer experience the world as it is. In *Time Trial 2*, A (mistakenly) experiences the world as one in which the race is run cleanly, and in which he is actually winning. But B's drug-taking makes A's experience of the world, throughout the race, untrue to the world as it is, and it is that, I submit, which harms A.

This thought—that events can affect our experience in that sense—underpins the suggestion that the case of the dead differs from the case of the wholly ignorant. Contrast *Time Trial 2* with *Time Trial 3*, in which A has good reasons to believe that B, who (in this case) he knows to be clean, and who is a cyclist of incomparably inferior skills, will never beat his time-trial record time. Suppose further that, two years after A's death, B starts taking performance-enhancing drugs and beats A's record. B's actions do not make a difference to A's experience, since A is no longer a subject of experiences. Not only does A experience neither B's drug-taking, nor the setback of witnessing his own record fall; the fact that B acts after his death means that A does not have a non-veridical experience of the world. Less quirkily perhaps, take the case of someone—Jack—who trusts his best friend, Jill, never to badmouth him behind his back.[11] Suppose that Jill betrays Jack's trust during Jack's life-time, that Jack will never know about it, and that his life will not be affected by it (his other friends will not turn away from him, he will not lose his job, etc). Imagine, alternatively, that Jill betrays Jack's trust after Jack's death. In the first case, or so I submit, Jill harms Jack precisely in so far as she makes his experience of his life untrue to his life as it is; in the latter, she does not harm him, or so I submit, precisely because he no longer has experiences—and, therefore, no longer has experiences of which it makes sense to say that they are, or not, veridical.

To recapitulate briefly, I have claimed (a) that we are harmed by some event only if the occurrence of that event makes a difference to our experience (which is why there is no such thing as a posthumous right); and (b) that we can be harmed by some event even if we do not experience this particular event itself or the setback to our interests which this event causes (which is why there can be such a thing as a right not to have certain things done to us while we are alive even though we are not, and never will be, aware of them).[12] My argument to that effect rests on a veridical account of experience, and will elicit the following, obvious objection. In *Time Trial 3*, B's drug-taking, after A's death, makes A's (*antemortem*) experience of the world (a world in which his record would never be broken) non-veridical. Likewise, if Jill badmouths Jack once he is dead, her behaviour makes his (*antemortem*) perception of Jill as someone who would never behave in that way untrue to the world as it was—just as her badmouthing him while he is alive falsifies his experience of her. What reason—it will be objected—is there to treat those two cases differently? To the extent that my veridical account of experience does support the claim that Jack is harmed by Jill's actions whilst alive even though he will never know about it, then, by the same token, it also supports the claim that Jack is harmed by Jill's posthumous badmouthing.

---

[11] I owe this example to Leif Wenar.

[12] Note that, on my account, the case of the dead is analogous to that of an Alzheimer's sufferer who has no awareness at all that his son, to whom he left his business in the hope and expectation that the latter would further expand it, has in fact run the company into the ground. (That is, not only does the father not remember leaving the company to his son, he does not even remember his son—indeed, does not even remember that he has a son.) I see no difficulty in accepting this implication of my argument. I owe this example to Kramer. He, Wenar, and Rowan Cruft have pressed me very hard on my account of the wholly ignorant, for which I am grateful. I am equally grateful to Katrin Flikschuh for helping me to clarify my response to their objections.

The objection has two variants. In its first variant, it might be taken to claim that Jill's behaviour after Jack's death, say at time t_{10}, causes Jack's perception of Jill while he was alive, at t, to have been false. If so, it is vulnerable to the charge that it relies on backward causation—which, in a world of purposeful agents (such as rights-holders and duty-bearers) leads to well-known absurdities.[13] In any event, in so far as there is no physical connection between Jill's conduct at t_{10} and Jack's experience at t, Jill does not cause anything to happen to Jack. Note, incidentally, that the point applies to the case where Jill, after restraining herself from badmouthing Jack at t, first does so at t_1, while he is still alive, but unbeknownst to him. Jill's conduct at t_1 does not cause Jack to be harmed at t; but it does cause him to be harmed from t_1 onwards (until he dies).

In its second variant, the objection claims, not that Jack's experience was made false to the world as it was by Jill's behaviour, but, rather, that the latter shows that Jack's perception of Jill as absolutely trustworthy was always false, and that Jack was always harmed by Jill (at least in that particular respect).

I concede that Jack's experience of the world, in that particular respect, was never veridical. However, that does not suffice to establish that Jill harms Jack (and it is that which must be established, you recall, for the notion of posthumous rights to make sense). As the objection under study concedes, it does not *become* true, as a result of Jill's conduct, that Jack was harmed all along. Rather, Jill's conduct merely has the heuristic effect of showing that Jack's (*antemortem*) experience of the world was not veridical. Now, to be sure, we—impartial observers—may feel regret that Jack's life should not have been the life he thought it was; we might even conclude that his life overall was the worse for Jill's deception. But (to reiterate) this is not the same as to say that Jack himself is harmed by Jill. For the latter claim to be true, it would have to be the case that Jill adversely affects his experience. In so far as, first, she actually does not cause anything to have happened to him, and as, second, at the point at which she acts, he does not have experiences of which we can say that they are (or not) veridical, it follows that she cannot harm him.

3.2 The Significance of Death

The second objection to the view defended here—that there is no such thing as a posthumous right, because there is no such thing as a posthumous harm—is that it both overplays and underplays the importance of death. Let me address

---

[13] Most notably, if an event E_1, occurring at time t_1, can be caused by another event E_3, occurring at t_3, then it must be possible for some agent A, at t_2 (that is, after the occurrence of E_1 but before that of E_3), to act in such a way as to forestall E_3, with the effect that E_1 will not happen—which is absurd. On backward causation, see, eg, Black 1956, Dummett 1964, Gorovitz 1964. On backward causation and posthumous harms, see Feinberg 1984, 90–1, Pitcher 1984, and Lomasky 1987 (where, incidentally, he criticizes the second variant of the objection, as set out in the next paragraph in the text, on grounds similar to mine).

the charge of overplaying first. As Jeff McMahan argues, to reject posthumous rights while conferring rights on the wholly ignorant supposes that death makes all the difference. Thus, imagine that someone's life-long work collapses unbeknownst to him. On the view I defend here, the collapse of his life's work is not a misfortune if it happens just after he dies, whereas it is 'a terrible misfortune' if it happens just before he dies. Surely, though, whether the collapse occurs shortly after or shortly before he dies cannot make such a difference (McMahan 1989, 38–9).[14]

And yet, I believe that it does make a difference. For although the man does not suffer a 'terrible misfortune' (or so I contend) if his life's work collapses shortly before he dies, he does incur some harm—the harm attendant on the fact that, in that brief moment between the destruction of what he holds dear and his death, he is, in fact, living a lie. Contrastingly, he does not suffer any misfortune if he dies just before the collapse. Note, though, that in the former case, the shorter the gap, the lesser the harm. So that death does make *all* the difference, but the difference may not, in fact, be that great at all.

The charge of underplaying is not so easily dismissed. It holds that the reasons why there cannot be posthumous rights imply that death cannot harm those to whom it happens. For consider. I argued that someone, X, can be harmed as a result of some event only if that event adversely affects his experience. This, I claimed, is why the dead cannot be harmed, whereas the living can, even if they will never know about it. However (the objection would press), the foregoing supposes that X is a subject of experience at the point at which the event occurs, since the event could not, otherwise, affect X's experience. Since X is no longer such a subject at the moment of his death, death cannot be bad for him. Put more generally, there can be no such thing as an interest in not being dead, and there thus can be no such thing as a right not to be killed.

To the extent that any account of rights which would rule out a right not to be killed ought to be rejected (or so I assume), the objection, if it works, is fatal to the Interest Theory. Accordingly, we can endorse the theory only if we can convincingly adopt either of the following strategies: (a) concede that there can be posthumous rights; (b) deny that there can be such rights *and* show that there nevertheless can be a right not to be killed. For aforementioned reasons, (a) is not a viable option. Yet, it is (I think) possible to defend (b). The fact that, at death, X is no longer a subject of experience need not pose a serious problem for my account of the reason why X cannot suffer posthumous setbacks to her interests: for what matters, when determining whether X is harmed by some event E at *t*, is not whether or not X is a subject of experience then but, rather, whether or not his experience is adversely affected by E at *t*. In so far as death destroys X's experience, it affects it. To be sure, whether or not this harms X depends on the extent

---

[14] Incidentally, in the case of the Alzheimer's sufferer, the charge would be that I overplay the importance of senility. *Mutatis mutandis*, my response to McMahan's objection applies there too.

to which it is beneficial to X to continue to be a subject of experiences—and that, in turn, depends on the kinds of goods, both present and future, of which death would deprive him.[15] Be that as it may, death can and will in some cases be bad for X to the extent that ending his experience is bad for him (McMahan 1989, 33). The Interest Theory thus need not deny that Red has a right not to be killed.[16] What it does deny, though, at least on the account of harm which I have defended here, is that Red, once he is dead, can still be harmed. As should be clear by now, this does not strike me as problematic.

I pointed out above that whether or not X exists at t is irrelevant to the determination of E as harmful to him. Even if that is incorrect, the Interest Theory still not need reject the claim that there is a right to be killed. The view that the Interest Theory must reject that claim can be construed as follows: 'X must exist at t in order to be harmed by E at t; X does not exist at death so death is not harmful to X; in so far as death is not harmful to X, X does not have a right not to be killed.' However, even if we accept, *arguendo*, that death is not harmful to X, the conclusion does not follow from the premises. For between E—the act which results in X's death—and X's dying, there is a lapse of time, however infinitesimally short, during which X still exists. The right not to be killed can thus be understood as a right that others not act in such a way as to bring about our death: those acts, and not death itself (*arguendo*), are harmful, and they are harmful precisely to the extent that they contribute to depriving us of the good of continued life. If that is correct, then one can on the one hand deny that there is such a thing as an interest-based posthumous right, and on the other hand claim (as one must) that there is such a thing as an interest-based right not to be killed.

---

[15] For subtle and interesting discussions of the badness of death, Feldman 1991, McMahan 1989, and Nagel 1979.

[16] Unlike the Will Theory, which is committed to the view that X has a right against Y that Y φ if and only if he is able to waive, or demand, remedies should Y fail to φ. In so far as, once dead, X will not be able to waive or demand remedies should Y kill him, X cannot have a right not to be killed. A Will theorist might be tempted to block this objection by dropping the requirement that being able to waive or demand remedies should Y fail to φ is a necessary condition for X to have a right against Y that φ. She might say, instead, that it is sufficient (as well as necessary) that X should be able to waive or demand the performance by Y of his duty to φ. However, this putative move would not rescue the Will Theory. For on the view mooted here, the theory is committed to the following pair of claims: (a) if Red is conscious before White inflicts one last kick on him, then Red can have a right that White not kill him; (b) however, if Red has lost consciousness at some point during this beating, then, in so far as he lacks the abilities to control White's actions at the point at which White inflicts the last kick, he cannot have a right that White not kill him—even if he would regain consciousness were the beating to stop. That, I believe, is wildly implausible. Surely the *temporary* loss of consciousness cannot make all the difference between having, and not having, a right not to be killed by a villainous attacker. It is worth noting, of course, that on the view I defend in this paper, the interest-based theory of rights is committed to the view that the irreversibly comatose cannot have rights (which is not to say that one cannot be held under any duty concerning them).

4 Conclusion

One is harmed by some event, I have argued, if, and only if, that event adversely affects one's experience, not necessarily in the sense that one feels, sees, and hears differently, but sometimes in the sense that one no longer has any experience, or that one's experience, though superficially unchanged, no longer fits with the world as it is. And it is precisely because one cannot be harmed unless one's experience is affected that neither the dead, nor the living, can have rights in respect of posthumous states of affairs. As I also noted, the claim, so defended, that the dead cannot be harmed is compatible with the view that the wholly ignorant can be harmed.

Of course, nothing I have said here precludes imposing on the living obligations with respect to the dead (although it does preclude obligations owed *to* the dead which do not correlate with rights, if there are such obligations at all). Thus, the claim that we cannot have a right against the living that they act in certain ways once we are dead is compatible with the view that the living are under an obligation to some other living person (for example, our next-of-kin) to act in certain ways regarding us. However, if the conclusions reached here are sound, and if the Interest Theory turns out to offer the most plausible account of rights, then we have to forego what is, for some of us, the deeply entrenched intuition that we do have a right that our will be respected and our grave not be desecrated; or that we do have a right that our reputation be restored if it has been wrongly destroyed, and this even if we are dead. In other words, we have to concede to Will theorists, most notably Hart, one of the key points which, according to their opponents, constitute a good reason for endorsing the Interest Theory.

13

Are There *Still* Any Natural Rights?

Hillel Steiner

Let me begin by saying that what this essay presents is more in the nature of a puzzlement than an argument and, in that respect, it's likely to leave you as dissatisfied as it does me. In that respect again, it's also a cry for help—an invitation to anyone who can shed some light on the puzzle it explores. What is that puzzle?

Among Hart's several works in moral and political philosophy, one of the two of greatest renown is unquestionably his essay 'Are There Any Natural Rights?', originally published in 1955 in the *Philosophical Review* (Hart 1955).[1] Over the ensuing decades, this essay was reprinted in numerous anthologies and edited collections, and generated an extensive responsive scholarly literature. The writings of many political philosophers (including my own) were heavily influenced by the central arguments of that essay.

Accordingly, for those persons, and many others as well, it was a cause of some surprise—and not a little dismay—that Hart declined to include it in his 1983 Oxford University Press collection of what he considered to be among his more significant papers, *Essays in Jurisprudence and Philosophy*. By way of explanation there, he offered only the brief and essentially unilluminating remark that

Though it attracted some attention I have not included it here, since its main argument seems to be mistaken and my errors not sufficiently illuminating to justify re-printing it now. (Hart 1983, 17)

Nor have any other persons, with whom I've thus far had the opportunity to discuss this matter, been able to shed any light on his reasons for this renunciation. For instance, Joseph Raz reports that

[Hart] became convinced, many many years ago, that the argument was not valid, but I do not remember why...I remember that he found it ironical that Rawls said somewhere,

---

[1] Reprinted in Quinton 1967. Page references are to the latter text and are accordingly designated as Hart 1967. The other famous work is Hart 1963.

or maybe in private, that that article set him on his own wild goose chase which led to thousands of books and articles being launched for no very good purpose.[2]

And, in similar vein, Nicola Lacey's recent biography simply records the fact of Hart's having later had doubts about his argument, without reporting any reasons for them (Lacey 2004, 169).

So I'm truly baffled. Here is this highly influential piece of work which, *inter alia* and as Neil MacCormick has suggested, seems unmistakably to form the justifying ground of Hart's liberal critique of legal moralism in his celebrated *Law, Liberty and Morality* lectures, published in 1963 (MacCormick 1981, 150). And yet, sometime over the following two decades and without (so far as we know) abandoning this liberal anti-moralism, Hart becomes thoroughly disenchanted with that seminal essay. Why? Or, what's not to like?

The present essay is simply an attempt to speculate about, and to assess, some possible reasons for that disenchantment. And I propose to do this by considering two issues: (1) What, for Hart, makes a *moral* right a *natural* right?, and (2) What, for Hart, makes a duty the correlate of a right? Hart's answers to these two questions are, of course, very closely connected to one another in that essay. So one thing that we'll also need to consider is whether there are any reasons to suppose that his eventual disenchantment with it was caused by some perceived break in that connection, due to some change in his views as to the proper answers to either or both of those questions.

Let's turn to the first issue first. For many, perhaps most, writers in the natural rights tradition—and for Hart too—one thing that makes a moral right a natural one is that it's a *foundational* right. A foundational right is one which is not inferable from any other right and from which other rights—*derivative* ones—are inferable. There are several different ways in which derivative rights can be derived from foundational ones and, for that matter, from other derivative rights. Thus a right to Y might be derived from a right to X by virtue of the fact that Y is a form or *instance* of X. This is plainly evident if Y is providing physical health and X is providing well-being, or if Y is non-incarceration and X is allowing someone freedom. Another mode of derivation is *instrumental*: thus, say, Y is providing medical treatment and X is securing physical health. Instantiating and instrumental derivations respectively conjoin conceptual and causal premises with the statement that there is a right to X, in order to derive their conclusion that there is a right to Y. That is, the duty to do Y is either a constitutive element of the correlative duty to do X, or doing Y is a means to doing X.

Still other modes of derivation invoke Hohfeldian considerations. One way in which a right to Y can be derived from a right to X is through the exercise of *powers* attached to the right to X. Your current Y right to that car was created by my exercising my antecedent X right to that car: that is, by my exercising the

---

[2] Personal communication, 30 January 2007.

power to transfer the ownership of the car to you. In exercising that power, I extinguish my X right that you (and others) not interfere with my possession of the car, and I create your Y right that others (including myself) not interfere with your possession of it. Similarly, Manchester University's Y right to my teaching services is derived from the exercise of powers attached to various of my X rights pertaining to my body and its labour. Yet another kind of derivation involves the exercise of *liberties*. Thus my X rights to (others' non-interference with) my possession of my supply of paper and my paper-shredding machine standardly give me a Y right to their non-interference with my possession of the shredded paper. Such 'Hohfeldian derivations' combine the statement asserting the X right with statements asserting (a) the existence of the relevant powers or liberties, and (b) the fact of their having been exercised, in order to infer the right to Y.

In Hart's analysis of natural rights, the primary modes of derivation are instantiation and exercises of powers. What he there calls *general rights*—his proffered examples are 'the right to say what I think' and 'the right to worship as I please'—are instantiations of his natural right. As he says, each of them is 'a particular *exemplification* of the equal right to be free' (Hart 1967, 64). To have these moral rights is to be equipped with a moral justification for demanding and, if necessary, enforcing others' non-interference with such acts of worship and speech. More strictly, these rights imply that their holder is vested with a variety of claims correlative to others' enforceable duties to forbear from actions which would standardly have the effect of preventing him or her from performing those speaking and worshipping acts. These general moral rights and their duty correlates, being simply particular instances of that natural right to equal freedom and its duty correlate, are, like them, not created nor conferred by any voluntary action and are of universal incidence—which, significantly, Hart takes to mean that they're vested in 'all persons capable of choice' (Hart 1967, 53, 64).

When we come to the mode of derivation of what Hart calls *special rights*, things are, however, somewhat less clear. What *is* clear is that special rights are modifications—indeed, truncations—of general rights. Interfering actions which persons' general rights would require others to forbear can, by dint of those others' special rights, become permissible and sometimes even obligatory to perform. How is this possible? How can there be moral rights that apparently encroach upon the most basic moral right, the right to equal freedom?

To this question, Hart offers several answers—the clearest of which runs as follows:

The most obvious cases of special rights are those that arise from promises. By promising to do or not do something, we voluntarily incur obligations and create or confer rights on those to whom we promise; we alter the existing moral independence of the parties' freedom of choice in relation to some action and create a new moral relationship between them, so that it becomes morally legitimate for the person to whom the promise is given to determine how the promisor shall act. The promisee has a temporary authority or sovereignty in relation to some specific matter over the other's will... But a promise is not the only kind of transaction whereby rights are conferred. They may be *accorded* by a person consenting or authorizing another to interfere in matters which but for this consent or authorization he would be free to determine for himself. (Hart 1967, 60, 61)

In these cases, the promisor or authorizer can be described as transferring, to another person, a portion of what we might refer to as his or her *rightful domain of discretion*. The promisor or authorizer loses some freedom and the promisee or 'authorizee' gains it. And to those philosophers who have found it mysterious that 'moral phenomena—rights and duties or obligations—can be brought into existence by the voluntary action of individuals', Hart's response is that

they have not clearly seen how special the moral notions of a right and obligation are, nor how peculiarly they are connected with the *distribution* of freedom of choice. (Hart 1967, 60, 61)

In other words, Hart believes that the *re*distributions of freedom, effected by the promisor's and authorizer's choices, are perfectly consonant with the distribution of freedom mandated by his basic moral right—the natural right to equal freedom. Their exercises of powers attached to the general rights composing that natural right are *not* to be understood as constituting contraventions of the kind of equality it mandates. Both the pre-promise distribution of rightful freedom, and its very different post-promise counterpart, can be consistent with that natural right. That is, consistent with a foundational right to equal freedom is the exercise of it by its possessor in such a way as to permit another person to curtail some of that freedom. Indeed, disabling that possessor from exercising it in that way would itself amount to an encroachment on that foundational right. Labour contracts and transfers of ownership are not, *per se*, violations of the natural right to equal freedom. Here it's worth noting that, in his essay, Hart does not go on, as perhaps he should have done, to consider what this more precisely implies about the sense in which his natural right to freedom is an *equal* one. But it's been argued elsewhere that the equal freedom distribution mandated by that natural right is thus best understood as an *initial* or *original* (or *starting-gate*) equality (Steiner 1994, 224–8).[3]

Hart's clearest explanation of the derivation of special rights from his natural right is, as I've said, his account of how they are created by exercising powers attached to that right. Far less clear is what he has to say about special rights which are *not* the correlates of such deliberately incurred obligations. Among these, he particularly singles out rights arising from special natural relationships such as that between a parent and a child, and what have since famously come to be called *rights of fair play*.

A right of fair play is said to exist in the following circumstances:

[W]hen a number of persons conduct any joint enterprise according to rules and thus restrict their liberty, those who have submitted to these restrictions when required have

---

[3] How such equality can be secured amongst persons, whose respective existences are only partly contemporaneous with one another, is a conceptually distinguishable and highly complex issue, which I set aside here; cf Steiner 1994, 270–3.

a right to a similar submission from those who have benefited by their submission. (Hart 1967, 61)

It's easy, I think, to see why such a right to similar submission might be thought of as fair. Less easy to understand, however, is how this right could be derived from a basic right to freedom. What is the mode of derivation relied upon here? Perhaps we might say that, when the activities of some persons produce such positive external effects for others, those others may be *presumed* to have consented to incur such duties of similar submission: that is, those others have *hypothetically* done the equivalent of what promisers and authorizers *actually* do. There are a number of familiar problems with this kind of explanation. One is simply that the fact that an activity produces a benefit for some persons does not, in itself, entail that this benefit outweighs any possible loss they might incur by acquiring that aforesaid freedom-restricting duty of similar submission. If their hypothetical consent is to be inferred at all here, the benefit involved must at least be a *net* benefit. But second, and even if it is a net benefit, it's unclear why fairness requires the activity producing it to be a *joint* enterprise conducted by *several* persons according to rules restricting their freedom. Why wouldn't fairness require that *any* activity that confers benefits on others—even one unilaterally undertaken by a single person—similarly give rise to some freedom-restricting reciprocal duties on the part of those recipients? And if the conferment of such unsolicited benefits *can* generate such duties on the part of their recipients, what then becomes of the common distinction, equally affirmed by Hart, between the respective domains of benevolence and rights?[4]

Equally unclear is the derivation of special rights from special natural relationships. Hart here instances parents' rights to obedience from their child. But he goes on immediately to note that this right to obedience would 'be thought to terminate when the child reaches the age "of discretion"' (Hart 1967, 63). And here we cannot avoid asking *why*. Why would it terminate at that point? After all, the natural relationship which is said to give rise to it doesn't. So presumably the answer must be that, if it were *not* to terminate at that point, it would constitute a contravention of the child's natural right to freedom. And if we then ask why it wasn't such a contravention prior to that point, the answer is supplied in the second sentence of Hart's essay, where he says that his natural right to freedom is to be understood as vesting in 'any adult human being capable of choice' (Hart 1967, 53). Prior to reaching the age of discretion—prior to becoming a person capable of choice—the child simply has no moral right to freedom to be contravened. Accordingly, the essay's central project—which, you'll recall, is to explain how interference with an action that would otherwise be an exercise of rightful freedom can be justified—simply has no application to such non-adult children, because none of their actions can count as such exercises. And that, in

[4] Yet a further problem besetting this idea of fair-play rights might be its apparent reliance on the *Cui bono?* test associated with the Interest Theory of rights; see below.

turn, is because, whatever freedom they may happen to have, it cannot be theirs by right. Lacking such moral rights, those children need not be presumed to be vested with moral obligations in order to justify curtailments of their freedom. And, indeed, the very same reason that they're here presumed to lack moral rights to freedom—namely, their incapacity for choice—is often taken to imply that they correspondingly lack moral obligations.

So, again and very much in the spirit of speculation, it looks as though one reason for Hart's disenchantment with his essay might have lain in a perception that its account of the special rights of fair play and special natural relationships fails suitably to derive them from his natural right. If there are any such moral rights, it would appear that their derivation must invoke some foundation other than the right to equal freedom, a right which would thereby lack the exclusive foundational status that he attributed to it. That said, however, I should also say that these deficiencies strike me as being, at most, marginal to the main thrust of the essay's argument, and hardly sufficient to warrant Hart's renunciation of it. So I think we need to look elsewhere if we are to find any such warrant.

In that respect, a different and far more significant—though not entirely unrelated—reason for that disenchantment might have arisen from his concerns with the Will Theory of rights itself, to which Hart famously gave considerable elucidation, in the form of what he more perspicuously labelled as the *Choice Theory*. Most discussions of 'Are There Any Natural Rights?' correctly identify the Choice Theory as forming the Kantian background—and, indeed, much of the foreground—of his central argument there (MacCormick 1981, 149). But here let me hasten to add two points. First, it's generally agreed that Hart's most developed articulation of the Choice Theory is to be found in his essay 'Bentham on Legal Rights'—an essay which did not appear until eighteen years after the natural rights essay and which, parenthetically, he did think worthy of inclusion in his subsequent 1982 collection, *Essays on Bentham*.[5] Second, in 'Bentham on Legal Rights' as well as elsewhere in his writings, Hart clearly sets out what he considers to be several limitations on the scope of the Choice Theory's capacity to serve as a conceptual tool for analysing certain kinds of *legal* provision: namely, those sustaining criminal law duties and constitutional immunities. So the conjecture I now propose to explore is that his disenchantment with his natural rights essay may in some way have been due to his subsequently acquiring a belief that those limitations seriously impair his account of natural rights.

It would, of course, take us too far afield to review the Choice Theory in all its detailed implications here; and, in any case, I assume that you're already acquainted with much of that detail (cf Steiner 1998, 233–302). Suffice it, then, to say that the familiar core thesis of that theory is that the holder of a right, in the strict sense of a claim-right, is whoever holds the powers both to waive,

---

[5] This essay first appeared in Simpson 1973. All my references to this essay are to the Hart 1982 text.

and alternatively to demand and if necessary enforce, compliance with the duty correlative to that claim. And much the same is true with respect to holders of immunity-rights, in the sense that they are the persons who are empowered both to extinguish the correlatively entailed disability of another person and, alternatively, to nullify putative exercises of some power which he or she *ipso facto* lacks. In thereby vesting claim-holders and immunity-holders with domains of discretionary control, the Choice Theory assigns to them spheres of freedom, in precisely the same way that we previously saw at work in Hart's natural rights essay. They are the persons enforcibly entitled to decide whether certain changes or continuities, in how the world is, should or need not occur.

Now, in relation to the conjecture we're about to explore, the significance of Hart's increasing involvement with the writings of Bentham can hardly be overestimated. Indeed, although his official attachment to the Bentham Project began only following his early retirement from the Chair of Jurisprudence in 1968, his fascination with Bentham was of much longer standing. As Lacey reports,

[E]ver since his inaugural lecture [published one year prior to his natural rights essay], his published works had demonstrated his regard for Bentham as a profound source of insight. (Lacey 2004, 298)[6]

As is well enough known, Bentham's hostility to the very idea of natural rights verged on the near-pathological. From his earlier period as a conservative Tory through his conversion to being a radical democrat, one theme that runs continuously throughout his thinking is the unintelligibility—*dangerous* unintelligibility—of that idea. Both the American *Declaration of Independence* and the French *Declaration of the Rights of Man and Citizen* were subjected to vitriolic denunciation, inasmuch as they centrally invoke what he considered to be the anarchistic claim that persons are naturally, pre-politically, vested with basic moral rights (cf Waldron 1987, 29–45).

It seems certain, however, that Hart's disenchantment with his own natural rights essay is very far from being simply a reflection of that Benthamite attitude. In the significant number of essays where he discusses Bentham's view of natural rights, he is constantly at pains to sort out what can be attributed to each of the several factors that converged to motivate that vehement hostility (cf Hart 1982, chs I–IV). Bentham's earlier fear and loathing of anarchism was, of course, one of these. And it robustly survived what Hart, in his 1978 article 'Utilitarianism and Natural Rights', describes as his eventual acquisition of

a deeply pessimistic view of all governments, the 'ruling few' as he called them. He viewed governments as gangs of potential criminals, tempted like robbers to pursue their own interests at the expense of those over whom they had power, the 'subject many'. But democracy, by placing the power of appointment and dismissal of governments in the hands

---

[6] Hart's inaugural lecture, delivered in 1953, was published in 1954 (see Hart 1954).

of the majority was, he thought, the best device for securing that governments worked for the general interest. (Hart 1983, 185)

It is democracy, and neither anarchism nor rapacious aristocracy, that will deliver the goods. As that passage further suggests, Hart finds a second motivating factor of Bentham's hostility to natural rights in his utilitarian conception of morality. Given the essential role that he believed government alone could play in attaining morally optimal states of affairs, the idea that individuals have moral claims and immunities, that might disable legislators from responding optimifically to changing circumstances, was regarded as simply anathema. The belief that responses to such changes should be solely a matter of individuals' choices was simply unacceptable, and doctrines of inalienable, imprescriptible rights were nothing but reactionary tools for obstructing moral progress.

There is, however, little evidence to suggest that Hart shared either Bentham's fear and loathing or his commitment to unqualified utilitarianism. So I think we need to look for the possible sources of his disenchantment in a third factor that was at work in Bentham's normative thinking: namely, his conception of rights *per se*.

In 'Bentham on Legal Rights' and elsewhere, Hart bestows a good deal of praise on Bentham's careful analysis of the concept, noting the impressive extent to which it anticipates the canonical account delivered by Hohfeld a century later and, indeed, drawing attention to a number of respects in which Bentham's analysis should be regarded as superior to that of Hohfeld.[7] But this enthusiasm is tempered by a number of significant reservations, the chief one of these being Bentham's adherence to the *Interest Theory* (which Hart also labels as the *Benefit Theory*) of rights. As is well enough known, the debate between the Will or Choice Theory of rights and the Interest or Benefit Theory is one of very long standing— dating back to at least the later Middle Ages—and is still ongoing (cf Kramer, Simmonds, and Steiner, 1998). Hart's 'Bentham on Legal Rights' is itself one of the more important contributions to that debate.

Again, as previously with the Choice Theory, I'll here refrain from reviewing the Interest Theory in all its detailed implications and, instead, simply assume that you're already acquainted with much of that detail. The main point on which we need to focus, for present purposes, is the basic difference between those two theories' respective tests for who is to be identified as the holder of the claim-right correlative to an enforceable duty. In the case of the Choice Theory, as we've seen, that test is a *formal* or *structural* one: that is, it asks 'Who chooses?'—who is vested with the powers both to waive, and alternatively to demand and if necessary enforce, compliance with that duty? In the case of the Interest Theory, the corresponding test is one of *content*: 'Who benefits?'—whose interests would be adversely affected by a breach of that duty? Whereas the validity of Choice

---

[7] Hart 1983, 162. Of particular significance was Bentham's distinction between naked and vested liberties.

Theory claims and immunities is independent of their myriad contents, the validity of their Interest Theory counterparts is not. This *Cui bono?* test—variously qualified by Bentham and others, so as to exclude certain counter-intuitive consequences[8]—tells us to whom those entitlements belong.

Hart, along with other writers in the Will Theory tradition, has expressed a number of doubts concerning the explanatory power of this model of rights. One of the most familiar of these, and one which is highly relevant for some issues to be discussed presently, is the problem of *third-party beneficiaries* of legal contracts. As Hart notes:

In many jurisdictions contracts expressly made for the benefit of third parties, e.g. a contract between two people to pay a third party a sum of money, is not enforceable by the third party and he cannot waive or release the obligation. In such a case although the third party is a direct beneficiary since breach of the contract constitutes a direct detriment to him, he has no legal control over the duty and so no legal right. On the other hand, the contracting party having the appropriate control has the legal right, though he is not the person intended to benefit by the performance of the contract. (Hart 1982, 187)

Here, then, is one class of cases where the Choice or Will Theory is clearly a better guide, than Bentham's *Cui bono?* test, to the correct identification of claimants. And, to that extent, Hart's natural rights argument's reliance on that theory should pose no problem for him.

To this, however, Bentham and other Interest theorists have rejoined with several *tu quoque* complaints. They have charged, and Hart concedes, that the explanatory power of the Will Theory model cannot extend to the enforceable duties of the criminal law. For here, the fact that the victim of a criminal offence might have consented—*ex ante* or *ex post*—to the offender's act, would not suffice to have extinguished that duty nor to exempt that offender from its enforcement. Hart's response here is essentially a two-fold one: (a) that such cases reflect the limits of *any* general theory of rights as a tool for analysing enforceable duties; and (b) that the Choice Theory's being thus limited is not sufficient grounds for embracing the rival Interest Theory, since it assigns no distinctive function to the concept of rights—renders them redundant—inasmuch as its analyses of rights are all fully translatable, without remainder, into the general language of duties (Hart 1982, 188–90).

That said, Hart does concede that this redundancy rejoinder

is no longer pertinent when what is to be considered are not rights under the ordinary law, but fundamental rights which may be said to be against the legislature, limiting its powers to make (or unmake) the ordinary law. (Hart 1982, 190)

---

[8] Such as vesting claims in an indefinitely large class of beneficiaries of a particular duty's performance.

However, this concession is not intended to offer any comfort to Bentham's Interest Theory since he maintains that it, too, is

not sufficient to provide an analysis of such constitutionally guaranteed rights. These require for their analysis the notion of an immunity. Bentham, unlike Hohfeld, did not isolate this notion in distinguishing different kinds or meanings of legal right, and indeed his attention was never seriously given to the analysis of fundamental legal rights. (Hart 1982, 190)

Such constitutional immunities, Hart believes, escape the Choice Theory net simply because they are unwaivable by individual citizens. But, in his view, they also escape Bentham's net

because, although, unlike Austin, he did not think that there were logical or conceptual objections to the notion of legal limitations of a sovereign legislature, he viewed with extreme suspicion any legal arrangements which would prevent the legislature enacting whatever measures appeared from time to time to be required by the dictates of general utility; and suspicion became contempt at the suggestion that such arrangements should be used to give legal form to doctrines of natural or fundamental individual rights. (Hart 1982, 190)

These constitutional immunities are best viewed, Hart says, as supplying persons with neither the protected choices of the Choice Theory nor the protected benefits of the Interest Theory, but rather with what Hart distinguishes from both of these, as individuals' basic or fundamental *needs* (Hart 1982, 190).

Now, the question I want to pose here is whether Hart's Choice Theory is necessarily bound to make the concessions he does make, concerning the analytical capacity of that theory in confronting the legal provisions for criminal law duties and constitutional immunities. What I'm *not* querying is the corresponding capacity of the Interest Theory to deal with such provisions: I have no doubt that, notwithstanding Hart's argument about Bentham on such immunities, the Interest Theory is perfectly able to account for these as rights—as well, of course, for those that it finds in criminal law provisions.[9]

Why does Hart suppose that criminal law duties entail no correlative claim-rights? We've seen that his grounds for this supposition are the absence of waiving powers in the potential victims of criminal offences. You and I cannot standardly consent to being assaulted or, at least, our consent to it—whether given *ex ante* or *ex post*—will neither release our assailant from his legal forbearance duty nor exempt him from prosecution for its breach. But why assume that it is *our* lack of such waiving powers that is decisive here?

The sole basis for such an assumption, it seems to me, is the thought that it is *we* who are the direct beneficiaries of others' compliance with that duty. That is, Hart's unwillingness to find rights correlative to criminal law duties is itself implicitly predicated on the *Cui bono?* test of the Interest Theory—a theory which he

[9] An important element of that account would doubtless be some form of rule utilitarianism.

explicitly rejects. So instead, and rather than conceding that such duties constitute a limitation on the Choice Theory's analytical capacities, what he should have considered is whether the law empowers someone else—typically, a legal official—to waive those duties. And here, as far as I'm aware, the answer is invariably 'Yes'. James Bond is, famously, licensed to kill, and presumably also to commit assault.

Now it's certainly true that the licensing official involved is unlikely to be an ordinary police officer or a junior public prosecutor, both of whom would typically be legally mandated to enforce such duties and thereby disabled from waiving them. But that mandate is issued to them by their superiors and can be withdrawn either by them or, if they too are mandated, by their superiors in turn. No doubt such mandate waivers are used sparingly, for obvious moral and political reasons. But that fact goes no distance at all toward sustaining a denial that, somewhere in the principal-agent hierarchy of legal officials, there are persons who are empowered to choose whether such mandates are to be imposed or alternatively withdrawn, and who therefore look like being prime candidates for the role of Choice Theory right-holders in the criminal law (cf Steiner 1994, 64–73, and Steiner 1998, 248–55). On this understanding, the role of ordinary citizens in relation to criminal law duties can perfectly adequately be described as that of *third-party beneficiaries*—a role which, as I noted previously, Hart found the Interest Theory to be incapable of correctly analysing when it comes to the provisions of some legal contracts.

I think that this same line of reasoning can further extend to what we saw Hart acknowledging as the other limitation on the Choice Theory's capacity to analyse legal provisions: namely, constitutional immunities against legislative enactments. For here too, it's suggested that it is the *ordinary citizen's* disability—in this case, to waive those immunities—that is sufficient to imply their imperviousness to Choice Theory characterization. Again though, it would appear that, in focusing on the question of whether such waiving powers are vested in ordinary citizens, Hart may once more be succumbing to the subliminal charms of some version of the *Cui bono?* test, inasmuch as he sees these immunities—correctly—as intended to protect provisions for basic or fundamental individual needs from the depredations that some legislators might otherwise inflict on them.

I would again suggest, however, that ordinary citizens' disabilities to waive these immunities do not imply that they are unwaivable. Hart is looking in the wrong place—at the wrong persons—in seeking, and failing to find, powers of waiver with respect to immunities against legislative enactments. For if citizens lack such powers, Hohfeldian logic tells us that they are thereby disabled, and that someone else is therefore vested with the immunity correlatively entailed by that disability. And a not very extended chain of reasoning is required to reach the conclusion that that someone else is going to be whoever is legally empowered to determine the meaning of such constitutional provisions. It is that someone else who is vested with the power to choose whether legislators' enactments are to be upheld or nullified. Accordingly, that someone else fills the role of a Choice Theory right-holder, with ordinary citizens again occupying the position of third-party beneficiaries though, in this case, with respect to constitutional immunities.

To all this unsought-for defence and extension of the Choice Theory, I can well imagine—I guess we can all imagine—Hart responding to the effect that this is all very well as an extension of Hohfeldian logic,[10] but it ill reflects a number of significant features of ordinary and professional legal usage. We just don't speak of legal rights against our being murdered, and legal immunities against laws abridging our freedom of worship, as entitlements vesting in legal officials—not even in constitutional judges.

This is, admittedly, true. But what's also true is that much of the analytical work on rights undertaken by Hohfeld and Bentham before him, and indeed by Hart himself, was motivated by a shared perception that both ordinary usage and that of lawyers, too, was seriously beset by numerous imprecisions and inconsistencies in their understanding of that concept—deficiencies which all too often led to invalid inferences being drawn in particular cases. Their respective attempts to bring a unifying coherence to the various senses in which that concept can be used—to bring forth a cosmos from a chaos—could hardly be expected to underwrite each and every aspect of prevailing usage, and they often explicitly noted such divergences.

In any case, the object of this long diversion into aspects of the Choice Theory has been, as you'll recall, to consider whether Hart's further development of it during the years following the publication of his natural rights essay, could somehow explain his disenchantment with that work. More specifically, and since the Choice Theory—albeit in more rudimentary form—clearly supplied the underpinning of his main argument there, we've been looking at whether the limitations he attributed to the theory's explanatory capacity might somehow have fostered his eventual belief that this main argument was mistaken. To this conjecture, I suppose the appropriate verdict must be 'Not proven'. For as I've tried to show, whatever shortcomings the Choice Theory may suffer from, Hart is himself mistaken in believing that it is beset by those limitations. It *can* serve as a perfectly general theory of rights, and his belief to the contrary is one that might well reflect, *inter alia*, some Benthamite influence, inasmuch as it seems implicitly to rest on the application of the *Cui bono?* test.

So I'll simply conclude here with the puzzlement with which I began. Neither of the two conjectures that I've explored, for Hart's disenchantment with his 1955 essay, seems to be compelling. And I therefore eagerly await further suggestions as to the explanation for this mystery.[11]

[10] Though not only Hohfeldian logic. For anticipations of this general argument, see: Holland 1906, 125–7, Gray 1921, 19–20 and 79–83, and Williams 1957, 264–5.

[11] Work on this paper was supported by a Leverhulme Trust Major Research Fellowship. It has also benefited from comments by John Finnis, Matthew Kramer, William Lucy, Neil MacCormick, Onora O'Neill, and Jeremy Waldron.

14

The Analysis of Rights

Leif Wenar

'Maine's reference to Bentham not as discovering or revealing the meaning of the expression "a right", but as *giving* a clear meaning to it is accurate; and raises a methodological issue of some importance.' (Hart 1982, 162–3)

'Faithfulness to the shape of common concepts is itself an act of normative significance.' (Raz 1986, 64)

1 Introduction

In some respects investigations into the nature of rights resemble investigations in the physical sciences. An investigation into the nature of a particular right, such as the right to remain silent or the right to pass a criminal sentence, will seek to describe the right in terms of its logical structure and its normative functions. This is analogous to an investigation of a particular chemical compound, which will attempt to describe the compound in terms of its physical structure and its standard causal properties.

Within the philosophy of science it is controversial whether scientists' generalizations should be interpreted as causal or nomic.[1] However all sides of this dispute agree that one scientific theory will be more powerful than another if it accounts for more phenomena, and if it accounts for the same phenomena using fewer basic concepts and relations. *Comprehensiveness* and *simplicity* are two primary dimensions along which scientific explanations should be measured. There is also broad consensus on which scientific theories have more explanatory power, at least for inter-paradigmatic comparisons. To take an obvious example, there is near-universal agreement that the explanatory framework of modern chemistry is superior to the medieval earth-air-fire-water-aether framework that it replaced. Although the modern periodic table of elements is not as simple as the medieval diagram of elements, the comprehensiveness of the modern theory makes it more powerful overall.

[1] Compare Hempel 1965, Salmon 1984, Kitcher 1989.

A theory of the nature of rights will also aim for greater explanatory power, where two primary measures of explanatory power are again comprehensiveness and simplicity. All else equal, a theory of rights will be more powerful when it accounts for more rights, and when it uses fewer basic concepts and relations. As with scientific theories no one believes that there is an exact schedule for trading comprehensiveness against simplicity. But there is no reason to think that there will be more dissensus when it comes to cases than there is in the comparison of scientific theories.

The 'phenomena' that a theory of rights ultimately aims to explain is *what rights there are and what rights there could be*. However, what lies within the extension of that concept is more controversial than what lies within the extension of the analogous concepts in many physical sciences (eg, 'what chemical compounds there are and could be'). This is because what moral rights there are and could be turns on which moral theory is correct, and what legal rights there are and could be turns on what is the correct theory of law. Which moral theory is correct, and which jurisprudential theory is correct, are matters of some dispute.

The theorist of the nature of rights therefore cannot simply set a list of the phenomena to be explained—the rights that there are and could be—without making hotly contentious assumptions outside of his domain of inquiry. Indeed there is doubled trouble here, as it will be controversial not only which moral or jurisprudential theory is correct, but also which rights are entailed by any such theory within a given set of circumstances.

In response to these difficulties rights theorists have adopted an indirect approach to their subject matter. They have tested the explanatory power of their theories not against what rights there are and could be, but against what rights *people say that* there are and could be. Theorists of rights have, in the main, taken an ordinary understanding of rights to set the phenomena to be explained. For example, a rights theorist will reject any theory that ascribes rights to tomato plants, or to ant colonies, because such a theory is incompatible with an ordinary understanding of rights. The same reason will be given for rejecting any theory that denies that it is coherent to ascribe rights to women. This indirect approach is attractive because what informed, thoughtful people believe about rights is much less contentious than what rights there actually are. Thoughtful people who are not theorists do have some familiar differences concerning what rights there are and can be—but moral and legal theorists share all of those differences and have many more disagreements as well.

The 'data' of ordinary understanding are therefore significantly less contentious than the 'data' of what rights there really are, and focusing on ordinary understanding allows debates over the nature of rights to refer to a common set of facts to be explained. By contrast if some theorist alleged that his theory of the nature of rights was superior because it fit with his preferred substantive theory of rights, he would immediately be challenged to show that his preferred substantive theory was correct. A debate on the terrain of 'conformity with some preferred moral or jurisprudential theory' would quickly become merely a proxy for a debate over which moral or jurisprudential theory is best.

For the most part, therefore, theorists have attempted to provide a conceptual analysis of the concept of a right as this concept is ordinarily understood. In the language of the Hart quotation that begins this article, theorists have been more concerned with 'discovering or revealing the meaning of the expression "a right"'; and less concerned with '*giving*' the concept a meaning. Nevertheless, as we will see in the final section of this article, rights theorists have also surreptitiously allowed a desire to bolster substantive theories to pull them toward revisionary definitions of the concept. Indeed rights theorists have surreptitiously yielded to this desire in a way that has contributed to making the debate over the nature of rights permanently intractable up to now.

2 The Will Theory and the Interest Theory

Of the two features of rights that a theory of the nature of rights is meant to explain—logical structure and normative function—there is much more consensus on the former than the latter. The Hohfeldian framework is by far the most widely accepted analysis of the logical structure of rights, and it is used by the majority of contemporary rights theorists. Regarding the functions of rights however there is a longstanding disagreement. Proponents of the will theory and the interest theory have struggled for decades if not centuries over which theory provides the more powerful explanation of what rights do for right-holders.[2] It is this debate over the functions of rights that is our main study here.

The question of the function of rights concerns what rights do for those who hold them. The will theory of rights asserts that the function of all rights is to give the right-holder choices. According to Hart's will theory, for instance, the function of a land owner's legal right is to give him the legally recognized power to waive or not to waive the duties that others have not to enter his land. As Hart describes the core idea of the will theory in the context of legal rights, 'One who has a right has a choice respected by the law' (Hart 1982, 171, 183–5, 188–9).[3]

The will theorist's view of the function of rights limits what he recognizes as a right: where there is no normatively respected choice, there can be no right. The will theorist's view also restricts the class of potential right-holders. Only those beings that have certain capacities—the capacities to exercise choice in controlling their own actions and the duties of others—are potential will theory right-holders.

---

[2] For some of this history, see Tuck 1997, Brett 1997. See also Simmonds's reflections on the history of the jurisprudence of rights (Kramer, Simmonds, and Steiner, 1998, 113–232).

[3] Besides Hart, influential advocates of a choice-based approach to rights include Savigny, Kelsen, Wellman, and Steiner.

The interest theory, by contrast, maintains that the function of all rights is to further their holders' interests. The most prominent interest theory analysis is Raz's: ' "X has a right" if and only if X can have rights, and, other things being equal, an aspect of X's well-being (his interest) is a sufficient reason for holding some other person(s) to be under a duty.' (Raz 1986, 166) Here rights do not give choices; rather rights are claims on the actions of others that are justified by the interests of the right-holder.

The advocates of each theory are deeply entrenched in their positions. At times the debate appears to be one—like the debate over Newcomb's problem—where each side can scarcely imagine that the other side has a reasonable view.[4] Thus Hart in laying out the will theory claims that 'it is hard to think of rights except as capable of *exercise*' (Hart 1982, 184) while Williams in opposition insists that 'no one ever has a right to do something; he only has a right that someone else shall do (or refrain from doing) something. In other words, every right in the strict sense relates to the conduct of another.' (Williams 1956, 1145)

These positions are entrenched despite the widely acknowledged fact that each theory is too narrow when judged against an ordinary understanding of rights. Each theory accounts for an insufficiently comprehensive range of rights, leaving large areas of commonly accepted rights unexplained. The ways in which each theory is too narrow are by now well understood. Indeed the debate between the two theories has generated a standard account of the shortcomings of each approach. Here I will just summarize this standard account of these shortcomings so as to set up a discussion of the strategies that the two groups of theorists have taken in response to the problem of narrowness.[5]

The narrowness of the will theory is apparent, first, in the types of actions that the theory can recognize as rights violations. Many important legal rights do correspond to Hart's legally-respected choices. But many do not. For example, you have no legal discretion to alter your entitlement against being enslaved, or your entitlement against being tortured to death. The will theory therefore does not recognize that you have a legal right against being enslaved, or against being tortured to death. Yet most would regard these unwaivable claims as rights, indeed as among the more important rights that individuals have.[6] Indeed the will theory does not recognize that the criminal law confers any rights on citizens, since the power to enforce the law rests not with citizens but with state officials (Kramer, Simmonds, and Steiner 1998, 230, Wellman 1985, 85). Yet most citizens would

---

[4] 'I have put this problem to a large number of people ... To almost everyone it is perfectly clear and obvious what should be done. The difficulty is that these people seem to divide almost evenly on the problem, with large numbers thinking that the opposing half is just being silly.' (Nozick 1969, 117)

[5] This summary draws from Wenar 2005.

[6] Despite not being able to recognize a person's claim against being tortured as a right, the will theory does recognize many negligible claims (such as your waivable claim not to be patted on the head) as rights (MacCormick 1977, 197).

find it surprising to hear that the criminal law did not ascribe to them a right against being murdered or raped.

The limitations of the will theory are also evident in its inability to account for the rights of certain kinds of right-holders: for example, for the rights of incompetent (eg, comatose) adults, and of children (MacCormick 1982, 154–66). The will theory can acknowledge rights only in those beings competent to exercise choices—which incompetent adults and children are not. Incompetent adults and children therefore are not possibly right-holders on this view. This result diverges significantly from an ordinary understanding of rights. Few thoughtful laymen would insist that it is a conceptual impossibility, for example, for the comatose to have rights against bodily mutilation.

Since the interest theory turns on interests instead of choices, it can recognize unwaivable rights against enslavement and torture. The interest theory can also accept children and incompetent adults as right-holders, since children and incompetent adults have interests that rights can protect.

Yet the interest theory is also inadequate to an ordinary understanding of rights. Staying with Raz's version of the interest theory, there are many rights for which the interests of the putative right-holder are not sufficient to hold other person(s) to be under a duty. For example, Raz himself allows that the interest of a journalist in protecting his sources is not itself sufficient reason to hold others to be under the corresponding duty (Raz 1986, 179, 247–8). It is rather the interests of the general public in an active and independent media that grounds the journalist's right to protect his sources. Yet as Kamm observes, 'If the satisfaction of the interests of others is the reason why the journalist gets a right to have his interest protected, his interest is *not sufficient* to give rise to the duty of non-interference with his speech' (Kamm 2002, 485). Nor does this difficulty only affect the rights of office-holders like journalists, as Raz admits that weighty rights such as the rights of free expression and freedom of contract are not justified solely by the interests of the individual citizens who hold them (Raz 1996a, 30–43, 131).

3 Three Strategies for Fitting Theory and Data

Both the will and the interest theories are, in their standard forms, too narrow. Each theory accounts for some but not all of the rights that any ordinary understanding of rights will accept.

Will and interest theorists have wrestled with this mismatch between the scope of their theories and the range of the phenomena for a long time. They have adopted three strategies in response to the problem of narrowness. The first strategy is to claim that their theories are only meant to describe a more limited range of the phenomena than was originally supposed. The second strategy is to attempt to expand the scope of their theories in order to explain more of the phenomena. The third strategy is to replace the set of phenomena to be explained with a different set. The three strategies could be summarized as narrowing the data, broadening the theory, and replacing the data-set.

We next examine some examples of each of the three types of strategies taken by the will and the interest theories in response to the problem of narrowness. While the three strategies are perfectly reasonable responses to the problem, the results of pursuing each of the strategies have been unsatisfactory. The reason for this repeated failure, as it turns out, is not contingent. As will be shown in the discussion afterwards, the two theories share a premise which prevents them from yielding an adequate understanding of rights, regardless of how the theories are recast.

3.1 Narrowing the Range of Phenomena to be Explained

The first response of rights theorists to the problem of narrowness has been to cut the domain of rights to be explained to fit the ambit of the explanatory theory. Thus Hart, when faced with counterexamples to the will theory involving constitutional immunities, confesses that his theory is satisfactory 'only at the level of the lawyer concerned with the working of the "ordinary" law', and is not adequate to handle individual rights at the level of constitutional law. Still less, Hart says, is his theory equipped to explain rights as they are understood by individualistic critics of the law and by social theorists (Hart 1982, 185–6, 192–3).

Hart attempts to make a virtue of this limitation by asserting that his will theory is only intended to explain rights within the 'ordinary' law. Yet even were we to grant Hart that his theory accounts for this limited domain, this first strategy makes a major concession. As with scientific theories, a more comprehensive account of the subject matter is always preferable to a less comprehensive account. This is particularly clear with rights. A theory that is adequate only to rights within one part of the law will at best satisfy certain specialists, and will not provide an analysis that is useful for understanding rights as a central concept in morality, in politics, and in the law viewed more broadly.

Interest theorists face the analogous difficulty that people's rights frequently outrun their interests. To take one type of example, because of ignorance or carelessness people often enter into promissory relations that vest in them rights to receive goods or services that they have no interest in receiving. Imagine, for instance, a budding auto enthusiast who finds in a newspaper what he thinks is a fine deal on a second-hand engine, and pays to have this engine delivered to his house the following week. As it turns out, this enthusiast has erred in buying this engine: as he does not yet realize, it does not fit his (or indeed any extant) car. The enthusiast has no interest whatsoever in having this useless and hard-to-dispose engine winched onto his driveway. As he will discover when he returns home from work and tries to install the engine, the delivery has made him significantly worse off. Yet as the lorry rumbles toward his house with the bulky engine in the back, there is no doubt that the lorry drivers are fulfilling the enthusiast's claim-right. The example shows that a person's well-being does not go up merely in virtue of promises to him being kept. A promisee can be in every way better off if the deal he has foolishly entered into goes unconsummated, and so his right remains unfulfilled.

In response to counterexamples where rights outrun interests, several interest theorists have framed their theories around weak generalizations, which only attempt to explain some but not all rights. MacCormick, for example, phrases his central thesis in terms of 'normal circumstances': 'To ascribe to all members of a class C a right to treatment T is to presuppose that T is, *in all normal circumstances*, a good for every member of C' (MacCormick 1982, 160, emphasis added). Similarly, Kramer presents his theory in terms of what is '*generally* beneficial for any *typical* human being or collectivity or non-human creature' (Kramer and Steiner 2007, 290, emphasis added). The qualifications 'normal circumstances', 'generally', and 'typical' limit the domain of rights that these theories will attempt to explain to a domain with certain rights (specifically, the counterexamples) removed.[7]

Weak generalizations are unsatisfying because of their lack of comprehensiveness. A linguist studying English will not rest content with the rule that *in all normal circumstances, 'i' comes before 'e'*. Nor will a toxicologist be satisfied with the thesis that *mushrooms are generally harmless when eaten*. It is unlikely that the best theory of rights takes the form: 'All rights have feature F (except for those that lack feature F)'.[8] A weak generalization can be better than another generalization that is weaker still, or better than no generalization at all. Yet a theory based on a weak generalization will always be discarded once a theory with greater explanatory scope is found.

3.2 Expanding the Scope of the Theory

The second strategy of rights theorists for overcoming the problem of narrowness has been to attempt to modify their theories so as to capture more rights. Both will and interest theorists have taken this path.

For example, Steiner has found new rights within the scope of the will theory in response to the charge that the will theory fails to recognize the rights of the 'powerless' (Kramer, Simmonds, and Steiner 1998, 258–62). Steiner's will theory cannot recognize the rights of children, comatose adults, and animals, because these beings lack the power to waive or enforce the duties of others. Nor can the will theory recognize the rights of criminal defendants, since such defendants do not have the power to waive others' duties against assaulting them, killing them,

---

[7] See also Raz 1986, 173–6.

[8] It is of course possible to try to recapture universal application by specifying some property specially rigged for the purpose, for example 'all rights share the property of belonging to a set whose members generally have feature F'. But the weak spot in the generalization will always remain.

and so on. Yet Steiner argues that his will theory *can* acknowledge rights that protect these unempowered beings—so long as those rights are seen to reside in beings besides those who have traditionally been taken to be the right-holder.

On Steiner's interpretation of the will theory the right-holder in these cases will not be the citizens, children, or animals who are protected by certain duties. Rather, the right-holders will be the 'power-possessors' who have the authority to waive or enforce those duties. So, for example, Steiner says that the right that a citizen not be assaulted is held not by that citizen, but by the magistrate who can decide whether to charge an assailant of that citizen. The right that the citizen not be assaulted is the magistrate's right. Similarly, the right that a particular child not be abused is vested not in that child, but in the judge who will decide whether to punish a person convicted of child abuse. It is the judge, not the child, who has the right that the child not be abused.

In response to the unnatural feeling of this location of rights in the case of children, the comatose, and animals, Steiner writes:

What scintilla of a practical or analytical difference can it make if we construe the rights correlative to those protection duties as one held by *those power-possessors* rather than one held by unempowerable creatures? As far as I can see, none. And if those power-possessors are indeed the holders of those rights, then, as we saw in the previous discussion of criminal law, the rights they hold are none other than will theory rights. (Kramer, Simmonds, and Steiner 1998, 261)

The difficulty that Steiner faces here is that he is both appealing to an ordinary understanding of rights to support his interpretation of the will theory, and also claiming that it makes no difference that this interpretation continues to conflict with such an ordinary understanding. Steiner's will theory acknowledges a greater number of rights than do other versions of the will theory, since on his interpretation it can be said that there are rights that protect citizens, children, and so on. This fits Steiner's will theory more closely to an ordinary understanding of rights. Yet Steiner's revised theory locates these extra rights in what are, on any common appreciation of rights, entirely the wrong places. Within Steiner's theory citizens still have no rights against criminal assault, children have no rights against abuse, and so on. So here there are more rights, which is welcome from an ordinary perspective; yet these rights are said to be vested in the wrong individuals, which is not. Steiner can legitimately commend his interpretation of the will theory for the ways in which it better captures an ordinary understanding of rights, but he can hardly then maintain that the ways in which his interpretation still conflicts with an ordinary understanding make no difference.

Kramer similarly considers expanding his interest theory to accommodate rights that seem beyond its reach.[9] Kramer suggests that within a 'capacious'

---

[9] I hesitate to address Kramer's interest theory, as Kramer has not yet had the chance to set out his evolving theory fully. This is evident in Kramer's last published writing on his interest theory (Kramer and Steiner 2007). For example, Kramer makes philosophically significant modifications

version of his interest theory (which he discusses but does not endorse) the powers and privileges belonging to various offices are properly classified as rights because those powers and privileges usually promote certain interests of the office-holders. This suggestion does not have much immediate appeal. For example, consider the fact that a judge's power to sentence criminals is properly classified as a right. It would sound odd to say that this fact is explained by the fact that the possession of this power is generally beneficial for the judge. Similarly with the fact that a policeman's liberty to detain a suspect is properly classified as a right. One might not think that this fact is explained by the fact that the possession of such a liberty is generally beneficial for the policeman.[10]

Yet that is what the 'expansive' version of Kramer's interest theory holds.[11] Within this expansive theory, if a norm (here a role) bestows a normative ability (a Hohfeldian power or privilege) on a person, then the fact that that normative ability is properly classified as a right is explained by the fact that their having

to his theory without having space to explain fully why he has done so or what the further implications might be, such as when he declares that a large class of interests (which he labels 'vicarious') are irrelevant to what rights there are (Kramer and Steiner 2007, 302–4). More broadly, Kramer has yet to set out a usable method for applying his theory's distinctive test for locating claim-right holders. Kramer's test says that X holds a claim-right if X's detriment is sufficient to establish a breach of a duty, yet Kramer has not yet said how one can tell whether X's detriment is in fact sufficient to establish a breach of a duty (without begging the question by surreptitiously relying on one's beliefs about whether X holds a claim-right). A full treatment of Kramer's interest theory must wait until Kramer has had the opportunity to present a complete statement of his revised theory, by explaining what he believes are the necessary and sufficient conditions for the ascription of a right, and by offering some systematic account of how one can tell whether these conditions have been met.

[10] Unlike Raz's interest theory, on the expansive version of Kramer's interest theory the interests of a right-holder are not necessarily what justifies the establishment of a right: they are not necessarily what justifies the imposition of duties or the creation of norms or roles. This can be seen from Kramer's test for right-holding (on the expansive interpretation of his view): 'If a norm or decision bestows a Hohfeldian entitlement on Q, and if the possession of that entitlement would usually be beneficial for someone in Q's situation, then Q is a right-holder under the norm or decision.' (Kramer and Steiner 2007, 290) Here the interest (what 'would usually be beneficial for someone in Q's situation') does not necessarily have any justificatory relation whatsoever to the norm. Rather the interest (partly) explains the fact that Q has a right by usually being present when the norm that bestows the relevant Hohfeldian entitlement is present: that is, by satisfying the second conjunct in the antecedent when the first conjunct is also satisfied. This is the sense in which, for example, the fact that a policeman's liberty to detain a suspect is properly classified as a right is explained by the fact that the possession of such a liberty is generally beneficial for the policeman.

[11] Kramer sets out the 'expansive' version of his interest theory at some length, and says it may be worth developing further, but in the end he does not accept it (Kramer and Steiner 2007, 290–5). This expansive version of the interest theory would need further explication in any case. For example, in setting out this theory Kramer appeals to a distinction between 'intrinsic' and 'extrinsic' effects of legal norms without defining these terms or saying how one might distinguish one from the other (293). Kramer also appeals to the purpose of legal norms to make sense of these cases (293), where a few pages earlier he had said that purposes had no 'determinative bearing' and were 'quite immaterial' in his theory (289, 290). I discuss the expansive version of Kramer's interest theory here because it is a serious attempt to broaden an interest theory so as to encompass the rights of offices and positions. Without some modification like this one, there seems little hope that Kramer's interest theory will be able to capture these rights.

this ability will normally make them better off. Within this theory the fact that a judge's power to sentence criminals is properly classified as a right is explained by the fact that having this power allows a judge 'to carry out his judicial responsibilities with smoothness and efficiency'. Within this theory the fact that a police patrolman's liberty to detain a suspect is properly classified as a right is explained by the fact that his having this liberty enables the patrolman to 'fulfill his duty to detain [the suspect], without exposing himself to penalties for so doing' (Kramer and Steiner 2007, 290, 291). Judges and policemen are made better off, the theory holds, by having the normative abilities to carry out their responsibilities. So these normative abilities further the interests of these role-bearers, and are therefore rights.

Such appeals to smooth and punishment-free discharge of responsibilities cannot help an interest theory to explain why the powers and privileges of offices are rights. For this line of reasoning simultaneously relies upon and misunderstands the norms that are roles. It is not as though there is a coherent role described as 'judge who has the responsibility to sentence but no power to sentence'—and then we make a separate determination that the life of someone filling that role would go better if they gained the power to sentence. The original description makes no sense: a role that assigns a responsibility to φ but with no normative ability to φ is not a role that fits into any recognizable human practice.[12] Similarly with the patrolman. There is no intelligible job that is 'policeman who has the duty not to detain suspects whenever he has the duty to detain suspects'. Such a job could be imagined only at the edges of a fantasy, if there; speculation about the interests of such a job-holder is moot. In reality, offices such as 'judge' and 'policeman' always pair the responsibilities of office with the normative abilities appropriate for carrying out these responsibilities. 'Rights of office' are not optional add-ons that help a person do a job; rather, rights of office are an integral part of every job's description.[13]

---

[12] Kramer might rather claim that a judge's responsibility is not *to sentence* but rather *to see that sentences are passed*. Yet imagining someone who has a responsibility to see that sentences are passed, but who has no power of his own to sentence, would not fit Kramer's words: such a person would not have 'judicial responsibilities' in this respect. Such a person would rather be the holder of some sort of administrative office. The powers of that administrative office (to see that sentences are passed) would presumably include powers to appoint, or perhaps simply to discipline, the judges who have the power to pass sentences. Whether it would be in the interest of someone holding such an administrative office for his office to be redefined so that he himself gains the power to sentence depends entirely on how we imagine his office to be currently defined (eg, how many judges he is responsible for overseeing, whether he is expected to have detailed understanding of sentencing procedures, what oversight he himself faces for discharging his responsibilities, etc). Within any well-designed system of roles there will be no presumption that overseeing officers have any such interest in their roles being redefined. (This reasoning applies also to the cases of the traffic warden and the army captain (Kramer and Steiner 2007, 290).)

[13] It might be noted here that this discussion is not concerned with whether it is in any individual's interests to hold a particular office in the first place. It may be beneficial for an individual to occupy some office, or it may be entirely a burden. It may or may not be in Jane's (or anyone's) interest to be a judge, but in either case Jane will have the rights of a judge if she is a judge. It might also

The expansive version of Kramer's interest theory cannot account for the fact that role-bearers' powers and liberties to do what they have duties to do are rights. Nor can it account for the fact that their discretionary liberties are rights. For example, a parent has the liberty either to punish or not to punish her child. Kramer attempts to explain why this first liberty (the liberty to punish) is a right as follows. Imagine a world in which a parent has no liberty to punish her child (ie, she has a duty not to punish), but in which she retains the liberty not to punish her child. In such a world, Kramer says, the parent would be better off if she gained the liberty to punish her child because then she would no longer be liable to penalties whenever she did punish (Kramer and Steiner 2007, 291–2).[14]

In Kramer's imagined world parents are prohibited from punishing their children. In this world parents also have no duty to punish their children. Why in this world would a parent be better off if she gained a liberty to punish her child? She will be better off gaining a liberty to punish her child only if she has some reason to punish her child. Yet there is no reason that Kramer can depend upon here.

Kramer appears to suggest that in his imagined world a parent would have a *role-based* reason to punish her child, and so would be better off with the liberty to punish. He says that with this liberty she would 'not have to worry about being penalized for taking steps which she reasonably deems necessary for the effective performance of her role as a parent' (Kramer and Steiner 2007, 292). Yet within this imagined world parents are prohibited from punishing their children, so their role is quite different than in our world. In this imagined world, the role of parent could at best be described as 'raising one's children well, so far as one can do so without punishing them'. Punishing one's child could not be a step reasonably deemed necessary for the effective performance of *that* role. In the imagined world, discipline is no part of a parent's job description. So Kramer has no role-based reason available to explain an interest in gaining the liberty to punish.

Kramer might instead venture that a parent in his imagined world would have some *non-role-based* reason to discipline her child.[15] Yet this depends entirely on how we imagine this world to be. For example, in this imagined world where parents have no duty to discipline their children and indeed are prohibited from doing so, the responsibility for disciplining children might well be (indeed likely

---

be mentioned that this discussion remains neutral concerning what justifies the creation of offices that are defined by specific duties and rights.

[14] Kramer notes that his reasoning is the same across two variants of this example. The discussion here concerns the variant in which the parent has a Hohfeldian privilege not to punish the child, and Kramer considers why the parent's privilege to punish is a right. The analysis of the other variant, where the parent has a duty to punish the child, is captured by the police patrolman example above.

[15] As mentioned in n 9 above, Kramer does not allow appeals to 'vicarious' interests within his theory (ie, interests that 'reside wholly in the furtherance of somebody else's interests' (Kramer and Steiner 2007, 303)). So whatever reason to discipline Kramer might posit here, it cannot be the reason that a parent has to discipline her child for the child's own good.

would be) assigned to someone else. Were we to posit that parents have an interest in punishing their children even when someone else is effectively doing so, we would seem to be making parents out to be simply cruel. Or again: parents in Kramer's imagined world might be just as glad, all things considered, to be legally prohibited from punishing their children. They might think that gaining the liberty to punish would result in their having endless headaches (familiar from our world) that they would just as soon avoid.[16]

An interest-theoretical approach such as this one cannot be the path toward understanding the rights of offices and positions. Rights of office cannot be explained by the interests of the individuals who occupy the office as currently defined. An interest theory needs to be expanded so as to capture these rights, but the interest framework does not provide the resources for the theory to do so.

3.3 Redefining the Phenomena to be Explained

The third strategy of will and interest theorists has been to assert that their theories are intended to account only for 'rights' in some technical sense of that term instead of in an ordinary sense. This third strategy resembles the first strategy in altering the domain over which the theory is meant to apply. Yet this strategy, unlike the first, applauds the fit between the theory and some *artificially constructed* concept that is given the name 'rights'. Interest theorists who take this path stipulate that their theories are not meant to account for rights as commonly understood, but only for 'rights' defined as Hohfeldian claim-rights. Will theorists who take this tack say that their theory is only intended to explain 'rights' defined as Hohfeldian claims accompanied by Hohfeldian powers of waiver or enforcement.

Thus when these theorists present their 'theories of rights', the term 'rights' is intended to refer to a *technical explanandum* (such as 'claims' or 'claims-with-powers'). 'Rights' no longer refers to the ordinary explanandum, which is the full catalogue of rights as commonly understood. As we will see, these theorists do not in the end repudiate 'fit with an ordinary understanding' as a criterion of success. Yet at least initially they take the phenomena to be explained as 'rights' in some specially defined sense.

---

[16] This example here resembles the case of John (Kramer and Steiner 2007, 292–3). Kramer addresses this case by invoking his weak generalization about what is generally in people's interests, and then asserting that it will be 'extremely rare' for people to be better off for facing a legal prohibition that disinclines them from doing something risky or difficult that they would otherwise do. But as the parent example shows, Kramer must face this kind of question all the time. Moreover, reflection on paternalistic legislation gives further reason to doubt Kramer's assertion. Paternalistic legislation is just an attempt to make people better off by instituting a legal prohibition that disinclines them from doing something risky or difficult that they would otherwise do. For Kramer to establish that it is extremely rare for a legal prohibition to further the interests of those restricted by it, he would need to show that it is extremely rare for paternalistic legislation to achieve its aims.

This substitution of the reference of 'rights' means that theorists using this third strategy speak a different dialect than that used by ordinary speakers such as judges, lawyers, and laymen. Thus when Wellman is confronted with the result that his will theory cannot recognize the rights of infants, he says:

> Surely it is confusing for me to insist that infants could not have legal rights as I conceive of a right but to admit that infants can and do have rights as judges and lawyers conceive of rights. Still, this confusion can be minimized, although probably not completely avoided, by distinguishing carefully between two spheres of discourse, the language of the law and the language of the philosophy of law. (Wellman 1995, 135)

Wellman here distinguishes the ordinary language of the law from the language in which his technical explanandum occurs: the 'language of the philosophy of law'. Kramer makes the same kind of distinction to justify a move to his own preferred technical explanandum. Kramer wishes to work within a sphere of discourse in which the referent of 'rights' is claim-rights. Like Wellman, Kramer faces the difficulty that ordinary discourse does not line up with his technical definition. In Kramer's case, one conflict is that claim-rights concern only the actions of others, while ordinary usage accepts many rights that give the rightholder themselves rights to act (eg, to speak, worship, promise). Faced with obvious cases where ordinary usage acknowledges rights to act, Kramer responds by disparaging ordinary language: 'Our ordinary ways of speaking about rights as entitlements to do various things are loose' (Kramer, Simmonds, and Steiner 1998, 13–14).

In Wellman's 'language of the philosophy of law', the term 'rights' refers to the technical concept 'claims-with-powers'. In Kramer's 'strict sense', the term 'rights' refers to the technical concept 'claims'. The question for the theorists of rights who deploy a technical concept is whether they can offer a rationale for moving the analysis away from ordinary language and toward their favoured technical explanandum in particular. One obviously inadequate justification would be to point out that redefining the explanandum makes the phenomena to be explained fit better with their favoured explanans. A will theorist, for instance, should not simply say that he prefers his technical definition of the term 'rights' because the will theory is so good at explaining 'rights' so defined. Yet putting such special pleading to the side, how else could a move to some particular technical explanandum be motivated?

Rights theorists who work within a technical discourse characteristically allege that this move is necessary because the ordinary discourse of rights is hopelessly vague, or because ordinary language speakers are prone to fall into contradictions when discussing rights (eg, Kramer and Steiner 2007, 295). As Kramer puts it in the quote above, ordinary ways of speaking about rights are 'loose'. No theory, these theorists say, can hope to explain a set of assertions if the assertions have extremely indeterminate or contradictory content. So, these theorists allege, they must aim their theories at an artificially-defined domain of 'rights' instead.

Interest theorists are particularly likely to cite Hohfeld in motivating their move to a technical discourse of rights, as Hohfeld was the originator of the thesis that in the 'strictest sense', all rights are claims (Hohfeld 1919, 36).[17] Will theorists take a differently-defined technical concept to be the object of their explanatory theory, which is more congenial to their thesis that rights endow their bearers with discretion over the duties of others.

Yet how then to decide *which* subset of the Hohfeldian incidents is the one that theories of rights should take as their focus? In fact, and surprisingly, the clearest and most repeated justification offered by the technical rights theorists for using their own favoured technical definition of 'rights' is that their favoured definition fits better with ordinary language (eg, Kramer and Steiner 2007, 296–7). Having spurned ordinary understanding in order to motivate the move to a technical concept, these theorists then emphasize the overlap between their favoured technical definition and an ordinary understanding in order to validate that definition. Indeed the debate between the technical will and interest theories has not infrequently turned into a debate over whether the area of overlap with common usage is greater using one technical definition of 'rights' rather than the other.

This appeal to ordinary language leaves the technical rights theorists in a precarious position. On the one hand, they attempt to cast enough aspersions on ordinary 'rights-talk' that there will appear to be no option but to shift from an ordinary to a technical explanandum. On the other hand each camp of technical theorists appeals to the fit between their favoured technical explanandum and ordinary understanding as the reason to judge their favoured explanandum superior. Interest theorists argue that the technical characterization of rights as claims is 'more acceptable to ordinary understanding', while will theorists argue that this honour is more fittingly given to their technical characterization of rights as claims-with-powers (Kramer, Simmonds, and Steiner 1998, 74).

The title character in Oliver Sacks's *The Man Who Mistook His Wife for a Hat* suffered from a certain kind of aphasia which led him to attempt to embrace his wife with his right arm at the same time as he attempted to push her away with his

---

[17] Hohfeld's curious, unargued stipulation that 'in the strictest sense' all rights are claims disables anyone who accepts it from giving a straightforward analysis of many commonly-asserted rights. For example, any analysis of legal rights should be able to explain a judge's legal right to sentence a convicted criminal. Some who adhere to Hohfeld's stipulation set aside the obvious analysis that this right consists in the judge's Hohfeldian power to impose duties on the convict, and say rather that the right consists in the claims protecting the judge from the interference of others when he exercises such a power (see for example Raz, who separates the power to promise from the 'right' against interference with one's promising (Raz 1986, 173–6)). However, construing such rights as claims against interference is strained. One can see this by imagining situations in which interference is literally impossible (eg, where judges pass sentences from impregnable strongholds, communicate telepathically, etc). Here a claim-right against interference makes no sense, but judges would still have a right to sentence. Similarly, anyone who accepts Hohfeld's stipulation will have difficulties explaining many (power- and privilege-) rights that religious believers have for centuries attributed to God (God has a right to make promises, to command his creations, to punish sinners, etc). These rights cannot possibly be construed as God's rights against interference, for such interference is literally unimaginable.

left (Sacks 1985, 8–22). The technical rights theorists have something of the same disposition toward the ordinary understanding of rights. These will and interest theorists are aware that their theories of the functions of rights cannot account for a large number of rights that are commonly accepted. They therefore insist that ordinary rights-talk is vague and inconsistent in order to attempt to shift attention toward their favoured technical recharacterizations of the term 'rights'. Yet when attention is so shifted, they once again attempt to embrace an ordinary understanding of rights as the guarantor of their theory's superiority. This position holds the ordinary understanding of rights to be so irremediably vague and inconsistent as to be useless as the object of theoretical explanation, but not so corrupt as to be useless in mediating between artificially constructed definitions of 'rights'.

This is an awkward posture to maintain, and in fact there is no need to assume it. The technical theorists' stated rationale for moving to a technical explanandum was to overcome the vague and contradictory nature of ordinary assertions about rights. However, vagueness and contradictoriness in ordinary language can be no reason whatsoever to switch to an artificial concept of rights.

First, technical rights theorists have not in fact established that ordinary discourse is frequently vague and contradictory, instead of being a discourse that systematically assigns different meanings to the same word in different contexts. Such systematic variation in meaning is familiar in common speech. For example there is nothing vague or contradictory in the statement that 'in a free market one is free to lend money interest-free'. 'Free' in this statement takes three different but determinate meanings, the meaning of each occurrence being determined by the context. Similarly in ordinary discourse one often hears the word 'right' used to refer variously to privilege-rights, claim-rights, power-rights, and immunity-rights, with the intended referent made clear by the context. Interpretations of ordinary speech that find vagueness or inconsistency instead of precise and determinate variation in usage are often just poor interpretations of ordinary speech.

Second, any vagueness and inconsistency within ordinary discourse about rights, insofar as it exists, does not justify a radical shift to a technical explanandum. For there is a straightforward solution to any problems with vagueness and contradiction, which is for rights theorists to use the Hohfeldian framework to discuss rights (as indeed most already do).

Using the Hohfeldian framework of privileges, claims, powers, and immunities gives maximum specificity to statements about rights, while simultaneously insuring against contradictions. So long as rights theorists use the Hohfeldian language correctly, they cannot commit errors of vagueness or inconsistency. Therefore once theorists are using this analytical framework, there is no further need for them artificially to designate some subset of the Hohfeldian incidents as the referent of the term 'rights'. Once theorists have agreed to use the Hohfeldian terminology, they would need an *extra* argument to motivate a redefinition of 'rights' either as 'claims', or as 'claims-with-powers', or indeed as

anything else. Any attempt by technical rights theorists to draw on the authority of (what these theorists allege is vague and contradictory) ordinary language
at this point cannot provide that required extra argument, and can only cause
confusion. Rights theorists utilizing the Hohfeldian framework make precise
and consistent statements about rights as they are commonly understood, so
there is no further rationale for these theorists to replace the object of analysis
with any technical concept.

It might nevertheless be thought that there exists an extra argument for will
and interest theorists to move to a technical explanandum, beyond the limp
argument just discussed of avoiding vagueness and contradiction in ordinary
language. It might be thought that a move to a technical explanandum could be
justified on the ground that a theory directed toward it would be not only more
comprehensive and simpler but also more *fruitful*. As Carnap says in the context
of scientific explananda, 'a scientific concept is the more fruitful the more it can
be brought into connection with other concepts on the basis of observed facts; in
other words, the more it can be used for the formulation of laws' (Carnap 1950, 6).
A scientific concept is more fruitful, in other words, the better it fits into a larger
system of explanatory generalizations. Perhaps a technical concept of rights could
also be more fruitful in this way.

It is fairly common for scientists to move from an ordinary to a technical
explanandum on grounds of fruitfulness. For example consider the concept of
'fruit' itself. Within a botanist's conceptual scheme, and in contrast to ordinary
usage, a tomato is a 'fruit' but a stalk of rhubarb is not. This is because botanists have
substituted a technical concept of 'fruit' for the ordinary one; to a botanist 'fruit'
means a 'seed-filled ripened ovary of a flowering plant'. The botanist will prefer
to work with his technical concept rather than the ordinary concept, because
the technical concept fits better into the larger botanical theory of the life-cycle
of plants. The botanical concept of 'fruit' is, given these general theories, more
fruitful.

Will and interest theorists might analogously argue that their move from an
ordinary to a technical explanandum is justified by the fruitfulness of their favoured
concept within more general theories of morality or the law. Thus Wellman in
motivating the move to his favoured technical explanandum suggests that 'a more
restricted application of the language of rights may be theoretically required in
order to provide a clearer and more revealing map of the law' (Wellman 1995,
136). While he does not elaborate upon this idea, what Wellman appears to
mean is that his favoured technical characterization of rights fits better within his
preferred jurisprudential theory—that is, it fits better with his view of what the
nature of the law is.

However unlike in the scientific case, such appeals to fruitfulness must be
illegitimate and for reasons we have already seen. As noted above, there is no
agreement on which substantive theory of morality or the law is correct. Will
and interest theorists cannot say that their favoured concepts are more fruitful

given the correct theory of morality or of the law, because unlike the theory of the life-cycle of plants these theories are not 'given'. Indeed, which substantive theory of morality or law is correct is a matter of fundamental dispute. An interest theorist who is told that a will-based definition of 'rights' fits more fruitfully into some controversial moral or jurisprudential theory will not believe that he has been given a reason to accept that definition (and vice versa). Of course it is vital that philosophers continue their debates within normative theory about which substantive theory of morality and of the law is the correct theory. However, within a conceptual analysis any appeal to a contentious substantive theory will merely infect that analysis with the contentiousness of the substantive theory appealed to.

All of the efforts of technical will and interest theorists to move away from 'fit with ordinary understanding' as the criterion for a successful analysis of the concept of a right are, finally, unsuccessful. The allegedly vague and contradictory nature of ordinary usage cannot justify such a move, nor can an appeal to fruitfulness. The only usable criterion for success in analysis remains that the analysis tracks the ways that informed, thoughtful speakers of the language use the concept—which is in fact the criterion that even technical rights theorists use, despite themselves, most frequently.

4 The Standoff

Neither the will nor the interest theory provides a comprehensive enough account of an ordinary understanding of rights. Neither theory succeeds, therefore, in achieving a fundamental goal of a theory of rights. Will theorists and interest theorists have explored three strategies of response to this problem in some detail. Yet as we have seen none of these lines of response—restricting the domain of application, attempting to expand the scope of the theory, or resorting to a technical discourse—has proved adequate. In this situation neither side of the debate is able to prevail conclusively in the main arena, nor can either side garner more resources or shift the field of play to one more favourable to its view. The result, as Wayne Sumner has said, is a kind of standoff (Sumner 1987, 51). This is a battle in which, despite the deployment of great ingenuity on each side for many years, there seems no chance that either side can emerge victorious.

Lacking the means to prove that their preferred theory is superior, will and interest theorists have resorted to turning up the volume in pointing out how the rival theory conflicts with ordinary understanding. Steiner is relatively civil in casting aspersions on the interest theory, pointing only to the 'grave implausibility' of its implications and how it 'places considerable strain on our ordinary understanding of rights' (Kramer, Simmonds, and Steiner 1998, 285, 287). MacCormick's frustration with the standoff between his own interest theory and the will theory leads him to more irritated pronouncements, wondering whether we must accept a theory that 'does such violence to common understanding':

We are entitled to ask somebody who stipulates that there shall be held to be 'rights' only where there are choices, whether that stipulation does not go wholly against common understanding, and whether there is any profit derived from it. (MacCormick 1977, 197)

Kramer's exasperation in being unable to dispose decisively of the rival theory results in an all-out high-decibel assault. 'One can scarcely help being puzzled', he says, about the will theory's 'arresting' claims and 'bizarre stipulations' that are 'needlessly odd' and 'flout too many entrenched linguistic intuitions to be very powerful'. The will theory is guilty of 'gratuitous contraventions of ordinary patterns of usage', and 'yields some results that tend to strike the ordinary observer as ridiculous'. Finally, he reviews the will theory in language usually reserved by critics for the year's worst film:

Many people would shrink from a theory which defines 'right' in a way that commits the proponents of the theory to the view that children and mentally infirm people have no rights at all. Even when stripped of its ghastliness by being carefully explained, such a view tends to sound outlandish when stated.[18]

When a long-running debate reaches this level of acrimony without coming any closer to producing a conclusive result, we may conclude that the debate is no longer progressing.

5 The Shared Restrictive Premise

In one way, the debate over the functions of rights is presently in a bad state. Theorists of the two leading views have been contesting for so long, and have become so familiar with the limited resources available on each side, that even the most stalwart defenders seem resigned to battle for the minor honor of holding the less starkly counter-intuitive theory.[19] In such a debate, as Schopenhauer said about diplomatic squabbles, each side complains about the other, and both sides are correct. Even more disheartening is when outsiders to this debate import either the will or the interest theory as a premise from which to derive further conclusions about rights in their normative theorizing. One cannot blame these outsiders for reaching for a leading theory in an area outside of their specialism.

---

[18] Kramer, Simmonds, and Steiner 1998, 72, 69, 73, 75, 69. In another essay Kramer describes the conclusions of the will theory as 'bizarre', 'preposterous', and 'jarringly and gratuitously at odds with ordinary patterns of discourse' (Kramer 2001, 71).

[19] Thus Steiner: 'Theories of rights don't come cheap. Buying either of them [the will theory or the interest theory] involves paying some price in the currency of counter-intuitiveness. Nor, I should add, has this centuries-long debate about the nature of rights ever revealed any distinct third theory that even approaches their levels of generality, let alone promises to undercut their prices.' (Kramer, Simmonds, and Steiner 1998, 298)

Yet these theorists do so without realizing the genetic weaknesses that their normative arguments thereby inherit.

There is, however, cause for optimism, as a broader view of the deadlock between the will and the interest theories shows where progress must come. The structure of the debate that we have seen is as follows. Each of the two theories explains some but not all of the relevant phenomena—in this case, an ordinary understanding of rights. Each of the theories has attempted predictable responses to its own narrowness. None of these responses has been adequate, even after many variations have been advanced. It seems quite likely that the correct diagnosis of this situation is that each theory captures part of the truth about the nature of rights, but that each also has within it some unremovable premise that prevents it from capturing the whole truth.

What could this premise be? We get an initial indication of the location of the premise by recalling two of the formal desiderata that these theories are attempting to fulfil: comprehensiveness and simplicity. Both the will and the interest theories, we have found, are insufficiently comprehensive. The natural suspicion must be, therefore, that they are excessively simple. There must be some oversimplified view of rights entrenched within these theories that prevents them from framing a thesis that would account for all of the phenomena to be explained. To put this the other way around, there must be some complexity in the nature of rights that these theories cannot acknowledge while they remain will or interest theories. If there were some way to rework these theories to capture this complexity, it seems that will or interest theorists would have found it by now.

Where more specifically is the restrictive premise within these theories? In this debate there are two theories, each professing that rights have a single function. Each of these theories appears to capture part—but only part—of the truth about what rights there are. The erroneous shared assumption must be that rights have a single function. The correct assumption therefore must be that rights have more functions than one. The difficulty faced by both will and interest theorists throughout their long debate is that they have each been advancing a monistic theory to account for pluralistic phenomena. This explains why the debate between them has been unresolvable. Each side can claim a certain domain as its own, and cast counter-examples at the other side. But neither side can give up its focus on just one function of rights without giving up the basic character of its theory. Thus the theories are stuck in the stalemate.

This situation has precursors in the history of physical theory. The pre-Socratics put forward contending monistic theories of the physical world. The debate between Thales' thesis 'all is water' and Anaximenes' thesis 'all is air' resembles the modern debate between the will thesis 'all rights give choices' and the interest thesis 'all rights further well-being'. Progress in scientific theory came only with the abandonment of the shared monistic premise. What post-Socratic scientific theories gave up in simplicity, they more than made up for in comprehensiveness. Progress in rights theory can be expected to come along the same path.

The truth about the functions of rights is that there must be more functions than one. And as the scientific example shows, the complete set of functions may not be merely a concatenation of the monistic functions. The Pre-Socratic monistic theories eventually gave way to the five-element Aristotelian framework (earth, air, fire, water, aether), which was itself then replaced by the modern 117-elemented table of chemical elements. The Aristotelian framework is quite a bit less simple than its monistic precursors, just as the periodic table is considerably less simple than it. Yet in each case the later theory yields more powerful explanations. We are willing, it seems, to sacrifice a good deal of simplicity in order to find a theory that captures all of the phenomena. If we look for a general answer to how many basic theoretical posits will render a theory insufficiently simple, the answer seems to be 'one more than in the simplest theory that explains all of the data'. In physical theory five posits were better than one, and as it turns out, 117 posits are better than five.

6 The Relation between Analytical and Substantive Theories of Rights

As we have seen both the will and the interest theories are based on a monistic premise, and each fails because it is so based. So far as an ordinary understanding of rights is concerned, any adequate analysis of the functions of rights must be pluralistic. All rights perform at least one function, but there is no single function that all rights perform.

The idea of a pluralistic analysis of ordinary rights-talk is not a difficult one. Indeed for a concept such as the concept of rights, which has been deployed in so many different contexts through a long history, it might be thought that a pluralistic analysis would be the assumption by default. There is no reason, after all, that we should think that the term 'rights' is in this respect different from other major normative terms that have a variety of senses, such as 'freedom' or 'justice'.[20] The struggle to claim each of these concepts for one ideology or another has been a feature of political debate throughout the modern era, and indeed even in earlier times. These struggles have left us with concepts stretched over a complex of overlapping senses, instead of with concepts that mind the strictures of some one-factored definition. Why, then, have rights theorists repeatedly presented monistic analyses?

The answer, it seems, lies in monistic theorists' desire to advance some controversial moral or jurisprudential theory of rights. Many theorists who put forward a theory of the nature of rights have done so not as an independent exercise in conceptual analysis, but as a prelude to introducing a substantive theory of what

---

[20] For 'freedom' see Wenar (2007).

rights there really are. So, for example, Steiner presents the will theory of rights as a preparation for his left-libertarian political theory, and Raz advances the interest theory as a step in the argument for his perfectionist account of social justice. The strategy here is to use a monistic analysis of an ordinary understanding of rights to relieve some of the justificatory burden from the substantive theory that will follow. On this strategy, if Steiner is accused of putting forward a substantive account of rights within which animals have no rights, he can reply that on the best analysis of an ordinary understanding of rights it is impossible for animals to have rights. If Raz is confronted by the objection that his political theory quite controversially rests the justification of rights on the interests (instead of, say, on the intrinsic dignity) of the right-holder, he can reply that on the best analysis of an ordinary understanding of rights the function of rights is to further the interest of the right-holder.

Monistic theories have continued to attract theorists, then, because such theories are useful for supporting one or another controversial substantive theory of rights. Within moral and political theory, the will theory has been used to support Kantian normative theories (which emphasize autonomy), while the interest theory has been used to support welfarist normative theories (which emphasize individual well-being). 'Fit with the theorist's preferred substantive theory' has in this way been a suppressed desideratum in presenting theories to account for an ordinary understanding of the nature of rights. As Raz himself puts it, 'Moral and political philosophy has for long embraced the literary device (not always clearly recognized as such) of presenting substantive arguments in the guise of conceptual explorations' (Raz 1986, 16).

This strategy is, of course, illicit. The fact that a monistic theory can be used to bolster a controversial moral or jurisprudential theory is no reason to accept such theories as a superior account of an ordinary understanding of rights.

Indeed the susceptibility of rights theorists to the invisible gravitational pull of their substantive theories has contributed to the continuing deadlock in the debate over the functions of rights. The pull of such substantive theories has dragged these theorists toward defending one of the two monistic theories as an account of an ordinary understanding of rights. Having been pulled into these positions, the debate over the function of rights has then become a proxy debate in the battle between the substantive (Kantian and welfarist) theories. Such a proxy debate has made no more progress than has the debate between the two substantive theories themselves.

As a subject of scholarly inquiry, an analysis of an ordinary understanding of rights has its own integrity. This integrity requires that the analysis be conducted independently of the pull of controversial substantive theories. If such an analysis is so conducted then, and only then, can it become useful as part of an inquiry into which substantive theory of rights is best.

For an unbiased analysis of an ordinary understanding of rights will be useful for weighing the justificatory burden that any substantive theory of rights must bear. Suppose we had such an unbiased analysis on hand. Then when a substantive theorist claimed that the set of rights that there really are or could be differs from the set of rights that is commonly acknowledged, we could ask him to demonstrate that his substantive theory is so compelling that the common understanding of rights must be adjusted where there are conflicts. We might ask Steiner, for example, to argue on the strength of his Kantian political theory that the common idea that animals have rights must be abandoned. Or a Millian might be asked to show that Mill's reforming definition of 'rights' should be accepted on the strength of Mill's utilitarian theory, despite its incomprehension of many rights assertions that would ordinarily be regarded as innocuous.[21]

Once we have achieved an analysis of the common concept of 'a right', we will be able to judge how much of our ordinary understanding of rights we are being asked to modify by theorists who advance some substantive account of rights or other. We will, that is, be able better to assess the proposals of those theorists who wish (as Hart said of Bentham) to *give* the term 'rights' a new meaning. We will be honouring Hart's method for the conceptual analysis of rights:

Hart's method implies, first, that conceptual analysis is a mode of inquiry that is distinct from and logically prior to substantive theory; and, second, that conceptual analysis aims at recovering some, perhaps idealized, common understandings, in the sense that it articulates but can never transcend the understanding already implicit in ordinary use and reflection. (Stavropoulos 2001, 71)

A reliable assessment of the ways that people do think about rights is the only common starting point for arguments about how people ought to think about rights. I have argued that a pluralistic analysis of an ordinary understanding of rights will be superior to any monistic account. If that is correct, then any substantive theory of rights will need such a pluralistic analysis as the background against which to present its own arguments for revisions in usage.

It is not enough, of course, simply to say that a pluralistic analysis must be the correct one. It is unreasonable to expect a single-function theorist of either variety to give up his theory until a plural-function theory of rights is available. There must be, that is, some place to jump. In other work I have set out an analysis of an ordinary understanding of rights in which I argue that rights have several specific functions (Wenar, 2005). That analysis is I believe a first step towards

---

[21] In *Utilitarianism* Mill presented a famous reforming definition of 'rights' as that which one has 'a valid claim on society to protect [one] in the possession of' (Mill 2002, 54). This definition of 'rights' fits very well within Mill's normative theory: it is 'worth it' in utilitarian terms to protect possession of certain things even at the cost of imposing social sanctions. However when we retain a grip on an ordinary understanding of rights we notice that Mill's reforming definition rejects many seemingly innocent rights as incoherent. There would ordinarily seem nothing amiss for example in attributing rights to people in society-less state of nature, or even in saying that every individual has the right to be free from society's protection. Yet neither of these ascriptions of rights could make sense within Mill's definition. To establish his definition of rights as the correct one, a Millian would need to show why the attractions of his normative theory are great enough to lead us to give up our ordinary understanding of rights in cases such as these.

a theory that is adequate to an ordinary understanding of rights. It might be (though I do not believe it so) that this particular pluralistic analysis is mistaken, and that rights have multiple functions different than those I have suggested. However this may be, pluralistic analyses of an ordinary understanding of rights should become the main topic for investigations into the nature of rights. The history and structure of the debate between the two monistic theories of the functions of rights show that these theories will always lack adequate explanatory power. Only a pluralistic theory can provide a sufficiently comprehensive analysis of rights.

PART VI

TOLERATION AND LIBERTY

15

On Being Tolerated

Leslie Green

[M]onstre, tu n'as pas ma religion, tu n'as donc point de religion...
Voltaire (1975, 40)

How does it feel to be tolerated? It feels a lot better than it does to be persecuted. There is, after all, a difference between a ghetto and a pogrom. But being the object of someone's toleration does not always feel very *good*, and that may be why many philosophical defences of toleration, and political attempts to make toleration real, are at some point accused of being hollow or even pernicious. We hear that toleration is not enough, or even that it is repressive, and that what is needed instead is acceptance.

It is easy to dismiss such complaints, especially when formulated as crudely as I just did. Yet they respond to a genuine worry, the sources and significance of which I explore here. First, I try to identify what it is about toleration that often makes it uncomfortable for the tolerated. Second, I want to explore how tolerators might respond to that discomfort. For these purposes I take for granted the validity of the principle of toleration. Much of my argument is meant to be faithful to the familiar ideal we inherit from Locke, Voltaire, and Mill. But I also want to propose something that has been less prominent, at least among contemporary liberal writers: we often need to supplement toleration with what I am going to call *understanding*. Here, we still have things to learn from H.L.A. Hart's famous dispute with Patrick Devlin about the propriety of enforcing conventional moral standards.

1 The Nature of Toleration

The sort of toleration I have in mind is a principle of restraint. It directs people who make adverse judgments about others not to act on those judgments in certain ways and to refrain from doing so for reasons of a certain type. A few words about this may help orient the discussion.

Practical judgments establish reasons to act; in the case of adverse judgments, reasons to avoid, oppose, resist, prevent, etc. A principle of toleration offers a reason not to act on some of those reasons. That marks it as a principle of restraint. Of course, it is not a principle of *complete* restraint. Toleration is consistent with many ways of acting on adverse judgments, including abstaining from conduct of which one disapproves, arguing against it, and in various ways discouraging it. In *A Letter Concerning Toleration*, Locke maintains that we even have a duty to do such things, provided we discharge it in a certain way: 'the care of each Man's Salvation belongs only to himself. But I would not have this understood, as if I meant thereby to condemn all charitable Admonitions, and affectionate Endeavours to reduce Men from Errors; which are indeed the Duty of a Christian. (…) But all Force and Compulsion are to be forborn. Nothing is to be done imperiously' (Locke 1983, 47). Toleration does not require us to ignore people's mistakes, vices, or deficiencies; it demands that we take special care in how we respond to them. Above all, it requires us to put aside force, coercion, and other forms of overbearing intervention that treat other people as if they were subjects of our own *imperium*. For brevity, let us join Locke and say that toleration requires refraining from imperious responses. There are obviously lots of borderline cases here, but it is worth remembering that they do not all mark the frontiers of coercion. Those philosophers who imagine that the only way of being intolerant is by coercing others have forgotten what every employee knows. If your boss or co-workers are intolerant of your politics or sexuality, they have plenty of ways of demonstrating it short of firing you, denying you promotion, or shunning you in the cafeteria. And every employer knows that if he wants to root out certain attitudes (or certain employees), then coercion, with its tendency to attract attention and to provoke backlash, may not be the best way to go about it. Coercive intolerance is just one special, though often especially worrying, case.

Tolerance, properly directed, is a virtue. Of course, some conduct is intolerable and to exercise restraint in responding to it would be a vice. For example, no one should tolerate egregious sexism amongst one's colleagues. And in addition to things that do not *allow* for restraint, there are also things that do not ideally *call* for restraint. Not all adverse judgments warrant any sort of other-regarding response. Judging that *John's hair is too long* does not give one a prima facie reason to hold John down and trim it, or even to upbraid him, and thus no reason for interference that needs to be restrained by a principle of toleration. Misguided busybodies may be intolerant, but the best remedy is not to teach them the virtues of tolerance, but to teach them why they have no reason to meddle in the first place.

We need a robust principle of toleration, however, because the best response may fail. We are often thrown together with people who diverge in high-stakes judgments which, if valid, would warrant interference and which, taken seriously, incline people to interfere. If you think that permitting same-sex couples to marry would destroy the entire institution of civil marriage, then (supposing that you also hold conventional views about the value of that institution) you are going to want to *do* something about it—just as you will if you judge that early abortions are murders, or that the irreligion of others is delaying the arrival of the Messiah. Here, it is hard to see how anything *other* than a principle of restraint would stop true believers from trying to prevent these disasters. When we are in what people conceive to be *ruat coelo* territory, toleration is a practical necessity.

One reason for adopting a principle of toleration is therefore evident. Since some people will do almost anything to advance their views, a sustainable *modus vivendi* needs a principle of restraint. It is fashionable to denigrate this argument as 'merely' prudential—as if prudence were not of the first importance, and as if there were in politics an important general distinction between prudence and principle. Be that as it may, there are also other good reasons for toleration, ones that do not aim at moderating social conflict. Liberals, for example, favour toleration because of its connection with liberty (which does not always make social life go more smoothly). When we cut each other some slack, individuals and groups are more likely to enjoy the autonomy and open futures that they deserve.[1] Toleration also sustains important shared goods, such as a public environment in which people can interact anonymously in a variety of social contexts without needing to see eye-to-eye on life, and without even needing to make their allegiances in this department very clear. This in turn makes discussion, cooperation, commerce, and many other forms of social interaction easier than they otherwise would be. Toleration is valuable also for the Burkean reasons that Hart invoked against Devlin's refusal to tolerate deviations from conventional sexual morality. Certain practices and institutions can have the value they do because they are organically connected with the life of a society. But it is a condition for the organic growth of things like marriage or the family that they be allowed free development in a climate of tolerance: 'To use coercion to maintain the moral *status quo* at any point in a society's history would be artificially to arrest the process which gives social institutions their value.'[2] Toleration thus draws support from many considerations, and it would be a mistake to think that any one of them is the most important, or the key to understanding its value.

2 Failures in Toleration

The importance of toleration surely does not come as news. Why then do those on the *receiving* end of tolerant treatment sometimes feel ill done by? Do they suppose that everyone else should simply agree with them? Doubtless that is

---

[1] It is not only children who are entitled to what Joel Feinberg (1980) aptly calls 'an open future'. This is not to endorse Feinberg's further and less plausible claim that this requires 'as many open opportunities as possible' (1980, 135).
[2] Hart 1963, 75. See also R Dworkin 2006, 74–5 and 88.

sometimes the case. But there are other reasons why even justified toleration can sting.

(1) Toleration can be resented because of its limited *scope*, because it is incomplete and partial. It is unfortunate that our leading theories of toleration, including H.L.A. Hart's, were worked out for the purpose of fixing the proper limits of the criminal sanction. When the Model Penal Code and the Wolfenden Report were being debated, the forces of intolerance rallied in favour of the *criminalization* of things like prostitution and homosexual conduct. It therefore became natural to suppose that toleration is mostly a matter of *de*criminalization, and that narrow interpretation remains surprisingly resilient. Presumably it was under its spell that Thomas Nagel could write, back in 1995, that 'there has recently developed in our culture a fairly widespread (though still far from dominant) attitude of toleration [of homosexuality] that is remarkable because it is not based on general sympathy or understanding' (Nagel 2002, 47). That was premature, coming as it did eight years before a murky and split decision of the Supreme Court finally decriminalized homosexuality throughout the country (*Lawrence v Texas* 2003). It was also somewhat flattering: *apart* from decriminalization there is slim evidence that sexual non-conformity is widely tolerated in the United States, where elections can still be won or lost on the issue of what to do about the gays and where, in areas from employment to family law, sexual minorities continue to experience harsh treatment now rare in liberal democracies.

Could we nonetheless plead that decriminalization is the leading indicator of tolerance—not everything, to be sure, but the first thing and the main thing? We could not. The significance of decriminalization depends on the reasons for it. Consider Catharine MacKinnon's campaign against pornography. It is easy to forget that she launched it with the argument that criminal obscenity laws ought to be abolished in favour of rights of civil action for women who can prove they have been harmed by pornography.[3] The idea behind this was not to tolerate the production or use of pornography. It was to free restrictions on pornography from the difficulties of securing criminal convictions and to target more sharply its supposed evils. MacKinnon's hope was that civil anti-pornography legislation would prove a better preventive—more precise and more effective—than had the criminal law of obscenity. Criminal penalties were an obstruction to a thoroughgoing intolerance of pornography; decriminalization would be the first crack in a real crackdown on vice.

(2) A second way toleration can go wrong is based not on its scope but its *grounds*. As I said, there are many good reasons for toleration. There are also

---

[3] A Dworkin & MacKinnon 1988, appendix D. I say 'easy to forget' because MacKinnon later welcomed the Supreme Court of Canada's decision to uphold criminal obscenity laws as 'a stunning legal victory for women ... of world historical importance' (Sallot 1992, A6).

morally suspect ones. J S Mill famously argued that we are entitled to 'the liberty of tastes and pursuits; of framing the plan of our life to suit our own character, of doing as we like, *subject to such consequences as may follow*: without impediment from our fellow-creatures, so long as what we do does not harm them...' (Mill 1981, 15). Notice that this statement of the harm principle also contains, in the passage I italicized, a warning to those granted the freedom to make their bed that they may need to lie in it. The harm principle secures their autonomy to choose the good *or* the bad; this is in the nature of liberty. Consider, then, one who tolerates another *in order to* make bad outcomes more likely, by securing a liberty with the intention or hope that it be used poorly.[4] It would be troubling if a government tolerated smoking because its actuaries discovered that smokers die early enough to yield net savings in pensions. Another example of tolerating for the wrong reasons is to be found in the opinion of one of the dissenters in *Lawrence v Texas* (2003). Justice Clarence Thomas rejected the idea that the US Constitution confers any liberty broad enough to protect private, consensual homosexual conduct between adults. But he also said that, were he a Texas legislator instead of a federal judge, he would have tolerated it—on the ground that the repression of homosexuals 'does not appear to be a worthy way to expend valuable law enforcement resources'. This suggests that homosexuality should be tolerated only because, and to the extent that, there are more serious wrongs to repress. Had that been accepted as the basis for toleration, gay Americans would rightly feel uneasy.

(3) Finally, toleration can go wrong in a more complex way, when it is afforded in the wrong *spirit*. It is often assumed, perhaps because it is sometimes true, that toleration is a grudging virtue. The explanation for this is not far to seek. Toleration requires that people not act on a judgment that they consider correct on the merits, and the more confidently they believe it to be correct the less they may be inclined to yield in the way of tolerance. Moreover, people can see the force of an argument for toleration without really taking it to heart, and they can feel compelled to conform without even seeing its force. Thus, while tolerating they can make it perfectly clear that they wish they didn't *have* to be tolerant. Personal cases easily come to mind: racial minorities whose arrival in a neighbourhood is tolerated but to whom few speak. There are also public cases. After the Supreme Court of Canada ruled it unconstitutional for the state to treat same-sex couples differently from unmarried different-sex couples, the then-Conservative government of Ontario enacted a bill bringing the Province's family law into grudging conformity with the Constitution. Respect for same-sex couples was proclaimed in a statute styled, *Amendments Because of the Supreme Court of Canada Decision in M v H*. Nobody wants to be tolerated grudgingly, especially when the grudge is this ostentatious. When we are entitled to a certain treatment, we want it to be

---

[4] For discussion of such examples, see Gardner 1993, 90; and Cohen 2004, 81–3.

delivered in a way consistent with the reasons that ground it. (People do not want to be admired grudgingly either.) But grudge need form no part of toleration, and that is our third corrective. One may even tolerate happily and generously, out of a sense of respect or wonder at the rich diversity of human lives. Here again, Locke is a reliable guide:

> No private Person has any Right, in any manner, to prejudice another Person in his Civil Enjoyments, because he is of another Church or Religion. (. . .) No Violence or Injury is to be offered him, whether he be Christian or Pagan. Nay, we must not content our selves with the narrow Measures of bare Justice: Charity, Bounty, and Liberality must be added to it. This the Gospel enjoyns, this Reason directs, and this that natural Fellowship we are born into requires of us. (Locke 1983, 31)

One of these lines of argument is directed at Christians who imagine their religious duties discharged when they accord others 'the narrow Measures of bare Justice', conforming to the morality of the Law but defying the gospel of Love. But Locke also mentions a non-theological argument that is meant to apply to all of us. We owe those whom we tolerate charity, bounty, and liberality as a rational expression of the 'natural Fellowship' of all humankind. I do not think that it matters whether we take this to be an argument for the importance of virtues complementary, but superadded, to toleration, or whether we take it to show that there is a web of closely-linked attitudes without which toleration is, in its own terms, deficient. Either way, we are being asked ensure that toleration reflects the moral status of the tolerated. Is there some kind of contradiction here?[5] After all, toleration arises only in the presence of *adverse* judgments and if Locke is telling us that we should be not only charitable toward those whom we must tolerate but also '*affectionate*', how can we retain the vigour of our aversion without backsliding (or indulging a smug self-satisfaction)? Actually, there is no contradiction. Locke is reminding us that the moral substratum for toleration is not just a logically necessary condition of one's being a possible recipient of tolerant attitudes; it is something that goes on to shape how those attitudes should develop and how toleration itself should be deployed. A grudging toleration is out of keeping with what we owe each other as members of *a natural fellowship*. Disagreements about what to do or how to live need to be understood as disputes amongst members of one species, who share common ancestors, and whose most basic needs, pains, and pleasures have no culture and no language. The reasons we have for tolerating other members demand that we do so in ways consistent with that status. We don't hear as much about these demands as we should, and were they restored to their proper place, toleration might seem less irksome than it sometimes does.

---

[5] There are similarities between this case and the (apparent) contradiction in thinking that a certain policy ought to be enacted, while fully accepting the authority of a contrary policy should one's preferred option be voted down. See Wollheim 1962.

3 Occasions for Toleration: Power

Because toleration can be deficient in scope, grounds, or spirit, the tolerated may well have reasons for complaint. Much of the burden of being tolerated may be explained by such deficiencies. But not all of it. It is possible for even a broad, principled, and generous toleration to chafe, owing to the very fact that it is needed. From the point of view of the tolerated, toleration is normally a second-best: they would rather not find themselves *having* to depend on the toleration of others.

One aspect of this has to do with the fact that toleration restrains the attempted *prevention* of disapproved conduct. D D Raphael observes, 'One can meaningfully speak of tolerating, i.e. of allowing or permitting, only if one is in a position to disallow. You must have the power to forbid or prevent, if you are to be in a position to permit' (Raphael 1988, 139). There is thus a connection between being tolerated and being subject to someone's power. Three cautions in construing this point: first, the relevant power is social power and there is no presumption that it is justified; it may be *de facto* power only. Second, it need not be coercive power; as mentioned above, people also try to prevent conduct by non-coercive interventions of many kinds. Third, the connection between toleration and power may be indirect. Raphael frames it in terms of *having* the power to prevent. Yet people may also adopt a principle of toleration if they *believe* that they have such power, and they may adopt it prophylactically, in case they should ever *come* to have the power to prevent.[6]

The significance of social power is seen in the common distinction between toleration on the one hand and endurance or resignation on the other. Herbert Marcuse criticized what he famously called 'repressive tolerance'; but he did not mean that toleration is always a repressive force. He thought that, too often, 'Tolerance is extended to policies, conditions, and modes of behaviour which should not be tolerated because they are impeding, if not destroying, the chances of creating an existence without fear and misery' (Marcuse 1965, 82). Marcuse thought this true of Americans who, he complained, tolerate their country's possession and use of nuclear weapons, the corruption of its politics by wealth, and 'the systematic moronization of children and adults alike by publicity and propaganda' (Marcuse 1965, 83). A grim picture. But Marcuse may have misread Americans. He was assuming that many of them would have affirmed (at any rate, in 1965) that these things were wrong but tolerable. It may have been worse than that: perhaps the average American acknowledged these facts but thought them unobjectionable. On the other hand, perhaps things were in one way better than Marcuse supposed: perhaps most people were vividly aware of these vices, but saw no way out. They weren't tolerating repressively, because they weren't tolerating at all: they were just resigned to a political and economic system well-armoured against fundamental change. If so, what Marcuse mistook for repressive

---

[6] I am indebted here to the helpful discussion in Cohen 2004, 93–4.

tolerance was actually resignation. And just as toleration is not always a virtue, resignation is not always a vice—for example, when there is in fact no hope of improvement.

Although toleration is thus bound up with power, it is worth stressing that none of this shows that it is a *form* of power, let alone a repressive or oppressive one. But it does point to the kernel of truth in those dramatic overstatements. Toleration is native to political environments in which power is, or may soon be, in play. Given the choice, eg, between (a) a situation in which someone can prevent you from praying as you want but will tolerate your doing it, and (b) a situation in which he lacks any such power, most religious people would prefer (b). Who wants to live by the grace and favour of the powerful? This is especially true when the tolerated have no similar power over their tolerators. In this respect, toleration shares something with other desirable but asymmetric relations, like offering mercy or taking pity, which can also be uncomfortable for their recipients. And when we consider people not as monads but as members of minority groups, then the fact of toleration may be an unhappy reminder of the social distribution of power. Thus, some traditionalist Muslim immigrants to the West have to resign themselves to many features of the societies around them, for example, to the fact that their girls will grow up seeing women wearing short skirts, flirting with strangers, drinking in bars, and so on. In contrast, members of the host societies can (we hope) learn to tolerate the fact that some of the Muslim girls will veil. Things being what they are, the host society has options that the immigrant group lacks. Toleration does not cause or legitimate that difference in power; but it does reflect it, and that is another thing that is unpleasant about being tolerated.

4 Occasions for Toleration: Judgement

We now have two explanations for why it can hurt to be tolerated: the toleration may be inadequate, or the fact that others are in a position to tolerate may be a matter for regret. Neither of these explains why complaints about being tolerated are so often framed in terms of a plea for *acceptance*. To understand that, we need to notice the importance of another point: toleration is called for only in the face of a judgement that the tolerated conduct (or, perhaps, state of affairs) is somehow wrong or deficient.[7]

Some kind of adverse judgement is essential to toleration. That is why a merely *permissive* attitude towards φ-ing does not show that one tolerates φ-ing. Thus: I, for one, cannot be said to tolerate homosexual conduct. Although I would never think of trying to prevent it, I also see nothing deficient in it, so restraint is not

---

[7] Among 'deficiencies' I include things like being incomplete, one-sided, and so on. These are not always moral vices, and they can be necessary conditions of having certain virtues: see Raz 1988, 165.

called for. Of course, I am not *in*tolerant of it; the issue does not arise. On the other hand, I do tolerate the ritual circumcision of infant males because, although I would not try to prevent that either, I think that unconsented amputations are wrong, at least when done only to satisfy someone's views about his own religious obligations towards the amputee. Some who share my permissive attitudes do so on the opposite footing: approving the cutting while deploring the loving. If so, they tolerate what I do not. Which acts we can be said to tolerate thus depends not only on what we are (not) willing to do about them, but also on the background judgements in light of which we act or refrain from acting.[8]

Naturally, the tolerated rarely share the adverse judgement. One might object: but how will they know that anyone endorses that judgement? Provided there is no overt grudge, won't they see only the permission? Perhaps; and when that is so, toleration may not sting. We are trying to understand how such feelings *may* arise—not how they *must* arise. (We know that they may arise, because we know that they *do* arise.) In practice, invisibility of the judgements underlying toleration is uncommon. Those who judge φ-ing deficient typically reveal that in various ways: by refraining from φ-ing, by arguing against φ-ing and, within the limits of toleration, by discouraging φ-ing. Moreover, in the cases that are politically most salient, toleration often cohabits with *generalized* adverse judgements that bear on conduct involving fundamental and even identity-constituting attitudes towards love, faith, work, and so on. Where the practices of religious, cultural, or sexual minorities face such broad hostility, it can limit the terms of political discourse within their societies. In extreme cases, it may seem that there is not even a recognized vocabulary in which they can dissent: the adverse judgements have become hegemonic. Do we feel tempted to say, 'Get over it'? That is a very hard saying. It would take a Socrates not to care about how others react in these circumstances, and it would be all too human to feel hurt by this sort of disapproval.

5 Acceptance

We now see why the burden of being tolerated is so often expressed as a demand for acceptance: that is a natural response to an adverse judgement of the sort that underlies toleration.

In political rhetoric, what 'acceptance' actually amounts to, however, varies a lot with context. Sometimes, it simply *means* toleration, or at least a more complete

---

[8] There are complications here worth flagging. First, there is a question of whether the judgement needs to be conscious. Should we say that someone tolerates an activity if she is 'committed' to an adverse judgement about it though she is herself unaware of that commitment? Second, does any old 'con-attitude', as they used to say, qualify as an adverse *judgement*, or does it need to be an attitude with a certain structure, or capable of taking a certain object? (Is blind hatred a judgement? Can racial difference be an object of toleration?) A study of these issues would take us too far afield for present purposes.

toleration. For example, when gay people say that want to be accepted in the US armed forces, and not merely tolerated under the Clinton policy of 'don't ask, don't tell', they are not hoping that their superiors will think that it swell that they are gay, or march with them in the Pride parade. They are objecting to the fact that being openly gay remains a ground for dismissal, and that they are therefore *not* now tolerated, or are tolerated only under extortionate conditions not imposed on any other group whose proximity makes some enlisted men feel uncomfortable.

A second notion of acceptance is closely related to accommodation. An employer must not only refrain from firing employees who have disabilities, it must also accept them into the workforce and then provide reasonable accommodations to enable them to work. Were we to set out the justifications for imposing such duties on employers, we would want to mention the fact that an accessible workplace acknowledges the dignity of, and expresses respect for the abilities of, people with disabilities. All of this is important, but it does not add up to the sort of acceptance that might assuage the tolerated. Providing accessible toilets or assistive technologies does not soften or qualify the judgement that it is a matter of *regret* that anyone needs them or that it would be better for the productivity of the firm if they did not. And the possibility of accommodation rests on a power to intervene in the lives of the accommodated, just as the possibility of toleration rests on a power to intervene in the lives of the tolerated.

We come closer to what we need with the notion of acceptance as involving something like the *valuing* of difference. The tolerated need not suppose that the tolerator will *share* the values that divide them, but can one value the fact that others have different values, and one can value them beyond or in spite of the difference in values. In this spirit, Audre Lorde writes, 'Difference must be not merely tolerated, but seen as a fund of necessary polarities between which our creativity can spark like a dialectic' (Lorde 1984, 111). These are hard days for dialectics, and even for differences. That aside, it is open to doubt to what extent the valuing of differences must express itself in the valuing of this very person with her different life and values. With respect to a given difference, there is the question of whether it generates any creative spark. Suppose we need a fund of polarities necessary to sustain moral creativity and experiments in living. It does not follow that we need all of the options that *our* culture makes available. We only need a broad enough range. History shows that we can get plenty of creative sparks flying between Anglicans and Presbyterians without any help from Catholics, to say nothing of Wiccans. Indeed, there may be options—benign but boring religions, for example—that could even be repressed in order to provide space and support for more interesting ones that would bring greater creative potential for experiments in living. To celebrate the differences among our *existing* options, one will need not only the abstract love of difference that Lorde seeks to promote, but a love of *our own* differences. Are we generally to transcend toleration through such love?

There are contexts in which that sort of love is appropriate. Parents, for example, should not merely tolerate the homosexuality of their child; they should accept it. The reason parents should do so is based in the sort of relationship they should aspire to have with their children. Yet acceptance is often difficult within such relationships, let alone outside them. Parents who think their child's sexuality a moral disorder, or a sickness, or simply disgusting, first need to let go of the idea that they can do anything about it. For some this will be an enormous step, requiring them to abandon their fantasies of parental power. But that is only the beginning. No child wants his parents to be merely resigned to his sexuality. The judgement that confirms is likely to deform the love that parents owe their children and to undermine the honesty with which children should engage their parents. Children need their parents to judge that their sexuality is no deficiency or, if it is one, that it is not the sort of deficiency that warrants any parental intervention.

I choose this example for two reasons. First, it is a case where acceptance has, for most of us anyway, powerful appeal. Parents who really *cannot* accept the sexuality of their children—and some are unable to do so—cannot enjoy full parental love for those children.[9] If their hostility drives their children into hiding, they may lose any authentic relationship with them. Second, the example also shows why it is idle to hope that the difficulties of toleration can normally be met by acceptance. Even parents, who have one of the strongest motivations to try, may still be unable to accept. The odds that weaker motivations—including appeals to the wonder of difference—can succeed where love fails are very slim.

What's more, even where acceptance is desirable and possible, it rarely comes without loss. If a parent is an adherent of a homophobic faith, how can he accept his child's sexuality without becoming an internal dissident, a believer in an affirming church, or a non-believer? Yet any of these options will also bring alienation from a way of life in which he is not only entrenched, but which normally has some virtues. Secular parents face challenges no less deep. They may need to re-examine their views about the boundaries of the family or about the significance of sex. Even now, heterosexual culture tries to keep sexuality under control, and it is no bad thing to have some space free of its distractions. However, owing to the salience of their difference, gay children often become proud of their sexuality in ways that embarrass the most liberal of parents. Secular parents who would find *moral* judgements about a child's sexuality unintelligible or perverse may nonetheless have a hard time accepting the exuberant prominence

---

[9] I do not deny that such parents have a partial or conditional love for their children, and I certainly do not assert that their incapacity for full love entails that they hate their children. (Though such cases are not unknown.) The parents' failure, though regrettable, may also be blameless. Acceptance is no more directly subject to our will than is belief. We cannot simply *decide* to accept that *p*, when we feel deep in our gut that *not-p*; and no cool, rational argument is likely to persuade us otherwise. We may therefore need to sneak up on *not-p*, exposing ourselves to influences that display the possibility that *p*, or try to interpret things on the footing that *p*, and so forth. Over time, we may therefore come to see that *p* is possible, eligible for endorsement, and finally, if we are lucky, acceptable. (When led to water some horses do drink.)

of sexuality in a gay child's life. And all parents, religious and secular, who accept their gay children will have to either reject or tolerate their own homophobic family, friends, and colleagues.

To the extent that the good is plural, such costs are inevitable. Robert Paul Wolff writes, 'Political toleration is that state of mind and condition of society which enables a pluralist democracy to function well and to realize the ideal of pluralism.' [10] Wolff offers this as an analysis, not a commendation, for he is sceptical of the pretensions of pluralist democracy (mainly on the ground that it is not as pluralist as it pretends). But his general point is correct: toleration is, among other things, a virtue needed for pluralism. Acceptance, on the other hand, is a virtue needed for unity. The pluralism that tolerance enables tends to compete with a full-blooded acceptance of others. That is why it is legitimate to hope for acceptance in some, usually intimate, relationships, and also why we should be sceptical about trying to give it a broad role in the polity.

6 Recognition

Our review of acceptance produced mostly negative results. But it tells us something about possible remedies. Any view that seeks to ameliorate the sting of toleration has to keep two balls in the air: it has to be consistent with some sort of adverse judgement (or else toleration is no longer called for), and it must also have the potential to take some of the sting out of that judgement (or else toleration is no less burdensome).

One approach that has the resources to do both is based on what is often called 'recognition'. Assume that we should tolerate religious clothing and symbols even when ostentatious, such as Catholic nuns wearing habits, Muslim women wearing the hijab, and Sikh men wearing their ceremonial dagger, the kirpan. None of these activities should be criminalized or rendered infeasible by other sorts of regulation, and they should be willingly tolerated even by those who think them superstitious, sexist, and so forth. There are, however, various routes to that conclusion. These include the idea that people are entitled to wear just whatever they like, at least when there is no countervailing reason of public interest. On this interpretation, the habit, hijab, and kirpan are all to be tolerated in the same way and for the same reason that we should tolerate loud dresses at funerals, students in 'gangsta' gear, and Scots wearing the *sgian dubh*. They all come under the liberty to dress as one pleases, which is one aspect of Mill's liberty of tastes and pursuits. And this is not a case of tolerating for bad reasons—the liberty of tastes is an important liberty, and one that grounds many arguments for toleration.

It is a fact, however, that most of the religious would not *themselves* value the tolerated activities under the description I just gave. It is extremely unlikely that

---

[10] Wolff 1965, 4. The most influential modern defence of this view is Raz 1986. I discuss some hazards of treating value pluralism as a general approach to cultural difference in Green 2001.

they would acknowledge them as expressions of a general liberty to dress as one pleases, for they are aspects of ways of life that reject that liberty. The habit, hijab, and kirpan are commonly worn in conformity to a perceived duty to dress in some ways, and to abstain from dressing in others. To represent them as instances of a liberty of tastes and pursuits might be useful in establishing political alliances or pushing a permissive policy without attracting too much attention to its consequences, but it would distort what the issue is really about. To tolerate without recognizing what the matter of dress is like for them combines a welcome permission with an unwelcome misprision.

Why does that matter, so long as we get to the bottom line? It matters because it may misconceive the injury of *in*tolerance, and that may affect our grasp of what the bottom line requires. Another example may make this clearer. Until it was struck down in 1967, all American states enjoyed the power to prohibit marriages between black people and white people, and a number of them exercised it. It goes without saying that this offended freedom of association. But to think that was what was at issue in *Loving v Virginia* (1967) is to miss the core evil of the anti-miscegenation laws. Of course they *did* interfere with freedom of association but, along with separate schools and train compartments, they did so in order to secure the central planks of apartheid. The point is not that 'restricting freedom of association' sounds too bland, too sanitary, to capture the profound assault on human dignity wrought by these laws. It is that it occludes the meaning of bans on interracial marriage in the relevant context. *Loving* attacked racism. That was the intolerance it targeted; race-hatred was its root. Had *Loving* been decided without naming the vice, it might have been a rhetorical success, but it would have been a moral failure. It is only by understanding what a ban on interracial marriage is like for those who would enter such marriages that we can understand the depth of the injury and shape of an adequate remedy. It is easy, especially for lawyers, to miss the importance of this point. The advocate is oriented towards winning, and to win may have to bring on board those who would rather not confront the fact that the legal system has been administering apartheid, and who may have little commitment to dismantling it. Advocates are therefore often tempted to rest their case on the most abstract, most watery, principles they can find, in the hope of building a coalition that will win in court, without worrying too much about what, if anything, might happen next. (The racist, too, learns to invoke freedom of association.)

These considerations support trying to see the issue as the tolerated do. Where the pertinent issues are bound up with one's social identity, there is another layer. Here, it is claimed, there is a need for mutual recognition (Taylor 1992, Honneth 1996).[11] On this view, our identities are elaborated in dialogue with others. Hegel

---

[11] In Galeotti 2002, recognition is associated with equal respect. This is somewhat different (though not incompatible) from the sense of 'recognition' I am exploring here, which is more identitarian in character.

suggested that this mutuality can transcend profound inequalities of power: he claimed that even a master is dependent on his slave for recognition. So perhaps our different faiths, sexualities, and cultures are also elaborated in a tangled interdependence. If self-knowledge requires the power to see ourselves as others see us, recognition requires the power to see others *as they see themselves*. People generally want such recognition and they take it as a kind of insult to be misrecognized (Taylor 1992, 25). In the case of radical misrecognition, we risk tolerating a fiction, someone who is not the very person before us but rather a character in our own narrative. Thus, if we tolerate the hijab or kirpan under the aspect of liberty of dress, we misrecognize their bearers even as we permit them to do what they wish. And, on the dialogic conception of identity, this is not only an injury to the tolerated, it is an injury also to the tolerator.

This sort of argument is immune to one of the objections to acceptance: recognition does not efface the difference it tolerates. On the contrary, recognition aims to represent it: the idea is not that I need to share your values but that I need you to know your identity. I do not need to accept Christ as my saviour in order to interact with you on the basis that *you* do. But, the argument continues, in order to properly represent this fact about you—a fact which may in some complex way also prove crucial to the shape of my own, different, identity—I must also get it *right*.

There are various doubts we might raise about this theory: how determinate and stable are these identities? What does it take to get them right? And just how interdependent are they? Let us skirt these objections and ask instead, how far could a recognitional account address our worries about toleration? I can certainly recognize your faith while rejecting it, but perhaps the idea that your difference somehow shapes my own identity suggests that we have at least a limited common stake here. Perhaps there are *kinds* of disapproval that are pragmatically at odds with the idea that our identities are dialogically related, and restricting the forms may therefore soften the harsher edges of adverse judgement. Could that be what underpins Locke's idea that intolerance is expressed not only in preventive coercion but also in imperious attitudes?

These are suggestive ideas, but there is reason to worry whether recognition, in the sense favoured by these philosophers, can give them life. It sets the bar too high. In aiming to represent people as they are, without any *mis*recognition, it makes demands that are as unrealizable as those of general acceptance. We may lack the concepts essential to reproducing the self-understanding of the other, since the ways she interprets her life may be so bound up with radically different practices that our nearest match may not be good enough. Perhaps the closest we can come to understanding an Afghan or African whose primary identity is tribal is to deploy some analogy to our concept of the family or the political party. That is likely to be inadequate; yet it may be the best we can do. Even when there is no serious conceptual difficulty, our own beliefs and attitudes may interfere with our getting a clear fix on other people and their practices. Nagel criticizes some arguments against tolerating pornography on the grounds that the meanings they impute to it (hatred, contempt, etc) are but projections of the sexual fears and fantasies of the intolerant, not authentic understandings of what the material means for its typical user. He writes,

> No one is polymorphously perverse enough to be able to enter with imaginative sympathy into the sexuality of all his fellow citizens. Any attempt to treat this psychic jungle of private worlds like a public space is much too likely to be an expression of one's own sexual fantasies, rather than being based on an accurate appreciation of the meaning of the sexuality of others. (Nagel 2002, 50)

The doubt that we can confidently move forward on the basis of 'an accurate appreciation of the meaning of the sexuality of others' is a good reason to suppose that authentic recognition is not generally possible.[12] The capacity of sexual imagery and stories to fix the human imagination means that one tends to react to them on the basis of how one would feel or respond if one were involved *oneself*. And sex is not unique in this. The same seems to be true also of food, where people also engage in wild projections when they contemplate the diversity of culinary habits, for instance, when they learn that in a certain culture people enjoy eating horses or dogs. Along such dimensions, our imaginations seem endemically limited and our prospects for authentic recognition proportionately poor.

7 Understanding

The failure of recognition is due to a key feature of that ideal as specified above: it holds that people have a need to be recognized *just as they are*, and that half-measures may be as bad as none. That sets a very high bar, probably an insurmountable one. But we could be more modest. Without hoping to either accept or truly recognize those with whom we differ, we might nonetheless strive to *understand* them. What I have in mind is related to what Nagel calls 'imaginative sympathy' and to the approach to historical understanding found in *Verstehendesoziologie*: the attempt to capture or recreate, to the extent that we can, the meanings that acts and symbols have for their agents.

In a helpful discussion, Nagel denies that those with sadistic or masochistic sexual fantasies simply attach a different valence to acts the rest of us abhor: 'it's not that they are delighted by *the same thing* that revolts me; it's something else

---

[12] Nagel also wants to use this fact to delimit the boundaries of the private sphere: it is *because* we lack agreed public meanings that public interference is wrong and toleration called for. This proves too much. There is also a riot of conflicting meanings in many areas that are assuredly within the public sphere—understandings about property, for example. I cannot enter with full imaginative sympathy into the world of an aboriginal person whose moral relationship to land is spiritual and non-proprietarian. But we are not on those grounds tempted to think that control over real property falls into the private sphere. We think that we need to negotiate a public accommodation between people with such different understandings.

that I don't understand, because it does not fit into the particular configuration of my sexual imagination...' (Nagel 2002, 50). Understanding, however, is a matter of degree, and Nagel's overly modest account actually lays claim to a significant degree of understanding. To begin, in order to know that the sadist is *not* delighted by the same thing that revolts me, I need to know at least that much— that we are not simply talking about someone who is, so to speak, wired backwards. As we shall see, that is already an empathetic achievement, and one that cannot simply be taken for granted. Importantly, Nagel understands that sadistic or masochistic desires *are* forms of sexual desire. And there is more. He also sees that such desires involve 'something having to do with the sense of one's body and the bodies of others, release of shame, disinhibition of physical control, transgression, and surrender—but I'm guessing'. That's a pretty good guess. At any rate, it is not unlike what those who are both reflective and brave enough to write about their sado-masochistic desires actually say.[13] Now, none of this is to deny that Nagel's sketch of sado-masochistic desire may be incomplete or imperfect—but why worry about that? If our goal were to develop an adequate phenomenology of sadomasochism, to know 'what it is like' to be a sadist or a masochist, then the limits of our sexual imaginations would be an obstacle. But we may have more modest ambitions. We may seek to understand as far as we are able, consistent with the limits of our concepts and our experience, while acknowledging that this may not add up to an accurate recognition of the other.

I am sure that I do not fully understand what it is like to feel the need to veil one's face in public; but I do know that it is not normally a fashion statement (and I also know, that those for whom it *is* only a fashion statement have rather different stakes in tolerance than do most Muslim women). What I know almost certainly involves misrecognition: there are aspects of its significance that elude me, perhaps necessarily. Nonetheless, I think I have some idea about the interaction among beliefs about personal modesty, the place of sexuality, and the value of tradition that inspires such a view, and therefore some idea of the *sort* of things that are at stake if we do not tolerate it, or if we tolerate it as if it were no more significant than a teenager's fashion crimes. Where I am already disposed to toleration, coming to understand the activity better may place my adverse judgement—it stills seems limiting and sexist—in a broader framework. It may even start to seem less like a gross error and more like a defective or deficient specimen of a kind of activity that is a genuine source of value. Having a better understanding of the stakes may also broaden my toleration, make me less grudging about it, or less likely to tolerate for the wrong reasons. And where I am *not* disposed to tolerate, understanding may encourage me to revisit that judgement, for it may give me a clearer sense of the harms of intolerance. There are no guarantees here—clear-sightedness about an activity may also sharpen our disapproval

---

[13] For example, Califia 1994, 164–74.

of it. But we cannot know that in advance, and remaining alert to the possibility that we have misunderstood expresses not only humility but also a humane openness towards the tolerated. The knowledge that tolerators are making good-faith efforts at understanding, that they are at least *trying* to grasp the stakes as they seem to the tolerated, provides some reassurance to the tolerated that they are indeed being addressed as members of our fellowship.

Toleration can go wrong when this sort of understanding is deficient. In the case of *R v Brown* (1993), the House of Lords considered whether consensual sadomasochism should be tolerated to the extent that consent should provide a defence to charge of assault. Lord Templeman, in the majority, confidently if blindly announced that, 'Society is entitled and bound to protect itself against a cult of violence. Pleasure derived from the infliction of pain is an evil thing. Cruelty is uncivilised.' Now, to think that consensual sado-masochistic encounters are but a 'cult of violence' can only be projection in full flight. With such a weak grasp of the facts, it was hardly surprising that the only serious argument for toleration that Lord Templeman considered (and of course rejected) was the blunt assertion that 'every person has a right to deal with his body as he pleases'. However loosely counsel may have spoken, no one in *Brown* was really claiming *that*, which would include a right to use his body to smother someone or a right to commit suicide. It was not simply an *irrelevant* fact that the activities in question were sexual, that they took place among a group of people sexually attracted to each other, that they came together on an organized basis in order to have just that sort of sex, and continued the ritual over several years. Like Nagel, I do not know what it is like to be a sadist or a masochist, but I can tell that it is not a cult of violence. Neither do I know what it is like to be a believer in Holy Communion, but I can tell that that is not a cult of cannibalism.

Whenever 'understanding' is mentioned in political contexts, it has to face, not only the contempt of those who think it unmanly and unfit to consort with muscular virtues of equality or justice, but also the charge that it is morally lax. As then-Prime Minister John Major once said about a supposed crime wave, they think that 'society needs to condemn a little more and understand a little less'. He meant, I suppose, that we should not let an understanding of criminogenic policies and environments become a standing excuse for the crimes that they inspire and reward. There is that much truth in the sound-bite. But there is a larger error. If we do come to understand *less*, how will we be so sure that we really need to condemn *more*? Doesn't an appropriate response depend on a sense of what the conduct actually is, what it means to the agent, why he might find it appealing in the circumstances, and so forth? Almost every aspect of toleration—its scope, its ground, its spirit—will be coloured by our answers to these questions.

H.L.A. Hart grasped this well. We sometimes forget that he deployed two independent lines of argument in favour of tolerating homosexual conduct. The first—dissected by a generation of scholars—was that homosexuality is harmless and that Patrick Devlin's assertions that we need to criminalize sexual deviance in order to prevent social disintegration were absurd. Hart's convincing attacks on such 'utilitarianism without facts' are all most people remember of his argument. It was, however, only half of his case. The second half was that this sort of repression is itself extremely *harmful*. Deployment of official coercion to enforce conventional sexual conduct causes two sorts of injury: the intended and collateral harms caused by the application of the penalties and a second injury, much wider in scope and significance, caused by the standing threat of their application. This not only interferes with experiments in living, it creates a special and chronic suffering because of the nature of the desires it frustrates and the role they play in human life. Imagine someone replying, 'We all have our dispositions to temptation, and we would not think that a thief's temptation to steal is a reason for decriminalizing theft, as if criminal law must place the same burdens on the crooked as on the honest.' Hart saw why this would be such a lame analogy. Not only is theft actually harmful, but the impulse to steal or kill is rarely 'a recurrent and insistent part of daily life' and thus, 'Resistance to the temptation to commit these crimes is not often, as the suppression of sexual impulses generally is, something which affects the development or balance of the individual's emotional life, happiness, and personality.'[14]

Those sentences go by quickly, and they are not developed and hedged in the ways they should be if we are to have a fully-paid-up distinction between innocent sexual conduct and sexualized crimes. Perhaps that is why we are apt to forget what an achievement of understanding they nonetheless represented in 1962, and how central they were to the argument of *Law, Liberty, and Morality*. When Hart wrote, the idea that the repression of homosexual impulses might *adversely* affect the development or balance of one's emotional life, happiness, and personality, was not exactly a received idea. This was an era in which gay men were offered, and sometimes tragically sought, 'cures' by hormone injection, surgery, aversion therapy, and prayer. It would be more than a decade before homosexuality was removed from the list of illnesses made up in the American Psychiatric Association's *Diagnostic and Statistical Manual*. Official harassment and entrapment of gay men and official toleration of private anti-gay violence were routine. In that context, understanding that the legal repression of these desires involved stakes utterly unlike those in ordinary crimes cut like a laser beam through a fog of prejudice and superstition.

Notice also the following. Hart's case for toleration makes no appeal to the *acceptance* of homosexuality and no demand for the *recognition* of those homosexually-inclined people who adopt (or are assigned) a gay identity. What matters is understanding that the repression of homosexuality falls under the description 'suppression of sexual impulses', together with a fairly sensitive grasp of what that means in a typical human life. This is not acceptance, because it does not

---

[14] Hart 1963, 21–2; and cf Hart 1994, 175.

preclude adverse judgements about these impulses.[15] Nor is it recognition, because it does not acknowledge any sort of identity—it need not even concede that variations in sexual appetites are sensible things around which to construct social identities. And it does not tell us much about what it is like to be homosexual or bisexual, save that in crucially relevant ways it is *nothing* like being a burglar or a tax-evader. A small point, you say? Maybe, but one with large implications for the development of toleration and for the way the tolerated receive it.

I've been stressing the place of understanding in Hart's argument for toleration, and its role in his deployment of the harm principle. It is worth noting that sometimes it is not only the tolerated, but also the tolerators, who need to be understood. It is tempting to say—I have said it often enough myself—that disapproval of homosexuality is not even a *candidate* moral view; it is simply an aversion. How could an otherwise licit sex act be permissible if performed by a female, yet impermissible if performed by a male? How could *that* fact make a moral difference?[16] Hart would have refused this line of thought. In addition to defending a broad concept of law, he also defended a broad concept of morality, demarcated by its role in individual and social life. He was well aware no rationale could be given for many of the taboos of conventional sexual morality: 'They are abhorred, not out of conviction of their social harmfulness, but simply as "unnatural" or in themselves repugnant.' But he also insisted that 'it would be absurd to deny the title of morality to social vetoes of this sort; indeed, sexual morality is the most prominent aspect of what plain men think morality to be' (Hart 1994, 174–5). In considering whether any sort of homophobia is tolerable, we are therefore going to have to take account of the fact that at least some people who abhor homosexuality do so as part of a sexual morality. The less it looks like a blind hatred and the more it looks like an attempt to live by an intelligible, if misguided, morality of intimate conduct, the more likely we are to have some kind fellow-feeling even for the homophobe. To treat him as simply confused would be a failure of understanding; it could not possibly 'represent the point of view of those who live by such a morality' (Hart 1994, 174; cf 182).

To students of jurisprudence, this should ring a bell. The idea that we need to understand a practice from the point of view of those who live in and with it lies at the core of Hart's argument against reductivist theories of law. To fully understand law, we need to see it, not as it might appear to the sort of sociologist, anthropologist, or economist who interprets it solely from the outside, but from the 'internal point of view' of one who actually uses its norms to guide and

---

[15] For example: one may think it a matter of regret that such impulses leave them with a small pool of potential mates, or make it unlikely they will share in whatever value attaches to raising children who share genetic material with themselves and their partners.

[16] Many religions that proscribe homosexual conduct acknowledge this. They proscribe it in virtue of some *other* general feature—such as being non-procreative. Such features are of course present in many heterosexual and autosexual acts. The peculiar obsession of some sects with homosexual species of the prohibited genus must be put down to bad faith, or to some kind of reaction formation.

appraise conduct. This has been long recognized as pivotal in Hart's jurisprudence. Curiously, those who have speculated about the normative significance of Hart's jurisprudence have missed this point arising from his methodology. Failure to take 'the internal point of view' is not only a source of interpretive error; as we see in Hart's criticism of Devlin, it is also a common source of *moral* error, not because the internal point of view is an approving one, but because it has to be an understanding one. It was this failure of the moral imagination rather than any utilitarian miscalculation that proved Devlin's undoing.

8 Conclusion

I arrive, finally, at my epigraph. As Voltaire saw, one of the roots of religious intolerance is the selfish supposition that 'religion' can be nothing other than *my* religion. Other faiths are not religions at all. We know how that line of thought continues: sexuality can be nothing other than *my* sort of sexuality; family can be nothing other than *my* sort of family, and so on. We also know where it too often ends up: in things like the claim that rough sex is an intolerable cult of violence, that same-sex unions aren't marriages at all, and so on.

Voltaire is not here pleading for acceptance of competing religions, and he is not trying to capture what it is like to be a Huguenot. He is urging us to take on board a more primitive point: we need to be open to the possibility that competing faiths might actually *be* religions. It is therefore wrong to suppose someone a moral monster merely on the ground that he worships different gods, or worships in a different way. Freed of Voltaire's polemical constraints we could go further, and acknowledge that we need to be open also to the possibility that both religion and irreligion can express valuable forms of conscientiousness. In the modern West, there thankfully aren't too many religious monstrosities left. Here, toleration and understanding have come together with reasonable success. But for our failures we need look no further than sexuality, where the figure of the grotesque homosexual is just giving way to that of the monstrous paedophile—a creature about whom intelligent discussion, to say nothing of humane response, is for now almost impossible.[17] It is even hard to see a point of entry here, unless it is the observation of the protagonist in Graham Greene's *The Power and the Glory*: 'When you visualized a man or woman carefully, you could always begin to feel pity...When you saw the corners of the eyes, the shape of the mouth, how the hair grew, it was impossible to hate. Hate was just a failure of imagination' (Greene 1940, 131).

[17] Witness the furious reaction to Judith Levine's moderate and careful book, *Harmful to Minors: The Perils of Protecting Children from Sex* (Levine 2002). Levine received death-threats and, from the state legislature, condemnation. To its discredit, a frightened University of Minnesota administration ordered an outside review of its Press's editorial policies, including the perfectly normal peer-review that endorsed publication of Levine's monograph (Benfer 2002).

How far can understanding round the edges of toleration? Only partially. Toleration remains, in the end, a principle of restraint, and for that reason it will never be totally comfortable to be tolerated. One reason for that lies in the power of the tolerator. Understanding leaves that power in place, though it may affect how it is deployed. Another reason lies in the adverse judgement which underlies toleration. Without supposing that tolerators should generally try to abandon that judgement, we can hope that it might be accompanied or preceded by an effort to understand the tolerated. Understanding what the disapproved conduct means for the agent, and how it fits into a human life, may make us revisit and sometimes revise that judgment. It may supplement toleration; it may make us better tolerators, especially when it gives us a grasp of what it is to be at the sharp end of a particular stick. That kind of understanding leaves room for disagreement in value, and room for correction of error. It does not bring acceptance or recognition. But the effort to understand affirms our fellowship with the objects of our toleration. Without that, toleration is poorer—and harder—than it needs to be.[18]

[18] I thank Ronald Dworkin, Claire Grant, David Miller, Thomas Nagel, Jeremy Waldron, and audiences at Cambridge, Oxford, and New York University for their tolerance and criticism.

16

Private Faces in Public Places[1]

Susan Mendus

Private Faces in Public Places are wiser and nicer than public faces in private places.

Auden

Discussions of the legacy of H.L.A. Hart tend to focus on his intellectual achievements in general and on his contributions to legal theory and political philosophy in particular. In the Preface to their 1977 Festschrift for Hart, published under the title *Law, Morality, and Society,* Peter Hacker and Joseph Raz write:

At mid-century political philosophy was said to be dead and legal philosophy appeared to be dying. The only fruits that could be obtained from that field of intellectual activity were the gleanings from ancestral sowings. A quarter of a century later a transformed landscape is revealed—legal philosophy flourishes as never before. The responsibility for this renaissance is H L A Hart's. His work provides the foundations of contemporary legal philosophy in the English speaking world and beyond. (Hacker and Raz 1977, v)

And they go on to argue that Hart did for twentieth-century legal philosophy what Jeremy Bentham did for eighteenth-century jurisprudence—he integrated it into the mainstream of general philosophical thought.

This assessment of Hart as the founding father of modern legal philosophy is echoed by Zenon Bankowski whose obituary of Hart looks back over 50 years of legal theory and concludes 'Then, there was only him. Now, a hundred flowers bloom. This is his lasting contribution' (as quoted in Lacey 2004, 361). And in similar vein, Ronald Dworkin's speech at the memorial service for Hart begins 'Nobody ever writes about Herbert's career without pointing to the transforming

[1] I am very grateful to Matthew Kramer and Claire Grant for inviting me to deliver this paper at their British Academy Symposium on 'The Legacy of H.L.A. Hart' which was held in Cambridge in July of 2007. In addition to benefiting enormously from discussion with many of the participants at the conference, I have also been greatly helped by conversations with colleagues and research students at the University of York. I would particularly like to thank Alex Bavister-Gould, Britain Brady, Alfonso Donoso, Matthew Festenstein, Ed Laws, Matt Matravers, and Jon Parkin whose comments and suggestions have been invaluable in helping me to clarify my thinking.

impact he had on legal and political philosophy. When he became Professor of Jurisprudence in Oxford, in 1952, those subjects were, to put it kindly, dead. When he left, in 1968, they were exciting growth industries. In the case of political philosophy that was in good part his doing; in the case of legal philosophy he did it nearly alone' (as quoted in Hart 1998, 213). The legacy, then, is widely agreed upon: Herbert Hart almost single-handedly transformed legal and political philosophy, first in Oxford, then in England, then in the English-speaking world.

What is not widely agreed upon, however, is whether, and to what extent, a complete understanding of that legacy requires consideration of more than philosophical material. In particular, whether it requires knowledge of Hart's character, temperament, and personal life as well as of his intellectual and philosophical convictions. The possibility that it does was raised by Dworkin when, in the speech quoted earlier, he claimed that Hart's character and style 'entered into the substance of his work' and that 'he was so effective because what he said grew so naturally and thoroughly out of who he was'. And Dworkin concludes, intriguingly, Hart was 'a liberal of temperament, not doctrine' (Hart 1998, 214–15).

However, the possibility that a complete understanding of Hart's legacy calls for a knowledge of his life, including his private life—is explored most fully and most controversially by Nicola Lacey in her biography, *A Life of H L A Hart: The Nightmare and the Noble Dream*. Lacey notes at the outset that the writing of biography poses dilemmas. She says:

One dilemma had to do with the very personal nature of some of his [Hart's] letters and diaries. My rule of thumb was to use only the personal material which sheds light on the development of his ideas and the course of his career. But this, it turned out, was usually the case, because Herbert Hart himself moved seamlessly back and forth in his diaries between personal and professional preoccupations, and sought increasingly to draw links between the two. Though some readers may feel that I have been too generous in my use of the personal material—particularly that relating to his feelings about his sexuality and his marriage—my judgement was that it was essential to any interpretation of him as a whole person. (Lacey 2004, xix–xx)

Lacey was correct in predicting that some might feel she had 'been too generous' in her use of personal material. While most reviews of the book were complimentary, Thomas Nagel wrote: 'When I finished this book I was left wondering why H L A Hart hadn't destroyed his diaries before he died...Perhaps he didn't care. One never knows how people will feel about what happens after their death. But having been acquainted with Hart for years and having known many of his friends, I felt I was learning too much that was none of my business' (Nagel 2005a, 12). And he then goes on to offer two reasons for objecting to the inclusion of so much personal material in an intellectual biography: first, and in this specific case, the decision to include such material sits uncomfortably, Nagel thinks, with Hart's own, very private, character; second, the personal material is in any case irrelevant for an understanding of Hart's, or indeed any philosopher's, intellectual achievements. On the former, Nagel writes: 'Hart was a figure notable, and admirable, for his discretion, reserve and unpretentious dignity. The turmoil that went on beneath that surface was his affair' (Nagel 2005a, 12); while on the latter he concludes robustly that Lacey's claim that 'the personal material is needed to write an intellectual biography is a pretence' (Nagel 2005a, 12).

There is, then, widespread agreement that Hart's legacy lies in his 'transformative' contributions to legal and political philosophy—contributions which, on at least some accounts, integrated those areas of intellectual interest into mainstream philosophy and which, on almost all accounts, resuscitated them from their moribund states. However, if we go on to ask what is needed in order to understand that legacy fully, agreement ceases. Some, such as Dworkin and Lacey, see Hart's life, including his personal life, his character, and his temperament, as significant factors informing the very substance of his philosophical position; others—notably Nagel—insist that such personal material is irrelevant to intellectual achievement and stands apart from philosophical commitment. Although these differences are often presented as comparatively minor matters— matters of personal taste or judgement—they strike me as being very significant disagreements, and ones which are of great importance in answering questions about the legacy of any thinker, but especially in answering questions about the legacy of H.L.A. Hart.

In this paper, therefore, I shall try to do two things: first, I shall try to offer some general reasons for thinking that knowledge of someone's personal life might be important for a full understanding of his or her work—including philosophical work; second, I shall try to exemplify that claim through discussion of a particular case—the case of H.L.A. Hart's famous 1973 article, 'Rawls on Liberty and its Priority'. It seems to me that our understanding of that article will be greatly enhanced if it is informed by knowledge of Hart's personality and of his personal circumstances at the time of its composition. I begin, though, with the first theme: the relationship between biography and philosophy, or between Life and Work.

1 Biography and Philosophy

Nagel offers two distinct objections to Lacey's use of personal material: first, and as has been noted already, he sees it as a kind of 'biographical voyeurism', and he believes this voyeurism to be especially distasteful in a biography of Hart because Hart was himself a very retiring and private person. Beyond that, however—and this is the second objection—Nagel denies that this personal material is relevant to the assessment of Hart's intellectual life and achievements. The two objections are distinct. The former appeals to sensitivity or good manners in the selection and publication of biographical material. It calls upon the biographer not to pry too deeply into private matters and to resist the temptation to publish personal material. The latter, by contrast, expresses a much more substantive claim about the relationship between a man's life and his work. It denies that personal material has any relevance to intellectual assessment. In his exchange with Simon Blackburn and Jeremy Waldron about the status of Lacey's biography, Nagel focuses on the former point (the point of sensitivity or manners) to the exclusion of the latter. He writes 'I agree…that the use of intimate personal material presents difficult issues, and that reasonable people can differ. My review expressed a personal view, that their use should be more restricted than is now customary, without the subject's express or implied consent, until a substantial time after his death' (Nagel 2005b).

It is undeniable that his review *did* express that personal view, but it also gave voice to a substantive claim about the relationship between someone's life and his or her academic or intellectual work. Moreover, this claim is one which Nagel has made on other occasions. Thus, in his review of the second volume of Ray Monk's biography of Bertrand Russell, he writes:

This is another of those painful biographies of a major creative figure that exposes personal failings and sexual agonies to the kind of intimate scrutiny that none of us could withstand. Those who read Monk's first volume may have felt, as I did, the indecency of being exposed to the depths of Russell's misery and the expression of his sexual passions. Why does a great philosopher, or a great artist or a great scientist, forfeit his privacy forever, so that we all get to read his love letters and sneer at his weaknesses? What such people create is far finer than they are. It is extracted from a flawed and messy self so that it can float free, detached from the imperfect life that produced it. (Nagel 2002, 63)

For Nagel, it seems, Life is one thing, Art another, and accounts of the intellectual life of a great man can and should be kept separate from the details of his private, personal, and (particularly) sexual life not only because good manners requires it, but also because the work both can and should 'float free' of the life that produced it.

These are contentious claims both about how a life is to be understood and about how a biography is to be written. While we may all agree that 'ideas and career' are different from 'the whole person', it does not follow that a biography—even an intellectual biography—can be written without attention to the 'whole person', and in concluding so speedily that this distinction can, and must, be maintained Nagel neglects a very large body of work on the serious problems and conflicts inherent in writing biography. In particular, he neglects—indeed he denies—the possibility that an understanding of someone's life (including their private life) may be important for an understanding of their work. This, however, is a possibility that literary biographers take very seriously indeed. John Updike goes so far as to refer to literary biography as a way of 'entering the mansion of the novel through the back door'. 'The biography', he writes, 'becomes a way of re-experiencing the novel, with a closeness, and a delight in seeing imagined details conjured back into real ones that only this particular writer could provide'

(Updike 1999). And in similar vein, Dana Greene notes that Leon Edel, the biographer of Henry James and 'spokesperson for biography at mid-century', saw his task as being to 'search for the figure under the carpet... the pattern exposed on the underside of life, one woven inextricably with the design of the top of the life, the public visage' (Greene 2006). In short, literary biographers are clear that personal detail can illuminate our understanding of a writer's work, even though they may disagree about the proper limits to biographical intrusion into the private lives of authors.

However, it may be said that even if this is a way of defending the inclusion of personal details in literary biography, it is not an appropriate approach to the biographies of philosophers. Here, the work really does—or should—'float free' of the life that created it, and this is because philosophy, unlike the writing of novels, is an abstract enterprise, not dependent on personality or temperament. But this, too, is questionable, and especially so if (as in the case of Hart) we are considering the work of a legal, social, and political philosopher rather than a logician or a philosopher of mathematics. It may be plausible to claim that *Tractatus Logico-Philosophicus* or *Principia Mathematica* can be fully understood without reference to their authors' personal lives or to the contexts in which they lived and wrote; it is much less plausible to suppose that the same is true of (say) *The Subjection of Women*, or the *Letter Concerning Toleration*, or *Law, Liberty, and Morality*. Moreover, to say this is not simply to say that there is no general answer to the question 'what is the relevance of a philosopher's life to his or her work?' (though I think it is true that there is no general answer to that question); it is also to note that legal philosophy and political philosophy may not be best understood as abstract enterprises and, in consequence, works of political and legal philosophy may not be best understood as 'floating free' of the lives of their authors. I will return to this point later. For now, I simply want to note, first, that it is not clear that the work of a great artist or a great philosopher can, as Nagel insists, 'float free, detached from the messy life that produced it', and second that, even if it can float free in some cases—specifically in cases of scientific thought, or of philosophical thought of a very abstract kind such as logic or metaphysics—it is not at all obvious that it can do so in the case of legal or political philosophy, nor indeed is it obvious that we should *want* it to do so in those cases.

The question that motivates this paper is a question about what is relevant to an assessment of H.L.A. Hart's intellectual legacy. More specifically, it is a question about whether at least some facts about Hart's private life might be important and illuminating. Thomas Nagel denies that they are and he denies this at least partly because he believes that private life is separable from intellectual life in general and from philosophical theory in particular. So far, I have suggested, in general terms, that the distinction between life and work, or between philosophy and biography, might be more complex than Nagel believes. However, Nagel's view rests on more than a contestable understanding of the relationship between life and work. It also rests on a rather simplistic conception of the public–private distinction and on a contestable understanding of the scope and aims of political philosophy. In the next two sections, therefore, I will say a bit more about each of these themes, and about the ways in which they might inform our assessment of Hart's legacy before going on to discuss a specific case—Hart's article 'Rawls on Liberty and Its Priority'. My aim here will be to show how our understanding of this piece of political philosophy might be illuminated by knowledge of some personal details of Hart's life and of the times in which he wrote. First, though, the public–private distinction and the status of political philosophy.

2 Public and Private

In arguing that intellectual (including philosophical) life is separable from personal life, Nagel assumes that the scope of the personal is clear and uncontroversial. This is evident in his complaints against Lacey's biography of Hart and also in his criticisms of Ray Monk's biography of Russell. In both cases he takes it for granted that we know and are agreed upon the boundaries between professional and personal matters. Moreover, this assumption is not confined to his reviews of biographical work, but is also evident in his writings on modern liberalism and modern politics. A recurring theme in Nagel's recent work is that modern society is becoming increasingly prurient, and he takes biographies such as Lacey's and Monk's to exemplify this general trend. What is more, he believes that the trend is one which exposes deep flaws in modern liberal societies and writes

everyone knows that something has gone wrong in the United States with the conventions of privacy. Increased tolerance for variation in sexual life seems to have brought with it a sharp increase in prurience and censorious attention to the sexual lives of public figures and famous persons, past and present. The culture seems to be growing more tolerant and more intolerant at the same time, though perhaps different parts of it are involved in the two movements. (Nagel 2002, 3)

However, in offering these comments on the state of modern America, Nagel never acknowledges either the (very familiar) difficulties inherent in deciding precisely where the line between public and private is to be drawn, or (more worryingly) the possibility that the distinction is problematic in itself and independent of where the line is drawn.

To take the first point first: in 'Concealment and Exposure' Nagel discusses the case of Clarence Thomas and Anita Hill. To recall, in July of 1991, President Bush nominated Clarence Thomas to the Supreme Court of the United States. Towards the end of the confirmation hearings it was alleged that Thomas had made sexually provocative statements to a number of female employees and had sexually harassed Anita Hill. In her testimony to the Committee, Hill stated that Thomas 'spoke about acts he had seen in pornographic films involving such matters as women having sex with animals and films showing group sex or rape scenes...On several occasions, Thomas told me of his own sexual prowess.' In his discussion of the Clarence Thomas case, Nagel allows that Thomas's nomination to the Supreme Court could legitimately have been rejected on grounds of competence and judicial philosophy, but goes on to insist that the challenge on the basis of his alleged sexual harassment of Anita Hill was unjustified. He writes: 'it is true that Hill was his [Thomas's] professional subordinate, but his essential fault was being personally crude and offensive. It was no more relevant than would have been a true charge of serious maltreatment from his ex-wife...This sort of bad personal conduct is completely irrelevant to the occupation of a position of public trust' (Nagel 2002, 23).

Nagel's insistence that Thomas's behaviour, while personally crude and offensive, was nonetheless irrelevant to his suitability for the job, is questionable along a number of dimensions. First, it is questionable whether improper behaviour exhibited in a professional context can properly be classed as 'personal'. In saying that it is questionable, I mean just that. The extent to which someone's character, temperament, and general social skills are personal rather than professional matters is, I think, a matter of context and judgement, not something that can be decided in the abstract: a self-employed furniture restorer may claim that his sexist, racist, or homophobic views are irrelevant to his ability to do his job; a GP, or a police officer, or a university teacher, would have greater difficulty in making the same claim with any plausibility. But the vast majority of jobs call for an ability to work with others, and if a candidate for a post is constitutionally inclined to make crude and offensive comments to and about women colleagues, that does not strike me as obviously irrelevant when considering his or her suitability for office. (To be clear, I am not claiming that Clarence Thomas *was* so inclined; only that *if* he was, then that would be a relevant consideration in determining his suitability for a job that involved working with women.)

Beyond that, it is at least arguable that people (like Clarence Thomas) who wish to occupy positions of public trust thereby render themselves more open to inspection both because they have voluntarily sought public office and (more importantly) because the decisions they take in that office will have far-reaching consequences for a large number of people, and insofar as decisions taken in public office reflect 'private' opinions or inclinations, the line between the public and the private may perhaps be drawn differently (and less sharply) in their case. This point is made by Amy Gutmann and Dennis Thompson when they write: 'when an attorney general belongs to a private club that discriminates against blacks and women, when the president's "drug czar" is addicted to cigarettes, when the enforcement chief of the Securities and Exchange Commission is accused of wife-beating, the public rightly takes notice' (Gutmann and Thompson 1996, 111). And I take it that the general thought here is that *even if* cigarette smoking or wife-beating are, in general, private vices, they are not necessarily private when discerned in public officials. What counts as public and what counts as private may vary depending on who we are talking about, and those who hold public office must accept that, in their case, the realm of privacy may be rather narrower than it is for the rest of us.

Whether Gutmann and Thompson are right in making this claim is not the point. The point is that this is a controversial area and one in which reasonable people may disagree. It is this that Nagel ignores when he asserts so boldly that Clarence Thomas's behaviour was a matter of personal crudity and offensiveness and, as such, irrelevant to his suitability for office. The line between the personal and the professional is rather more vague and fuzzy than Nagel is inclined to suppose, and it is also a line that may, perhaps, be drawn in different places for different people.

Moreover, there is a second, and deeper, point to be made here—a point about the problematic character of the public–private distinction independent of where the line between the two is drawn. The case of Clarence Thomas draws our attention to the fact that publicity and privacy are both important liberal values, but they are also values that conflict one with another. Thus, having claimed that the allegations made against Thomas were indeed relevant to his suitability for office, Gutmann and Thompson go on to note that in deciding how to deal with Anita Hill's allegations the Judiciary Committee 'confronted a dilemma. The Committee could ignore the charges, in which case they would fail in their constitutional duty to examine Thomas's qualifications thoroughly. Or they could consider the charges without telling Thomas, in which case they would violate Thomas's right to confront his accusers—a basic liberty. The Committee could escape this dilemma only by persuading Hill to accept a lesser degree of confidentiality than she had initially requested' (Gutmann and Thompson 1996, 113). In short, Thomas's right to know what allegations were being made against him was in tension with Hill's understandable desire for confidentiality and privacy.

The point can be, and has been, generalised. In 'Theoretical Foundations of Liberalism' Jeremy Waldron notes the 'Enlightenment impulse' that society should be a 'transparent order, in the sense that its workings and principles should be well-known and available for public apprehension and scrutiny' and he goes on to ask whether that impulse is in tension with the equally characteristic liberal commitment to privacy in certain areas of social life. He concludes

The problem is that privacy here is not usually the privacy of solitude, but rather the privacy of the family and (in classical but not in modern liberalism) the privacy of the workplace. But these are areas in which, on any realistic understanding, important issues of power and hence legitimacy arise. That leads to a genuine dilemma. Some liberals may be happy with the panopticism of a Bentham... but others will view this with alarm. Freedom from the public gaze, they will argue, is an indispensable condition for the nurture of moral agency: people need space and intimacy in order to develop their liberty... to the extent that these lines of thought are taken seriously, liberals leave themselves open to the charge of being less than wholehearted about the legitimation of *all* structures of power in modern society. (Waldron 1993, 58–9)

In short, then, Nagel takes the public–private distinction to be clear and unproblematic. However, in doing so he ignores a vast body of literature which stretches back at least as far as 1970s feminism on the controversial character of that distinction. The controversy ranges both over questions of scope and over questions of stability: it includes questions about what should count as public and what private; it raises the possibility that the line is differently drawn for different people (arguably, at least, those who voluntarily occupy positions of public trust cannot expect the same degree of privacy as the rest of us); and it also includes questions about the stability of the overall relationship between liberal commitment to privacy and liberal commitment to transparency and publicity.

Additionally, Nagel claims that the shifting of the public–private boundary, the increased 'prurience' (as he calls it) that is characteristic of modern society is a sign that 'something has gone wrong' in liberal society. But the other possibility is that this intrusion of the public gaze into what was previously thought of as private life is, if not inevitable, then at least a danger that is structurally inherent in liberalism itself. In other words, it may not be the case that 'something has gone wrong'; it may rather be the case that a single, significant, strand of liberal thinking has been taken to its practical, if not its logical, conclusion and that the simultaneous growth of toleration in the political sphere and its demise in the cultural or moral sphere are connected. However, before considering that possibility in more detail, I will first say something about the second set of questions prompted by Nagel's work: the scope and aims of political philosophy.

3 Political Philosophy

The question which stands at the heart of this paper is a question about whether, and to what extent, facts about Hart's personal life may be relevant to an understanding of his philosophical work and to an assessment of his intellectual legacy. In the preceding section I took issue with the claim that facts about his personal life are irrelevant to an assessment of his legacy and I did so in part because the claim that personal details are irrelevant presupposes that there is clarity about what counts as personal and this, for reasons offered, seems to me to be untrue. So, one reason for questioning the claim that personal details are irrelevant to an assessment of intellectual legacy is because the scope of the personal is both controversial and indeterminate.

A second reason for questioning the claim that personal details are irrelevant to an assessment of intellectual, and particularly philosophical, legacy is because there may be dispute about the nature of philosophy and, in particular, about the nature of political and legal philosophy. Earlier in the paper I noted that Nagel's insistence on the irrelevance of personal life to intellectual legacy depends, in part, on his belief that philosophical work can 'float free' of the messy life that produced it, and I wondered whether that belief could be sustained in the case of political and legal philosophy, even if it is defensible in the case of logic or metaphysics.

Perhaps the simplest way of voicing my concerns here is to return to the conception of philosophy which seems to underpin Nagel's denial that personal details are relevant to philosophical legacy. In insisting that philosophical work should float free of the imperfections of the life that produced it, Nagel implicitly commits himself to an understanding of philosophy as an abstract enterprise, one which aims to rise above the detail and contingency of the world and to deliver timeless, objective, and eternal truths. While this may be an appropriate way of thinking of metaphysics, for instance, or of philosophy of mathematics, it is far from clear that it is the appropriate way to conceive of the enterprise of political philosophy.

To see the difficulty here, recall John Rawls' insistence that 'the aims of political philosophy depend on the society it addresses': Herbert Hart's society was one in which homosexuality was a criminal offence; John Stuart Mill's society was one in which adultery was scandalous and divorce close to impossible; John Locke's society was one in which it was assumed that the magistrate had both a right and a duty to impose religious orthodoxy. It is difficult to believe that, in these cases, the work can properly be assessed without reference to the context in which it was written and the location of the philosopher within that context. Nor, I think, is that a matter for regret. To suppose that political philosophy either can or should be 'pure' in the sense implied by Nagel is to adopt a peculiarly narrow view of the discipline and one which, at least on some accounts, has been damaging to it.

In his essay, 'Political Philosophy and the Analytical Tradition' Bernard Williams identifies a 'law' which, he says, is 'so far as I know exceptionless, but not for all that transparent—that living political philosophy arises only in a context of political urgency' (Williams 2006, 155). And he goes on to associate this 'law' with the uneasy relationship between political philosophy and the analytic tradition: the latter aims to be pure and non-normative, while the former can only be impure and normative. It is, he says, this conflict between the character of political philosophy and the character of analytic philosophy that accounts, in part, for the death of political philosophy during the heyday of the analytic.

But if, as Williams suggests, political philosophy is essentially impure and normative—if, in particular, it arises in contexts of political urgency—then the distinction between it and sociology may be rather less stark than is implied in the correspondence between Nagel, on the one hand, and Blackburn and Waldron on the other. We do not need to concur with Alasdair MacIntyre's insistence that every 'moral philosophy presupposes a sociology' (MacIntyre 1981, 22) in order to doubt whether sociological considerations either can or should be deemed utterly irrelevant to philosophical theories.

Clearly, the issues here run very deep and I have neither the time nor the skill to discuss them in detail. All I want to suggest is that Nagel's insistence on the desirability of keeping philosophical argument pure and untainted by personal and social considerations bespeaks a controversial understanding of the scope and aims of philosophy in general, and an especially questionable understanding of the nature and ambitions of political philosophy—an understanding, moreover, that was implicated in the premature death of political philosophy.

So far, then, I have suggested that Nagel's views reflect a controversial understanding of the relationship between Life and Work, an optimistic commitment to the clarity of the public–private distinction, and a contentious conception of the proper aims and scope of political philosophy. Beyond that (and this is my third theme), I am puzzled by his claim that the increased prurience of modern society is a sign that 'something has gone wrong' (Nagel 2002, 3). It is not clear to me that our society does, in fact, display increased prurience, but even if it does, the conclusion that this is a sign that 'something has gone wrong' requires explanation and defence.

In the next section, I will consider a different possibility—one that calls for direct engagement with the work of H.L.A. Hart and which aims, via the use of a specific example, to explain how an understanding of Hart's personal life might contribute to a fuller understanding of his intellectual and philosophical legacy.

4 The Structure of Liberty

In discussing Gutmann and Thompson's account of the Clarence Thomas affair, I noted that they emphasize the tension between two important liberal values— the value of privacy and the value of publicity. And similarly in commenting on the public–private distinction, I noted Jeremy Waldron's identification of a tension between liberal demands for transparency and liberal commitment to privacy. The fact that liberals embrace values which may conflict is an important and familiar one. Indeed, it is something Nagel himself makes much of in his discussion of Rawls' liberalism when he identifies liberalism as responding to two moral impulses—the impulse to liberty and the impulse to equality. He writes: 'However much is required of the state in a positive direction to curb the development of deep institutional and structural inequalities, it may not violate the basic rights to liberty of individual citizens when carrying out this charge. Putting these impulses together in a coherent theory is not always easy' (Nagel 2002, 89).

However, and despite the famous motto 'freedom for the fox is death for the chicken', the possibility of tension *within* a single value (within the value of liberty, for example) is not often acknowledged. It is that possibility that I now want to explore. The exploration will focus on Hart's famous paper, 'Rawls on Liberty and Its Priority', and my reason for focusing on this paper is that I believe it shows how an understanding of Hart's personal life might illuminate his philosophical legacy.

'Rawls on Liberty and Its Priority' was first published in 1973 and is one of Hart's most famous papers. It is also one of the few papers to which Rawls responded at length, and in his response (Rawls 1993, Lecture VIII) he conceded that Hart had exposed serious difficulties and incompatibilities in *A Theory of Justice*. It is not my intention to rehearse the debate between Hart and Rawls here, but only to draw attention to one part of Hart's critique—the part in which he asks what is meant by Rawls' claim that liberty may be restricted only for the sake of liberty. In discussing this question Hart notes that although there will be some cases in which the notion of limiting liberty for the sake of greater liberty will have application, what is more generally true is that not only the quantity, but the value of liberty must be taken into consideration. He writes: 'But there certainly are important cases of conflict between basic liberties where, as in the simple rules of debate case, the resolution of conflict must involve consideration of the relative *value* of different modes of conduct, and not merely the extent or amount of freedom' (Hart 1973, 543–4, emphasis added).

Additionally, and crucially for Hart, questions about value draw our attention to differences of temperament. He writes: 'suppose the legislator has to determine the scope of the rights of exclusion comprised in the private ownership of land, which is for Rawls a basic liberty, when this basic liberty conflicts with others. Some people may prefer freedom of movement not to be limited by the rights of landowners supported by laws about trespass; others, whether they are landowners or not, may prefer that there be some limitations' (Hart 1973, 546–7). And later in the paper he underlines this consideration when he says 'the most important general point which emerges from these separate criticisms is as follows. Any scheme providing for the general distribution in society of liberty of action necessarily does two things: first, it confers on individuals the advantage of that liberty, but secondly it exposes them to whatever disadvantages the practice of that liberty by others may entail for them' (Hart 1973, 550).

Hart's emphasis on the costs exacted by liberty and on the fact that those costs will be different for people of different temperament has not, I think, received the attention it deserves, nor have its implications been fully explored. In his contribution to this volume Philip Pettit notes Hart's claim that there will not always be a unique answer to questions about basic liberties, and he concurs with the contention that this will, in part, be traceable to differences of temperament, where 'temperament' may refer to the temperament of a society as well as to the temperament of the individuals within that society. He writes: 'Communitarians would argue for allowing householders to extend or decorate their houses but only under common rules of zoning, development, and heritage preservation. And they would argue for giving people the liberty to own guns but only subject to strict rules for the possession and use of firearms; these rules might make it impossible for many people to have access to guns. Rugged individualists would insist that such regulations are unnecessary…they may hail diversity in house styles as attractive' (Pettit 2008, 219).

And as a way of acknowledging these differences, he proposes that basic liberties be understood as 'in a certain sense' culture-specific: all societies will have basic liberties of broadly the same universal character (liberties of speech and of ownership, for example) but those liberties will have fewer associated restrictions in 'ruggedly individualistic' societies than they will have in more communitarian societies. There will, in short, be theme and variation in the application of basic liberties: the themes are the universal values; the variations reflect the culture and mores of the particular society under consideration. So Pettit concludes 'the system of rules in any society, while it may be challenging in some respects, ought to have the minimal fit with social mores that is likely to be required for the system to prove resilient. Thus, the appropriate rules may be subject to a degree of cultural variation' (Pettit 2008, 219–20).

I confess, I do not find this strategy entirely persuasive. For one thing, it is not clear to me how it will 'play out' in multicultural societies where (almost by definition) there is no single set of social mores to be reflected. Beyond that, however, some of the most significant debates about liberty are precisely ones in which the character of the society cannot be antecedently identified as, for example, ruggedly individualist or communitarian, because their overall character is precisely what is at stake. The Hart-Devlin debate about the legal enforcement of morality is, of course, a classic example of this, since it raises questions not only about whether morality can properly be legally enforced but also about what the morality of the society is. As Peter Cane has noted, 'the very establishment of the Wolfenden Committee witnesses to the fact that social attitudes towards homosexuality in Britain were in a state of flux in the 1950s... whereas the Wolfenden Committee said that [homosexual] behaviour was a matter of private morality and not the law's business, others were apparently of the view that it was not morality's business either' (Cane 2006, 27).

The fundamental point here is simply that Pettit's proposal supposes that we first establish whether a society is ruggedly individualist or communitarian, and then take decisions about the rules governing the basic liberties which reflect that assessment. But some societies (multicultural societies, for example) lack a single character, while other societies (Britain in the mid-twentieth century) stand at moral or cultural crossroads. In cases such as these, the appeal to cultural variation can only, and at most, identify the problem. It cannot provide the solution.

Moreover, even if the character of a particular society can be characterized as ruggedly individualist or communitarian, it remains true that decisions about the scope and extent of liberty will exact costs from those individuals whose temperament is 'abnormal' vis-à-vis the society as a whole: communitarian societies exact a price from rugged individualists, and ruggedly individualist societies exact a price from those of a more communitarian temperament. The point is not often fully acknowledged, but it is important, and indeed doubly so if taken in conjunction with a second claim made by Hart—namely that, even if there is no justification for the *legal* enforcement of morality, there is nonetheless room for the preservation of morality by extra-legal methods. In *Law, Liberty, and Morality* he is at pains to emphasize that 'the distinction between the use of coercion to enforce morality and other methods which we in fact use to preserve it, such as argument, advice, and exhortation, is both very important and much neglected' (Hart 1963, 75). And he concludes 'it is a disastrous misunderstanding of morality to think that where we cannot use coercion in its support we must be silent and indifferent' (Hart 1963, 76).

Put simply, the choice for Hart is not a choice between enforcement and endorsement. He is quite open to the legitimacy of preserving the morality of a society by extra-legal means, and indeed he flirts with the idea that society is defined as 'a body of men who hold certain moral views in common' (Hart 1963, 51), but in 'Rawls on Liberty and its Priority' he shows himself to be equally alert to the fact that the preservation of a social morality is not costless, and this is true whatever kind of society one lives in. Hence his astonishment at Rawls' claim that it would be rational to want as large a share of liberty as possible because (Rawls claims) 'no-one suffers from a greater liberty'. 'This', Hart says, 'I find misleading because it seems to miss the vital point that, whatever advantage for any individual there may be in the exercise of some liberty taken in itself, this may be outweighed by the disadvantages for him involved in the general distribution of that liberty in the society of which he is a member' (Hart 1973, 551). Again, liberty exacts costs, and the fact that people have different temperaments, when combined with the fact that societies have social mores which are reflected in their rules and conventions, serves to highlight the inescapability of those costs.

Lacey's biography emphasizes Hart's understanding of himself as 'an outsider on the inside' (Lacey 2004, 2–7). There are several dimensions to this self-understanding: Hart was a Jew in a Christian society (and few parts of that society were more Christian than the University of Oxford); he was a lawyer in a world where the queen of disciplines was philosophy; and he was a homosexual at a time when homosexuality was a criminal offence. His religion, his ethnic origins, his academic expertise, and his sexuality all served to put him 'on the outside' even though he appeared to the wider world to be firmly 'on the inside'. As Lacey puts it:

What is particularly intriguing about Hart's interior life is that, though he would widely be regarded as a quintessential 'insider', the fact is that he felt himself to be very much an outsider. This contrast between his public and private worlds raises fascinating questions not only about Hart's background and personality, but also about the nature of his intellectual creativity and about the quality of the social world, with its various intersecting hierarchies, in which he lived. (Lacey 2004, 3)

The suggestion that Hart was, at root, 'an outsider on the inside' takes us back to 'Rawls on Liberty and Its Priority' and to Hart's recognition that liberty will exact costs from those who are 'outsiders' or who are, in a literal sense, 'abnormal'. He is almost alone in making this point, either against Rawls or more generally, and it may be that his sensitivity to it was due in no small part to the facts of his own personal life. As an outsider on the inside he was well-placed to see that liberty has costs—that a society in which there is extensive freedom of speech, for example, will be one in which the private and retiring person may suffer, or that a society in which there is extensive sexual liberty will be one in which those who prefer to keep such matters to themselves may find that they cannot do so. But he also insisted that the existence of these costs should not lead us to abandon the liberties. He was, as Ronald Dworkin put it, a liberal of temperament.

Of course, it does not follow from this that knowledge of Hart's private life is needed in order to grasp the brute philosophical point he is making in 'Rawls on Liberty and Its Priority'. The fact that a more extensive system of liberties may be costly for some people is one which stands or falls independent of Hart's own character or personal life. Nonetheless, once we do know something of Hart's life, both the point and the significance of his position may be seen more clearly, and if these facts do not substantially alter the content of his argument, they certainly add poignancy to it and prompt us to wonder (again) whether political philosophy is best understood as a series of abstract propositions or whether (as I suspect) it is more fully and richly represented through the lives and contexts that give rise to it.

17

Hart and the Liberalism of Fear

Alan Ryan

1

This paper is celebratory rather than argumentative. Since it celebrates Herbert Hart's liberalism, it implies arguments whose conclusions I rely on without rehearsing them. The most important is that the best (but by no means the only) place to found liberalism is on a commitment to the avoidance of cruelty, especially the cruelty of the state; another is that we should not smuggle liberal values into the definition of democracy: the old view that democracy brings in its train the danger of majority tyranny, especially the tyranny of opinion, is not to be despised, nor disposed of by definitional sleight of hand. I do not think that Ronald Dworkin's conflation of liberal-democracy with democracy *tout court* quite goes so far, but I much prefer the robustness of Schumpeter (Dworkin 1996, Schumpeter 1943). A third is that there is a limit to the extent to which liberal convictions can be reduced to one core value, even that of freedom. Liberalism is a historical phenomenon, and what freedoms liberals concentrate on depends on what they perceive as immediate and urgent threats. Our intuitive sense that one can be an 'x-liberal'—eg a sexual liberal—without being a 'y-liberal'—eg an economic liberal—requires no elaborate defence. Even if a rich homosexual in Texas prior to 2003 resented his tax bill more than the danger of being jailed under the sodomy statute then in force, observers might think that the sodomy statute was an illiberal interference with his sexual freedom while the first was merely a charge for the services of the several governments under which he lived, without which he would have had neither property nor an income to be taxed.

Hart's liberalism was founded on an abhorrence of cruelty; it was in Dita Shklar's sense a liberalism of fear (Shklar 1984); it was distrustful of public opinion—though more systematically distrustful of some strands of elite opinion; and like the political thinking of Hart's contemporaries and colleagues such as Berlin, Hampshire, and Williams, it was built on value-pluralism. Although I argued with Hart at length over many years about the merits of Mill's attempted redefinition of the concept of morality and about its role in founding the right to non-interference, I shan't here pursue that hare (or wild goose). Without resiling

from my view of the importance of Mill's *analytical* enterprise and its connection
with Mill's propagandist aims, I agree that the politically important aspect of
Mill for our concerns a hundred and fifty years later is his recognition of the
irreducible plurality of ultimate values, and that Hart's view of his own affinities
was right.

2007 is not only the centenary of Herbert Hart's birth, but the fiftieth
anniversary of the publication of the Wolfenden Report. These events are closely
connected. Sir John Wolfenden's report adopted as its touchstone for the justification of legislation that criminalized sexual activity between consenting adults a
version of Mill's notorious 'harm principle'. 'In this field, its function, as we see it,
is to preserve public order and decency, to protect the subject from what is offensive or injurious, and to provide sufficient safeguards against exploitation and
corruption of others, particularly those who are specially vulnerable because they
are young, weak in body or mind, inexperienced, or in a state of special physical, official or economic dependence.' (Committee on Homosexual Offences
and Prostitution 1957, ¶ 13) The purpose of the criminal law was not to make
us better people. 'Unless a deliberate attempt is to be made by society, acting
through the agency of the law, to equate the sphere of crime with that of sin, there
must remain a realm of private morality and immorality which is in brief and
crude terms, not the law's business.' (Committee on Homosexual Offences and
Prostitution 1957, ¶ 224) That proposition provoked some energetic reactions:
the most distinguished of those reactions was Lord Devlin's Maccabean Lecture
on 'The Enforcement of Morals'.

Devlin was infinitely far from being a sexual radical, but he was at any rate
a man of unbrutal leanings and in favour of repealing the laws that criminalized homosexual acts between consenting adults in private. Devlin's position was
complicated: he had no doubt that homosexuality was a perversion, and no doubt
that leading boys into corruption was intrinsically criminal; but where corruption was not at issue, he thought the law was clumsy and ineffectual. 'I agree
with everyone who has written or spoken on the subject that homosexuality is
usually a miserable way of life and that it is the duty of society, if it can, to save
any youth from being led into it. I think that duty has to be discharged although
it may mean much suffering by incurable perverts who seem unable to resist the
corruption of boys. But if there is no danger of corruption, I do not think that
there is any good the law can do that outweighs that misery that exposure and
imprisonment causes to addicts who cannot find satisfaction in any other way of
life.' (Devlin 1965, v) He was, however, entirely hostile to the thought that there
was a realm of private morality that ought in principle to be placed beyond the
coercive reach of the law; like other judges of the day, he was attracted to the idea
that acts *contra bonos mores* were criminal at common law, whether or not their
prosecution was prudent.

This was more than an interesting jurisprudential quirk. In a now long forgotten
case, the publisher of *The Ladies Directory*—an illustrated pamphlet advertising

the services of Soho prostitutes—was convicted *inter alia* of conspiracy to corrupt public morals. Not only the judge at first instance, but the Court of Appeal, and then the House of Lords were happy to revive Lord Mansfield's opinion that such an offence existed at common law. Lord Reid stood out alone against his fellow Law Lords. Devlin sided with the majority in a later essay on the subject, arguing that in the last resort the common law provided the resources to criminalize behaviour of a sufficient degree of wickedness whether or not that behaviour harmed anyone. The example of such an act provided by Devlin was writing in praise of homosexuality.

Herbert Hart's attack on Devlin, and thereafter on the House of Lords decision in *Shaw v Director of Public Prosecutions*, first made him something more than a distinguished but not otherwise very visible professor of jurisprudence. It also showed him the master of a polemical style that he had no doubt honed at the bar before the war, in which the most complete courtesy of manner hardly veiled an equally complete contempt for the argumentative capacities of the English judiciary. There are moments in *Law, Liberty, and Morality* when one recalls the unfortunate (and possibly apocryphal) judge who rebuked F E Smith: 'Are you trying to show contempt for this court, Mr Smith?' 'No, m'lud, I am trying to conceal it.' Indeed, Hart's predecessor in the chair of jurisprudence at Oxford was apprehensive that Hart's plainspokenness about the judiciary would imperil relations between them and the Oxford faculty; but Arthur Goodhart was, I think, unique among academic commentators in approving of the judiciary's *démarche* in *Shaw*. Devlin himself complained very mildly only that he had been rebuked 'in rather strong language'. Hart's first foray was in an article in *The Listener*, 'Immorality and Treason', where he pointed out that Devlin's claim that it was the task of law to repress immorality 'as such' was familiar from James Fitzjames Stephen's *Liberty Equality, and Fraternity* and in which he treated the engagement between Wolfenden and Devlin as a variation on the argument between Mill and Stephen (Hart 1969). Devlin was astonished to find that he had plagiarized a work he had never heard of, and as he later recounted in the book that reprinted *Enforcement* and other essays, he set out to find *Liberty, Equality, and Fraternity*; the search was fruitless until he found a battered copy in Holborn Public Library. It was held together with rubber bands; but once he had got into it, Devlin found in Stephen much to admire and endorse.

At this distance, it is hard to recall the climate of the time; that itself is some cause for celebration. There were, as the title of the *Report* suggested, two issues on the Home Office's mind. The first was homosexuality. Statute law criminalizing male to male sexual activity in particular came relatively late. In 1885, Henry Labouchere responded to the widespread panic about underage girls being sold into prostitution by introducing a clause into the Criminal Law Amendment Act to provide that any man who committed an act of 'gross indecency' with another man, whether in public or in private, was guilty of a criminal act punishable by two years at hard labour. Its relevance to underage female prostitution was indirect, but it may have reflected a sense that upper class men had been exploiting working class children of both sexes with impunity. This was the law under which Oscar Wilde was jailed, and under which the great majority of convictions were subsequently secured. The offence of gross indecency was not defined in the statute, and it was left to the jury, assisted by the police, prosecutors, and judge to decide whether whatever it was that had happened was sufficiently disgusting to constitute a criminal offence. The law was a blackmailer's charter, and a standing temptation to the police to engage in entrapment; like most anti-vice legislation, one of its most obvious and predictable effects was to corrupt the police charged with its enforcement.

The second concern for the Home Office was the sense that street-based prostitution had got out of hand, especially in central London. Wolfenden's *Report* treated soliciting as an issue of public order, therein including decency, rather than one of deep moral significance, and the Street Offences Act did more or less what was intended, which was to drive prostitution off the streets of London. It was, of course, the greater difficulty of street-walking that made Shaw's clients resort to printed advertisements.

Homosexual law reform was another matter, though the double context suggests something of the way the Committee saw its job: decency and the avoidance of offence were salient, but neither a rethinking of the ethics of selling sexual services to willing purchasers was so, nor was a concern to allow gays absolute legal equality with their straight fellow citizens. A new Street Offences Act was easy to pass; getting rid of Labouchere's amendment was less easy. It was a decade before the law was changed to decriminalize homosexual acts between consenting adults in private; even then, the final measure was timid: the age of consent was fixed at twenty-one, lowered in stages over the next thirty years to eighteen and then to sixteen. It was also timid inasmuch as, in deference to local sensibilities, the law was initially not changed in Northern Ireland, and was changed subsequently only as the result of a ruling in the European Court of Human Rights.

The pressure to re-examine the law stemmed from the unease induced by the 1954 trial and conviction of Edward Montagu, Michael Pitt-Rivers, and Peter Wildeblood on charges of gross indecency. It was felt by many people that the police had behaved badly, that they had gone out of their way to secure convictions by promising immunity from prosecution to shady characters who might be induced to testify against the defendants. The police had unsuccessfully prosecuted Lord Montagu in 1953 on a charge of gross indecency involving a fourteen-year-old Boy Scout, and it was widely thought that the next prosecution was police revenge for their failure in the 1953 case. In the early 1950s there had been a witch hunt against homosexuals that many observers thought had got out of hand. One underlying cause of the witch hunt was political; when Burgess and Maclean defected to the Soviet Union more than one commentator linked their homosexuality to their political deviancy, and it is said that the CIA leaned on the

British government to root out homosexuals from government service. Connoisseurs of *nemesis* will recall the fate of Senator Joe McCarthy's assistant Roy Cohn. But, the initial post-war crack-down on the public aspects of homosexual life in London antedated those events, and is not easy to explain other than as part of a general desire to return to what was imagined as a more 'respectable' pre-war era.

Even before Lord Montagu and his friends had been convicted, there were discussions among politicians, clergy, and others about the potential for barbarity inherent in the existing law. The criminal law with respect to homosexuality was in part based on the 1861 Offences Against the Person Act, and enshrined a very old common-law prohibition of buggery that had been enshrined in statute in the 1533 Act Against Buggery which was itself repealed and re-enacted over the years; the law was modified in 1817 to distinguish—as much American law does not—between buggery in the proper sense and genital-oral sex, and modified again in 1861 to take buggery off the list of capital offences. Buggery remained punishable under some circumstances by life imprisonment even after the 1967 Sexual Offences Act got rid of Labouchere's amendment. It was also illegal without distinction of sex, and like other assaults could not be consented to, even as between husband and consenting wife. The law was not fully tidied up until 2002, when the absence of consent became the crucial feature of almost all sexual offences, other than bestiality, which was made a specific offence rather than being swept up with other forms of buggery.

The *Report* took three years to compile. Home Office anxieties about the effect on their office staff of having to type material relating to homosexuals and prostitutes were so acute that they were referred to as 'Huntleys' and 'Palmers' (Ryan 2007). The committee was made up of impeccably respectable persons, including the head of the Glasgow Girl Guides; with one dissenting opinion it came down on the side of decriminalizing homosexual acts done in private between consenting adults. In doing so, it repudiated the bulk of psychiatric and medical opinion presented to it; one nowadays forgets how nearly unanimous medical opinion was that homosexuality was deviant not just in the sense of being a minority taste but in constituting an illness. The Committee was more sensible, arguing that the only symptom of the supposed illness was the homosexuality itself; for the purposes of everyday life, homosexuals functioned as effectively as heterosexuals, and did not need to be 'cured' of anything. It was, of course, patently crazy to think that locking up a male homosexual in the company of other men was likely to induce a change of sexual allegiance. One might as well try to cure an alcoholic by locking him up in a distillery.

The Conservative government of the day very much disliked the part of the *Report* concerned with homosexuality, and the then Home Secretary immediately rejected its proposals. It didn't help matters that a junior minister was coincidentally arrested for having sex with a guardsman in St James's Park. Nor did it help that substantial numbers of Tory backbenchers shared Blackstone's view that the crime against nature was not fit to be named and certainly not fit to be discussed in Parliament. What they did or did not remember of what had happened in their boarding schools after 'Lights Out' defies speculation. But they were not eager for a handbagging from the blue-rinsed hangers and floggers of their constituency associations for excessive kindness to lipstick-wearing nancy boys. It is unkind to single out Tory backbenchers; at the time of the passage of the 1967 Act, Richard Crossman confided to his diary that he shared his constituents' doubts about Labour MPs spending their time attending to the welfare of buggers in Westminster rather than the unemployed in Coventry. Labour MPs for heavily Catholic areas had their own grounds for anxiety. On the other hand, nobody felt quite comfortable about what had happened to people like Peter Wildeblood, a quiet, harmless, respectable, and timid literary editor banged up for eighteen months in the company of a lot of illiterate thugs sent to the Scrubs on their third or fourth conviction for GBH. That looked like gratuitous cruelty. And mounting evidence of police corruption subverted confidence in the law and those who enforced it. Nonetheless, no Tory government could act, and sexual scandals both gay and straight kept on derailing the argument, especially because they almost invariably involved issues of national security. The opposition of elderly military figures also got in the way—Field Marshal Montgomery feared a 'brush fire' of homosexuality sweeping the land if the law was relaxed. So things advanced pretty slowly until the inevitable outcome.

2

That, at all events, is the background against which Hart took on Devlin in a return bout of *Mill v Stephen*; but when Hart delivered the Harry Camp Lectures at Stanford in 1962 and published them as *Law, Liberty, and Morality*, the UK legislation decriminalizing homosexual acts between consenting adults was five years off, the Federal Government would not change its rules automatically dismissing anyone suspected of homosexuality until 1975, and the Supreme Court's decisive judgment in the Texas sodomy case was forty years in the future (*Lawrence et al v Texas* 2003). The way Hart approached the relations of law and morality in the lectures reflected not only his doubts about the potential for cruelty in legislation on sexual matters but his commitment to the positivist separation of law and morals that he had defended against Lon Fuller some years before, and in *The Concept of Law*. We need not take sides on those jurisprudential issues beyond acknowledging a distinction between *critical* and *positive* morality.

In what follows, I rehearse Devlin's criticisms of Wolfenden and by implication of Mill, then Hart's criticisms of Devlin and Stephen; then I venture a few observations about some of the interesting topics that Mill said nothing about but that Hart was deeply, but somewhat opaquely, concerned with: such as decency, privacy, and sexual identity. Devlin said in the preface to *Enforcement*—the book contains seven essays—that he 'had read with complete approval its [the

Report's] formulation of the functions of the criminal law in matters of morality' (Devlin 1965, v). As we have seen, the *Report's* remit had a lot to do with sparing people encounters with offensive and indecent conduct; the *Report* recommended changes to the law, not the wholesale reconstruction of conventional views about either the Huntleys or the Palmers. The committee was not hospitable to—for instance—the view later put forward by Robert Nozick that persons possessed an indefeasible freehold interest in their own bodies, so that they are entitled to engage in whatever sexual activities they choose, either from affection or for financial reasons, subject always to the condition that all parties freely consent to what goes on.

This opened the door to Devlin. The committee did not ask Mill's question in Mill's terms. He had asked whether the 'likings and dislikings' of mankind should be allowed to decide whether an individual should be coerced into behaving in some particular fashion or be threatened with ill consequences if he did other than he was required. Mill's answer was straightforward. Likings and dislikings had no moral authority. Moral disapproval must rest on a well-founded judgement that the conduct from which someone was to be deterred was calculated to cause harm to others, or in the alternative to damage their interests, or in another variation to undermine arrangements that enhanced everyone's lives on a fair-shares basis. 'Mere' likings and dislikings got short shrift, and decency was dealt with in half a sentence. The *Report* did not engage in moral philosophy; I no longer regret the fact, and not because Sir John Wolfenden and his committee would have made a mess of the task. Common sense would have carried them a long way. The *Report* prescinded from moral argument; the thought was that whether or not homosexual conduct was intrinsically wicked and/or disgusting, it was not offensive if done privately, and if allowed only between consenting adults it was not likely to 'corrupt' those who took part, since their 'corruption', if it was that, was established. In Millian terms, there were no unconsenting victims. Nonetheless, the committee's evasion of the contentious question—*was* there anything intrinsically wrong with homosexual relations, given the committee's view that they were not evidence of mental illness?—allowed Devlin to conflate three questions: how much do (most) people dislike some activity or other, whether it be buggery, incest, bigamy, or sex between persons of the same sex; what is the basis of their dislike; and how are we to strike a balance between the wishes of those whose conduct is restricted and those who would be distressed if the restrictions were to be removed? Devlin eventually, if awkwardly, disentangled those questions, but at the cost of embroiling himself in some complex sociological and philosophical issues.

It is worth distinguishing Devlin's view from the agreeably vulgar populism that is energetically defended by Justice Scalia when sodomy cases come before the Supreme Court: in a democracy, the majority has *ceteris paribus* the right to legislate as it chooses. Only where some clear-cut provision of the Constitution is violated, is there any limit to that authority. If the majority wants to criminalize

oral sex, that's that. I am not hostile to that view as a matter of jurisprudence;
democracies are capable of behaving in stupid and oppressive ways, and a positivist
is likely to think that what the local legislature enacts as law *is* by and large law.
Fitzjames Stephen came close to the Scalia doctrine, but did not quite endorse
it, and the same was true of Devlin. Scalia is concerned for the constitutionality of *statute*, but the argument put forward by Devlin was about the common
law's hospitality to the moral intuitions of English juries. Devlin, like Stephen,
handed the issue to the jury, 'the man on the Clapham omnibus'. If the man
on the Clapham omnibus felt strongly enough that conduct alleged to be criminal was indeed criminal, that showed that 'the limits of toleration' were being
reached. The awkwardness of this argument is obvious: it confuses the empirical
and the normative. It is one thing to observe that juries will do their best to jail
people whose behaviour they dislike, and another to suggest that they are right to
do so. The 'limits of toleration' might mean either that we have reached the point
at which the local population will for whatever reason react coercively, or that
we have reached the point at which it would be right to do so. Conflating the
sociological *is* with the normative *ought* is a recipe for confusion.

Devlin had what emerged as two distinct views that he initially did not distinguish; the first that strong sentiments of revulsion were *evidence* that a practice
was somehow bad for a society, the other that a society was *constituted* by widely
shared sentiments of this sort. The second is, or can be made to be, a more or less
Durkheimian view, and with a little pushing and tugging can be made to support the first view. A society on this view is not constituted simply as an enterprise for mutual protection, but it is structured around a conception of 'normal'
behaviour. If people behave *non-normally*, they undermine social cohesion. The
positive morality of a society is *constitutive* of the society. Given Durkheim's view
of the coercive nature of the *conscience collective*, the line between law and positive morality will in all societies but the most modern be pretty blurred. Nor is
it surprising that morals should be backed up by metaphysics—that homosexuality, for instance, should be condemned as unnatural; all societies endeavour
to enshrine their moral convictions in a conception of the way in which the natural order is structured. The conflation of morals and metaphysics is not a quirk
that western legal systems have inherited from Leviticus and Deuteronomy, but
part of the apparatus for the preservation of good order that all societies employ.
Mary Douglas's *Purity and Danger* and *Natural Symbols* were written in that
Durkheimian mode, and one is much more likely to understand why people
couch so much of their moral condemnation in terms such as *disgusting* or *corrupt* by reading Mary Douglas than by reading Mill or Hart. It is important that
Hart took it for granted that people had such reactions and did not dig further
into the question of what such feelings were based on. Hart took the *Report* on its
own terms.

The thought that animated Devlin and sparked off Hart's reaction in his
Listener article was that there was no distinction between private morality and

public morality; trying to understand what Devlin meant is made no easier by Devlin's conflation of immorality and sin and his view that the clergy were 'experts' on ethics. Because Devlin saw morality as a system of requirements and prohibitions that gained their authority from a source—divine commandment— rather than from their content, the distinction that Mill drew between what concerns ourselves only and what concerns others had no force. The question was whether conduct had been divinely required or prohibited. Viewed in that light, there is no such thing as 'private morality'. If one drops God out of the equation and replaces him with the *conscience collective*, nothing changes. All morality is public, because conceptions of right and wrong, the tolerable and intolerable, the pure and the filthy, the decent and the indecent, form our identities and 'hold society together'. As we saw, Devlin insisted that a society was a community of ideas. These ideas are its morality. He went on to equate the depth of feeling behind convictions of the wrongness of homosexuality and other forms of sexual deviation as a sign that these were 'spiritual' convictions, about which I shall say something later. The task of a jury was to decide whether the breach of this common, or public, sense of moral order was severe enough to demand punishment.

3

Hart's assault depended on nothing more elaborate than making Devlin draw distinctions that did not come naturally to him, but which came naturally to anyone practising philosophy in the 1950s mode. Was the jury supposed to consult only its own reactions? This was the view that what made the plain man sick was illegal. If the jury was supposed to stand back and reflect on its reactions, with what apparatus? What ethical standards was it supposed to apply? Or was it not supposed to apply ethical reasoning, but something closer to sociological analysis, to consider whether society would be undermined by a failure to enforce uniformity in whatever area was at stake? The Obscene Publications Act of 1959 asked the jury to do both these things; they first had to decide whether an item would tend to deprave and corrupt its readers or viewers and then whether it nonetheless had such artistic merit that it should be published. This is how *Lady Chatterley's Lover* finally got past the censors; the jury decided that in spite of the risks to the morals of our wives, daughters, and maidservants to which the Attorney General drew the jury's attention, the book's literary merits justified publication. The question of exactly what form of depravity and corruption its reading would lead to was never clearly established in this or any other case. The only case I know of where someone willingly avowed that they had been corrupted was particularly absurd: Sir Basil Blackwell claimed that *Last Exit to Brooklyn* had corrupted him. What he meant was that he felt the book was filthy and that some of the filth had washed off on him; it is unlikely that he meant to suggest that he had become a less reliable partner in the matter of buying and selling books.

Devlin was unlike Fitzjames Stephen in one respect. Stephen was a utilitarian; he had no doubt that it was the task of the political and legal system to advance the welfare of the population for whom the government and the judiciary were responsible, and that the interesting question was how they might best achieve it. Mill was a renegade utilitarian, since he wanted to set barriers in the way of the robust, no nonsense, no holds barred promotion of the general welfare that Stephen thought right. The man on the Clapham omnibus was a better guide to what would promote the general well-being and what was in the interests of the public. Mill's wish to protect obnoxious individuals from the rigours of the law so long as they did not actively damage the interests of others was a needless complication. Sexual conduct of any sort was not something Stephen would discuss at all; he hardly dared tackle Mill's arguments in *The Subjection of Women* because all talk about intimate relations between the sexes was indecent. This squeamishness did not prevent him fathering ten children. Like others who have wanted to combine a conservative tenderness for uniformity of opinion with a progressive and rationalist view of the way the law might promote the public welfare, Stephen had some difficulty in knowing just what the argument from the man on the Clapham omnibus was supposed to achieve, but one can construct some arguments that do not fall straight down the hole labelled 'if it makes the average member of the public sick, it is illegal'.

One is that the maintenance of a consensus on moral issues makes for general happiness by reassuring us about the way in which other people can be expected to behave. Another is that philosophical inquiry into the bases of right and wrong gets into difficulties that the plain man's intuitions do not. A third is that an element of moral paternalism is essential. There will be some people who hold out against the moral consensus, and suffer for it, but many more will find the suasion of legal and moral pressure helpful. There is no sociological finesse in Stephen, other than a very rough and ready acceptance of a form of social evolution, so there is no anticipation of, say, the views of Durkheim. Nor is there any tenderness towards Christianity and its role in creating or stabilizing the moral sentiments of the English. Stephen's arguments are meticulously—to the extent that meticulousness was his mode—reversible; it is as permissible for the Romans to execute anyone who mocked the auguries as for an English court to convict a man of blasphemous libel.

The burden of Hart's argument against Devlin was that the claim that *all* morality is public in any sense that elides the distinction between what is 'done in private' and 'done in public' was misguided. Certainly, the whole ensemble of ideas that constituted the positive morality of the British public was the possession of the public and a public phenomenon. But at least one element in the conventional morality of the British public was a concern for privacy and hostility to its invasion. Hart relied, as anyone must, on a simple distinction between positive and critical morality analogous to Bentham's distinction between positive and censorial jurisprudence. If restrictions on people's behaviour are *ceteris paribus* a bad thing because they stop people doing what they choose to do and either cause distress or reduce happiness, Hart's question was whether the good done by restricting freedom in sexual matters was sufficient to justify the distress that restriction caused. Taking a view endorsed by Bentham himself, though one he never published, Hart emphasized the peculiarly intense misery that criminalization of people's sexual preferences entailed. Unlike the urge to steal or to murder, which are rarely part of a person's deepest personal characteristics, sexual desire is notoriously just that. Frustrating its satisfaction causes particular pain and hurt. The conclusion followed that the Wolfenden Report was right in its recommendations.

Had the matter ended there, it would have been one more battle between those who wanted to reduce the role of the criminal law in sexual matters and those who felt vaguely that if the law did not criminalize a good deal of behaviour that was private in the sense of done 'in private' or done between consenting adults, something terrible would happen. It did not end there. One of Hart's arguments was that Devlin's insistence that society was a community of ideas and that it would fall apart if that community was not maintained was equivocal. If society is *defined* by its current set of ideas and attachments, a change in those ideas means the dissolution of the society and its replacement by another society, defined by *its* ideas. But then, it does not seem to matter if society is dissolved, since it will be replaced by a closely adjacent society; indeed, few people would notice the process of dissolution and reconstitution. If the claim was not that society was constituted by its ideas definitionally, but that a society would fall to pieces in some more familiar way—rioting in the streets, the impossibility of transacting business, a constant danger of violence, all the things that Hobbes ascribed to the state of nature—if the law retracted its coercive support for the moral convictions of the right-minded man, then the claim was incredible. In any event, there were some societies that might be better off disintegrating; that Hitler's regime would have collapsed if nobody had believed in the racial inferiority of Jews might or might not be true, but the collapse of Hitler's regime would itself have been a good thing.

Devlin reacted by taking the sociological route; the right-minded member of the jury was to consult his sentiments and to answer the question whether those sentiments sprang from, or were attached to, a well-founded belief that society would come to harm if the behaviour towards which they were directed was allowed. He somewhat simplified the task by reiterating more than once that the question the member of the jury must ask was a simple factual question: what was the public morality of the day? Of course, the question was not simple, but highly speculative: how much of that morality might be eroded before damage—that is, damage other than the change in moral sentiment itself—was done? Arguing in this fashion was embracing a lost cause. Unless he retreated to the definitional strategy of asserting the coincidence between society and its current moral attachments, Devlin was letting himself be drawn onto the moral terrain of the secular utilitarian. On that, he was sure to be defeated.

Devlin's more effective tactic was not to defend a positive case but to point out the implausibility of Hart's explanations of those parts of the law that Hart had no quarrel with. On the issue of not allowing consent as a defence against charges of the commission of violent assault, Devlin could at best hope for a draw. If I were to encourage my sadistic lover to inflict mild but definite damage on me, the law would still not excuse him (or her) from the charge of ABH; Hart's view was that the point of the law was to refuse to allow murderers the defence of consent, since a dead victim could not testify to the genuineness of his consent, and could not testify that his killer had not simply gone too far in playing rough games to which the victim had, initially, been a willing party. This is perfectly plausible. Where Devlin has more of a chance is in areas that most philosophers hesitate to risk themselves on: incest, bigamy, and bestiality for instance.

4

Hart accepted without much further discussion that the law might properly be used to spare people shock, although this was giving hostages to fortune; he also allowed a role for paternalistic coercion, and acknowledged that he was moving away from Mill's uncompromising opposition to coercion for our own good. Among the fascinating subjects he did not further engage with, one is the question of where the onus lies to avoid shock; old jokes about elderly ladies who complain that if they stand on the edge of the bath, and peer through the window, they can see something shocking going on next door that clearly ought to be stopped make a simple point. But it is not a wholly simple question what we should say about people who take advantage of other people's shockability to inflict distress on them. I shall shortly say a few speculative things about the realm of the shocking, disgusting, obscene, or whatever we might choose to call it, and then deploy a final paragraph in celebratory mode to say something about Hart's positive views. Devlin focused, quite rightly, on topics where Hart's utilitarian analysis of the point of the criminal law ran into trouble. Sometimes Hart seemed unwilling to employ some fairly simple pieces of apparatus to secure his position; but sometimes simple apparatus does not do the trick. Thus with bigamy, Hart suggested that the law prohibiting bigamy was a way of avoiding outrage to persons with deeply religious sensibilities. But, as Devlin said, the proportion of the population who saw marriage as a sacrament and bigamy as a sort of blasphemy was not very high. The simple route is Millian or Benthamite; societies need some institutionalized way of allocating the care of children and the passing of property, and marriage is one element of it; what a society *counts* as a valid marriage is a local option. What is not a local option is the need to make people follow whatever the local rules are once those rules exist.

If we were to allow—say—a variation under which a man might take two wives with the consent of each, and a woman might take two husbands with the consent of each, there might well be some interesting complexities about the sorts of family that such arrangements would produce, but the idea of organizing married life in such a way would not be *shocking*. However, in virtue of being a legal arrangement which entailed rights and obligations of the familiar sort, it would still have to be policed to ensure that people weren't taken advantage of to their detriment. The objection to bigamy generally speaking is that a man has more often than not taken a good many more than two unsuspecting women for a ride, financially and emotionally. There is a Millian wrinkle to the argument. Since it is optional what forms of privileged cohabitation a society enshrines in law, there will be arguments for monogamy in modern societies such as ours that might not make anything like the same sense in very different, less economically developed societies. We—mostly—have a view about the possibilities of companianate marriage that might well lead us to privilege monogamous marriage; these ideals were not shared in the ancient world. The intellectual apparatus required to explain the wrongness of bigamy applies *ceteris paribus* to the explanation of the law's unwillingness to enforce contracts for immoral purposes; and what cannot be explained in those terms is by and large indefensible as in the case of the old rule that prevented a landlord from suing for his rent if he knowingly let his property to an unmarried couple.

Now for the difficult argument. To my eye, Hart never offered a satisfactory answer to Devlin's query about what one might describe as the Leviticus shopping list (*Leviticus* 17–21): things described as *abominations*. Take the prohibition on incest. Suppose brother–sister twins in their twenties go to the opera and are swept away by *Die Valküre*, ending the evening by consummating their affection for one another. Are we really outraged by the idea? Do we regard *Wälsungenblut*, the short story by Thomas Mann in which exactly this incident occurs, as obscene? There are good reasons of policy for prohibiting incestuous liaisons, though many of those reasons relate to the incapacity of young children to give their free and unforced consent to sexual relations rather than to incest itself. Those who are outraged by incest are not, I think, outraged because they recall the blood-curdling prohibitions in Leviticus. They are outraged because, roughly, we draw very sharp lines between licit and illicit sexual partners. Take the prohibition on bestiality; it is not obvious that it rests on a concern for cruelty to animals, though it is certainly true that the animal is a non-consenting partner, so bestiality violates the principle that all sexual relations should be consensual. The principle to which these prohibitions seem to pay allegiance is 'you can't do that sort of thing with that sort of partner'. One reason for thinking that morality has little to do with the matter is that if sex with the wrong sort of entity is one of the great areas of line-drawing and absolute prohibition marked by terms like 'abomination' and 'disgusting', the other is defecation. Nobody thinks that defecation as such is *malum in se*, as Devlin would have put it. But defecating in the middle of a crowded street is another matter entirely. 'Not that there', we say.

None of this would be of any great interest if it was not for the fact that it is precisely to these requirements and prohibitions that our most uncontrollable and violent reactions are attached. The so-called 'yuck' response is attached most readily to bodily fluids, the display of human organs, and—again roughly—to those things where we have a very strong sentiment of 'not in that form' or 'not here'. One philosopher who picked up this point was Hannah Arendt, who disapproved of space travel on the grounds that the earth was not meant to be seen from outside so to speak, just as the bodily organs were not meant to be seen on public display. The row over Gunther von Hagens' 'plastinated' human (and other) bodies, as also some of Damien Hirst's pickled animals suggests that Ms Arendt picked up, as she often did, a familiar reaction. Here, too, it is worth remembering that *where* any of this happens is crucial; we do not complain of the blood and gore of an operating theatre, but of it being put on public display. The only point I want to make, however, is that our intensity of reaction has nothing to do with 'spiritual' considerations. There is an interesting question, to which I have no answer, about the indispensability of some such drawing of lines in the process of turning infants into adult human beings. In Kant's anthropology, which secularized *Genesis* to considerable effect, covering our sexual organs and acquiring a sense of shame is the first step in becoming *human*. No particular set of devices to enforce the human/animal binary seems to be uniquely required, but the existence of *some* set of such devices is. If there is such a device, it needs to be ingrained in the consciousness of small children so that it takes with sufficient strength. I was surprised forty years ago, and remain surprised now, that Hart was not interested in the genesis and nature of taboo. The fact was that he was not. And yet, our ideas about what is private, intimate, not to be invaded must certainly as a matter of their genesis have a lot to do with the way in which we are taught as children to treat our faeces as something other than playthings and to control our infantile polymorphic sexual impulses. Since Hart's most eloquent defence of the *Report*'s conclusions relied on the intensity of the misery caused by invasions of privacy, one might have expected more curiosity than he displayed.

This would not have undermined a liberal and humane view of the legal regulation of sexual conduct; the persecution of adult homosexuals was manifestly a bad thing for humanitarian reasons—as well as because the law tended to corrupt the police. It would not, on the other hand, have strengthened it either. He briefly took an interest in Durkheim's distinction between mechanical and organic solidarity, and someone who wanted to maintain a strongly liberal view about the sanctity of private life while acknowledging the insights, real or supposed, of the sociology of law could have found worse places to start. He did not pursue the matter. It was enough that a liberal would approach the criminal law in relation to sexual activity with one question in mind—does it prevent more harm than it causes?—and would have an acute sense of the harm done by the law in a sensitive area of life. There are, of course, areas where the question is hard to answer and knowing when to invoke the criminal law is very difficult; it is notoriously hard to draw up sensible rules for the age of consent—itself a very modern idea—and catch the forty-year-old preying on gullible twelve-year-old girls while not jailing an excited seventeen-year-old who has had sex with a sophisticated fifteen-year-old. As to the complexities of accommodating the different, but equally intense, reactions of persons from different cultures in a supposedly multicultural Britain, there is no room here to say more than that there is no room here to say anything.

The subject of sex and the law is inexhaustible, and *Law, Liberty, and Morality* is a very short book which mostly criticizes the attitudes of the English judiciary of the day; it seems proper to end with Hart's contribution, not to the subject of law and sex, but to liberal ideas about law. One reason he drew on Mill's ideas in the essay *On Liberty* and yet devoted little effort to refining or extending them was that he took two things for granted. The first was that law is an immensely useful device for making our lives predictable and manageable; only with an efficient regime of, for instance, property rights and rules for the making and enforcing of contracts, can we make the most of our talents and energies, and provide people with the incentive to develop their abilities and with the scope to expand their tastes and interests. This view permeates *On Liberty*. It comes with a health warning. Rights and rules are intended to enable us to constrain each other to act and forbear in predictable ways; although rights and rules should not be defined in terms of coercive force, they must be liberty-limiting in order to be choice-expanding, and a system of rights and rules could not function if no coercive mechanism backed it up. We expand the range of things we can do at the price of making it risky to break our obligations. Moreover, the machinery which we have to employ to preserve predictability is in obvious ways somewhat clumsy. It takes no great insight to see Hart's impact on the report of the Committee on Obscenity that Bernard Williams chaired in the mid-seventies.

The second is that anyone who understands the world in these terms is well on the way to understanding that we are, or at least can become, creatures who pursue an open-ended and indefinite variety of goals. An appreciation of the variousness of the ends that might be pursued by both ourselves and others is both an aid to happiness in itself and a curb on the urge to force any particular lifestyle on others, save when self-defence, good order, and a minimal degree of protection against self-harm demand it. Hart's liberalism was not libertarian in the American sense; he did not see the world in terms that gave property rights priority, nor did he think property rights a model for all rights in the way the Nozick of *Anarchy* did. It certainly rested on a Hobbesian or Berlinian concern for negative or 'let-alone' liberty, but that did not preclude the pursuit of all sorts of goals to which liberty might have to be sacrificed; moderate redistributive measures of the kind pursued by the postwar Labour government required the trading off of liberty and either equality for its own sake or welfare on the assumption that the worse-off would gain more than the better-off would lose. Because he accepted that there was a plurality of acceptable ends, Hart did not attempt to show that curtailing the amount of money people could derive from the sale of their services or whatever else was not 'really' a curtailing of their liberty; rather, the liberal was recognizable as the person who set a specially high value on minimizing not only coercion in general but particularly the more intrusive and invasive kinds of coercion, and who was reluctant to pursue any one value *à l'outrance*. On my reading of the matter, this is not the only way to be a liberal, but it is a particularly good way to be one, and sustained a delicacy and a deftness of touch that not all writers on these subjects have managed.

Bibliography of Works Cited

Alldridge, Peter. 1990. 'Rules for Courts and Rules for Citizens.' 10 *Oxford Journal of Legal Studies* 487–504.

Allen, James (ed). *Without Sanctuary: Lynching Photography in America*. Santa Fe, NM: Twin Palms.

Altman, Andrew and Wellman, Christopher. 2004. 'A Defense of International Criminal Law.' 115 *Ethics* 35–67.

American Heritage Dictionary of the English Language. 1992. Third Edition. Boston: Houghton Mifflin.

Anscombe, Elizabeth. 1957. *Intention*. Oxford: Blackwell.

Anscombe, Elizabeth. 1958. 'Modern Moral Philosophy.' 33 *Philosophy* 1–19.

Aquinas, Thomas. 1959. *Selected Political Writings*. Edited by A P d'Entreves. Oxford: Basil Blackwell.

Arendt, Hannah. 1973. *On Revolution*. Harmondsworth: Penguin Books.

Aristotle. 1996. *Politics*. Translated by Stephen Everson. Cambridge: Cambridge University Press.

Ashworth, Andrew. 2002. 'Testing Fidelity to Legal Values: Official Involvement and Criminal Justice.' In Stephen Shute and Andrew Simester (eds), *Criminal Law Theory: Doctrines of the General Part*. Oxford: Oxford University Press.

Austin, JL. 1962. *How to Do Things with Words*. Cambridge, MA: Harvard University Press.

Baier, Annette. 1980. 'The Rights of Past and Future Persons.' In Ernest Partridge (ed), *Responsibilities to Future Generations*. Buffalo, NY: Prometheus Books.

Barker, Craig. 2007. 'The Politics of International Law-Making: Constructing Security in Response to Global Terrorism.' 3 *Journal of International Law and International Relations* 5–29.

Baron, Marcia. 2005. 'Justifications and Excuses.' 2 *Ohio State Journal of Criminal Law* 387–413.

Bazelon, David. 1976. 'The Morality of the Criminal Law.' 49 *Southern California Law Review* 385–405.

Benfer, Amy. 2002. 'What is So Bad about Good Sex?' URL: http://archive.salon.com/mwt/feature/2002/04/19/levine_talks/index.html.

Bennett, Jonathan. 1988. *Events and their Names*. Oxford: Oxford University Press.

Bentham, Jeremy. 1776. 'Preparatory Principle.' Bentham Manuscripts, University College London. Box LXIX, Folios 70–75.

Bentham, Jeremy. 1838–43. *Works*. Edited by John Bowring. Eleven volumes. Edinburgh: William Tait.

Bentham, Jeremy. 1970a. *Introduction to the Principles of Morals and Legislation*. Edited by J H Burns and H L A Hart. London: Athlone Press.

Bentham, Jeremy. 1970b. *Of Laws in General*. Edited by H L A Hart. London: Athlone Press.

Bentham, Jeremy. 1977. '*Comment on the Commentaries*' and '*A Fragment on Government*'. Edited by J H Burns and H L A Hart. London: Athlone Press.

Bentham, Jeremy. 1996. *Introduction to the Principles of Morals and Legislation*. Edited by J H Burns and H L A Hart. Oxford: Clarendon Press.

Bentham, Jeremy. 1998. *Legislator of the World: Writings on Codification, Law, and Education*. Edited by Philip Schofield and Jonathan Harris. Oxford: Clarendon Press.

Berman, Harold. 1983. *Law and Revolution*. Cambridge, MA: Harvard University Press.

Berman, Mitchell. 2003. 'Justification and Excuse, Law and Morality.' 53 *Duke Law Journal* 1–78.

Besson, Samantha and Tasioulas, John (eds). 2008. *Philosophy of International Law*. Oxford: Oxford University Press.

Black, Max. 1956. 'Why Cannot an Effect Precede Its Cause?' 16 *Analysis*, 49–58.

Blackstone, Sir William. 1765–9. *Commentaries on the Laws of England*. 4 volumes. Oxford: Clarendon Press. Available at the following URL: <http://www.yale.edu/lawweb/avalon/blackstone/blacksto.htm>.

Bohannan, Paul. 1965. 'The Differing Realms of Law.' 67 *American Anthropologist* 33–42.

Bolling v Sharpe. 1954. 347 *United States Reports* 497–500.

Braithwaite, John and Pettit, Philip. 1990. *Not Just Deserts: A Republican Theory of Criminal Justice*. Oxford: Oxford University Press.

Brett, Annabel. 1997. *Liberty, Right, and Nature*. Cambridge: Cambridge University Press.

Brophy, Alfred. 2002. *Reconstructing the Dreamland*. New York: Oxford University Press.

Brown v Board of Education. 1954. 347 *United State Reports* 483–96.

Buchanan, Allen and Golove, David. 2002. 'The Philosophy of International Law.' In Coleman and Shapiro 2002.

Burns, Robert. 1999. *A Theory of the Trial*. Princeton NJ: Princeton University Press.

Califia, Pat. 1994. 'Feminism and Sadomasochism.' In *Public Sex: The Culture of Radical Sex*. Pittsburgh: Cleis.

Callahan, Joan. 1987. 'On Harming the Dead.' 97 *Ethics* 341–52.

Campbell, Kenneth. 1987. 'Offence and Defence.' In Ian Dennis (ed), *Criminal Law and Justice*. London: Sweet & Maxwell.

Cane, Peter. 2006. 'Taking Law Seriously: Starting Points of the Hart/Devlin Debate.' 10 *Journal of Ethics* 21–51.

Carnap, Rudolf. 1950. *The Logical Foundations of Probability*. Chicago: University of Chicago Press.

Carter, Ian. 1999. *A Measure of Freedom*. Oxford: Oxford University Press.

Casey, John. 1971. 'Actions and Consequences.' In John Casey (ed), *Morality and Moral Reasoning*. London: Methuen.

Christodoulidis, Emilios. 2004. 'The Objection that Cannot be Heard: Communication and Legitimacy in the Courtroom.' In Antony Duff, Lindsay Farmer, Sandra Marshall, and Victor Tadros (eds), *The Trial on Trial I: Truth and Due Process*. Oxford: Hart Publishing.

Christopher, Russell. 1995. 'Unknowing Justification and the Logical Necessity of the *Dadson* Principle in Self-Defense.' 15 *Oxford Journal of Legal Studies* 229–51.

Civil Rights Act. 1875. 18 *United States Statutes at Large* 335–7.

Civil Rights Act. 1964. 78 *United States Statutes at Large* 241–68.

Civil Rights Cases. 1883. 109 *United States Reports* 3–62.

Cohen, Andrew Jason. 2004. 'What Toleration Is.' 115 *Ethics* 68–95.

Cohen, Gerald. 1979. 'Capitalism, Freedom, and the Proletariat.' In Alan Ryan (ed), *The Idea of Freedom*. Oxford: Oxford University Press.

Cohen, Gerry. 1989. 'On the Currency of Egalitarian Justice.' 99 *Ethics* 906–44.

Coke, Sir Edward. 1628. *Institutes of the Laws of England*. 3 volumes. London: Society of Stationers.

Coleman, Jules. 1982. 'Negative and Positive Positivism.' 11 *Journal of Legal Studies* 139–64.

Coleman, Jules. 2001a. 'Incorporationism, Conventionality, and the Practical Difference Thesis.' In Jules Coleman (ed), *Hart's Postscript: Essays on the Postscript of 'The Concept of Law'*. Oxford: Oxford University Press.

Coleman, Jules. 2001b. *The Practice of Principle*. Oxford: Oxford University Press.

Coleman, Jules and Shapiro, Scott. 2002. *Oxford Handbook of Jurisprudence and Philosophy of Law*. Oxford: Oxford University Press.

Collingwood, R G. 1999. *The Principles of History and Other Writings in Philosophy of History*. Edited by W H Dray and W J Van der Dussen. New York: Oxford University Press.

Collins, John; Hall, Ned; and Paul, Laurie. 2004a. 'Counterfactuals and Causation: History, Problems, and Prospects.' In Collins, Hall, and Paul 2004b.

Collins, John; Hall, Ned; and Paul, Laurie (eds). 2004b. *Causation and Counterfactuals*. Cambridge, MA: MIT Press.

Committee on Homosexual Offences and Prostitution. 1957. *Report of the Committee on Homosexual Offences and Prostitution*. London: Her Majesty's Stationery Office.

Constitution of the United States. 1789.

Cotterrell, Roger. 1995. *Law's Community*. Oxford: Oxford University Press.

Crisp, Roger. 1997. *Mill on Utilitarianism*. London: Routledge.

Crisp, Roger. 2006. *Reasons and the Good*. Oxford: Oxford University Press.

Cruft, Rowan. 2004. 'Rights: Beyond Interest Theory and Will Theory?' 23 *Law and Philosophy* 347–97.

Dan-Cohen, Meir. 1984. 'Decision Rules and Conduct Rules: On Acoustic Separation in Criminal Law.' 97 *Harvard Law Review* 625–77.

Delgado, Richard. 1985. ' "Rotten Social Background": Should the Criminal Law Recognize a Defense of Severe Environmental Deprivation?' 3 *Law and Inequality* 9–90.

Dennis, Ian. 2007. *The Law of Evidence*. Third edition. London: Sweet and Maxwell.

Devlin, Patrick. 1965. *The Enforcement of Morals*. Oxford: Oxford University Press.

Dicey, Albert. 1982. *Introduction to the Study of the Law of the Constitution*. Eighth Edition of 1915. Indianapolis, IN: Liberty Classics.

Dietrich, Franz and List, Christian. Forthcoming. 'A Liberal Paradox for Judgment Aggregation.' *Social Choice and Welfare*.

Dittmer, John. 1994. *Local People*. Urbana, IL: University of Illinois Press.

Dixon, Julie. 2001. *Evaluation and Legal Theory*. Oxford: Hart Publishing.

Dred Scott v Sandford. 1857. 60 *United States Reports* 393–632.

Dressler, Joshua. 1984. 'New Thoughts about the Concept of Justification in the Criminal Law: A Critique of Fletcher's Thinking and Rethinking.' 32 *UCLA Law Review* 61–99.

Dubber, Markus. 2002. *Criminal Law: Model Penal Code*. New York: Foundation Press.

Duff, Antony. 1998. 'Law, Language, and Community: Some Preconditions of Criminal Liability.' 18 *Oxford Journal of Legal Studies* 189–206.

Duff, Antony. 2001. *Punishment, Communication, and Community.* New York: Oxford University Press.

Duff, Antony. 2007. *Answering for Crime: Responsibility and Liability in the Criminal Law.* Oxford: Hart Publishing.

Duff, Antony; Farmer, Lindsay; Marshall, Sandra; and Tadros, Victor. 2007. *The Trial on Trial III: Towards a Normative Theory of the Criminal Trial.* Oxford: Hart Publishing.

Dummett, Michael. 1964. 'Bringing About the Past.' 73 *The Philosophical Review* 338–59.

Dworkin, Andrea and MacKinnon, Catharine. 1988. *Pornography and Civil Rights.* Minneapolis, MN: Organizing against Pornography.

Dworkin, Ronald. 1967. 'The Model of Rules.' 35 *University of Chicago Law Review* 14–46.

Dworkin, Ronald. 1986. *Law's Empire.* Cambridge, MA: Harvard University Press.

Dworkin, Ronald. 1996. *Freedom's Law: The Moral Reading of the American Constitution.* Cambridge, MA: Harvard University Press.

Dworkin, Ronald. 2000. *Sovereign Virtue.* Cambridge, MA: Harvard University Press.

Dworkin, Ronald. 2002. 'Thirty Years On.' 115 *Harvard Law Review* 1655–87.

Dworkin, Ronald. 2006. *Is Democracy Possible Here?* Princeton, NJ: Princeton University Press.

Eekelaar, John. 1973. 'Principles of Revolutionary Legality.' In Simpson 1973.

Fabre, Cécile. Forthcoming in 2009. 'Preconception Rights.' In Ian Carter, Matthew H Kramer, and Steven de Wijze (eds), *Hillel Steiner and Political Philosophy.* New York: Routledge.

Fehrenbacher, Don. 1978. *The Dred Scott Case.* New York: Oxford University Press.

Feinberg, Joel. 1970. *Doing and Deserving.* Princeton, NJ: Princeton University Press.

Feinberg, Joel. 1973. *Social Philosophy.* Englewood Cliffs, NJ: Prentice-Hall.

Feinberg, Joel. 1974. 'The Rights of Animals and Unborn Generations.' In William Blackstone (ed), *Philosophy and Environmental Crisis.* Athens: University of Georgia Press.

Feinberg, Joel. 1980a. 'Noncomparative Justice.' In *Rights, Justice, and the Bounds of Liberty.* Princeton: Princeton University Press.

Feinberg, Joel. 1980b. 'A Child's Right to an Open Future.' In William Aiken and Hugh LaFollette (eds), *Whose Child? Parental Rights, Parental Authority, and State Power.* Totowa, NJ: Littlefield, Adams.

Feinberg, Joel. 1984. *Harm to Others.* Oxford: Clarendon Press.

Feinberg, Joel. 1986. *Harm to Self.* New York: Oxford University Press.

Feinberg, Joel. 1988a. 'Responsibility *Tout Court.*' 14 *Philosophy Research Archives* 73–92.

Feinberg, Joel. 1988b. 'Responsibility for the Future.' 14 *Philosophy Research Archives* 93–113.

Feinberg, Joel. 1992. 'Wrongful Life and the Counterfactual Element in Harming.' In *Freedom and Fulfillment.* Princeton: Princeton University Press.

Feldman, Fred. 1991. 'Some Puzzles About the Evil of Death.' 100 *Philosophical Review* 205–27.

Finnis, John. 1968. 'Review of H.L.A. Hart, *Punishment and Responsibility.*' 8 *Oxford Review* 73–80.

Finnis, John. 1973. 'Revolutions and Continuity of Law.' In Simpson 1973.

Finnis, John. 1977. 'Scepticism, Self-Refutation, and the Good of Truth.' In Peter Hacker and Joseph Raz (eds), *Law, Morality, and Society*. Oxford: Clarendon Press.

Finnis, John. 1980. *Natural Law and Natural Rights*. Oxford: Clarendon Press.

Finnis, John. 1983. *Fundamentals of Ethics*. Oxford: Oxford University Press.

Finnis, John. 1984. 'The Authority of Law in the Predicament of Contemporary Social Theory.' 1 *Notre Dame Journal of Law, Ethics, and Public Policy* 115–37.

Finnis, John. 1987. 'On Positivism and the Foundations of Legal Authority.' In Ruth Gavison (ed), *Issues in Contemporary Legal Philosophy: The Influence of H.L.A. Hart*. Oxford: Oxford University Press.

Finnis, John. 1989. 'Law as Coordination.' 2 *Ratio Juris* 97–104.

Finnis, John. 1991. 'Object and Intention in Moral Judgments according to St. Thomas Aquinas.' 55 *The Thomist* 1–27.

Finnis, John. 1992. 'Natural Law and Legal Reasoning.' In Robert George (ed), *Natural Law Theory: Contemporary Essays*. Oxford: Oxford University Press.

Finnis, John. 1994. 'On Conditional Intentions and Preparatory Intentions.' In Luke Gormally (ed), *Moral Truth and Moral Tradition: Essays in Honour of Peter Geach and Elizabeth Anscombe*. Dublin: Four Courts Press.

Finnis, John. 1997. 'Commensuration and Public Reason.' In Ruth Chang (ed), *Incommensurability, Comparability, and Practical Reasoning*. Cambridge, MA: Harvard University Press.

Finnis, John. 1998. *Aquinas: Moral, Political, and Legal Theory*. Oxford: Oxford University Press.

Finnis, John. 2002. 'Natural Law: The Classical Tradition.' In Coleman and Shapiro 2002.

Finnis, John. 2003. 'Law and What I Truly Should Decide.' 48 *American Journal of Jurisprudence* 107–29.

Finnis, John. 2004. 'Self-referential (or Performative) Inconsistency: Its Significance for Truth.' 78 *Proceedings of the American Catholic Philosophical Association* 13–21.

Finnis, John. 2005a. 'Foundations of Practical Reason Revisited.' 50 *American Journal of Jurisprudence* 109–31.

Finnis, John. 2005b. 'The Thing I Am: Personal Identity in Aquinas and Shakespeare.' 22 *Social Philosophy and Policy* 250–82.

Finnis, John. 2007. 'Natural Law Theories of Law.' In Edward Zalta (ed), *The Stanford Encyclopedia of Philosophy (Spring 2007 Edition)*. URL: <http://plato.stanford.edu/archives/spr2007/entries/natural-law-theories/>.

Fischer, John and Ravizza, Mark. 1998. *Responsibility and Control*. Cambridge: Cambridge University Press.

Fletcher, George. 1978. *Rethinking Criminal Law*. Boston: Little, Brown.

Fleurbaey, Marc; Tungodden, Bertil; and Vallentyne, Peter. 2009. 'On the Possibility of Non-Aggregative Priority for the Worst Off.' 28 *Social Philosophy and Policy*, forthcoming.

Foner, Eric. 1988. *Reconstruction*. New York: Harper & Row.

Fugitive Slave Act. 1793. 1 *United States Statutes at Large* 302–5.

Fugitive Slave Act. 1850. 9 *United States Statutes at Large* 462–5.

Fuller, Lon. 1958. 'Positivism and Fidelity to Law: A Reply to Hart.' 71 *Harvard Law Review* 630–72.

Fuller, Lon. 1969. *The Morality of Law*. Revised Edition. New Haven, CT: Yale University Press.

Bibliography

Fuller, Lon. 1978. 'The Forms and Limits of Adjudication.' 92 *Harvard Law Review* 353–409.

Galeotti, Anna Elisabetta. 2002. *Toleration as Recognition*. Cambridge: Cambridge University Press.

Gardner, John. 1996. 'Justifications and Reasons.' In Andrew Simester and A T H Smith (eds), *Harm and Culpability*. Oxford: Oxford University Press.

Gardner, John. 1998. 'The Gist of Excuses.' 1 *Buffalo Criminal Law Review* 575–98.

Gardner, John. 2000. 'The Virtue of Justice and the Character of Law.' 53 *Current Legal Problems* 1–29.

Gardner, John. 2001. 'Legal Positivism: 5½ Myths.' 46 *American Journal of Jurisprudence* 199–227.

Gardner, John. 2003. 'The Mark of Responsibility.' 23 *Oxford Journal of Legal Studies* 157–71.

Gardner, John. 2004. 'Fletcher on Offences and Defences.' 39 *Tulsa Law Review* 817–27.

Gardner, John. 2007a. 'Nearly Natural Law.' 52 *American Journal of Jurisprudence* 1–23.

Gardner, John. 2007b. *Offences and Defences*. Oxford: Oxford University Press.

Gardner, John and Macklem, Timothy. 2002. 'Reasons.' In Coleman and Shapiro 2002.

Gardner, Peter. 1993. 'Tolerance and Education.' In John Horton (ed), *Liberalism, Multiculturalism, and Toleration*. New York: St Martin's Press.

Gayle v Browder. 1954. 352 *United States Reports* 903.

Giudice, Michael. 2002. 'Unconstitutionality, Invalidity, and Charter Challenges.' 15 *Canadian Journal of Law and Jurisprudence* 69–83.

Glannon, Walter. 2001. 'Persons, Lives, and Posthumous Harms.' 32 *Journal of Social Philosophy* 127–42.

Goldberg, John. 1990. 'Community and the Common Law Judge: Reconstructing Cardozo's Theoretical Writings.' 65 *New York University Law Review* 1324–72.

Golding, Martin and Edmundson, William. 2005. *Blackwell Guide to the Philosophy of Law and Legal Theory*. Oxford: Blackwell Publishing.

Goldsmith, Jack and Posner, Eric. 2005. *The Limits of International Law*. Oxford: Oxford University Press.

Gorovitz, Samuel. 1964. 'Leaving the Past Alone.' 73 *The Philosophical Review* 360–71.

Gosseries, Axel. 2003. 'A-t-on des obligations envers les morts?' 101 *Revue Philosophique de Louvain* 80–104.

Grant, Claire. 2006. 'Promulgation and the Law.' 2(3) *International Journal of Law in Context* 105–15.

Grant, Claire. 2008. 'Knowing the Law.' In Michael Freeman (ed), *Current Legal Issues: Law, Mind, and Brain*. Oxford: Oxford University Press.

Gray, John Chipman. 1921. *The Nature and Sources of the Law*. New York: Macmillan.

Green, Leslie. 2001. 'Pluralism, Social Conflict, and Tolerance.' In Arend Soeteman (ed), *Pluralism and Law*. Dordrecht: Kluwer.

Green, Leslie. 2003. 'Legal Positivism.' In Edward Zalta (ed), *The Stanford Encyclopedia of Philosophy (Spring 2003 Edition)*. URL: <http://plato.stanford.edu/archives/spr2003/entries/legal-positivism/>

Green, Leslie. 2005. 'The Germ of Justice.' URL: <http://www.trinitinture.com/documents/green.pdf>

Greenawalt, Kent. 1984. 'The Perplexing Borders of Justification and Excuse.' 84 *Columbia Law Review* 1897–1927.

Greene, Dana. 2006. 'Biography and the Search for Meaning.' May 5th *National Catholic Reporter*. URL: <http://www.ncronline.org/NCR_Online/archives2/2006b/050506/050506t.php>.

Greene, Graham. 1940. *The Power and the Glory*. London: Penguin.

Greene, Mark. 'Loss and Modality.' Unpublished paper.

Gutmann, Amy and Thompson, Dennis. 1996. *Democracy and Disagreement*. Cambridge, MA: Harvard University Press.

Hacker, Peter and Raz, Joseph (eds). 1977. *Law, Morality, and Society: Essays in Honour of H.L.A. Hart*. Oxford: Clarendon Press.

Hall, Ned. 2004. 'Two Concepts of Causation.' In Collins, Hall, and Paul 2004b.

Hampshire, Stuart and Hart, Herbert. 1958. 'Decision, Intention, and Certainty.' 67 *Mind* 1–12.

Hart, Herbert. 1948. 'The Ascription of Responsibility and Rights.' 49 *Proceedings of the Aristotelian Society* 71–94.

Hart, Herbert. 1953. 'Philosophy of Law and Jurisprudence in Britain (1945–1952).' 2 *American Journal of Comparative Law* 355–64.

Hart, Herbert. 1955. 'Are There Any Natural Rights?' 64 *Philosophical Review* 175–91.

Hart, Herbert. 1958. 'Positivism and the Separation of Law and Morals.' 71 *Harvard Law Review* 593–629.

Hart, Herbert. 1959. 'Immorality and Treason.' July 30th *Listener* 162–3.

Hart, Herbert. 1961. *The Concept of Law*. Oxford: Clarendon Press.

Hart, Herbert. 1963. *Law, Liberty, and Morality*. Oxford: Oxford University Press.

Hart, Herbert. 1965a. 'Book Review: *The Morality of Law* by Lon Fuller.' 78 *Harvard Law Review* 1281–96.

Hart, Herbert. 1965b. 'Review: *Crime and the Criminal Law* by Barbara Wootton.' 74 *Yale Law Journal* 1325–31.

Hart, Herbert. 1967a. 'Are There any Natural Rights?' In Quinton 1967.

Hart, Herbert. 1967b. 'Varieties of Responsibility.' 83 *Law Quarterly Review* 346–64.

Hart, Herbert. 1967c. 'Philosophy of Law, Problems of.' In Paul Edwards (ed), *Encyclopedia of Philosophy*. Volume 6. London: Macmillan.

Hart, Herbert. 1968. *Punishment and Responsibility*. Oxford: Clarendon Press.

Hart, Herbert. 1973. 'Rawls on Liberty and its Priority.' 40 *University of Chicago Law Review* 534–55.

Hart, Herbert. 1977. 'American Jurisprudence through English Eyes: The Nightmare and the Noble Dream.' 11 *Georgia Law Review* 969–89.

Hart, Herbert. 1979. 'Between Utility and Rights.' In Alan Ryan (ed), *The Idea of Freedom*. Oxford: Clarendon Press.

Hart, Herbert. 1982. *Essays on Bentham*. Oxford: Clarendon Press.

Hart, Herbert. 1983. *Essays in Jurisprudence and Philosophy*. Oxford: Clarendon Press.

Hart, Herbert. 1986. 'Who can Tell Right from Wrong?' July 17th *New York Review of Books* 49–52.

Hart, Herbert. 1994. *The Concept of Law*. Second Edition. Oxford: Clarendon Press.

Hart, Herbert. 2008. *Punishment and Responsibility*. Second Edition. Introduced by John Gardner. Oxford: Clarendon Press.

Hart, Herbert and Honoré, Tony. 1959. *Causation in the Law*. Oxford: Clarendon Press.

Hart, Herbert and Honoré, Tony. 1985. *Causation in the Law*. Second Edition. Oxford: Clarendon Press.

Hart, Jenifer. 1998. *Ask Me No More: An Autobiography*. London: Peter Halban.

Heffernan, William and Kleinig, John. 2000. *From Social Justice to Criminal Justice: Poverty and the Administration of Criminal Law*. New York: Oxford University Press.

Hempel, Carl. 1965. *Aspects of Scientific Explanation and Other Essays in the Philosophy of Science*. New York: Free Press.

Hobbes, Thomas. 1990. *Behemoth or The Long Parliament*. Edited by Ferdinand Toennies. Chicago: University of Chicago Press.

Hobbes, Thomas. 1996. *Leviathan*. Edited by Richard Tuck. Cambridge: Cambridge University Press.

Hohfeld, Wesley. 1923. *Fundamental Legal Conceptions*. New Haven, CT: Yale University Press.

Holden-Smith, Barbara. 1996. 'Lynching, Federalism, and the Intersection of Race and Gender in the Progressive Era.' 8 *Yale Journal of Law and Feminism* 31–78.

Holland, Thomas Erskine. 1906. *The Elements of Jurisprudence*. Tenth Edition. Oxford: Oxford University Press.

Honneth, Axel. 1996. *The Struggle for Recognition: Moral Grammar of Social Conflicts*. Translated by Joel Anderson. London: Polity Press.

Honoré, Tony. 1995. 'Necessary and Sufficient Conditions in Tort Law.' In David Owen (ed), *Philosophical Foundations of Tort Law*. Oxford: Oxford University Press.

Horder, Jeremy. 2004. *Excusing Crime*. Oxford: Oxford University Press.

Howard, Benjamin (ed). 1857. *A Report of the Decision of the Supreme Court of the United States and the Opinions of the Judges Thereof, in the Case of Dred Scott versus John F.A. Sandford*. New York: D. Appleton.

Hudson, Barbara. 1995. 'Beyond Proportionate Punishment: Difficult Cases and the 1991 Criminal Justice Act.' 22 *Crime, Law & Social Change* 59–78.

Husak, Douglas. 1987. *Philosophy of Criminal Law*. Totowa, NJ: Rowman & Littlefield.

Huxley, Aldous. 1928. *Point Counter Point*. London: Chatto & Windus.

Jones, Harry. 1969. *The Efficacy of Law*. Evanston, IL: Northwestern University Press.

Kagan, Shelly. 1994. 'Me and My Life.' 94 *Proceedings of the Aristotelian Society* 309–24.

Kamm, Frances. 2002. 'Rights.' In Coleman and Shapiro 2002.

Kammen, Michael. 1986. *A Machine that Would Go by Itself*. New York: Knopf.

Kelsen, Hans. 1945. *General Theory of Law and State*. Translated by Anders Wedberg. Cambridge, MA: Harvard University Press.

Kennedy, Randall. 1997. *Race, Crime, and the Law*. New York: Vintage Books.

Kenny, Anthony. 1978. *Freewill and Responsibility*. Oxford: Oxford University Press.

Kitcher, Philip. 1989. 'Explanatory Unification and the Causal Structure of the World.' In Philip Kitcher and Wesley Salmon (eds), *Scientific Explanation*. Minneapolis, MN: University of Minnesota Press.

Korsgaard, Christine. 1997. 'The Normativity of Instrumental Reason.' In Garrett Cullity and Berys Gaut (eds), *Ethics and Practical Reason*. Oxford: Oxford University Press.

Kramer, Matthew. 1998. 'Rights Without Trimmings.' In Kramer, Simmonds, and Steiner 1998.

Kramer, Matthew. 1999. *In Defense of Legal Positivism*. Oxford: Oxford University Press.

Kramer, Matthew. 2001. 'Getting Rights Right.' In Matthew H Kramer (ed), *Rights, Wrongs, and Responsibilities*. Basingstoke: Palgrave.

Kramer, Matthew. 2003. *The Quality of Freedom*. Oxford: Oxford University Press.

Kramer, Matthew. 2004. *Where Law and Morality Meet*. Oxford: Oxford University Press.

Kramer, Matthew. 2005. 'Moral Rights and the Limits of the "Ought"-Implies-"Can" Principle: Why Impeccable Precautions are No Excuse.' 48 *Inquiry* 307–55.

Kramer, Matthew. 2007. *Objectivity and the Rule of Law*. Cambridge: Cambridge University Press.

Kramer, Matthew; Simmonds, Nigel; and Steiner, Hillel. 1998. *A Debate over Rights*. Oxford: Oxford University Press.

Kramer, Matthew and Steiner, Hillel. 2007. 'Theories of Rights: Is There a Third Way?' 27 *Oxford Journal of Legal Studies* 281–310.

Kymlicka, Will. 1989. *Liberalism, Community, and Culture*. Oxford: Oxford University Press.

Lacey, Nicola. 2004. *A Life of H.L.A. Hart: The Nightmare and the Noble Dream*. Oxford: Oxford University Press.

LaFave, Wayne; Israel, Jerold; and King, Nancy. 2004. *Criminal Procedure*. Fourth Edition. St Paul, MN: West Group.

Lawrence et al v Texas. 2003. 539 *United States Reports* 558–606.

Leiter, Brian. 2007. *Naturalizing Jurisprudence: Essays on American Legal Realism and Naturalism in Legal Philosophy*. Oxford: Oxford University Press.

Levenbook, Barbara. 1984. 'Harming Someone After his Death.' 94 *Ethics* 407–19.

Levenbook, Barbara. 1985. 'Harming the Dead, Once Again.' 95 *Ethics* 162–4.

Levine, Judith. 2002. *Harmful to Minors: The Perils of Protecting Children from Sex*. Minneapolis, MN: University of Minnesota Press.

Lewis, David. 1969. *Convention*. Cambridge, MA: Harvard University Press.

Lewis, David. 1973a. 'Causation.' 70 *Journal of Philosophy* 556–67.

Lewis, David. 1973b. *Counterfactuals*. Cambridge, MA: Harvard University Press.

Lewis, David. 1979. 'Counterfactual Dependence and Time's Arrow.' 13 *Noûs* 455–76.

Lewis, David. 1986. *Philosophical Papers, Volume II*. Oxford: Oxford University Press.

Llewellyn, Karl. 1951. *The Bramble Bush*. Dobbs Ferry, NY: Oceana Publications.

Locke, John. 1983. *A Letter Concerning Toleration*. Edited by James Tully. Indianapolis, IN: Hackett Publishing.

Lomasky, Loren. 1987. *Persons, Rights and Moral Community*. Oxford: Oxford University Press.

Lorde, Audre. 1984. 'The Master's Tools will Never Dismantle the Master's House.' In *Sister Outsider: Essays and Speeches by Audre Lorde*. Freedom, CA: Crossing.

Loving v Virginia. 1967. 388 *United States Reports* 1.

Luban, David. 2004. 'A Theory of Crimes Against Humanity.' 29 *Yale Journal of International Law* 85–167.

Lucas, John. 1993. *Responsibility*. Oxford: Oxford University Press.

Lucas, John. 2007. 'The Ascription of Actions.' URL: <http://users.ox.ac.uk/~jrlucas/ascript.html>.

Lynch, A C E 1982. 'The Mental Element in the Actus Reus.' 98 *Law Quarterly Review* 109–42.

Lyons, David. 1973. 'On Formal Justice.' 58 *Cornell Law Review* 833–61.

Lyons, David. 1998. 'Moral Judgment, Historical Reality, and Civil Disobedience.' 27 *Philosophy and Public Affairs* 31–49.

Lyons, David. 2007. 'Racial Junctures in U.S. History and Their Legacy.' In Michael Martin and Marilyn Yaquinto (eds), *Redress for Historical Injustices in the United States*. Durham, NC: Duke University Press.

MacCormick, Neil. 1977. 'Rights in Legislation.' In Hacker and Raz 1977.

MacCormick, Neil. 1978. *Legal Reasoning and Legal Theory*. Oxford: Clarendon Press.

MacCormick, Neil. 1981. *H.L.A. Hart*. London: Edward Arnold.

MacCormick, Neil. 1982. *Legal Right and Social Democracy*. Oxford: Oxford University Press.

MacCormick, Neil. 1985. 'A Moralistic Case for Amoralistic Law?' 20 *Valparaiso Law Review* 1–41.

MacCormick, Neil. 2005. *Rhetoric and the Rule of Law: A Theory of Legal Reasoning*. Oxford: Oxford University Press.

MacCormick, Neil. 2007a. 'Legal Positivism: Hart's Last Word.' URL: <http://www.cflpp.law.cam.ac.uk/past_events/the_legacy_of_hla_hart:_papers.php>.

MacCormick, Neil. 2007b. *Institutions of Law*. Oxford: Oxford University Press.

MacIntyre, Alasdair. 1981. *After Virtue*. London: Duckworth.

Mackie, John. 1974. *The Cement of the Universe*. Oxford: Clarendon Press.

Mackie, John. 1977. 'The Third Theory of Law.' 7 *Philosophy and Public Affairs* 3–16.

Marcuse, Herbert. 1965. 'Repressive Tolerance.' In Robert Paul Wolff, Barrington Moore, Jr, and Herbert Marcuse, *A Critique of Pure Tolerance*. Boston: Beacon Press.

Marmor, Andrei. 2001. *Positive Law and Objective Values*. Oxford: Oxford University Press.

Marshall, Sandra and Duff, Antony. 1998. 'Criminalization and Sharing Wrongs.' 11 *Canadian Journal of Law & Jurisprudence* 7–22.

May, Larry. 2005. *Crimes against Humanity: A Normative Account*. Cambridge: Cambridge University Press.

McGinnis, John and Somin, Ilya. 2007. 'Should International Law be Part of Our Law?' 59 *Stanford Law Review* 1175–247.

McMahan, Jeff. 1989. 'Death and the Value of Life.' 99 *Ethics* 32–59.

McMahan, Jeff. 1994. 'Innocence, Self-Defense, and Killing in War.' 2 *Journal of Political Philosophy* 193–221.

Mendelson, Maurice H 1998. 'Formation of Customary International Law.' In *Recueil des cours (Collected Courses of the Hague Academy of International Law)*. The Hague: Martinus Nijhoff.

Mill, John Stuart. 1872. *A System of Logic: Ratiocinative and Inductive*. Eighth Edition. London: Longmans, Green & Co.

Mill, John Stuart. 1981. *On Liberty*. New York: Modern Library.

Mill, John Stuart. 2002. *Utilitarianism*. Edited by George Sher. Indianapolis, IN: Hackett.

Miller, David. 1999. *Principles of Social Justice*. Cambridge, MA: Harvard University Press.

Moore, Michael. 1997. *Placing Blame: A General Theory of the Criminal Law*. Oxford: Oxford University Press.

Morris, Christopher. 1991. 'Punishment and Loss of Moral Standing.' 21 *Canadian Journal of Philosophy* 53–79.

Morse, Stephen. 1998. 'Excusing and the New Excuse Defenses: A Legal and Conceptual Review.' 23 *Crime and Justice: An Annual Review of Research* 329–406.

Mulgan, Timothy. 1999. 'The Place of the Dead in Liberal Political Philosophy.' 7 *Journal of Political Philosophy* 52–70.

Murphy, Liam. 2001. 'The Political Question of the Concept of Law.' In Jules Coleman (ed), *Hart's Postscript: Essays on the Postscript to 'The Concept of Law'*. Oxford: Oxford University Press.

Myrdal, Gunnar. 1944. *An American Dilemma*. New York: Harper & Brothers.

Nagel, Thomas. 1979. 'Death.' In *Mortal Questions*. Cambridge: Cambridge University Press, 1979.

Nagel, Thomas. 2002. *Concealment and Exposure and Other Essays*. Oxford: Oxford University Press.

Nagel, Thomas. 2005a. 'The Central Questions.' February 3rd *London Review of Books* 12–13.

Nagel, Thomas. 2005b. 'Letter.' February 17th *London Review of Books*. URL: <http://lrb.co.uk/v27/n04/letters.html>.

Norman, Richard. 1995. *Ethics, Killing, and War*. Cambridge: Cambridge University Press.

Norrie, Alan. 2001. *Crime, Reason, and History*. Second Edition. London: Butterworths.

Nozick, Robert. 1969. 'Newcomb's Problem and Two Principles of Choice.' In Nicholas Rescher (ed), *Essays in Honor of Carl G. Hempel*. Dordrecht: D Reidel.

Nussbaum, Martha. 1992. 'Human Functioning and Social Justice.' 20 *Political Theory* 202–46.

Olsaretti, Serena. 2003. 'Distributive Justice and Compensatory Desert.' In Serena Olsaretti (ed), *Desert and Justice*. Oxford: Clarendon Press.

O'Neill, Onora. 1979–80. 'The Most Extensive Liberty.' 80 *Proceedings of the Aristotelian Society* 45–59.

Ormerod, David. 2005. *Smith & Hogan Criminal Law*. Eleventh Edition. Oxford: Oxford University Press.

Parfit, Derek. 1984. *Reasons and Persons*. Oxford: Oxford University Press.

Partridge, Ernest. 1981. 'Posthumous Interests and Posthumous Respect.' 91 *Ethics* 243–64.

Perry, Stephen. 'Hart's Methodological Positivism.' In Jules Coleman (ed), *Hart's Postscript: Essays on the Postscript of 'The Concept of Law'*. Oxford: Oxford University Press.

Pettit, Philip. 1986. 'Free Riding and Foul Dealing.' 83 *Journal of Philosophy* 361–79.

Pettit, Philip. 1997. *Republicanism: A Theory of Freedom and Government*. Oxford: Oxford University Press.

Pettit, Philip. 2001. 'Capability and Freedom: A Defense of Sen.' 17 *Economics and Philosophy* 1–20.

Pettit, Philip. 2006. 'Freedom in the Market.' 5 *Politics, Philosophy, and Economics* 131–49.

Pettit, Philip. 2007. 'Free Persons and Free Choices.' 28 *History of Political Thought*.

Pettit, Philip. 2008. 'Republican Liberty: Three Axioms, Four Theorems.' In Cécile Laborde and John Maynor (eds), *Republicanism and Political Theory*. Oxford: Blackwell Publishing.

Pitcher, George. 1984. 'The Misfortunes of the Dead.' 21 *American Philosophical Quarterly* 183–8.

Plato. 1967–8. *Laws*. Translated by R G Bury. Cambridge. MA: Harvard Univerity Press.

Plessy v Ferguson. 1896. 163 *United States Reports* 537–64.

Porter, Jean. 2007. 'Custom, Ordinance and Natural Right in Gratian's *Decretum*.' In Amanda Perreau-Saussine and James Bernard Murphy (eds), *The Nature of Customary Law*. Cambridge: Cambridge University Press.

Postema, Gerald. 1986. *Bentham and the Common Law Tradition*. Oxford: Oxford University Press.

Postema, Gerald. 1994. 'Implicit Law.' 13 *Law and Philosophy* 361–87.

Postema, Gerald. 2006. 'Bentham's Utilitarianism.' In Henry West (ed), *A Guide to Mill's Utilitarianism*. Oxford: Blackwell.

Postema, Gerald. 2007. 'Custom in International Law: A Normative Practice Account.' In Amanda Perreau-Saussine and James Bernard Murphy (eds), *The Nature of Customary Law*. Cambridge: Cambridge University Press.

Postema, Gerald. 2008. 'Salience Reasoning.' *Topoi*, forthcoming.

President's Committee on Civil Rights. 1947. *To Secure These Rights*. Washington, DC: United States Government Printing Office.

Prigg v Pennsylvania. 1842. 41 *United States Reports* 539–674.

Quinton, Anthony (ed). 1967. *Political Philosophy*. Oxford: Oxford University Press.

R. v Brown. 1993. 2 *All England Reports* 75.

Rabkin, Jeremy. 2006. 'American Self-Defense Shouldn't be too Distracted by International Law.' 30 *Harvard Journal of Law and Public Policy* 31–63.

Rainbolt, George. 2006. *The Concept of Rights*. Dordrecht: Springer.

Raphael, D D. 1988. 'The Intolerable.' In Susan Mendus (ed), *Justifying Toleration: Conceptual and Historical Perspectives*. Cambridge: Cambridge University Press.

Rawls, John. 1958. 'Justice as Fairness.' 67 *Philosophical Review* 164–94.

Rawls, John. 1971. *A Theory of Justice*. Cambridge, MA: Harvard University Press.

Rawls, John. 1982. 'Social Utility and Primary Goods.' In Amartya Sen and Bernard Williams (eds), *Utilitarianism and Beyond*. Cambridge: Cambridge University Press.

Rawls, John. 1993. *Political Liberalism*. New York: Columbia University Press.

Rawls, John. 1999. *The Law of Peoples*. Cambridge, MA: Harvard University Press.

Rawls, John. 2001. *Justice as Fairness: A Restatement*. Cambridge, MA: Harvard University Press.

Raz, Joseph. 1979. *The Authority of Law*. Oxford: Clarendon Press.

Raz, Joseph. 1986. *The Morality of Freedom*. Oxford: Clarendon Press.

Raz, Joseph. 1988. 'Autonomy, Toleration, and the Harm Principle.' In Susan Mendus (ed), *Justifying Toleration: Conceptual and Historical Perspectives*. Cambridge: Cambridge University Press.

Raz, Joseph. 1993. 'The Autonomy of Legal Reasoning.' 6 *Ratio Juris* 1–15.

Raz, Joseph. 1996a. *Ethics in the Public Domain: Essays in the Morality of Law and Politics*. Revised Edition. Oxford: Oxford University Press.

Raz, Joseph. 1996b. 'The Inner Logic of the Law.' In Raz 1996a.

Raz, Joseph. 1996c. 'Authority, Law, and Morality.' In Raz 1996a.

Raz, Joseph. 2001. 'Two Views of the Nature of the Theory of Law: A Partial Comparison.' In Jules Coleman (ed), *Hart's Postscript*. Oxford: Oxford University Press.

Roberts, Paul. 1995. 'Taking the Burden of Proof Seriously.' *Criminal Law Review* 783–98.

Roberts, Paul. 2002. 'The Presumption of Innocence Brought Home? Kebilene Deconstructed.' 118 *Law Quarterly Review* 41–71.

Robinson, Paul. 1984. *Criminal Law Defenses*. 2 volumes. St Paul, MN: West Group.

Robinson, Paul. 1993. 'Should the Criminal Law Abandon the Actus Reus/Mens Rea Distinction?' In Stephen Shute, John Gardner, and Jeremy Horder (eds), *Action and Value in Criminal Law*. Oxford: Oxford University Press.

Robinson, Paul. 1997. *Structure and Function in Criminal Law*. Oxford: Oxford University Press.

Ryan, Joanna. 2007. 'The Privacy of the Bedroom? Fifty Years on from the Wolfenden Report Reforms.' 1 *Sitegeist: Journal of Psychoanalysis and Philosophy.*

Sacks, Oliver. 1985. *The Man who Mistook His Wife for a Hat.* New York: Summit.

Salmon, Wesley. 1984. *Scientific Explanation and the Causal Structure of the World.* Princeton: Princeton University Press.

Sallot, Jeff. 1992. 'Legal Victory Bittersweet', *Globe and Mail* 29 February. Toronto, Canada.

Scanlon, Thomas. 1988. 'The Significance of Choice.' In Sterling McMurrin (ed), *The Tanner Lectures on Human Values, Volume 8.* Salt Lake City, UT: University of Utah Press.

Schaffer, Jonathan. 2007. 'The Metaphysics of Causation.' In Edward Zalta (ed), *Stanford Encyclopedia of Philosophy (Winter 2007 Edition).* URL: <http://plato.stanford.edu/archives/win2007/entries/causation-metaphysics>.

Schauer, Frederick. 1991. *Playing by the Rules.* Oxford: Oxford University Press.

Schopp, Robert. 1998. *Justification Defenses and Just Convictions.* Cambridge: Cambridge University Press.

Schumpeter, Joseph. 1943. *Capitalism, Socialism, and Democracy.* London: Allen & Unwin.

Searle, John. 1989. 'How Performatives Work.' 12 *Linguistics and Philosophy* 535–58.

Sen, Amartya. 1983. 'Poor, Relatively Speaking.' 35 *Oxford Economic Papers* 153–68.

Sen, Amartya. 1985. *Commodities and Capabilities.* Amsterdam: North-Holland.

Shapiro, Scott. 1998. 'On Hart's Way Out.' 4 *Legal Theory* 469–507.

Shapiro, Scott. 2000. 'Law, Morality, and the Guidance of Conduct.' 6 *Legal Theory* 127–70.

Shapiro, Scott. 2002. 'Law, Plans, and Practical Reason.' 8 *Legal Theory* 387–441.

Shklar, Judith. 1984. *Ordinary Vices.* Cambridge, MA: Harvard University Press.

Simester, Andrew and Sullivan, G R 2007. *Criminal Law: Theory and Doctrine.* Third Edition. Oxford: Hart Publishing.

Simmonds, Nigel 1991. 'Between Positivism and Idealism.' 50 *Cambridge Law Journal* 308–29.

Simmonds, Nigel 1998. 'Rights at the Cutting Edge.' In Kramer, Simmonds, and Steiner 1998.

Simmonds, Nigel 2007. *Law as a Moral Idea.* Oxford: Oxford University Press.

Simpson, A W B (ed). 1973. *Oxford Essays in Jurisprudence, Second Series.* Oxford: Clarendon Press.

Skinner, Quentin. 1998. *Liberty before Liberalism.* Cambridge: Cambridge University Press.

Skinner, Quentin. 2006. 'Rethinking Political Liberty.' 61 *History Workshop Journal* 156–70.

Skinner, Quentin. 2007. *Freedom as Independence.* Cambridge: Cambridge University Press.

Slaughterhouse Cases. 1873. 83 *United States Reports* 36–130.

Smith, A T H 1978. 'On Actus Reus and Mens Rea.' In Peter Glazebrook (ed), *Reshaping the Criminal Law.* London: Stevens.

Sperling, Daniel. Forthcoming. *Posthumous Interests: Legal and Ethical Perspectives.* Cambridge: Cambridge University Press.

Sprack, John. 2006. *A Practical Approach to Criminal Procedure.* Eleventh Edition. Oxford: Oxford University Press.

Squires, Dan. 2006. 'The Problem with Entrapment.' 26 *Oxford Journal of Legal Studies* 351–76.

Sreevenisan, Gopal. 2005. 'A Hybrid Theory of Claim-Rights.' 25 *Oxford Journal of Legal Studies* 257–74.

Stalnaker, Robert. 1968. 'A Theory of Conditionals.' In Nicholas Rescher (ed), *Studies in Logical Theory.* Oxford: Blackwell.

Stavropoulos, Nicos. 2001. 'Hart's Semantics.' In Jules Coleman (ed), *Hart's Postscript.* Oxford: Oxford University Press.

Steiner, Hillel. 1994. *An Essay on Rights.* Oxford: Blackwell.

Steiner, Hillel. 1998. 'Working Rights.' In Kramer, Simmonds, and Steiner 1998.

Stewart, Hamish. 1999. 'Legality and Morality in H.L.A. Hart's Theory of Criminal Law.' 52 *Southern Methodist University Law Review* 201–27.

Strevens, Michael. 2007. 'Mackie Remixed.' In Joseph Keim Campbell, Michael O'Rourke, and David Shier (eds), *Causation and Explanation.* Cambridge, MA: MIT Press.

Sumner, L W 1987. *The Moral Foundation of Rights.* Oxford: Clarendon Press.

Tadros, Victor. 2005. *Criminal Responsibility.* Oxford: Oxford University Press.

Tadros, Victor and Tierney, Stephen. 2004. 'The Presumption of Innocence and the Human Rights Act.' 67 *Modern Law Review* 402–34.

Tamanaha, Brian. 2001. *A General Jurisprudence of Law and Society.* Oxford: Oxford University Press.

Taylor, Charles. 1992. 'The Politics of Recognition.' In Amy Gutmann (ed), *Multiculturalism and the Politics of Recognition.* Princeton, NJ: Princeton University Press.

Thomson, Judith Jarvis. 2003. 'Causation: Omissions.' 66 *Philosophy and Phenomenological Research* 81–103.

Tierney, Brian. 1997. *The Idea of Natural Rights.* Atlanta, GA: Scholars Press.

Tuck, Richard. 1979. *Natural Rights Theories.* Cambridge: Cambridge University Press.

Twining, William. 1973. *Karl Llewellyn and the Realist Movement.* London: Weidenfeld & Nicholson.

Twining, William. 1998. 'R.G. Collingwood's Autobiography: One Reader's Response.' 25 *Journal of Law and Society* 603–20.

United States v Reese. 1875. 92 *United States Reports* 214–56.

Updike, John. 1999. 'One Cheer for Literary Biography.' February 4th *New York Review of Books.* URL: <http://www.nybooks.com/articles/607>.

Van Parijs, Philippe. 1995. *Real Freedom for All.* Oxford: Oxford University Press.

Voltaire, François Marie Arouet. 1975. *Traité sur la tolérance.* Paris: Éditions Gallimard.

Waldron, Jeremy. 1989. 'The Rule of Law in Contemporary Liberal Theory.' 2 *Ratio Juris* 79–96.

Waldron, Jeremy (ed). 1987. *Nonsense upon Stilts: Bentham, Burke and Marx on the Rights of Man.* London: Methuen.

Waldron, Jeremy. 1993. *Liberal Rights.* Cambridge: Cambridge University Press.

Waldron, Jeremy. 1999. 'All We Like Sheep.' 12 *Canadian Journal of Law and Jurisprudence* 169–86.

Waldron, Jeremy. 2006a. 'Are Constitutional Norms Legal Norms?' 75 *Fordham Law Review* 1697–713.

Waldron, Jeremy. 2006b. 'The Concept and the Rule of Law.' URL: <http://www.law.nyu.edu/clppt/program2006/readings/Concept%20and%20Rule%20of%20Law%20WALDRON.pdf>.

Wallace, R Jay. 1994. *Responsibility and the Moral Sentiments*. Cambridge, MA: Harvard University Press.

Waluchow, Wilfrid. 1986. 'Feinberg's Theory of "Preposthumous Harm." ' 25 *Dialogue* 727–34.

Waluchow, Wilfrid. 1994. *Inclusive Legal Positivism*. Oxford: Oxford University Press.

Waluchow, Wilfrid. 2000. 'Authority and the Practical Difference Thesis: A Defence of Inclusive Legal Positivism.' 6 *Legal Theory* 45–81.

Waluchow, Wilfrid. 2007. *A Common-Law Theory of Judicial Review: The Living Tree*. Cambridge: Cambridge University Press.

Watson, Gary. 2001. 'Reasons and Responsibility.' 111 *Ethics* 374–94.

Wellman, Carl. 1985. *A Theory of Rights*. Totowa, NJ: Rowman and Allenheld.

Wellman Carl. 1995. *Real Rights*. Oxford: Oxford University Press.

Wenar, Leif. 2005. 'The Nature of Rights.' 33 *Philosophy and Public Affairs* 223–52.

Wenar, Leif. 2007. 'The Meanings of Freedom.' In Laurence Thomas (ed), *Contemporary Debates in Social Philosophy*. Oxford: Blackwell Publishing.

Wiggins, David. 1991. 'Claims of Need.' In *Needs, Values, Truth*. Second Edition. Oxford: Blackwell Publishers.

Wikipedia. 2007. 'List of Race Riots.' URL: <http://en.wikipedia.org/wiki/List_of_race_riots> (viewed in October 2007).

Williams, Bernard. 2006. *Philosophy as a Humanistic Discipline*. Princeton: Princeton University Press.

Williams, Glanville. 1956. 'The Concept of Legal Liberty.' 56 *Columbia Law Review* 1129–50.

Williams, Glanville. 1957. *Salmond on Jurisprudence*. Eleventh Edition. London: Sweet & Maxwell.

Williams, Glanville. 1982. 'Offences and Defences.' 2 *Legal Studies* 233–56.

Wirszubski, Chaim. 1968. *Libertas as a Political Ideal at Rome*. Oxford: Oxford University Press.

Wolff, Robert Paul. 1965. 'Beyond Toleration.' In Robert Paul Wolff, Barrington Moore, Jr, and Herbert Marcuse, *A Critique of Pure Tolerance*. Boston: Beacon Press.

Wollheim, Richard. 1962. 'A Paradox in Democracy.' In Peter Laslett and W G Runciman (eds), *Philosophy, Politics, and Society*. Second Series. Oxford: Blackwell.

Woodward, C Vann. 1955. *The Strange Career of Jim Crow*. New York: Oxford University Press.

Wootton, Barbara. 1981. *Crime and the Criminal Law: Reflections of a Magistrate and Social Scientist*. Second Edition. London: Allen & Unwin.

Wright, Richard. 1985. 'Causation in Tort Law.' 73 *California Law Review* 1735–828.

Wright, Richard. 1988. 'Causation, Responsibility, Risk, Probability, Naked Statistics, and Proof: Pruning the Bramble Bush by Clarifying the Concepts.' 73 *Iowa Law Review* 1001–77.

Wright, Richard. 1999. 'Principled Adjudication: Tort Law and Beyond.' 7 *Canterbury Law Review* 265–96.

Wright, Richard. 2000. 'The Principles of Justice.' 75 *Notre Dame Law Review* 1859–92.

Wright, Richard. 2001. 'Once More into the Bramble Bush: Duty, Causal Contribution, and the Extent of Legal Responsibility.' 54 *Vanderbilt Law Review* 1071–132.

Wright, Richard. 2003. 'The Grounds and Extent of Legal Responsibility.' 40 *San Diego Law Review* 1425–531.

Wright, Richard. 2007. 'Acts and Omissions as Positive and Negative Causes.' In Jason Neyers, Erika Chamberlain, and Stephen Pitel (eds), *Emerging Issues in Tort Law*. Oxford: Hart Publishing.

Zimmerman, Michael. 1988. *An Essay on Moral Responsibility*. Totowa, NJ: Rowman & Littlefield.

Zipursky, Benjamin. 2006. 'Legal Obligations and the Internal Aspect of Rules.' 75 *Fordham Law Review* 1229–52.

Zucca, Lorenzo. 2007. *Constitutional Dilemmas: Conflicts of Fundamental Legal Rights in Europe and the USA*. Oxford: Oxford University Press.

Index